Pacific Microphone

PACIFIC MICROPHONE

William J. Dunn

FOREWORD BY MIKE WALLACE

TEXAS A&M UNIVERSITY PRESS
College Station

The paper used in this book meets the minimum requirements
of the American National Standard for Permanence
of Paper for Printed Library Materials, Z39.48-1984.
Binding materials have been chosen for durability.

Library of Congress Cataloging-in-Publication Data

Dunn, William J.
   Pacific microphone by William J. Dunn. — 1st ed.
     p.   cm. — (Texas A&M University military history series ; 8)
   ISBN 0-89096-339-8 (alk. paper) : $19.95
   1. Dunn, William J. 2. World War, 1939–1945—Journalists—
Biography. 3. World War, 1939–1945—Personal narratives, American.
4. World War, 1939–1945—Pacific Area. I. Title. II. Series.
D799.P16D86   1988
940.54'81'73—dc19   88-12193
                                                       CIP

To my two granddaughters,
AMANDA of England and NAGAKO of Japan,
lovely proof that peaceful coexistence
can be richly rewarding

CONTENTS

Part IV

SPECIAL REPORTS

LIST OF ILLUSTRATIONS

MAPS

FOREWORD

There was only one American broadcast war correspondent who covered the Pacific war from Day One—the Japanese attack on Pearl Harbor—through VJ Day, victory over Japan, almost four years later. His name is Bill Dunn. His network was CBS News.

There was no television, there were no satellites, no high-tech methods of communication. Just minimal, erratic voice channels, telephone lines, telegraph, typewriter, pencil and paper. Broadcast technology from 1941 to 1945 was about as primitive as the jungles in which men fought. But when Gen. Douglas MacArthur stepped ashore on the island of Leyte fulfilling a promise ("I shall return!"), CBS correspondent Bill Dunn was at his side, typewriter in hand.

Bill Dunn has some unexpected, and fascinating memories of MacArthur that add to our collective historical knowledge. Dunn had already met the General before the attack on Pearl Harbor because CBS News had sent him out to the Pacific in anticipation of war breaking out there.

This is a careful, detailed, on-the-ground history by an accomplished reporter, a first-rate description of how the news was carried from the war front to the civilian rear, and an altogether inspiring memoir of what it was like out there in the bloody, traumatic Pacific war.

Mike Wallace
CBS News/60 Minutes

PREFACE

When is a Japanese a "Jap?"

That's easy! It's when he's flying an enemy plane, occupying an enemy bunker, pacing the bridge of an enemy warship or merely trying to eliminate you from this earth.

Since World War II I have twice lived in Japan and have visited the country several times. For the purpose of putting the record straight, I must report that in all that time I never really met a "Jap." Today, more than forty years since they surrendered their empire to superior strength, it's doubtful that many of the men we so identified are still with us. May they rest in peace!

In writing this study of an unhappy era, I have tried to limit my use of the word to a minimum but if I haven't been entirely successful (after those long years of using no other), I refer the reader to my dedication of this book. Incidentally, it might be enlightening to learn some of the endearing terms those "Japs" dedicated to our men during that cruel and bitter war.

Also, I wish to apologize to any officer whom I may have invested with a lesser rank than he had earned by the end of the conflict. When you cover a major headquarters with its many military satellites over a period of more than four combat years, almost none of your uniformed friends will leave you wearing the same chevron, bar, leaf, eagle, or star they wore when you first met. Even Douglas MacArthur "faded away" with more stars than any of his predecessors knew existed. So, if I refer to Colonel Bogie as Major, I apologize. After all, he was a captain when we first met.

Now, having dispensed the caveats, I wish to express my appreciation of the important help given me by four particular friends, each of whom had enough to do on his or her own without taking the time to help a struggling penny-a-liner:

Ann M. Sperber, editor, biographer (*Murrow: His Life and Times*), who gave the time necessary to chart the course *Pacific Microphone* had to follow in order to reach its intended goal;

the Reverend Theodore M. ("Father Ted") Hesburgh, president emeritus of the University of Notre Dame, who provided archival facilities for nearly a thousand original World War II broadcast scripts on which *Pacific Microphone* is based and who has cheered the idea of this book for more than a decade;

Margie Gewirtz, manager of the Wings Club, New York, whose logistic support during the creation of *Pacific Microphone* has been exceeded only by her encouraging confidence in the ultimate success of the project;

finally, but certainly not least, Joseph Wershba, editor, writer, veteran producer for CBS News's *60 Minutes*, who has been untiring in his support and invaluable in matters of research, rhetorical guidance, and the boosting of flagging morale. Joe's influence on *Pacific Microphone* has done much to make it a better book.

Without the interest and support of these four persons this would be, at least, a very different book, if in fact it had been carried to completion. I am grateful to them and to the countless others who contributed, but I appreciate most of all the loyal friendship which brought them to my aid.

Pacific Microphone

PROLOGUE

Certainly the arrival of our armada off the coast of Leyte Island had been scheduled for a moonless night, but no military planning board could have forecast the heavy cloud layer that made our cover complete. The hundreds of ships that surrounded the U.S.S. *Nashville* clear to the invisible horizons had been swallowed by darkness. We might have been alone except for the periodic emergence of great, shadowy ghost ships looming out of the murk and passing in eerie semi-silence.

We lay-to outside the entrance to Leyte Gulf shortly before midnight to wait for dawn and the official start of hostilities. General George Kenney joined me on the main deck as he had every night since we lift Hollandia in New Guinea. Together, we tried vainly to sight the coastline as we talked about the morrow, the general doing most of the talking.

What George Kenney wanted, urgently, was a piece of real estate that could be converted into an airstrip *right now!* In his mind, and few could dispute his premise, the ultimate success or failure of this campaign would depend on how quickly he could get his Far East Air Forces into position to support the ground operations of General Walter Kreuger's Sixth Army. Kenney didn't underestimate the necessity or value of naval air power, but like all air corps men he was convinced that adequate, continuing support of ground troops could never originate from the deck of a carrier, and it still seems a reasonable premise.

The *Nashville* command had provided comfortable quarters in a relatively quiet cabin for the four correspondents assigned to the mission, and we all stretched out on our berths, trying to get some sleep in the few hours left, but it was no use. Long before daylight we were back on deck, watching in anticipation for the first rays of dawn that would signal the assault. The bombardment erupted exactly on schedule, and the *Nashville* immediately weighed anchor and headed into the gulf. The threat of a tropical rain was heavy in the air.

It's almost impossible to describe the kaleidoscope and cacophony of a naval bombardment. As we moved into Leyte Gulf, zigzagging a path through the mined waters, most of the ships participating in

the shelling were behind us, and their seemingly uncoordinated salvos, signalled by the roar and flash of their guns, were immediately
echoed by the distant, muted coughs of the shells as they burst on
shore.

As long as the darkness of early dawn continued, we could see the
tracer shells moving in great arcs overhead, steady on their course
and amazing in their lethargy. It was an illusion, of course, but the
great balls of fire seemed to move with the slow deliberation of a freight
train. As the darkness lifted, the criss-cross of white rocket trails became visible against the mottled sky, and high above, great waves of
navy fighter planes maneuvered in fine coordination in quest of an
enemy that seemed to have been taken completely by surprise.

There was no pause. From the hoarse belch of the first gun until
the barrage lifted, signalling the first wave of troop-laden barges ashore,
the din was ear-splitting and continuous and I could feel the concus-
sions throughout my whole body. I had been impressed by the bombardment of the beaches at Cape Gloucester months before, but this
was incomparably greater.

From the first rays of daylight we could see General MacArthur
on the bridge with Capt. C. E. Coney, our skipper, his eyes scanning
the beaches and the waters in between. At that moment MacArthur's
role was reduced to that of an observer. His work had been completed
before we left New Guinea. Now he could only watch, alert for the
unexpected, and pray that his plans were being properly executed.

From what we could see from the main deck and learn from scuttlebutt around the ship, everything seemed to be progressing as planned.
There was opposition along the whole shoreline, from Dulag on the
south end of what had been designated as White Beach to Tacloban
at the north end of Red Beach, but our troops were more than holding
our own, and the situation appeared to be stable.

One welcome sight to this radio reporter was the appearance of
the broadcast ship, *Apache*, which came alongside the *Nashville* during the morning so Col. Abe Schechter, General Diller's radio officer,
could come aboard and get a copy of the first official communiqué
announcing the landing. When I had left Sydney, the *Apache* had been
under construction and there was doubt whether she would be ready
for this campaign. Because the entire fleet was under enforced radio
silence during the northward cruise, her facilities still had not been
tested in actual operation, but a few minutes later she relayed the
communiqué to the West Coast with complete success.

We had been told in an earlier briefing that General MacArthur would not go ashore, would not in fact leave his command post on the bridge, until the situation was under control and could be left in the hands of individual commanders. We had no way, of course, of knowing when that would be, probably some time after noon.

About eleven o'clock word came down that the General would like to meet the correspondents. Accordingly, we all mounted to the bridge. I was the only one who knew the General personally, from Manila, so I introduced the others: William B. Dickinson of the United Press, representing the newspapers and press associations, Frank Prist of Acme Newsphotos, chosen to represent the still photographers, and Earle Crotchett of Paramount, who carried the camera for the news-reels. I represented the combined U.S. radio networks.

The General was in excellent spirits, smoking the inevitable corn-cob as he kept a constant eye on the distant beach and the waters of the crowded gulf. He greeted us individually, assured us all was going according to plan, and after a few minutes told us the story he had asked us up to hear. Exactly forty-one years before, he told us, on October 20, 1903, 2d Lt. Douglas MacArthur, just commissioned out of West Point, had arrived in Tacloban, Philippines, assigned to the U.S. Army Corps of Engineers. That little city, he said, looked very much the same from our distance aboard U.S.S. *Nashville* as it had to the eyes of a youthful shavetail standing on the deck of an inter-island freighter. To this day I believe that anniversary fixed October 20 as the date for our formal return to the Philippines. When a command decision was made to make Leyte the primary target instead of Mindanao, advancing the entire campaign by two months, no one day had any advantage over another. But Douglas MacArthur was a man of great sentiment, and the date chosen would have had a special significance for him.

Just before we left the bridge, I asked the General if he remembered a promise he had made me at his first press conference in Melbourne after he arrived from Corregidor, when I was myself a refugee from Java. "I certainly do, Bill," he replied. "I told you that if you stuck with me, I would take you back to Manila." He waved a hand at the shoreline. "And here you are!"

In his *Reminiscences* MacArthur said he decided to go ashore with the third wave, but most of the coordinated movements of the great barge fleet seemed to have been concluded when, shortly after noon, a landing barge pulled alongside the *Nashville* and we all climbed aboard. Besides the General and ourselves, the group included Lt. Gen. George Kenney, chief of the Far East Air Forces; Maj. Gen. Richard K. Sutherland, MacArthur's chief of staff; Col. Courtney Whitney, liaison officer with the onshore guerrillas; and a half-dozen or so staff members. As we moved away from the *Nashville*, MacArthur and Sutherland perched side by side on top of the engine housing, both continuing to scan the busy waters. Suddenly MacArthur, with obvious emotion, gestured toward the shore, then slapped Sutherland on the knee. "Believe it or not, Dick, *we're back!*"

Our first stop was a nearby transport, where we were joined by Philippines President Sergio Osmeña; Maj. Gen. Basilio Valdez, chief of staff of the Philippines Army; and Brig. Gen. Carlos P. Romulo, an aide to President Osmeña and one of his nation's most eloquent spokesmen. I had known Rommy ever since I first arrived in the Philippines, when he was the editor of a Manila newspaper who had just won a Pulitzer Prize. We had a brief but warm reunion.

When President Osmeña joined us, the General greeted him warmly and helped him to a seat on the engine housing. All the time, however, his first attention was on the action surrounding us. Hundreds of barges and landing craft were shuttling men and materiel between the anchored fleet and the beaches. One barge was heading directly toward us, coming from the beach, and MacArthur ordered our coxswain, "Hail that barge."

Our cox gave the hail and the barge moved closer. This time it was the General who did the shouting. To the pop-eyed sailor at the other helm, who obviously didn't expect to meet his commander in chief in the middle of Leyte Gulf, the General called, "Son, where is the hardest fighting going on?" The astounded helmsman pointed to a spot on Red Beach, almost directly ahead of us, and the General thanked him. Then, to our own cox, pointing to the same spot: "Head for that beach, son." I was never quite sure what knowledge an able-bodied seaman afloat had of combat conditions ashore, but there was no doubt that Douglas MacArthur was looking for trouble!

The entire eastern shore of Leyte Island consists of sandy beaches that extend far into the water. As a result, our craft was grounded some twenty to thirty yards from dry land, and we had to wade the remaining distance. In addition to Prist and Crotchett, the army had a staff photographer aboard, and Dickinson was carrying his own camera. As soon as the ramp dropped, these four dashed into the surf in quest of good camera angles. I was carrying only my trusty typewriter, so I stayed with the main group.

The famous picture of that landing, published thousands of times all over the world, was made by military photographer Maj. Gaetano Faillace, who carried a movie camera. Despite persistent reports to the contrary, it was strictly a one-time shot. The idea that Douglas MacArthur would actually pose for the picture or that he made several treks between the landing craft and shore to ensure good camera angles is one of the most ludicrous misconceptions to come out of that war. Once that ramp dropped, he had no interest in anything except getting ashore as quickly as possible to see for himself how the situation was evolving.

I have been asked scores of times why I was the only member of the group not wearing a cap or helmet. I don't like hats and have never owned one except when required by uniform regulations. When the word came that we were ready to go ashore, I dashed below to get my typewriter and helmet. I knew we would broadcast from the beach, and I thought I might need a script. The faithful Hermes was where I had left it, but the helmet wasn't handy so I hurried back to the deck without it. No one paid the slightest heed, and I'm sure my shock of hair (much thinner now) gave me as much protection as the General got from his famous campaign cap.

In his own account of the landing, General MacArthur leaves the impression, unintentionally I'm sure, that among the first things he did, once ashore, was to make his historic broadcast to the people of the Philippines. Actually, it took more than an hour for the Signal Corps to get a transmitter into position and tuned for the job. Although the Signal Corps knew the broadcast would be made and had a transmitter standing by, mounted in a weapon carrier, no one knew where along that twenty-mile stretch of beach the General's craft would touch. Not until he established personal contact with the nearest command post did the technicians learn where to bring the transmitter, probably a distance of several miles.

Once we reached dry land, the word that General MacArthur was on the beach spread rapidly, and curious GI's appeared from everywhere in spite of the staccato of rifle and machine-gun fire in actual combat only a few yards distant. You wondered who was tending the store. The General asked directions to the nearest command post and then set a pace through the soft, yielding sand that had some of us

General Douglas MacArthur's landing at Leyte. This, the official picture of the *only* landing MacArthur made on October 20, was taken by Maj. Gaetano Faillace, a photographer attached to GHQ. *Left*, Pres. Sergio Osmeña, Col. Courtney Whitney, Brig. Gen. Carlos Romulo, General MacArthur, Maj. Gen. Richard Sutherland, myself, and Sgt. Francis Saveron.

juniors panting to hold our own. He spent most of that first hour moving tirelessly about the beachhead, on foot, talking with unit commanders, inspecting positions, and asking endless questions.

After a time the Signal Corps arrived with the transmitter mounted in its weapon carrier and moved it into position at the edge of a nearby palm grove. The major in charge handed me the microphone and asked for a voice level while he finished tuning. I took the mike, which resembled a hand-held telephone, and began to speak. "People of the Philippines, in a few minutes you will hear the voices of Gen. Douglas MacArthur and your own president, Sergio Osmeña, speaking to you from Philippines soil. You will hear them on the wave length to which you are now tuned." The broadcast was to be transmitted on

Ignoring a tropical deluge that blurred this picture, General MacArthur delivers his historic pronouncement, "I have returned!" from a palm grove on Leyte's Red Beach after having been introduced by me (left). Directly behind me, wearing a helmet, is Bill Chickering of Time-Life, and on Bill's left, wearing a water-soaked uniform, is Maj. Phil North, whose landing barge had been sunk.

several frequencies known to be used by the guerrilla forces and familiar to civilians with clandestine receivers. I repeated those words, with variations, for fifteen or twenty minutes while the technicians did their work.

Finally the major indicated that the circuits were ready, and I motioned to General MacArthur, who was waiting nearby with President Osmeña. Rain clouds had threatened all morning, and a brisk shower began to fall as I again took up the microphone. "People of the Philippines, the next voice you hear will be that of Gen. Douglas MacArthur, speaking from a beach on the island of Leyte. The General will be followed by your own president, the honorable Sergio Osmeña. Now, here he is, Gen. Douglas MacArthur."

This is the hand-held microphone used by Gen. Douglas MacArthur to announce his return to the Philippines from a rain-swept beach on the island of Leyte. Preserved by the U.S. Signal Corps and presented to the MacArthur Memorial in Norfolk, the mike occupies a prominent place among the General's memorabilia. *Courtesy MacArthur Memorial, Norfolk*

The General accepted the microphone and began to speak. "People of the Philippines, I *have* returned! By the grace of Almighty God our forces now stand again on Philippines soil—soil consecrated by the blood of our two people. . . ." He continued, ignoring the rain, which was now a real tropical downpour. When finished, he introduced President Osmeña, who delivered a stirring message to his people.

(Some years later, during the Korean War, I was talking to the General on the airstrip at Taegu, our first meeting in over a year. Suddenly he asked, "Bill, do you remember that day on the beach at Leyte when you introduced me on the radio and I spoke to the people of the Philippines?" More than a little astonished at the question, I assured him I certainly had not forgotten. To which he responded, "My, you have a remarkable memory." After nearly four and a half decades, I am still trying to sort that one out!)

As the rain abated somewhat, the General and the president walked into the grove a few meters and sat down on a palm log for a protracted conversation while the rest of us kept a discreet distance. As they talked, a couple of enemy planes managed to penetrate the naval air patrol and dropped one or two bombs nearby. I would gladly have hit the dirt until they left, but General MacArthur characteristically chose to ignore them (he did mention them in his memoirs), so the rest of us remained staunchly, if unenthusiastically, erect.

As we went back to the barge for the return to the *Nashville*, we learned that enemy planes had attacked the U.S.S. *Indianapolis*, sister ship of the *Nashville*, inflicting considerable damage. It was thought that the Japanese might have been after our own ship, which was carrying the C-in-C. At any rate, as soon as we were all back on board, the *Nashville* weighed anchor and headed out into the Pacific to spend the night in evasive maneuvers.

Soon after we boarded, I went up to the ship's communications room and, using a relay via the *Apache*, made my first report to the combined American networks on MacArthur's return to the Philippines, a brief broadcast encapsulating the events of a memorable day for what was probably the largest audience I ever addressed. Fortunately, reception in the States was reported as very good.

Later on, after the evening meal, I was asked to join General MacArthur in the communications room and again I introduced him as he repeated the speech he had made on the beach, this time beamed to the United States, also via the *Apache*. As we stood talking, waiting for the go-ahead from San Francisco, I noticed that the General's hands were trembling slightly as he held his script. It actually was a minor affliction of his latter years, but I, with remarkable lack of tact, asked him if the microphone made him nervous. He looked at me reprovingly and shook his head. "Bill," he said, "I am *never* nervous."

PART 1

CHAPTER 1

"90-Day" Assignment

I could tell by his expression and by the way he waved me to a chair he had something special on his mind. Paul White, Chief of CBS News, delighted in making a production out of anything unusual, and this apparently was something unusual. He let me get seated, then said, "Bill, we know there's going to be a war in the Pacific, probably sooner than most people think, and CBS will have to cover it. If we are going to do the job right, we'll need a lot more information than we can get in this office. How would you like to take a three-month trip to the Far East. . . ."

As he spoke the phone rang, his private line, and he stopped in mid-sentence to pick it up, leaving me to sit there in utter disbelief, trying to convince myself I had heard him correctly. No American network had ever sent a correspondent halfway around the world for any reason, and even a hint that I might be the first was hard to digest. Finally he hung up the phone and turned back. "Well, what about it?" Paul had been watching me covertly as he talked, and I have always believed he arranged that interruption just to enjoy my reaction. It would have been entirely typical. I sparred. "Paul, what's this all about?"

There was a microphone on his desk that we used to talk to Ed Murrow and our other overseas correspondents before they made their reports on the morning and evening news shows. Paul pulled the mike over to him and examined it carefully before he answered. "I've been talking to Ed Klauber (the vice-president to whom CBS News then reported), and he agrees we should be getting ready for trouble in the Pacific. Someone has to go out there and make a complete reconnaissance to put CBS in position to report whatever happens. There's no way I can leave, and you're next in seniority. The assignment is yours if you want it."

"Will there be any broadcasting?" Paul laughed. We both knew I had (and still have) one of the worst Hoosier twangs ever to aggravate a microphone, and he often kidded me about it. Fortunately for me, however, White was one radio news editor who rated knowledge and experience above vocal cords. "I don't give a damn about your voice as long as you cover the story and keep CBS in evidence. We'll schedule you whenever your facilities are available and acceptable. We want to establish CBS in our listeners' minds as first in the Far East. The rest is right down your alley: organization, locating facilities, making contacts, pinpointing news sources, and lining up correspondents."

I sat there in deep thought for a good minute while he moved the mike into yet another position, still watching me. Finally, he broke it up. "Okay, talk it over with Catherine. Think it over and get back to me as soon as you can. The quicker we get started, the better. Now, get the hell out of here. I'm busy."

Headquarters of CBS News in those formative years occupied most of the seventeenth floor at 485 Madison Avenue, home base of the network. Both White and I had our own offices, but I never used mine, occupying instead a desk that commanded a view of the entire newsroom and broadcast studio. It was to this desk I returned, my head spinning.

What was the Orient actually like? How do people react with war staring them in the face? How do the potential aggressors act while getting ready to strike? There was half a world in this assignment, stretching from Japan to Australia; it was impossible to digest the enormity of the concept all at once. To be honest, I had made up my mind instantly, just as White knew I had, but it was necessary to clear the idea with my wife and daughter and to take a few hours to arrange my own thoughts and emotions.

I doubted from the first Paul's ninety-day estimate, and I told Catherine I was sure it would take much longer. As a network news editor, I knew enough about geography and the state of the world to understand the distances and the difficulties involved. Air transportation was sketchy to nonexistent over most of the area, and much of my assignment would have to be covered by sea or overland. Catherine agreed it was an opportunity I couldn't refuse, as I was sure she would. In over half a century she has never tried to influence any decision pertaining to my career. She might have expressed some solid doubts, however, had she realized that the projected ninety days would stretch into over five years during which we would be apart for all but ninety days.

Once my decision had been formalized, I struggled to arrange a quick departure. I had to handle the red tape myself, no proxies. Thanks to Hitler and Mussolini, who then controlled almost all of Europe and much of North Africa, anything connected with international travel was automatically difficult. It was impossible to get a passport until you satisfied the State Department that your proposed travels were less than frivolous, if not absolutely essential, and when, or if, you received the document, it would declare large areas of the globe, not necessarily contested areas, off-limits to you.

The New York passport office advised me to take my application directly to Washington to avoid possibly weeks of delay. I followed that advice and scored in just three days, but even then I had to go back on the fourth day for an amendment permitting travel to India and Singapore, both originally banned for unexplained reasons. The all-important matter of visas, however, presented no problem except that it took time. Even the Japanese at this stage were cooperative, but world turmoil generated a marked increase in the red tape so dear to all government functionaries, regardless of flag.

The first transportation problem arose when I applied to Pan American for passage to Manila. Five years earlier Pan Am's heralded *China Clipper* had pioneered the first, and at that time the only, air route across the Pacific. Consequently I assumed I would cover the 11,000 miles to Manila by air, but I was wrong. Pan American advised against flying from San Francisco to Honolulu (actually Pearl Harbor), explaining that their flying boats could not carry a normal payload on that 2,400-mile flight unless the weather was perfect. If there was any possibility of bad weather or adverse winds, passengers had to be off-loaded for fuel. Instead, Pan Am booked me on the M.S. *Matsonia* for what proved to be the most delightful five days of the sixteen it took me to reach the Philippines.

There still remained the inevitable immunization shots and vaccinations, a routine I would gladly have skipped on the theory that the unhappy diseases they were designed to prevent couldn't have been any worse than the reactions I invariably suffered. Smallpox vaccinations weren't too bad, but the cholera and typhoid shots required at that time, particularly the latter, were something else. I'd already been given two typhoid shots and was scheduled for the last on the day of departure. By that time my right arm was swollen and inflamed, and I asked that the third be postponed, at least until I reached the West Coast. The doctor was adamant, however, and I got the final shot in the left arm. The results were immediate and superpositive and lasted all the way to Honolulu. I think I would still opt for typhoid.

Finally the essentials were completed. I had all the necessary pa-

pers and shots and tons of advice from everyone who had ever heard
of the Orient. At five o'clock on the afternoon of January 14, 1941,
I bade farewell to my wife and daughter and took off from LaGuardia
on the longest "three-month" tour on record. With me were my passport, heavily visaed, two stopwatches, one typewriter, two very sore
arms, and a fever. All that was missing was a microphone.

By the time I reached Honolulu eight days later, the effects of the
shots had diminished, but I had contracted a deep cold that reacted
like laryngitis and left me with almost no voice, hardly an ideal situation for a radio correspondent.

At least I learned en route that I am a good sailor. The *Matsonia*
ran into rough weather on the second night out of the Golden Gate,
and before she reached Diamond Head several thousands of dollars'
worth of fittings and furniture, smashed by the careening of the ship,
had been dumped overboard. For two days the first-class dining room
was almost empty as our fellow passengers battled *mal-de-mer* in their
staterooms. The only five that never missed a meal were a husband
and wife from Chicago, a naval commander, a navy wife en route to
join her husband, and an almost speechless radio reporter.

I had radioed New York about my vanishing voice, and White delayed my first scheduled report by two days. I spent the first in bed
while a doctor tried to coax my vocal cords back into service. The
second day, however, I spent inspecting naval and military facilities
at Hickam Field, Schofield Barracks, and Pearl Harbor. And the one
lesson that was drilled into me at every point was that thanks to the
army, navy, and air corps, Oahu was absolutely impregnable. "Safer
here than on the west coast" was the universal word, and I must admit I bought it.

My guide at Pearl Harbor was Lt. Jack Pierce, commander of the
Narwhal, at that time the largest submarine in our navy. Jack was
not only a distinguished submariner, he was also an accomplished
salesman who knew Pearl Harbor as well as his own backyard. By
the time we finished the tour, I was convinced Hawaii was more secure than San Francisco Bay. I managed to croak through my first report from outside the continental limits the following day—Saturday,
January 24—and I left no doubt in the minds of my listeners that I
was reporting from one American citadel no enemy could ever penetrate. I have often wondered if my vocal difficulties actually meant
that the Good Lord was trying to tell me something.

On Sunday morning I took off in Pan Am's *Philippines Clipper* from Pearl Harbor and four days later, after overnight stops at Midway, Wake, and Guam, landed in Cavite harbor on Manila Bay, just south of the city.

From the first, I had intended to establish headquarters in Manila from which I could move in any direction—Japan, China, Singapore, India, Burma, Indochina, Thailand, or the Netherlands Indies. The Philippines, still under the American flag, would provide a secure base for possessions or information I didn't want to take into potentially hostile territory. More importantly, Manila in 1941 was truly the crossroads of the Orient. It was almost impossible to travel any distance in the Far East at that time without touching at Manila or Hong Kong.

Pan American had one weekly round trip between Manila and Hong Kong while KNILM, the KLM subsidiary in the Indies, operated infrequent flights between Manila, Batavia (now Jakarta), Singapore, and Saigon, with an occasional schedule to India via Rangoon. China National Airways Corporation (CNAC) flew unheralded flights from Hong Kong to Chungking, Kunming, and Rangoon.

With the exception of Pan Am's Hong Kong flight, it was impossible to schedule a plane trip in advance. You could only let your desires be known, stand by more or less patiently for a few hours or a few days, then rush to complete departure preparations in a matter of minutes. Schedules were top secret in most instances in order to confuse the enemy.

The maritime situation was a little better. British, Dutch, Japanese, and American freighters provided more consistent, if still irregular, transportation. The shipping lines tried to maintain some semblance of order, but it wasn't easy. Everything was always subject to change without notice because of a war on the other side of the world or because of the Sino-Japanese conflict, which at that time saw large portions of the Chinese mainland occupied militarily by Japan. Of all the countries offering transport, only the United States was not actively at war somewhere.

For these reasons, and in view of the magnitude of my territorial assignment, it was sensible to be headquartered in the center of the area where whatever transportation was available would likely find its way. Manila would be my far eastern base. The original ninety-day schedule was forgotten.

CHAPTER 2

Douglas MacArthur

The Manila of 1941 was a unique Manila . . . a Manila that had never existed before . . . a Manila that would never exist again.

Despite the thunderheads mounting to the north, the Manila of 1941 was truly the Pearl of the Orient, a city whose rising prosperity made even the thought of total war impossible for the average person to comprehend. Although a paternal Uncle Sam had ordered all diplomatic and military families back to the States, and many businessmen had followed that lead, few thought such action really necessary.

American influence in the Philippines reached its zenith in that fateful year. Although the Philippines was a commonwealth steadily moving toward promised independence, its capital, Manila, was essentially an American city. The government of President Manuel Quezon was completely subordinate to the office of the U.S. high commissioner, Francis Sayre, and the economy of the entire archipelago carried a "Made in USA" label.

Almost all the leading business firms were American or European controlled. Of the two largest newspapers, one was American owned and edited and the other had an American editor. All major newspapers were printed in English. Even the Rotary and Lions clubs were presided over by Americans, although plans were being made to allow the Filipino to preside at least every other year.

To live in Manila in 1941 was to experience the good life. The currency was based on the dollar-backed peso and was officially traded at two pesos to the dollar. In fact, the Philippines peso had almost the same purchasing power as the 1941 dollar in the States. The pack of American cigarettes that cost fifteen cents in New York in those days cost fifteen centavos in Manila, exactly half price, and the five-peso dinner, regarded as expensive in any top Manila restaurant, would have brought at least five dollars in Manhattan. Amenities of every sort were available on a similar scale.

Further, the American family stationed in the Philippines, whether for diplomatic, military, or personal business reasons, could equip its menage with a good cook, houseboy or girl, *lavendera* (laundress), and a competent chauffeur, for the peso equivalent of about a hundred dollars a month, and the servants considered themselves well rewarded. Who could visualize the horrors of war while living such a life under benign tropical skies?

My first few days in Manila were exploratory and organizational. I made immediate contact with RCA Communications (RCAC), which would provide my broadcast link to the States, and with radio station KZRM, which had a loose affiliation with CBS and would provide me with a broadcast studio. In working with these organizations and the United Press (UP), I made three friends who rendered wholehearted and invaluable assistance in getting me settled and oriented in a new and strange environment. All remained close personal friends throughout their lives.

Earle ("B. G.") Baumgartner, local head of RCAC, had all the technical information I needed, knew the important people in Malacañan Palace, the presidential mansion, and gave me my first view of the Philippines countryside surrounding his transmission facilities some miles outside the city.

Dave Sternberg of KZRM knew the political situation in the islands as well as any man I could hope to meet. Confined to a wheelchair by childhood polio, Dave more than made up mentally for the weakness of his frail little body, and he was an excellent mentor. He provided details from both the domestic and American viewpoints that would have taken me months to learn on my own.

Finally, Dick Wilson, UP bureau chief, had been in Manila long enough to know all the angles necessary to the gathering of news. He supplied me with contacts in the high commissioner's office, Malacañan, and the American military, a windfall for a newly arrived reporter. He also knew all the best restaurants and had access to all the better clubs. Radio reporters can't live on kilowatts alone!

Although their contributions were independent and in no way coordinated, these three men quickly tuned me in on the right wave lengths to realize practically all my needs, and in a wholehearted manner that few would have bothered to waste on a stranger. (I was able to repay B. G. and Dave for some of their help three years later when I discovered Baumgartner in a Japanese prison camp at Cabanatuan, and Sternberg in the Santo Tomás internment camp in Manila. Dick Wilson was in Hong Kong on a business,trip at the time of Pearl Harbor and spent his internment in that defenseless colony.)

Soon after my arrival I paid courtesy calls on President Manuel Quezon, fighting a losing battle against tuberculosis but still mentally keen and determined to function in what he recognized as a major crisis for his people, and on Francis Sayre, the high commissioner, an erudite man with no illusions about the gathering storm. But the man I wanted most to talk to was Douglas MacArthur, at that time on leave from the U.S. Army, acting as military advisor to President Quezon and supervising organization of the Commonwealth Army, which would serve the nation after the advent of promised independence.

I got little encouragement from members of the regular U.S. Army in the Philippines, however. Most of the officers with whom I spoke dismissed MacArthur as superannuated, on loan to the Philippines government to keep him occupied until retirement. I would be wasting my time talking to a has-been. Nevertheless, I felt that MacArthur could fill me in on the overall Asian picture and provide background information that would be invaluable as I moved on to the other countries in my assignment. He was not in the news at the moment, of course, but as a newcomer to the Orient, I wanted to hear the views of a seasoned Far East veteran.

To my surprise, the unidentified person who accepted my call at MacArthur's headquarters gave me a flat turn-down. "Sorry, but the General is much too busy at present to grant interviews . . . perhaps at a later . . ." Frankly, I didn't believe what I heard, but I didn't persist. Instead, I placed a call to Malacañan Palace, to the aide who had fixed my appointment with President Quezon. Very quickly I had a call from Commonwealth Army headquarters telling me that General MacArthur would like very much to meet with me, and an appointment was made. It was my first experience with the protective cordon his subordinates always tried to maintain around him, without, I am sure, his knowledge or consent.

When I arrived at the designated time, the major in the outer office greeted me quite cordially but cautioned me not to usurp too much of the General's time. I was not to exceed my allotted fifteen minutes. Those determined efforts to limit the duration of interviews or casual visits was quite unnecessary. Once you gained access to that inner office, all signals were called by the General. You were never in doubt if he wanted you to remain, and when he decided the session was over, he made that decision cordially clear. My interview lasted over an hour and a half, during which we discussed (my contribution consisting of a few questions and a pair of eager ears) everything from the new Commonwealth Army to the war in Europe and the storm-clouds gathering over Asia.

General of the Army Douglas MacArthur

To my surprise, he told me that President Roosevelt had assured him he would be called home to command the American combat forces if, or when, the United States was drawn into the European conflict. Until that time or until events in Asia indicated otherwise, he assured me, he would remain at his post in the Philippines. His agreement with President Quezon had some five years to run.

Although MacArthur then held the rank of field marshal in the Commonwealth Army, he never wore a uniform during all those furloughed years. He never explained his reason, but those who knew him best believed that because of his deep respect for the uniform he had worn almost all his adult life, he could never bring himself to wear any other. The General was wearing tropical white linens when he received me, and tropical white linens were here his standard "uniform" until he was called back to his original uniform the following July as commander of the newly formed United States Armed Forces in the Far East (USAFFE).

When I entered his office, he came out from behind his desk to greet me, and within minutes I realized I was in the presence of a great conversationalist. He talked with the assurance that comes only with knowledge, and he made his points as precisely as if reading a script but was never stilted nor pedantic. Frankly, until now I had regarded him as just another general. Before I left that office, I already had begun to change my mind.

During much of the time he smoked a black cigar—cigars—which I judged to be one of Manila's famous "ropes." I did not see the famous corncob until later. The office was in an old Spanish mansion atop the great stone wall that had once enclosed the original Manila. Its large windows looked out across the Luneta, a broad common, to Manila Bay beyond, and the General moved between his desk and this vista every few minutes during our entire conversation. It was as if his active mind wouldn't let his body relax.

Finally, when he decided we had covered the designated ground, he came smiling out of his chair, hand extended, and I understood that our "fifteen minutes" had elapsed. It would have been just as impossible to extend my visit beyond that handshake as it would have been to terminate it earlier.

In spite of an immediate affection for Manila and the Philippines, which has lasted to this day, I was anxious to get on with my assignment. I still had the remainder of the Far East and possibly Australia to cover, and there was no way to judge how much time remained. My original plan had been to visit Tokyo almost immediately, before a menacing situation became worse. Only a few weeks before my arrival in Manila, a correspondent for Reuters News Agency had jumped, or been pushed, to his death from a window in the Tokyo police headquarters while being questioned by Japanese authorities. Understandably, after that incident, Tokyo was no longer regarded as a reporter's paradise.

I didn't want to be trapped in Japan if the worst did happen, a view Paul White shared completely. In fact, Paul at first had questioned the value of my visiting Tokyo at all. We certainly would not be broadcasting from there if war did come. Still, he was very unhappy with the string correspondent he had hired by cable, and a second choice made the same way might be no better. Finally, we decided to include Tokyo but early on the schedule. I therefore began looking for transportation as soon as I established my Manila base. The U.S.S. *President Coolidge*, I learned, would depart Manila for Kobe about three weeks after my arrival in the Far East, the only ship scheduled from Manila to a Japanese port in the next sixty days. I booked passage and began packing.

That plan had to be scrapped immediately, however. For some reason he didn't explain, Paul decided I should delay my departure and stand by in Manila. It was fortunate that he did, because the trip would have been impossible at that time. My passport, only four weeks old, was outdated. The State Department had changed the color of passport covers from maroon to green. Mine was perfectly valid for another two years, but Irving Ross, passport officer, thought I risked serious misunderstanding by some "flunky" (the word was his) in some remote immigration office, and he offered to issue me a new one. The drawback, of course, was that my maroon document carried all the visas I had to have to complete my assignment, so he proposed stapling the two together. I agreed. Unfortunately, the "flunky" Ross had feared proved to be in his own office. While my new document was being prepared, this youngster busied himself stamping "Cancelled" across the face of every visa except that for the Netherlands Indies, the last one in the book. The culprit was checked before he reached that one, but the damage was done.

A highly embarrassed passport officer immediately got on the phone and called his counterparts at all the concerned consulates, explained the situation, and asked for duplicates. No one objected except the Japanese. They were terribly sorry, of course, but a matter as grave as the accidental cancellation of a visa could be rectified only on orders from Tokyo, and they had no idea how long it might take to get the word from Tokyo. We pleaded, but they were flatly adamant. White didn't know of this predicament when he decided to delay the Japan trip, and I didn't tell him. Ross insisted I would get the visa eventually, so I recommended going south to Batavia, Singapore, and Saigon rather than standing by in Manila where I was pretty well organized, and Paul agreed.

. The only air link between Manila and the Indies was by KNILM, the Dutch line that operated a nonscheduled flight between Manila and Batavia every ten days or two weeks, and they had a flight set up for February 27, only a couple of days after I decided to go south. The flight would take me through the southern Philippines and Borneo, with an overnight stop in Balikpapan, second largest oil field in the Far East.

Dick Wilson offered to drive me to the airport for my 7:00 A.M. departure. Nichols Field was then Manila's leading airfield, used by both the civil and military air. Dick's driver was well on the way to Nichols when I realized that my ticket specified Makati Field, a little-used grass strip about two miles distant. We immediately changed direction, but by the time we reached Makati, the DC-2 was already at the end of the field and poised for takeoff. The field manager, who obviously had been waiting for me, waved us onto the field, and we dashed out to the waiting plane. As we raced up beside the plane, the copilot opened the door, I swung my typewriter and bag aboard, and then Wilson and his driver boosted me through the doorway into the waiting arms of the copilot. One minute later we were in the air, heading for Borneo and the Netherlands Indies.

Our route lay almost directly south from Manila across the Visayan Islands with a brief stop at Iloilo, then south again and slightly west across the Sulu and Celebes seas to Tarakan, a little island off the northeast tip of Borneo, site of the third largest oil fields in the Indies. We set down at Tarakan at noon and drove from the plane through the largest assemblage of oil derricks I had ever seen to arrive at an excellent luncheon, courtesy of Shell Oil Company.

The crude oil pumped from the wells of Tarakan was famous for its very high quality, and the Dutch knew it was a prize high on Japan's list of priorities. Military activity here gave plenty of indication that the Dutch were anticipating serious trouble and doing their best to prepare for it.

The flight to Balikpapan was memorable as my first view of equatorial jungles. From Manila to Tarakan, our plane carried us mostly over water and scattered islands. From Tarakan south to Balikpapan, however, we were over the densest part of the Borneo jungles. It took little imagination to envision what a power failure would mean. In that entire 330-mile flight, I saw no clearing large enough to offer room even for a crash-landing. (I would later learn that New Guinea's jungles, while formidable, couldn't compare.) I concentrated on trying to estimate the distance of the Macassar Straits, which paralleled our route some miles to the east.

At Balikpapan military preparations were again everywhere evident. Once more we were driven through a mammoth forest of derricks, this time to an attractive little club on the shore of the straits, obviously a recreation facility for Shell Oil employees who operated the huge fields and refineries. Each of us five passengers was assigned a room in a type of dormitory, plain but immaculately clean. After seeing us settled, our captain, Dick von Rees, suggested we take a few minutes to freshen up, then join him in the lounge for an "hour of grog." The excellent dinner that followed, and the "hour" itself, hardly fit my preconceived ideas of the wilds of Borneo, but, with the memory of those deep jungles still fresh in my mind, I was content!

CHAPTER 3

Doubt and Belief

The direct airline route from Balikpapen to Batavia carries the traveler once again over some of Borneo's most forbidding jungles so it was welcome word when von Rees told us we would make a cargo stop at Sourabaya, which is almost directly south of Balikpapen on the eastern end of Java. We would be cruising over the Makassar Straits and the Java Sea for most of the five hours and would also have a better view of both Borneo and Java.

Although the Philippines and the Indies appear as parts of one great archipelago when viewed on a map, there definitely is a visible physical difference. As you move south across the equator the foliage somehow seems greener, with both the sky and the sea a more brilliant blue. But in 1941 there was another and more vital difference, apparent from the first time you touched Indonesian soil.

Moving from the Philippines to the Netherlands East Indies (NEI) and Singapore-Malaya in 1941 was moving from serious doubt to certain belief. The civilian population of the Philippines, Filipino and American alike, had never experienced all-out war and simply could not believe in it. The Dutch in the NEI, however, already had lost their Netherlands homeland to a vicious Nazi blitzkrieg, and the British in Singapore had the fresh memory of the Battle of Britain to convince them it could happen anywhere.

Dutch and British attitudes toward the menace of war with Japan differed, however. The Dutch held no illusions except, perhaps, too much faith in their allies. They knew they could never hold out alone against a large-scale invasion, and they based their defence plans on the hope—futile, as it turned out—that if they prepared themselves to the last man and proved their ability and determination to fight when the blow fell, then the United States and their other allies would certainly provide the massive aid they had been led to expect. In contrast, the British fully expected the Japanese to move against them eventually but clung to the myth of the impregnable Singapore superfortress, wholly confident they could handle whatever situation developed.

These were the impressions I was to gather in the next few weeks as I traveled through both areas and talked with the people, civilians, military, businessmen, and members of the governments. The probable reaction of the ethnic populations, mostly Islamic, would be doubtful until the actual test came. Almost none of them could have any real conception of modern warfare. The Dutch expected the Indonesians, as a people, to remain loyal; the British in Malaya and Singapore weren't so sure.

It was good to find there would be no major transmission problems in the NEI. The Dutch had an excellent intercontinental facility in the Bandoeng hills, south of Batavia, linked by land lines to Batavia, to Sourabaya, and to Bandoeng itself. The facility had been developed, of course, to provide reliable communication with the Netherlands, but it functioned just as efficiently across the Pacific.

Consequently my stay in Java was regrettably brief. Despite the heavy overtones of military preparation, Batavia in 1941 was a delightful place. The Dutch were most cooperative because they wanted the world to know their story, to understand their determination to meet whatever came with every resource at their command. I established Jack Raleigh as the CBS string correspondent, made my own contacts with the government offices, and continued on to Singapore in less than a week.

Singapore proved to be an entirely different story. First of all, the transmission facilities were not geared for intercontinental communication. Even more important, the British colonials didn't seem to have the same sense of urgency as the Dutch. I found them cooperative but not enthusiastically so. Sure of their superfortress, they would accept outside help but didn't consider it imperative. They had, after all, repulsed Hitler's Luftwaffe in the Battle of Britain only a few months earlier, and Japan could never mount a more serious threat. When the U.S. Congress passed the Lend-Lease Act in March, 1941, which authorized the president to send war supplies to countries whose defense was vital to the United States, the news was greeted in the colony with very mixed reactions.

The broad verandah of the venerable Raffles Hotel was the meeting place late each afternoon for Singapore's journalists, minor government officials, officers, and visiting correspondents. We gathered to discuss the latest news, usually the news from abroad, aided by the ubiquitous *stengah*, the local term for whisky (scotch) and water. On this particular afternoon the enactment, a day earlier, of the Lend-Lease bill topped the agenda, and someone immediately questioned the news judgment of the *Straits Times*, Singapore's leading paper, in burying the story deep on an inside page. The editor defended his decision stubbornly, insisting that because everyone knew the bill was going to pass, it really wasn't news. He seemed offended when asked if one day he would bury the story of King George's death, since everyone knew he was going to die.

Another British brother was more outspoken. "This," he declared, "is a typical example of American arrogance in trying to foist their help on people who don't need and don't want it!" I was dumbfounded. Only a month earlier Winston Churchill in a broadcast from London had declared he was going to tell President Roosevelt: "Give us the tools and we will finish the job!"

I pulled out my notebook and made a show of taking notes. My senator-uncle (fictional) in Washington, I said, would be very interested in these opinions, having helped to sponsor the measure. That brought immediate protests from others in the group who assured me that lend-lease was indeed needed and certainly welcome. But there was no real enthusiasm on the part of any of my English cohorts. It was a strange reaction and one not shared, I am certain, by bomb-battered Londoners. I have often pondered that session at Raffles, particularly a year later when things were going so badly for the British in the jungles of Malaya.

Despite Bob Hope's cherished memories of nights in Singapore, that "far away city with its strange-sounding name" in 1941 was just plain dull. There was the verandah at Raffles, of course, and there were movies, mostly American, and some of the theaters even had air conditioning. There was a low-key night club run by two American expatriates, Stan Cowen and Bill Bailey, old-time vaudevillians. Stan and Bill also provided the entertainment while Stelle, Stan's wife, supervised the kitchen and the cash register. Grand people but hardly thrilling.

Aside from those amenities, you were on your own. I probably read more books in those few weeks than in any comparable period before or since. The military was very much in evidence with uniforms of every type from OD's (olive drabs) to tartan kilts visible on the verandah each night. On Sunday evenings the Gordon Highlanders regimental band set up shop next to the verandah and provided some rather good music. On Sundays, too, a correspondent might be invited out to the Dogras or some other regimental mess for a Pimm's cup or to the home of a regimental officer for a curry tiffin, always memorable, good food, drinks, and conversation.

The one experience that stays with me, even after over four decades, was the Sunday tiffin at the home of Capt. Jack McNaughton, of the Loyal North Lancasters, where I was offered as a Sunday libation, gin with quinine water. I thought it was a joke. I had had youthful experience with quinine (my English friends pronounce it "quaneen"), and even the thought of that bitter additive in any kind of a drink was impossible. My host protested its merits, among them prevention of malaria. He also insisted that I would enjoy it, and, strangely, I did. But it never occurred to me that gin and tonic (Indian tonic, according to the label on the bottle) would flood my own country as soon as the war ended, driving the long-reigning Tom Collins virtually out of business.

My problem in Singapore, as a radio reporter, lay in the knowledge that the Malayan Broadcasting Corporation (MBC) was not equipped for the short-wave transmission necessary for distant projection. Local facilities on the broadcast band were excellent but limited in range, designed only for coverage of the peninsula and of Singapore Island. In order to reach San Francisco with an effective voice signal, it was necessary to arrange a relay by some short-wave facility near enough to receive the MBC signal clearly. That meant either Manila or Batavia, and tests were arranged. RCAC in Manila made several tests but reported in the negative. Batavia, nearly nine hundred miles closer, was able to handle the relay with fair success.

We would be able to put the required signal into San Francisco and onto the network under favorable atmospheric conditions, but there was one major drawback. The words of the reporter, intended only for an American audience, could be heard by anyone in the Malaya-Singapore area who had an ordinary home radio. That would mean more stringent censorship, of course, because the government would be more concerned with what you (involuntarily) told the people of the colony than what you reported to the United States. But there was no alternative. Arrangements were completed, and I made my first broadcast at 4:00 A.M. on March 12, 1941 (6:00 P.M. on March 11 in New York). The circuit was acceptable.

CHAPTER 4

Gem in the Tiara

While waiting to hear whether the San Francisco circuits via Batavia were adequate, I decided to make a quick trip north to Saigon, cultural capital of what was then French Indochina, France's largest Asian colony that included all of what is now Cambodia, Laos, and Vietnam. Saigon is almost exactly 750 miles north and a little east of Singapore. My friends at KNILM informed me they would have a DC-2 scheduled for the flight around March 18, and promised a second flight for my return in about a week or ten days. I immediately booked both flights.

Neither Paul White nor I believed there was much chance that Indochina, politically linked with pro-Axis Vichy France, could contribute to our potential war coverage, but we agreed we should find out for ourselves. It didn't take long to learn we were right. Indochina was already under heavy pressure from Japan. Gen. Georges Catroux, the governor general who had advocated a middle course, had been ousted shortly before, and in that seat was Adm. Jean Decoux, an avowed Vichyite who was willing to listen to Tokyo. The Haiphong railroad, which had been moving supplies from the Hanoi port in North Vietnam to China, had been closed at about the same time and a number of Japanese troops were allowed access to the Haiphong area. Two trade treaties, one concluded in January, 1941, and a second being negotiated at the time of my visit in March, gave Japan almost a complete monopoly on Indochinese rice and rubber, and Tokyo even then was seeking permission, later granted, to station more troops inside the country on the Thai border.

The Vichy-controlled government clearly had no regard for the United States, although no overt hostilities existed. No welcome mat was spread for American reporters. I had been unable to obtain a visa for Indochina in Washington but was advised that the French consulate in Singapore would accommodate me. I had my doubts. Shortly after I reached Singapore, however, I was introduced to a Frenchman, an import-export trader with headquarters in Saigon, an office in Singapore, and, apparently, connections wherever they were important. For some reason I never discovered, he took a very helpful interest. He arranged my visa with no delay, wired his Saigon office to make my hotel reservations, assigned an English member of his firm to introduce me to Saigon, and proved himself generally useful.

As often happens in the shadow of war, quite a few people cautioned me to be wary of my newfound friend. No one made any specific charges except to point out that he was shuttling between Saigon and Singapore as often as transportation was available, and that alone seemed suspicious to some. Undoubtedly, I was warned, he would be looking for ways to make use of a naive correspondent still unfamiliar with the ways of the mysterious Orient. Disappointingly, perhaps, nothing of the sort happened. My friend asked no favors and posed no leading questions. James Bond wouldn't have wasted the time of day on him. If I had encountered more such "doubtful" characters along my route, however, my assignment might have been much easier.

My stay in Saigon lasted exactly nine days, the time that elapsed between consecutive KNILM flights. There was no other air service, and very few ships were plying the route. Actually, I could have accomplished the same result had I remained on the original flight and returned to Singapore the following day. Aside from recognizing that Saigon—and this will undoubtedly sound strange to some of my later colleagues who covered Vietnam at its worst—was the most beautiful city in the Far East by western standards, it held nothing for me or for CBS News's blueprint for covering a war.

In Saigon the French had built a modern European-style city, on the surface at least, with wide boulevards, enticing cafes and restaurants, comfortable hotels with all the amenities, and a sanitation system that kept the sidewalks immaculately clean. But Saigon in 1941 was the gem in the tiara of a colony linked to a defeated nation, and the air of defeatism was everywhere apparent. In their own words, the predominant spirit was that of *laissez faire*.

The Hotel Continental, my billet, was fronted by a wide sidewalk terrace-cafe remindful of the Cote d'Azur, a gathering place that rivaled the Raffles verandah in midday and afternoon popularity. The Continental also featured something this Hoosier schoolboy had never before encountered—a plentiful supply of opium! No one, to my personal knowledge, smoked opium on the sidewalk terrace, but the unmistakable scent was prevalent in the hotel corridors, for the tropical ventilation of the building allowed the redolent air to pass freely through the rooms.

Opium, of course, was completely legal, proof of which was the government-owned and operated opium factory only a few meters from the hotel, and the drug seemed to be as popular with the Occidentals as with the Asiatics. Most Americans in Saigon at that time worked for one of several large oil companies—Texaco, Socony, Shell, and others—and I hasten to exclude them from that generalization. There may have been exceptions—there usually are—but, as a group, these Americans were a close-knit group who stayed together in their doubtful environment, regardless of corporate rivalries. With normal business drastically restricted, they had plenty of time for leisure activity, but they used that leisure without any assist from the juice of the poppy.

Every American I met agreed that if Japan struck the United States anywhere in the Pacific, Saigon, on signal from Vichy, would immediately espouse Tokyo's cause and the whole of Indochina would be enemy territory to Americans, certainly no base for American reporters. As soon as I returned to Singapore, I relayed the word to White and to CBS News.

I had hoped to make at least one broadcast report to the network during my abbreviated fortnight, but there was no chance. Jacques le Bourgeois, manager of Radio Saigon, couldn't have been more hospitable—or less cooperative. He personally escorted me on a tour of his facilities, studios, and transmitter complex, and he invited me to his home for dinner, unusual for a Frenchman. Even Madame le Bourgeois, a delightful English lady, took me to their country club for cocktails. But that was hospitality *only.* Le Bouregois lamented the "fact" that his modest facilities could never reach either Batavia or Manila, but he offered no evidence that any such tests had ever been attempted. I got the firm impression that the world's most powerful short-wave transmitter, based in Indochina, would never reach San Francisco if there was an American at the mike.

The truth was that most of the French in Indochina were unhappy about what had happened to their homeland and their probable future in Asia, and they wanted just as little international exposure as possible. Moreover, personal feelings aside, they were unwilling to risk the ire of the ruling powers and their allies.

I spent a day at the Terre Rouge rubber plantation, then the largest in Indochina, where the manager, Jean O'Brien by name but just as French as Hennessy, showed me the process of rubber production from the tapping of the tree to the baling of the finished raw product. As a result of that visit, I was able throughout the Pacific war to visualize where the rubber that cushioned the Japanese war machine originated and how it was processed.

The night before my return flight to Singapore, I encountered Dick von Rees of KNILM, the pilot who had flown me to Java from Manila, by now an old friend. He was with a party in one of Saigon's leading restaurants, and although he assured me he would take me south the following morning, he obviously wasn't going to let that obligation blunt his enjoyment of the evening. The following morning Dick and his copilot appeared at the airport, escorting two of the lovely French girls who had been in their party the night before. They bade the ladies fond adieu, and we all climbed aboard the trusty DC-2. Dick took off immediately, without bothering to warm up the engines (standard operational procedure for Dutch airline pilots in 1941), and as soon as we cleared the ground, he turned back and buzzed the loading area in final salute to the demoiselles! Shortly after we gained altitude, von Rees came back for a brief chat and then returned to the controls, or so I thought.

About ten miles north of Singapore, across the Straits of Johore, lies the little city of Johore Bahru, capital of the sultanate of Johore (now a state of Malaysia) noted for the magnificent palace of its sultan. After an uneventful flight, I suddenly realized we were in a tight spiral, and I looked up from my book. Below us in all its splendor was the famous palace, and we were perfectly positioned to view it in detail. I felt quite appreciative of Dick's thoughtfulness, but when we repeated the circle, I began to wonder, and when we began a third one, I rose from my seat and inspected the cabin ahead of me. There, fast asleep on a front seat, was our dauntless captain, oblivious to the palace and everything else. When I aimed a pillow, accurately, at the back of his head, he awoke with a start, glanced about the cabin, then out the window. Then, with a wave of his hand, he went forward and brought us in for the landing, something his copilot apparently was not authorized to do.

In fairness to Dick von Rees, I must digress long enough to report that some months later, after the Japanese had made their move, Dick was shot down over Borneo in an unarmed plane with passengers. Although seriously wounded, he crash-landed the plane in a jungle clearing and made his way on foot to a native village, where he found help to rescue his injured passengers without a fatality. He was rewarded by the Netherlands Indies government with its highest civilian award. Dick von Rees was not only a dedicated *bon vivant*, he was also, and first of all, a magnificent pilot.

CHAPTER 5

Singapore to Tokyo

Back in Singapore I began needling New York for permission to move north. With little or no immediate news to be reported from the Straits Settlements, the colony's official designation at that time, I was anxious to complete my Japanese reconnaissance as quickly as possible. If Tokyo did intend to strike, as we believed, further delays only brought us closer to the unknown target day, and I had no desire to spend a war interned in the enemy's land, of no value to myself or to CBS News.

White, however, believed Singapore probably would be the first, or one of the first, targets when the enemy finally did strike, and he seemed perfectly willing for me to remain there indefinitely. Personally, I thought the Philippines might well be the prime target. Those islands lay directly in the path of any drive the Japanese might mount to the south toward the oil of the Indies and the rubber of Malaya and Indochina, absolutely essential to the successful conduct of a war in Southeast Asia. I wanted to be within reach of Manila if that happened. White didn't argue, but he still favored Singapore. Needless to say, neither of us ever gave a thought to Hawaii and Pearl Harbor.

Transmission facilities in Singapore were far from ideal, but they did work when conditions were right, and the authorities were trying with some success to improve them. But there simply was no real news worthy of even poor facilities. With other correspondents, I toured the famous naval base, heart of the colony's defense and Great Britain's principal salient in the Far East. I had a long interview with an apparently optimistic Vice Admiral Sir Geoffrey Layton, who commanded the Royal Navy in those waters. Aside from background information not for public consumption, however, there was almost nothing to report that might be of interest to network listeners.

Finally in mid-April White consented to my trip north and for the first time indicated that he might send someone, unnamed at that time, to backstop me in Singapore while I continued with the rest of my assignment. We agreed that Jack Raleigh should stay in Batavia, where he understood the situation and had the local contacts. He would be given a staff assignment if the conflict erupted.

En route to or from Japan I wanted to check out short-wave facilities in both Hong Kong and Shanghai. I knew that such facilities, suitable for voice transmission, were not then available, but RCA Communications in Manila had advised me to check with the postmaster general in the crown colony with the thought that adequate facilities might be arranged. I also wanted to return briefly to Manila to leave all my notes, personal papers, and incidentals acquired in the swing south. Far East veterans told me to take nothing into Japan that might be of even minimal interest to a censor.

KNILM was not operating to Hong Kong, and to board one of their infrequent flights to Manila, I would have had to return to Batavia and wait for a departure. It took me almost a week to arrange passage to Hong Kong on a China coast freighter and another five days to reach the Crown Colony. There was no hardship involved—*au contraire*—but the snail's pace was irksome. Today one can leave Singapore on a morning jet, stop briefly in Manila, and stroll the Ginza that same evening. In 1941, with necessary stops in Hong Kong and Shanghai, it took me almost a month to reach Tokyo aboard a British, Dutch, and two American ships.

As I had expected, neither Hong Kong nor Shanghai had anything to offer an electronic reporter. In the Crown Colony the postmaster general told me frankly that although there was a close association with RCAC in Manila, there were no voice circuits of broadcast quality and, in view of the overall political situation in the Far East, further investments would be limited to what was necessary to maintain commercial message communication. George Baxter, head of the United Press bureau in Hong Kong, was more blunt. "Hell, the Japs can take Hong Kong by telephone!" He said he expected to be interned. In Shanghai, where both RCAC and Press Wireless were represented, the story was very much the same. The only difference was that the Japanese were already on the outskirts of the city, poised to move when the time came. Both communications systems were geared to handle routine commercial traffic, and both were convinced that any further investment would merely be a gift to a waiting enemy.

Ten days of the month it took me to move from Singapore to Tokyo could have been eliminated if the Japanese consul had been more cooperative concerning the visa cancelled in Manila. He had spent time in the United States and spent more time telling me what a great poker player he was. He made a great point of trying to be helpful but insisted the final okay had to come from a higher authority. As a result, I missed passage on one American President liner and turned to the Japanese K.K.K. Line for help. As always, the Japanese were courteous and "perfectly understanding" of my situation, but nothing happened. Finally, on the ninth day, my poker-playing friend sent word that my visa was approved, and the American President Lines found space for me on the *President Taft* departing the following night. I finally arrived in Tokyo on May 28. The only valid reason for my visiting Tokyo other than White's desire to have CBS make the first broadcast report by a staff correspondent was my own curiosity concerning the capital of a nation I was certain would soon be at war with my own. We knew that transpacific transmission was excellent, and we also knew that that transmission would be of no use to us once the line was drawn. As far as news was concerned, the trip was a complete waste of time. I made several broadcast reports to the network, but in each case my script had to be submitted to the censor forty-eight hours in advance, and it was not returned until I sat down at the microphone. There was barely time to scan it and see what changes or deletions had been made before getting the go-ahead.

Not having physical control of the script led to an incident that created quite a stir in New York. I was staying at the Imperial Hotel about a block from Radio Tokyo, and I had to be in the studio around five o'clock in the morning to make a broadcast that would be heard on the network at 7:00 P.M. On this particular morning, I was awakened by a phone call from Shigeru Satow, at the studio, asking if I was going to make the broadcast. I glanced at my watch and realized the hotel hadn't called me. I had barely fifteen minutes before air time. Satowsan said he would send me a Radio Tokyo car, and I jumped into my clothes and dashed for the lobby.

The car was waiting, and I lost no time reaching the studio—even the ceremonial cup of tea was omitted—but I missed by a few seconds. One of the engineers, who spoke good English but with a Ginza accent, was seated in front of the mike, reading my script. He motioned for me to take over, but I had violated the first rule of broadcasting (never run to a microphone) and was out of breath. I shook my head, and he continued. I had expected him to sign off as one reporting *for* the missing reporter, but to my chagrin he read the script verbatim, concluding: "This is William J. Dunn in Tokyo. I return you now . . ."

There was nothing to be done. I thanked him, and Satowsan took me back to the hotel. I invited him in for breakfast, and we had barely seated ourselves when I heard myself being paged. It was an overseas call from Elmer Davis, at that time the top commentator for CBS news: "Is this Bill Dunn?" "Sure, Elmer. What's up?" "What is your daughter's name?" "Patricia Lee . . ." He cut me short: "What was the score of the Notre Dame–Army game last fall?" I told him, then asked "What the hell's this all about?" "We wanted to be sure we were talking to you and that you are all right. That wasn't you who made that broadcast."

The contrast between Tokyo and the other cities I had visited since crossing the international date line was anticipated but still remarkable. This was a no-nonsense capital of a nation preparing for war. The first thing you noticed was the brown-out, a dimming of lights and the elimination of all but the most essential, not for security reasons but for conservation. Petroleum and other fossil fuels, of course, are the lifeblood of modern warfare, and Japan had to rely on outside sources for all its petroleum and much of its other fuels, so conservation was almost a religion there in 1941. New motor cars were not available to the man in the street, and the venerable vehicles that were operating were usually equipped with great gas bags on their tops or converters for other fuels. Ersatz was a way of life as the nation strove to hold on to whatever resources it had on hand and to acquire and stockpile others as swiftly as possible. Although other capitals and major cities of the Far East were preparing for what lay ahead, none could match the Japanese in the intensity of their efforts.

The press corps in Tokyo at that time included all the major wire services, the *New York Times* and *Herald Tribune,* and several British and Australian papers. Shortly after my arrival in Tokyo, Walter Winchell headed one of his columns with a story of how the Japanese information authorities had saluted me by announcing that all future press conferences would be held in Japanese. It was a good story, but there wasn't a word of truth in it. Sessions at the Ministry of Information seldom contained anything newsworthy, but we all enjoyed the ubiquitous cup of tea and the chance to get together at some place other than the American Club.

There were two important foreign clubs in Tokyo in 1941, the Tokyo Club and the American Club. The former was predominantly British, but memberships intermingled and many members of the foreign community belonged to both. Inasmuch as the foreign press corps was predominantly American, the American Club also served as an informal press club, with the public rooms of the Imperial Hotel a close second.

Since Tokyo's foreign community consisted largely of executives with minimal duties, the clubs were more popular than usual. When the Tokyo representative of the Gargantuan Oil Company reached his office on any given morning, he would find little to do. Tightening Japanese regulations had brought normal trade to a standstill, and most company representatives were there primarily "to watch our investment." It wasn't unusual to see businessmen, traders, and executives of foreign corporations arriving at the American Club early on Monday morning to start a rubber of bridge that might extend indefinitely.

It was not a rugged life for a foreign correspondent if he could carry the burden of having no news to report, news that the censor might approve. The shadow of threatening internment hung over the entire community, however. All my Tokyo friends, except two who were transferred or called home, eventually spent long unhappy months in Japanese internment. But that was their assignment and they accepted it.

There was little social intercourse with the Japanese, except for old Japan hands who had been in the country for years and had made friendships that eventually outlasted the war. My associates at Radio Tokyo were very cooperative and for the most part quite friendly. I had met Satowsan in New York a year or so earlier, and he was acquainted in a general way with the CBS News operation. He was always helpful and seemed eager to repay what he termed our courtesies to him while he was in New York. When I left, he presented me with a beautiful damascene cigarette case engraved, in gold, "From your friends at Radio Tokyo." (I left the case in Manila for safekeeping when I went to China and never saw it again.)

But that was essentially a business relationship between two men in the same field. The one friend I made during my weeks in Tokyo who had nothing to do with news or broadcasting was James Kawasaki, a prominent member of that industrial family, whose friends all called him Jimmy. Kawasaki had been educated in the United States and Great Britain, and he had no illusions concerning the future. At his home in Zuci, a lovely little waterfront village about thirty-five miles from Tokyo, Jimmy talked frankly to me and two other correspondents permanently assigned to Japan who had known him for a long time. His message, if not his exact words, was as follows:

> Just consider my situation. There is no doubt that my country is going to attack yours, and that we have no chance whatever of winning. I know the potential strength of the United States, and I know we are underestimating you. I am going to lose everything I have in the world, and so are my friends, but there is absolutely nothing to be done. I have already been accused of being subversive and warned to quit talking, but my situation is desperate. If the navy were in charge here, things might be different. The naval commanders have traveled and know more about the world. But Japan is run by the army and the army is provincial. They have no realization of the odds against us, and they won't listen. It's heartbreaking to see your beloved country headed for disaster and not be able even to speak up.

Jimmy Kawasaki was the only Japanese I ever knew personally who would admit his country would be the aggressor—and would fail. He survived the war only long enough to address a meeting of the *zaibatsu* (the great family-controlled banking and industrial combines), called to protest the reforms of Douglas MacArthur. What he said, according to inside sources, was, "I told you so five years ago, but none of you would listen." He died very shortly thereafter, before I could see him again, but I have never forgotten that evening in his home, the intensity of his feeling, and the clarity of his vision.

If there had been any lingering doubts in my mind as to the certainty of war in the Pacific, with Japan as the aggressor, that month in Japan erased them completely. The only questions now in my mind were when and where the first blow would fall.

CHAPTER 6

The "Final" Stages

By mid-June I was ready to quit Japan for the final stages of my assignment, Chungking, Rangoon, and Bangkok. With a few lucky breaks in transportation, I might even be home in time for the World Series, an exhilarating prospect. According to the tentative schedule I cabled New York, I would return briefly to my base in Manila, then take Pan American to Hong Kong and China National Airways Corporation (CNAC) to Chungking. From there I would take available transportation to Rangoon and Bangkok and return to Manila, where I could take the *Clipper* home. There had been talk of Australia, but I didn't mention that. There would be no World Series, no Army–Notre Dame game if White decided to include that distant continent.

One matter remained to be resolved before my departure: the appointment of a string correspondent to represent CBS after I left. With New York's approval, I fixed on an American free-lancer named W. R. Wills. Bud, as everyone called him, had had some radio experience and was highly regarded in the American community. He was one of the press corps who had sworn to remain in Japan until "the situation was resolved," simply another way to describe waiting for internment. I greatly admired their dedication but had no desire to emulate them.

On June 19 I boarded the M.S. *Asami Maru* in Yokohama, ticketed for Manila with a stop in Shanghai. All ships plying those waters in those years were freighters with passenger facilities, but this was my first trip on a Japanese freighter. It was a delightful ship, immaculately clean with impeccable service. In only a few months I traveled on Dutch, British, and Japanese ships, as well as a couple of American vessels. My own country suffered by comparison in almost every aspect of service, a reflection of the sad state of our merchant marine in the past half-century.

The most surprising thing about the *Asami Maru* on this particular voyage was the great number of well-dressed Japanese businessmen who crammed every public room as we moved out into Tokyo

Bay. It looked like a major sales convention afloat, and I wondered where they were headed. The answer came from Clarke Lee of the Associated Press, a fellow passenger returning to his permanent base in Shanghai. The men were indeed members of the business community and would all be leaving us the following day in Kobe after a holiday free from the restrictions of the Japanese mainland. In 1941 Japan had an ersatz scotch whisky called "*Sun Tory.*" (They have since improved on it.) But there was nothing ersatz aboard that ship. Lee and I combined to do a thorough recco of the bars and public rooms, but we didn't find a single bottle of the Ginza specialty. The scotch actually came from Scotland, and the food was good enough to be almost unpatriotic! When we berthed in Kobe shortly after noon the following day, our friends all departed, leaving only a score of us in the first-class section.

Two days after leaving Kobe, on June 23, we were off the mouth of the Yangtze River when someone called my attention to a bulletin just posted on the board where the ship's news-sheet was put up each day. Germany had declared war on the Soviet Union and was moving huge armies across the Russian frontier on a thousand-mile front that extended from the Baltic to the Black Sea. This was stunning news. Hitler, master of the double cross, had ignored his nonaggression treaty with the USSR, which had made possible Stalin's invasion of Poland and which now enabled the Nazis to catch the Russians themselves completely off guard. When we went ashore in Shanghai, I found that our skipper had withheld the news for twenty-four hours before posting it. Apparently the Japanese, as members of a tripartite pact for mutual defense with the Berlin-Rome Axis, were also confused by this unexpected development.

Earthshaking as the news was, I didn't see how it could have any immediate effect on my mission. Russia's European borders were thousands of miles distant, and my own country was not yet at war. I went ashore, met some fellow correspondents, and prepared to enjoy a quiet evening before resuming my trek to Manila the following day.

Four of us were enjoying an excellent meal in a little restaurant in the French section when a waiter approached our table, paging me by name. I couldn't believe it. No one knew where I was except those who were with me. It had to be a gag, but I went to the phone. The voice at the other end purported to be an employee of Press Wireless, and the message from Paul White, which he read me, tersely ordered me to stay in Shanghai pending a visa for Moscow. I asked for Al Lucey, manager of Press Wireless, but he was away from his office. Still unconvinced, I waited a few minutes and called Press Wireless. The voice that answered was totally familiar. "Why, yes, Mr. Dunn, I just read you the message." There went the World Series and the football season! It was my first experience with Shanghai's famous "bamboo telegraph." The Chinese knew where every Occidental was at all times, or they would find out in short order. I returned to my table, finished my dinner, and then left for the *Asami Maru* to cancel my passage and gather my personal effects.

New York obviously considered an active war preferable from a news standpoint to a probable war, but White had no success whatever getting my Russian visa, and no one in Shanghai could help. I found myself isolated again, forced to confine whatever information I did uncover to cables or Press Wireless. Meanwhile I haunted the wire services for news from Russia, all of it bad. The Nazis had taken the Russian army completely by surprise, and nowhere along that thousand-mile front were they facing anything stronger than token resistance.

After two weeks in which New York, through its Washington connections, had made absolutely no progress, I decided to see if my friends in Tokyo's U.S. Embassy could help. I called Chip Bohlen, an attaché with whom I had played golf and a little poker, who promised to investigate and call me back. In a couple of days Bohlen, too, reported failure. The Russians were doing so poorly militarily, he said, that they would not admit any correspondent if they could reasonably refuse. Pressure would have to be applied in high places. The Washington approach was having no effect, however; the only word I received from New York was to be patient. The Tokyo embassy did reveal that the State Department was quietly advising getting ready for the worst. The situation in Russia was deteriorating so rapidly that a total collapse was feared in the very near future.

There were worse places to be stranded in 1941 than Shanghai, a city of unbelievable paradoxes. The Chinese already were at war with Japan, of course, and Japanese troops virtually surrounded the city. But inside the city itself was a peaceful amalgam of opulence and abject poverty. The sea lanes were open, and there was no lack of anything, even luxuries, for those who could pay. That included almost all the foreign community as well as the wealthy Chinese. There were no duties as such on imports, and that kept prices down. A bottle of Dewars or any standard scotch usually cost less than two dollars, and other liquors and wines were comparably priced. Scores of restaurants offered excellent European food, usually French or Russian, at amazingly low prices, and Chinese restaurants featured the varied cuisines of the native provinces exquisitely prepared and served. Theaters ran American and British movies, night clubs never closed, a race track operated with parimutuel betting, and there were plenty of other diversions for the foreign businessman with no business other than "keeping an eye on the investment."

The *yuan*, usually referred to as the "Mex" dollar as distinguished from the "gold" dollar, traded at about 18-to-1, but better rates were available. The fact that the U.S. dollar had gone off the gold standard years before made no difference in 1941 Shanghai, nor was I able to determine where Mexico got into the act, but everything was priced in dollars, "Mex" or "gold."

But Shanghai was also a sinkhole of poverty, heavily overpopulated and sadly lacking in employment opportunities. Beggars slept on the sidewalks even in the better parts of the city, and death from malnutrition or just plain starvation was commonplace. It was physically dangerous to give a coin to a beggar because the donor would be surrounded immediately by an army of other beggars demanding the same. The presence of the United States, France, and Great Britain had kept the Japanese outside the city, but it had done nothing to alleviate the plight of the poor.

The Fourth U.S. Marine Regiment had been stationed in Shanghai for years to help protect the foreign population. The marines were not conspicuous, but their presence was ever felt and served to keep in power the foreigners who had no moral right to be there. The Fourth of July was always celebrated with a baseball game between the Fourth Marines and the American Club. I was present at the last game ever played and witnessed a long stride toward Anglo-American solidarity when an *Englishman* hit a towering home run in the ninth inning to seal an American Club victory!

All this, though interesting, was not what I had been sent halfway around the world for, and I was getting restless. I was convinced I would never get that Moscow visa. Members of the Russian press corps didn't mingle too freely with the rest of us, but I did get to talk to Boris Rogoff, Tass representative in Shanghai. He assured me he had no jurisdiction but would wire Tass in Moscow and see if someone in the head office might help. Nothing resulted, as I expected, and I wanted to be on my way. On July 19, after almost a month, New York finally admitted defeat and okayed my departure for Manila. With great good fortune I was able to book passage on the *Nitta Maru* for the twentieth, a Sunday, and I began to prepare for departure.

I had adopted the universal Shanghai practice of not paying cash for anything. If you were an Occidental with a clean shirt you could sign for meals, movies, taxis, even race track tickets, and even if the proprietor had never seen you before. I remarked to an old Shanghai hand that it would now be a major nuisance trying to track down all those chits and settling them. He laughed. "Relax, Bill, you'll not leave Shanghai owing anyone a penny." Sure enough, on Sunday morning a bevy of smiling Chinese appeared in the hotel lobby, each carrying his share of the chits I had signed. The bamboo telegraph was functioning with its usual infallibility.

CHAPTER 7

"Hitler Didn't Read His History."

A surprise awaited me in Manila. I returned from Japan convinced that war in the Pacific was as certain as the sunset, to find my friends all minimizing or refusing to admit the danger. Despite the blows Hitler was scoring on a disorganized Russian army, the evidence of Nazi viciousness in the Battle of Britain, and the news that Japan had openly allied itself with the Berlin-Rome Axis, a large portion of the American community had convinced itself that nothing was going to happen in the Philippines.

In late 1940, before I reached the islands, the armed forces had ordered all U.S. Army families back to the States, and Francis Sayre, the American high commissioner, had recommended that all civilians also leave. Sayre, of course, had no authority to order civilian families home, but probably a majority accepted his recommendation. Manila, when I first saw it, had an American community almost empty of wives and children. Now intelligent businessmen whose families had been safely home in the States four months before had brought these families back to the islands, and the good life was again in vogue, just as though the menace of Japan didn't exist. The fact that the high commissioner did not follow his own advice, but kept

Mrs. Sayre and a number of women members of his staff in the city, probably affected the final decisions of many who had heeded him in the first place.

The attitude was not confined to the civilians. Quite a few government workers belittled the threat of war and openly wished they could bring their own families back to join them. Those, of course, were personal opinions and, in theory at least, would affect no one but themselves and their families. But they were not alone. One Sunday I was invited by Dr. Victor Buencamino, head of the Food Conservation Agency, to join him, the governor of Rizal province, a representative of the high commissioner, and the Manila head of the American Red Cross on an inspection tour of the surrounding countryside to see what progress was being made in the accelerated production of foodstuffs. I found it an intriguing trip and learned a lot about how the Filipino farmer lives and works.

As we were inspecting one excellent farm, the Red Cross chief drew me to one side and confided, "We have to go along with this sort of thing, of course, but it's a complete waste of time. Nothing is going to happen." I looked at him in amazement. "That's not the impression I got in Japan." My friend shrugged and, as he turned away, asked me not to quote him. I have often wondered how his attitude affected the operation of the Red Cross in the Philippines when the impossible finally did happen.

Within forty-eight hours after my return from Tokyo and Shanghai, General MacArthur was recalled to active duty by Gen. George C. Marshall, American army chief of staff, and given command of the newly formed United States Armed Forces in the Far East (USAFFE) with the rank of lieutenant general, a signal ignored by the American community. MacArthur had been in the Philippines for half a dozen years, and his change in status, decisive though it was, attracted little attention.

Informed authorities, both civil and military, tried with small success to arouse people to an awareness of impending danger. A series of practice blackouts proved to be little more than an excuse for more conviviality. ("How about coming over to my house for the blackout tomorrow night? The Joneses and the Smiths will be there, and we'll play a little bridge.") Incredible as it may seem, it actually happened. The good life prevailed. Had I not seen the Japanese in action, their conservation program, their obvious preparation for something besides a harvest moon festival, I probably would have had the same attitude. In retrospect, I believe the informed Filipinos took the situation with deeper regard than their alien guests, but they were not in charge of their own country and there was little, if anything, they could do.

As soon as word was released of General MacArthur's recall to active duty, I contacted G-2, the intelligence office, and was told that the General was in the midst of an organizational program. The major promised, however, to pass my message to him and ask for an appointment at his convenience. The next day I was informed that MacArthur would like to see me at ten the following Monday morning, August 4.

As usual, I was cautioned to keep the interview brief (I think fifteen minutes was mentioned) and, also as usual, the duration of my stay remained completely in the hands of the General and ran closer to an hour. He was very interested in my impressions of Japanese civilian activity and questioned me closely on several points. On the matter of his own work, just being brought to conclusion, he said he was satisfied with the progress made to that time in the organization of a Philippines defense force, but he clearly would have liked more time.

His most amazing observation came when I spoke of the overwhelming success the German armies were having on their drive into Russia. He had just lighted another cigar, and he studied the thin blue smoke for a moment and then said, "This marks the beginning of the end for Adolf Hitler."

It was a flat statement without qualification, and I probably indicated my surprise. In six weeks, the progress of the Nazis had been slowed only by their own lengthening supply lines. MacArthur, of course, understood all this better than I did, and he nodded when I told him what our embassy in Tokyo had said concerning the threat of a total Russian collapse.

"They haven't studied their history. Napoleon made the same mistake, and Hitler will wind up just as Bonaparte did, and with infinitely greater losses. The Russians will never surrender. They have unlimited manpower, and they can retreat, mile by mile, clear across Siberia. In two months the rains will start, and a month later the Russian winter will set in. No people in the world can withstand a Russian winter like the Russians, certainly not the Germans."

There was no escape clause in this positive prediction, the first word I had heard since the invasion on June 22, from any source, encouraging to the Russians. I was not about to argue with a master strategist like Douglas MacArthur, and I went away impressed but unconvinced.

Immediately on my return to Manila, New York scheduled me for four broadcasts in the next five days, and White indicated he wanted me to remain there while we thoroughly tested our new network of Far East correspondents, almost but not quite complete. I had lined up facilities in Manila, Batavia, Singapore, and Tokyo, with string correspondents in all except Singapore. There just wasn't a suitable candidate for the job when I went through there, so White hired a full-time reporter, Cecil Brown, in Europe and sent him out to fill a spot vital to the overall program.

Actually, the business of hiring part-time correspondents in foreign cities wasn't as easy as it might sound. Most of the really good men were already working for one of the wire services or syndicates or were representing one of the larger stateside newspapers and were not permitted to represent a potential media rival on the side. But we were successful for the most part.

I knew we would have a problem in Manila when I left because the reporter I had named to handle the bureau during my previous absences just wasn't heavy enough for the job. I had tried to hire Ford Wilkins, managing editor of the *Manila Bulletin* who was a top-ranking newsman with a comprehensive knowledge of the Philippines and the Far East. Unfortunately Wilkins was reluctant, feeling a primary obligation to his publisher, an American for whom he had worked for several years, and not wanting to take the CBS assignment lightly. I understood his position, but the only alternate available had shown very bad judgment on at least one story, and I was afraid to trust him without supervision. We finally reached an agreement whereby Wilkins would handle the assignment unless the pressure of war (which he agreed was certain) proved too heavy, in which case he would turn the schedule over to the alternate but would check each script before it was broadcast.

For more than two months, however, I covered the beat myself, averaging from three to five broadcasts a week, getting a valuable knowledge of the Philippines, the government, military, and civilian news sources. The Philippines had been promised early independence, but the American government was still firmly in control, more than it might have been if Manuel Quezon, president of the commonwealth, hadn't been such an ill man. I had paid him a courtesy visit soon after my first arrival in Manila, but now, six months later, I was advised not to try to see him for reasons of his health. On the evening of August 19, Vice-President Henry Wallace made a broadcast to the Philippines that was carried locally in Manila and answered by President Quezon. I introduced the president, who spoke from his private study in Malacañan Palace, and I was shocked by the way he had aged in those few months. He spoke so softly I could hardly hear him from a distance of ten feet, but San Francisco reported excellent reception. He had to be helped from his desk and retired to his bed immediately, although it was early evening.

Although White vigorously denied it when I broached the subject some years later, I believe he had no intention of bringing me home before war actually broke. He wanted someone he knew in the Far East when the shooting started, and I was his pigeon. Our relationship extended back to 1928, when we both worked for United Press down in the old *New York World* building. He was responsible for my joining CBS back when Hitler annexed Austria. We knew each other's methods and limitations from long cooperation. And I was the only full-time radio correspondent in the Pacific who knew anything about network operation on Madison Avenue.

My original assignment could never have been carried out in six weeks, but six months *was* possible had he wanted it that way. Instead, he found excuses to slow me down. I spent much more time in Manila, Singapore, and Japan than necessary; he kept me idle for a full month in Shanghai waiting for a visa he must have known the Russians would never grant, then three months in Manila again, performing duties my stringers could have handled neatly. It was the end of September before White finally allowed me to continue to Chungking. Had we not needed a reliable man in China, whom I was to locate and hire, I doubtless would have remained in Manila attending practise blackouts and advising my friends to send their families home.

Just before my departure for China on October 3, I met General MacArthur at a cocktail party given by visiting Clare Booth Luce. Russia was still in deep trouble, but the ultimate outcome was no longer in doubt, and I complimented him on his earlier prediction. He smiled. "History, Bill, just history! It was all there, but Hitler didn't read it, or else he didn't believe it."

CHAPTER 8

Shattered City

It was impossible to book transportation direct from Manila to Chung-king. With great portions of the Chinese mainland occupied by the Japanese, the only access was by air, and that service was limited to a small fleet of Douglas DC-3's operated out of Hong Kong by China National Airways Corporation (CNAC) on a very irregular schedule. Almost the whole of the 750-mile flight was over enemy territory, the planes operated only at night, and departure times were never publicized. Reservations were made only in the Hong Kong offices of CNAC, and the only information given the prospective traveler was the approximate departure date.

Pan American was operating a weekly flight from Manila to Hong Kong with flying boats, and I had only a four-day wait for departure. Back in January, I had made the trip from Pearl Harbor to Manila aboard the *Philippines Clipper*, a Martin flying boat that cruised around a hundred knots. When I appeared for the Hong Kong flight, I was delighted to find myself on the brand new *California Clipper*, a Boeing 314 flying boat, quite the largest plane I had ever seen and considerably faster than the Martin.

Fortunately, one of the first persons I met in Hong Kong was Charles Sharp, local manager of CNAC, who promised to put me on the first flight to Chungking, probably late the following week. He explained the need for absolute secrecy, told me we would make the flight in a blacked-out plane, and assured me it would be extremely difficult for a Japanese pilot to spot us en route.

During the next few days I spent considerable time with Mel Jacoby, a *Time* magazine correspondent just arrived from Chungking who supplied me with a wealth of valuable information on that war-torn provisional Chinese capital. He also gave me a small jewel case to deliver to Miss Annalee Whitmore, who was there working for Chinese relief. It was the engagement ring he hadn't been able to buy in Chungking.

On Tuesday Chuck Sharp sent me a message telling me to be ready to leave any time after the next twenty-four hours. All I needed was my exit visa, which presented no problem except that the British obviously weren't as interested in airline security as CNAC. In a large office filled with unknowns of various nationalities, the immigration officer asked for my destination. Trying to keep my voice down, I told him Chungking, which he repeated in a loud voice. He then asked when I was leaving. When I told him I didn't have the schedule, he informed me, still in a roundhouse voice, it would probably be the following evening.

He was absolutely right, and despite this "security breach," the flight proved to be entirely without incident. In addition to an effective blackout, however, the plane's heating system didn't work, and the half-dozen of us who left Kai Tak airport just as the dusk was turning to darkness spent some four and a half hours huddled under blankets, trying to keep from freezing.

Chungking's main airport is located on an island in the Yangtze River, not far from the heart of the city, but our midnight arrival inexplicably was routed into a military airport some thirty-five miles from the city. We were told it was a new airport, but all we saw was a huge expanse of flatlands with no trace of a runway or a hangar. A makeshift shelter housed the operations office, immigration, and customs. A battered old truck with narrow board seats provided transportation to the city. The ride was beautiful beyond description as a bright moon highlighted the magnificent mountains of Szechuan province, but the combination of a narrow board and no springs made it difficult to enjoy.

One of my fellow passengers, a New Yorker named Martin Gold, had spent many years in China representing a large trading firm. Through his Chungking office, he was one of the very few civilians in the city with a car, not much of a car, it's true, but a car that *usually* ran. During the two or more hours it took to reach our destination, he lamented the fact that he had been unable to notify his office of his schedule. His car, he explained, for all its other shortcomings, did have cushioned seats. For the only time in a lifetime of travel, I found actual bruises on my derrière when I finally reached the hotel.

The Chai-ling House, Chungking's only European-style hotel, definitely had no affiliation with Hilton or Sheraton. It was a three-story structure that had been bombed and patched repeatedly, and even the patches had patches on them. When it rained, which was quite often, the roof admitted the water in large quantities, and the floor above my first-floor room was almost as leaky. Oiled paper had replaced most of the shattered windows, and there was no running water closer than the Yangtze River. When the generator failed, not unusual, candles provided the only light. Chungking can get quite chilly as early as

October; the sole source of heat came from charcoal braziers, and charcoal was in short supply.

The alternate choice of quarters for the media was the press hostel a couple of miles distant, a new one-story structure built of bamboo and clay that resembled a paddock stable. It had a nearly weatherproof roof but only a dirt floor. The original press hostel had been destroyed by an enemy air raid only a few weeks before my arrival. Sleeping accommodations at both the hotel and the hostel were limited to bamboo cots, but they did have woven bamboo "springs" instead of the solid boards that distinguished authentic Chinese beds.

Since I was was only to be in the city for a few weeks, I had been assigned to the hotel. The hostel, filled to capacity with media, was considerably closer to the Ministry of Information, however, an important advantage in a city where public transportation consisted only of rickety rickshaws and a few aging sedan chairs too small for my generous proportions. For the next six weeks, 90 percent of my personal travel would be on foot.

I have heard reporters complain bitterly about accommodations in some of America's finest hotels, but there was no complaining in Chungking. We all knew we were using the only facilities available in a city that had been battered unmercifully for years. Also, no other reporter-correspondent was getting a better break.

An unanticipated task presented itself the morning after my arrival. A boy seated me in the nearly deserted hotel dining room and left for the kitchen. I examined my table carefully, then those nearby. An Englishman across the room confirmed my suspicions: "Relax, friend, there are no knives and forks." I waved my understanding and set to work, clumsily, on the food the waiter produced. I have no memory of the food, only of the chopsticks. It is amazing how quickly one can adapt when there are no alternatives!

My next task was to establish contact with the Ministry of Information, less difficult but entailing a two-mile walk through the rice fields along a narrow dirt walkway barely wide enough for two persons to pass. Another route followed roads all the way, but was at least a mile longer. Consequently the short-cut was preferred in daylight, but in darkness it had to be the roadway. One step off that narrow path and you would sink to your ankles in night soil (human excrement used as fertilizer). The encircling fields also served as outdoor toilets for men, women, and children, day or night, standing or seated. It was startling at first for a newcomer, but you became unconcerned very quickly, as long as you remained safely on that path. I made a note: "The Chungking folk have few compunctions / About their so-called personal functions."

Fortunately, the Ministry of Information, the Ministry of Communications, and the cable office were all located close together. My broadcast reports would originate from the studios of the Ministry of Communications after being censored (I was in a war zone now) by Hollington Tong, the minister of information, or by one of his aides.

My biggest travel problem came whenever I was notified by the American Embassy that mail had arrived for me. The embassy was located on the south side of the Yangtze atop a high hill. There was a ferry across the river at the foot of a flight of 492 steps (I counted them every trip; they varied three or four steps with the height of the Yangtze, but 492 was a good average), which led from the river to the heart of the city. In order to reach the embassy, I had to walk three miles to the Yangtze, down those 492 steps, ferry to the south bank, then up another 300 or so steps. The return was exactly the reverse, except that those 492 steps seemed infinitely steeper in ascent.

The first time I made the trip, I picked the wrong hill on the south bank and would up at the Royal Dutch Shell House, also some 300 steps above the water. Shell provided me with a welcome beer and pointed out the American flag on the building that topped the adjoining hill. An extra 300 steps down and 300 steps back up, and my mission finally accomplished, I returned across the river and looked upward with trepidation.

The stone steps were about twenty feet wide, but they mounted continuously, without flights. There was no place to rest for a moment. Scores of Chinese were running up and down the steps as if on level ground. There was no way I could run, but I did start out staunchly, lifting one foot above and ahead of the other with determination. After about 200 steps, I had to stop for a breather. Immediately every coolie on the steps stopped as well, and a dozen grouped around me to see why I had called a halt right there in the middle of nowhere. Embarrassed, I pulled out my notebook, pretended to study it for a moment, then continued my climb, reaching the top without further pause. Although I never could take those steps two at a time like my Chinese friends, I was able before too long to climb those steps without stopping and to repeat on the south bank.

Actually, those six weeks afoot among the Chungking hills was probably the best thing that could have happened to me at that par-

ticular time. Rough days lay ahead, and the weeks of forced exercise
put me in better physical condition than I had been in in years.

   The ostensible reason for my going to Chungking was to hire a first-
class reporter who would work as a stringer, with the understanding
he would go on the staff if and when war spread to the Pacific. Just
before I left Manila, however, Paul White informed me he had hired
a stringer named James Stewart on the basis of test broadcasts, and
he asked me to check him out. Of course, New York already had approved Stewart's mike style and subject material, and I was not likely
to find him otherwise unacceptable. Still, Paul obviously wanted me
to go to Chungking, so I did.

The choice of Stewart proved to be an excellent one. Jimmy and
his wife, a young couple probably in their twenties, were true old
China hands. Both were from missionary families, born and basically
educated in China, with college in the States. They were in Chungking because they felt a deep sympathy for the land of their birth in
its struggle against a vicious invader, but they obviously were not growing wealthy on the sketchy assignments that came Jim's way. He came
to the Chai-ling House that first afternoon, having learned of my arrival through his friends at CNAC, and our long conversation, which
touched on many points, confirmed by initial impression. My first
job was completed the day of my arrival.

My second assignment had nothing to do with New York. I had
to deliver the ring Mel Jacoby had given me in Hong Kong to Annalee Whitmore. Annalee was living at the Chai-ling House, and Mel
had told her to expect me. It was my only time I played Cupid, and
I mentally saluted Jacoby. Annalee Whitmore was a charming girl from
Washington, D.C., who had become deeply interested in China and
its problems through diplomatic connections. She didn't work directly
for the Chinese, but for one of the agencies organized for China's aid,
and she had been in Chungking several months. Talented and well-
informed, she would prove a valuable source of information for a reporter new to the scene.

My Chungking routine revolved around the Ministry of Information and the Ministry of Communications. New York provided a regular schedule of broadcasts averaging three to four a week. Frequent
press conferences advised us of the situation on the outlying fronts,
all of which were unusually quiet during my tenure. Although the
Japanese had ravaged Chungking with four years of constant air raids,

Annalee Whitmore (later Jacoby) pauses halfway up Chungking's Yangtze River steps (492 at low tide) and can still smile.

not one Japanese plane was reported over the city while I was there, a lull due no doubt to Japan's preparation for war on an infinitely greater scale.

The first really ominous sign from Tokyo came on October 17, 1941, when Gen. Hideki Tojo succeeded Prince Fumimaro Konoye as prime minister (we learned of it a day later). Although Prince Konoye had served as a front for the militarists in 1937, he had altered his views considerably over the years and had become a negotiator strongly advocating an agreement with the United States that would give Japan a free hand in Asia without war. Tojo was a militarist of the old school who believed the only way Japan would get what she wanted was to go out and take it. He was one of the jingoists Jimmy Kawasaki had told us about, a career soldier, parochial in his outlook and, as it turned out, overconfident of the military strength at his command. The correspondents then in Chungking who had covered assignments in Tokyo all agreed that the supplanting of Prince Konoye was indeed an ominous development.

That same evening Dr. Tong gave a dinner party for the media, and the Konoye resignation was the principal topic of conversation, at least when the talk dwelt on serious subjects, which in truth was only briefly. When a Chinese host decrees that his guests enjoy themselves, not even war or threat of war can dampen the occasion, and Hollington Tong was one of the finest of Chinese hosts. Unfortunately, even the minister of information could do nothing about the heavy rain that fell all day and most of the evening. Consequently, we of the Chailing House contingent had to plod the two miles back through a sea of mud, but we had been happily fortified by a generous supply of rice wine.

My primary contact at Chungking Radio was T. S. Peng, the manager, who called on me almost immediately after my arrival and was always available for help whenever I needed it. Only a couple of days after we met, Peng told me he wanted to show me his station and introduce me to some of the men who would be handling my broadcasts. I was delighted, although my technical knowledge of the wireless world was, and is, negligible. The engineers were responsible for any technical successes.

Nevertheless, the inspection tour was really special. After I had been shown what made Chungking Radio tick, I was the guest of honor at a dinner hosted by Peng and attended by just about every member of his staff. The food was surprisingly good to have been secured and prepared in a war-torn capital, but the food wasn't the only feature of the evening. A chorus of students from the nearby Central China University sang some inspiring battle songs for us, then surrounded me and demanded my autograph, certainly a first!

Meanwhile my hosts and fellow guests were happily initiating me into the ancient ritual of *kan pai*. At a Chinese dinner you are automatically served a small porcelain container of rice wine that you must drain on signal or risk offending your host. If, having fulfilled your obligation to your host, you return your cup to the table upside down, no more wine will be served you. The cups hold little more than a thimbleful, so you are lulled into a false sense of security. You return your cup right side up, and *immediately* it is filled again. Now you are fair game for anyone around the table. A fellow guest lifts his own glass to you with the command *kan pai!* (Literally, "bottoms up," and pronounced "gam*bay.*") You both drain your drinks, and you are then free to propose the toast to any other guest whose cup remains upturned. Fortunately your hosts and fellow guests are too well mannered to gang up on you. But it is never wise to underestimate the potential of a tiny thimbleful of rice wine. Still, it did provide a welcome buffer against the determined elements of a Chungking autumn.

It might seem strange that a group like ours could enjoy an evening of genuine fun and pleasure in the midst of the devastation wrought by a bitter, unremitting war, but it was to me an early manifestation of a precept I would hear many times during the next few years from men who had long lived with war: "Take your pleasure when and where you find it. It may be a long time between drinks." Chungking certainly had little occasion to salute anything in the nature of a success.

There was no shortage of news in China's wartime capital. The Chinese wanted to keep the western world aware of their travail, and frequent press conferences under Dr. Tong's aegis kept us informed of the military developments and government information. The numerous embassies and ministries in the provisional capital gave us access to diplomatic activities. Unfortunately most diplomatic activity took place south of the Yangtze, which had suffered less than the main section of the city, but we managed. Finally, there was a constant movement of correspondents from all parts of the globe bringing firsthand information of developments elsewhere.

A temporary but tenuous truce was in effect between Generalissimo Chiang Kai-shek's nationalist government and Mao Tse-tung's

communist opposition. Chairman Mao was represented in Chungking by Gen. Chou En-lai, but the nationalists downplayed his presence and prohibited contact between Chou and the foreign press. None-
theless, four of us at the Chai-ling House—Vincent Sheean and Edgar
Ansell Mowrer, syndicated columnists, Leland Stowe of the *Chicago
Daily News,* and I—determined to meet with Chou. We doubted he
would say anything of import, and, of course, any attempt to file or
broadcast a story quoting him would be an admission that we had
evaded the ban. Still, none of us expected to remain in Chungking
long, and we all were naturally curious about this man who was second only to Mao in the communist hierarchy.

Our persistence resulted in a midnight rendezvous at a point that
would be known to none of us. A guide met us at a designated spot
inside the main city and conducted us on a weird labyrinthine tour
of dark alleys and corridors that was like something Hollywood might
do with Fu Manchu. General Chou was waiting for us in a dimly
lighted room (all Chungking was dimly lighted) furnished with only
a table and a few chairs. He greeted each of us individually and ge-
nially, just as if we all were brothers in a great cause. We talked for
about an hour and, as expected, learned almost nothing except that
Chou was indeed affable when he chose to be.

He side-stepped any questions that might be difficult but did so
with a skill you had to admire. He himself had one question to which
no one of us could venture a guess. "When is the United States coming into this war?" It was a question we encountered all over Chungking. The Chinese obviously felt that American military aid would
bring their years of agony to a much earlier conclusion. I got the distinct impression that Chou En-lai wanted an end to this Japanese affair so that he and Mao could move on to more important matters.

There was no such rigamarole surrounding the Generalissimo, although he consistently declined to be interviewed. He did occasion-
ally make public appearances, and he left the impression that any
reticence on his part was due to his pressing duties as head of a nation fighting for its very existence. I first met him at a tea he and
Madame Chiang gave in their home to which all correspondents were
invited. It was a late afternoon affair in which China's traditional rice
wine played no part, given Madame's steadfast stand against alcohol
in any form. The feature of the soiree was unscheduled and more than
a little eerie.

I was standing next to the Generalissimo, on his left, and a Tass correspondent was on his right. Suddenly, without warning, the generator (each important edifice had its own generator) went dead, throwing the room into total darkness. I could feel the Gissimo's presence there beside me, but I couldn't see him or my fellow correspondent from the USSR. I spoke to the Gissimo, but his answer was unintelligible. No one around us moved, but there was activity near the door as servants went for candles. The total darkness couldn't have lasted more than a couple of minutes, but it seemed much longer. It was a perfect *setting* for a real international incident but hardly the right *place*. The Gissimo was always well, if not obviously, guarded. When the first candles arrived, I looked at the Gissimo, and he smiled thinly. I too smiled, but our friend from Tass remained impassive.

I had met Madame Chiang when she gave a baby giant panda to New York City's Bronx Zoo and wanted CBS to carry the presentation on the network. The first request came from T. S. Peng. I told him I thought New York might be interested, thereby laying the foundation for the biggest single headache of my Chungking sojourn. New York did like the idea but wanted a firm date immediately, since the network schedule would have to be shuffled to accommodate a half-hour broadcast in prime time. An immediate date was impossible, however. The Madame chose that moment to leave Chungking on a trip, and no one would admit knowing how to reach her. The panda was coming from Chengto but no one knew when. And Dr. John Tee Van of the Bronx Zoo executive staff, in China on a research mission, had agreed to accept the gift and escort the animal to its new home, but no one knew when Dr. Tee Van would be available.

There was nothing to do except stall, and after a few querulous messages I began to hope New York would cancel. It took two weeks to get all parties agreed on a date and another to clear the network time, during which I had to explain the delay to Peng, who was under pressure from both Madame Chiang and Holly Tong.

Then Tong asked me to invite the ambassador, Clarence E. Gauss, to appear on the program with the Madame. Annalee Whitmore, who was preparing the script, and I walked to the embassy to make the request. In answer to the ambassador's direct question, we had to admit the hour would be 4:00 A.M., Chungking time, and we left with a less than enthusiastic "I'll let you know."

A couple of correspondents who had been covering Chungking almost from the first advised me confidentially that I was wasting my time. Madame Chiang, they said, was resented in some high places, and plenty of people in Chungking would not be happy to see her enjoy a major public relations break on a nationwide broadcast in the United States. I first thought of broaching that subject with Hollington Tong, but decided instead to talk to T. S. Peng. Peng did not deny some attempt might be made to prevent the broadcast, but assured me there was no chance it would succeed. Twin microphones in the studio would be connected to two separate transmitters by separate land lines and powered by separate power plants. If one failed for any reason, the other would carry on. It sounded encouraging.

On the day before the scheduled broadcast, the Russian Embassy held a reception in honor of the twenty-fourth anniversary of the October Revolution, which had put the Soviets in power. It was a very low-keyed assemblage because the Germans were still in the ascendency inside Soviet borders, but all the Chungking diplomatic corps was present. I took the opportunity to get from Ambassador Gauss the reply I expected: "Dunn, I'm hanged if I'm going to get up at four in the morning to appear on anyone's broadcast." I thanked him. The next morning as all the participating parties were gathering in the studio, Madame Chiang turned to me with a half-smile. "I understand Ambassador Gauss doesn't like to get up early." It was an observation that required no answer, so I just nodded and went on about my duties.

Technically, our broadcast was to be beamed to RCA Communications in Manila and relayed on to San Francisco. As soon as Jimmy Stewart and I arrived at the studio, Fung Chien, chief engineer, informed us the outlook wasn't promising. It was impossible to contact Manila. We had no choice but to do the broadcast blind, and, although everything went smoothly in the studio, we had no idea if we were getting through. As a matter of record, we did not. New Yorkers had to rely on the daily press for news of their new giant baby panda and Madame Chiang Kai-shek's largess.

It took us several hours to get a message from San Francisco with the bad news, and all information pointed directly to "atmospheric conditions beyond our control." When we first realized our failure, I immediately thought of the warning given me some days earlier. Sober consideration, however, finally convinced me that no one on this mortal planet, male or female, possessed enemies powerful enough to control the "atmospherics." Paul White's reaction had nothing to do with atmospherics or technicalities. He wired, "Hope you never see another panda!"

CHAPTER 9

The Burma Road

The first time I mentioned the Burma Road to Paul White, I confidently anticipated a quick negative. That tortuous highway, hacked, dug, and blasted out of the rugged mountains of Yunan province in the preceding three years, was China's main lifeline in its war with Japan, the artery that fed China with the supplies and materiel that made resistance possible. The modern airlift was unknown in 1941, and the Yangtze, which normally linked Chungking with the sea, had been closed by the Japanese to all important shipping.

A trip down the Burma Road might yield one or two stories but no broadcast reports, and it would take as much as a week longer to reach Rangoon, my next objective. The World Series was over and the football season nearing its close, but I still hoped to spend Christmas with my two girls. I had done all there was for me to do in Chungking, and I wanted to move. To my surprise, Paul seemed taken with the idea of a survey trip down the road. Again I got that feeling he was hoping to keep me in Asia until the Japanese struck. He indicated it would be a good idea for me to learn as much as possible about the Far East–Pacific while I could. So I began checking local transportation.

Jimmy and Eleanor Stewart had to be glad to see me planning to leave. A stringer, who gets paid on the basis of assignments, is always happy to see a staffer depart, for economic reasons if no other. It's hard to realize much of an income while someone from the home office is monopolizing the microphone.

The Stewarts were a grand couple who had been a big help to me, and I still treasure the memory of a dinner party they gave for Annalee, Marty Gold, and me. Their home was an abandoned generator house at the radio station, a room probably ten feet square furnished with a bed that doubled as a sofa, a table, and four chairs, none of which matched any other. A tiny shack adjoining served as the kitchen (a W.C. was never a problem in China), and light was supplied by a line from the station. There were five unmatched forks, two table knives, and a large knife for carving. More amazing were the utensils in the kitchen—an assortment of tin cans! A big two- or three-gallon dried-milk can served to cook the pot roast and gravy, perfectly prepared. Vegetables required a smaller tin, and the home-made mushroom soup was served from another. Oranges and pomolos provided dessert for a meal I'll never forget.

A couple of days before I left Chungking, Annalee and I were invited to join Dr. Tee Van at lunch with Madame Chiang and Madame H. H. Kung at the latter's home. It was a delicious meal, but the Soong sisters couldn't serve more graciously in that spacious mansion than the Stewarts did in their ramshackle generator shed. Not all correspondents enjoy the luxury of London's Savoy hotel all the time.

In order to travel down the Burma Road, it was customary to go to Kunming, about four hundred miles southwest of Chungking, the northern terminal of the road. There truck convoys formed for the trek to Lashio across the border in Burma. I was advised to wait until I reached Kunming to contact one of the commercial firms, most of them British, that operated the convoys. That was the only positive advice I received. Most of the officials I talked to, both Chinese and American, strongly opposed the trip as both strenuous and dangerous. I wasn't worried about the former, and danger is hard to imagine in advance. Besides, I had already committed myself to New York and wouldn't consider a change of heart.

An American gunboat, the U.S.S. *Tutuila*, permanently stationed in the Yangtze at Chungking, was a favorite oasis for Americans looking for home-side cooking. When a Colonel Mayer, military attaché at the embassy, was unable to talk me into abandoning the project, he went down to the ship and requisitioned two pairs of long underwear for me so at least I wouldn't freeze in the high altitudes. It took nearly ten days to book a CNAC flight to Kunming, and I would be making the trip in late November. The idea of long underwear was suddenly attractive.

One of the first men I met in Kunming was Capt. Martin Wright, an American advisor to the road authority. After making his own bid to change my mind, he gave me the names of several firms engaged in the operations with instructions on how to locate them. Fortunately, the first firm I contacted, Steele Brothers and Company, not only had a convoy leaving the following morning but the manager, Ian Mackay, told me the convoy leader would be an Indian who spoke English, and he promised me space on a truck whose driver, probably Chinese, was similarly gifted. Mackay issued no warnings, but neither did he brief me on the condition of the dozen vehicles that would make up our convoy, information that might well have discouraged me. Instead, he invited me to lunch, advised me to buy up some canned goods, and told me to report to the Steele depot not later than seven the next morning.

My shopping safari gave me a chance to see something of Kunming, a very attractive place and the first Chinese city I had visited that wasn't dominated by foreign influence or blasted beyond recognition. The shopping was a failure, however. All I could turn up were three tins of California sardines and three cans of Chinese peanut brittle. I couldn't find a single can of beans, spaghetti, corned beef, or soup. I did, however, have a large can of a hundred bouillon cubes, the gift of Mme. Gladys Savary, proprietress of Manila's finest restaurant, "in case you get hungry on the Burma Road." Her choice couldn't have been better for one who was heading into a country where boiling water was standard fare wherever you went.

The Hotel de l'Europe awakened me on schedule, accepted my *yuan*, and summoned a coolie to take my gear to the *airport*. Fortunately I did recognize that single word in the directions given the guide and was able to protest. When the message finally got through that I was going to ride a *truck*, I clearly had lost face.

Ian Mackay was a gracious gentlemen, but he obviously had little knowledge of Steele Brothers convoy schedules. I arrived at the depot a few minutes before seven to find the gates locked and no sign of activity anywhere. I banged on the gate with my fist, but nothing happened. As I waited, an American couple with three small children came up and introduced themselves. They were missionaries, the Reverend and Mrs. John Bolton, returning via truck to their station in Tali about a third of the way down the road. Their appearance struck me as a good omen. If this American family could brave the alleged rigors of the Burma Road, surely the reports of danger had been grossly exaggerated. Bolton told me not to worry about the gate, it would open eventually. Things seldom happen on schedule in China, he explained. Patience was the only answer.

By 7:30 the depot was fully active, and with good reason. Almost every truck had something wrong with it, and two had to have new springs installed. Bolton obviously was acquainted with the Steele operation, and he introduced me to Jagdish Rai, a tall slender Indian who was the convoy leader. I gave Rai the identifying letter Mackay had given me, and he shoved it into a pocket without a glance.

When the time finally arrived for the first trucks to start, Rai introduced me to a Chinese named Yung Chu-tsin who would be my driver. Yung did indeed speak good English, having been educated by the British in Malaya, his home. He explained that the first trucks to leave (it was almost eleven o'clock by this time) would be those with Burmese drivers, followed by the Indians. Our truck and two others driven by Chinese would bring up the rear. The reason, Bolton explained later, was that the Chinese were the best drivers and the Burmese the poorest, an explanation confirmed every evening when the order of arrival at each destination reversed the order of departure.

One happy feature of the Burma Road was the prevalence of kilometer markers. The engineers who created this unbelievable highway had placed a marker at every kilometer interval. Although some markers had been destroyed by attrition or by vandals, you usually had fairly accurate knowledge of your location in relation to Kunming, where the zero marker was fixed.

Mackay had assigned the Boltons to a single truck, also driven by a Chinese and already loaded to capacity, as were all the trucks. I still wonder where they stowed themselves, but they seemed quite happy with the arrangement and waved as their truck moved out, promising to see me at the next stop. I had no such problem. Yung shared his seat in the cab with me and kept up a running commentary for my education and entertainment. We were not the first to leave, but within a very few kilometers we had taken the lead with Yung performing like a favorite in the Grand Prix.

All went smoothly until we reached the 50 kilometer marker and realized we were out of water. We came to a dead stop at 51 kilometers, and Yung got out to investigate. The nearest water was in a rice paddy about fifty feet distant, and the only container was a pith sun helmet Yung pulled from under our seat. Carrying water in a helmet that has four air vents in the crown is not easy, but he managed to fill the radiator partially, and we limped on a few kilometers to where the occupant of a roadside hut loaned Yung an earthenware crock.

This refill got us over a 6,560-foot pass, and we descended into a valley by means of the tightest hairpin turns I've ever seen. The *lacets* of the Alpes Maritimes can't compare! The breathtaking beauty of the Yunnan mountains partially compensated for the breathtaking driving of Yung Chu-tsin. He was truly a superb driver, and he needed to be on a highway just barely wide enough for two trucks to pass, where one mistake could send you hurtling into seemingly bottomless canyons.

Our faulty radiator has cost us the lead, which was fine with me;

I had lost my desire for speed. When we reached the little village of Tufung, we found Jagdish Rai waiting for us. Although it was only a little after two o'clock, Rai announced we would stop there for the night. The protests were unanimous, so he finally agreed to let the three Chinese drivers continue as far as Tsuyung, another 72 kilometers. The first 40 took us into the Ipingling Gorge through which ran the Lufung River, a small but beautifully ferocious mountain stream. Paralleling the road we could see the grading being done for the proposed Yunnan-Burma railroad, another dream that died aborning.

Once out of the gorge, we started climbing again, this time to top a 7,020-foot pass. By now the sun had begun to drop into the west, directly in front of us and focusing on our windshield. Approaching trucks churned up great clouds of dust, each particle spotlighted and polished by the sun's rays. It blinded me, but Yung seemed to have a built-in radar, and the great, shadowy forms of trucks lurching suddenly out of the glare found him always alert and deft.

As we neared the top of the mountain our truck, true to form, ran out of water again, this time with no stream, house, or even a rice field handy. Yung elected to continue, pulling slowly up the hills, then free-wheeling down the other side with the engine shut off. By now it was getting dark, but Yung never hesitated. He told me we would find a house on the left just before we entered the final and highest pass. As usual he was right, although I would never have spotted it by the feeble light of a lone candle that flickered behind a window.

Once again we filled the radiator and completed the climb. Then came the descent in the dark, and for the first time the reputed perils of the Burma Road seemed credible. Yung was an excellent driver, praise be, but we still had several near misses with only fractional inches to spare. The sight of a less fortunate truck sprawled in a ditch about twenty feet below us added no reassurance.

There was no driving in the left lane on this highway. The surface was just wide enough for one truck riding the middle with barely enough room to clear on-coming traffic with your two left wheels riding an inadequate shoulder if your luck held out. Yung made that descent with the aid of blinding headlights and screeching horns, ours and scores of others, and all the speed of an express elevator, finessing the countless hairpins and dodging countertraffic with a skill that both pleased and scared the hell out of me.

Strangely, perhaps, the spectacular "21 Curves" shown above, while the most photo-genic part of the Burma Road, did not offer its greatest challenges. Here the grade of ascent was constant but more moderate than elsewhere, and the road was wide enough to allow two trucks to pass. No matter how high the road climbed, the rice terraces that had fed China's millions for centuries were always visible. *Courtesy U.S. Army Signal Corps*

The last few kilometers into Tsuyung were bumpy but blessedly level. We pulled up beside the city wall about seven-thirty, and Yung directed me to a hotel just a few meters inside the wall. I found it easily enough, but the place was full and I couldn't find an employee who could speak English. I returned to the truck, and Yung took charge. Any other hotel would be "common," he informed me, and I would be attacked by bugs, which he illustrated by scratching himself enthusiastically until I got the point. Instead, he would fix himself a bunk inside the truck, and I could have the driver's seat to myself.

It was getting cold, and the cab would at least offer some protection from the night breezes; besides, there didn't seem to be any choice. Forgetting that I had had nothing to eat, I curled up on the seat, my legs wrapped around the steering column and my head pillowed on an old towel coat. I was feeling very much alone and nostalgic for the many soft, warm beds I had not really appreciated down through the years. Behind me Yung was preparing his own billet, singing as he worked, not in his usual Chinese falsetto but with clear, if accented, lyrics:

> Have you ever been lonely?
> Have you ever been blue?"

I have no idea where he learned those words, but they certainly spelled out my innermost feelings at the end of a hectic day. Hunger and discomfort lost out, however, and I was asleep in minutes, Yung's lullaby still in my mind.

Any hope we may have had of making time on our journey were dashed the next morning when Rai announced we would have to wait for the arrival of four Burmese-driven trucks that hadn't showed up the evening before. I joined the Boltons in a walk through the little city and finally, when noon arrived before the missing trucks, I treated them to an excellent luncheon in a little restaurant they discovered.

It was almost one o'clock before Rai finally gave the word for us to proceed as far as Sha Chao, another 55 kilometers. The only incident of the day came when Yung, filling the radiator as usual, lost the radiator cap. After a futile search, we set out, the cap replaced by a handkerchief. Still, the water lasted for the entire 55 kilometers, and we rolled into Sha Chao well before sundown, stopping directly in front of what looked to be a brand new hotel constructed of wood and bamboo matting.

The Boltons were already there, and Reverend Bolton explained

there were only two rooms on the upper floor (the lower was a restaurant), one of which they proposed to occupy and the second available. The charge for each room was on a per-bed basis, each bed cost-
ing the *yuan* equivalent of seventy-five cents. To assure privacy I
elected to take all four, a decision that amazed the proprietor, but
for a mere three dollars I could afford to be a big spender! Each bed,
I found, consisted of two sawhorses with three planks laid across
them. There were no linens or covers of any type. The only entrance
to my room was through the Boltons', but I considered this a plus because it was more insurance of privacy.

I gladly joined the Boltons for dinner, my own culinary knowledge
being limited to the realization that Chinese food as the Chinese
themselves eat it can be very good. It was hard to remember that only
a brief year before I wouldn't touch rice in any form, proving there
were some four hundred million people in China who were smarter
than I was.

When the Boltons assured me my typing would not annoy them,
I retired to the privacy of my quarters to do a little work. First, I re-
arranged two beds to form a table and a bench for the typewriter.
Then I placed a number of candles in a semicircle around the machine. It wasn't ideal, but it worked. I typed for a few moments, then
paused to ponder the next word. As I did I heard a rustling sound behind me and turned to find a half-dozen Chinese surrounding me, obviously intrigued by the blond, pasty-skinned foreigner and his con-
traption. Startled at first, I relaxed when they gave me friendly grins.
I grinned back and returned to my typing.

The next morning the Reverend Bolton told me I had been the sensation of Sha Chao. Why would anyone spend money for four beds
when he could sleep on only one? Why would one man need a dozen
candles just for himself? Finally, what was that strange machine he
used to put characters on paper? The only way to satisfy such curiosity was by personal investigation, so there had been a constant
stream of silent, shadowy figures passing through the Boltons' room
into and out of my own private quarters to see this strange sight for
themselves.

When I finally closed the machine and settled down to read by the
light of a single candle, the procession ended as eerily and quietly
as it had begun. The bed I finally chose had little to offer in the way
of creature comforts, but neither did it have the bugs that Yung de-

tested. And there was the soothing *click-click-click* of mah-jongg tiles in the room below to lull me to early slumber.

One of the many wonders of the Burma Road was that it was ever able to serve the purpose for which it was built. It represented a staggering and continuing investment of money, engineering skills, physical effort, and human lives. It was the main and vital lifeline for a besieged and ravaged China, yet the Chinese government did almost nothing to police it, and thievery, piracy, smuggling, and senseless violence plagued it from the very beginning.

Despite the physical inadequacy of the highway, its narrow width, lack of shoulders, and brutal stone surface that could cut a tire to pieces on a single trip, no effort was made to get maximum service from a facility so essential to a nation's existence. In my brief experience I saw drivers, stopping for food or drink, leave their trucks right in the middle of the road even when there was room to pull off, which created traffic jams that extended for miles as other trucks struggled to get by.

Too, the road was beset by a breed of bandits known as "yellow fishes," ostensibly free-lance drivers looking for jobs. They would drive a truck to Kunming, then hitchhike back to Burma for another hire. When they did get a truck, they all carried contraband, known as "pigeon," that consisted of anything saleable in China, and almost everything was saleable once smuggled into China. Some of the "yellow fishes" carried hand guns to protect their "pigeon" and themselves, which was completely illegal but almost never punished.

In the entire 1,146 kilometers (712 miles) from Kunming to Lashio I saw no armed guards at any point except the two great bridges that spanned the Mekong and Salween rivers. Military units guarded those spans, but no civil police were ever in evidence. Obviously, the flow of supplies carried by these trucks and tankers was of sufficient quantity to minimize the loss to the "yellow fishes" and other criminals.

We left Sha Chao early the next morning, a glorious day. Yung said we would go only as far as Hsaikuan, 104 kilometers distant, where the entire convoy would stop for very necessary repairs. Almost every truck had something wrong with it, he said, and we might be there for a couple of days. The first 40 kilometers were magnificent. We climbed and climbed, doubling back and forth as the highway rose to its highest pass, a col that topped 8,528 feet. The scenery was indescribably beautiful, but we didn't make much time because our camion insisted on frequent stops for water while the brakes showed signs of going on strike.

Soon after topping the pass, at the 292-kilometer marker, we came upon a small plateau, little more than a wide place in the road, and a ramshackle tea house. Yung decided it was time for refreshment. He pulled off the road, parked the truck, and I followed him into the shop. He ordered tea and peanuts boiled in hot oil that had to be eaten with chopsticks. We went outside and sat down on a sawhorse to enjoy the break. We were almost ready to leave when another truck pulled into the clearing and a half-dozen "yellow fishes" jumped out and made straight for Yung, jabbering madly in Chinese. One of them carried a length of rope with which he tried to whip Yung. Another picked up a sawhorse and threw it at him. He started to run and I started to yell, but no one listened. Then I saw the gun, apparently a six-shooter, that one of the goons had stuck under his belt. I decided not to intervene.

Yung was obviously putting up no resistance, merely trying to fend off the blows, all the time retreating back toward the pass. I ran to the truck, opened both doors to the cab, climbed inside, and shouted to Yung to make a run for it. I don't know if he heard me, but when another driver intervened, he did circle the group and ran to join me. Just as he reached the door one of the thugs hit him with a rock as big as a fist, right at the base of the brain. He dropped like a plummet, unconscious. That seemed to satisfy the thugs, and the attack (it was never a fight) ended. Two of the drivers came over, picked Yung up, and shoved him into the cab beside me. Then they all retired to the tea house and emerged a few moments later with bowls of rice that they proceeded to consume with great nonchalance, squatting by the roadside.

There was nothing to do but sit there. I had never been checked out on a Dodge truck, nor was I equipped to navigate the Burma Road. After several minutes Yung began to stir. When he did regain consciousness he was too dazed to talk, certainly in no condition to drive. Finally still another driver came up and spoke to Yung in Chinese. Yung made no response, but he did slide over to the center of the seat. His friend (I sincerely hoped) moved in under the steering wheel, and a few seconds later we were back on the road again, this time with a stranger at the wheel and a passenger who had no idea what the onset was all about.

After a few kilometers Yung began to sit up and take notice. He conversed with the stranger, apparently on the best of terms, and that at least was a relief. As Yung slowly regained full consciousness, he filled me in on the cause of the attack. He spoke carefully, for the beating he had taken seemed to affect his speech. It had all begun in Sha Chao when this group of "yellow fishes" had asked Jagdish Rai for a lift. Rai had refused, and they took out after him with the gun, firing several shots but missing. For some reason they had decided that Yung was responsible for the refusal, so they commandeered a truck and set out for Hsiakuan, overtaking us at the scene of their attack. Yung said he didn't dare fight back because they would have used that as an excuse to kill him. Such killings had happened before, he assured me, and no one was ever punished.

In the meantime Yung had moved back behind the wheel and was obviously unhappy with the truck's performance. At the 315-kilometer mark he pulled up at the side of the road and announced we were entirely without brakes. The hydraulic system had sprung a leak and all the fluid was gone. As we debated our next move, four trucks of our convoy pulled in behind us, all driven by Indians, one of them a very shaken Jagdish Rai, who confirmed having been shot at and expressed his not too surprising opinion that "all Chinese drivers very bad." For some reason, however, he didn't include Malay-born Yung in that category, and the two of them went into an immediate huddle to discuss our brakes. The decision was for Yung to continue to Hsiakuan where Steele Brothers had a depot. Yung insisted he could make it safely, and Rai seemed to agree with him. I wanted to protest, but their minds were made up. My options were two: either I would have to trust Yung to get us over another towering pass, or I could ask Rai to put me in another truck with a driver who could not communicate with me and whose driving skills were questionable. I stayed with Yung.

I have already classified Yung Chu-tsin as an excellent driver, but the next eighty-seven kilometers definitely moved him into the superlative class. We drove slowly past Yunanyi Lake and then started up the face of a mountain on a road that was really only a ledge carved out of solid rock, nine kilometers always upward, with Yung in complete control. We topped the pass at 7,700 feet and then began our brakeless descent, a feat I could hardly believe even while experiencing it.

Using the engine as a brake, we moved downward in low gear with never a heartstopper. We saw a number of trucks off the road, their cargoes strewn about, one with a dead driver beside it. Yung dismissed them all as bad drivers. "Good drivers never do." I hate to think what that kind of driving does to an automotive engine, but it seemed certain that the firms or the government agencies operating on this destructive road had to anticipate an early write-off on all equipment.

We moved slowly but so skillfully that even I began to relax. We pulled into the Steele depot in Hsiakuan about seven-thirty and found the Boltons waiting for us. It was then that I learned that the commandeered truck that had carried the goons had also been carrying my own personal luggage. The Reverend Bolton had salvaged my gear, and Mrs. Bolton had made a reservation for me at the local *pen-kwan* (guest house), the last space available.

This time the room had two beds instead of four, and they were deluxe beds by Chinese standards, each having a woven cane foundation instead of wooden planks. The linen consisted of one quilt-like spread on each bed. If I had been less exhausted I might have questioned the purity of those spreads, but all I wanted was to pass into oblivion as quickly as possible. I made a cup of bouillon to go with the inevitable tea, lay down on one spread, and pulled the other one over me. Sleep came swiftly.

I don't know what time it was when I was awakened by the sound of chopsticks falling on a bare floor. I had used them to stir my bouillon and left them on the table beside the bed. I grabbed my flashlight and immediately spotted a rat, nearly as large as a kitten, trying to break into my can of bouillon cubes. I gave a chase, saved the cubes, and stashed them inside my suitcase. I tried unsuccessfully for more sleep and lay there in the dark reviewing the events of the preceding day.

The Boltons still had eight miles to go to reach their home station in Tali, an ancient city noted for its marble quarries. Steele Brothers had loaned or rented them a truck, and they invited me to go with them to see how missionaries live in the far corners of China. Yung could not leave before late that afternoon, so I consented. Their home proved to be a very comfortable Chinese house that the Reverend Bolton had remodeled and modernized himself. Of particular interest was the first electric power plant I had seen since leaving Kunming, a small hydro-operated generator fed by the little mountain stream that flowed briskly past their kitchen window. It produced enough power to light the house and activate some small appliances but certainly insufficient power to carry a reporter's voice all the way to San Francisco and the network! I left the Boltons with regret. They had been helpful far beyond the call of duty, and I had become Uncle Bill to their three youngsters. By way of farewell they presented me with a can of pork and beans, and I reciprocated with a pair of flashlight batteries.

Back in Hsiakuan I found the *pen-kwan* had rented my room and learned that there would be no chance of leaving that day. It looked like another night in Yung's front seat until I remembered David Lloyd of Socony-Vacuum whom I had met in Kunming and who told me he was the only non-Asiatic stationed in Hsiakuan. He might possibly have a spare bed. It took me some time to locate his home, but my luck had really turned. Lloyd had returned from Kunming almost coincidental with my visit, traveling in a Buick sedan that belonged to the Bank of China. With him were Hu Fu-yon, who represented the bank, and Jack Hall of Shell Oil, a pipeline engineer. The latter two were continuing to Burma, and Lloyd's seat would be vacant. An Yu-heng of the road administration was also at Lloyd's when I arrived, and he offered me a bed in his home nearby. Finally, we all had a very excellent dinner. Bed, board and transportation! I was a very happy reporter.

Mr. An loaned me a pair of coolies, and I returned to the depot for my gear. Yung seemed genuinely sorry to see me leave, particularly since the brakes were fixed. That was indeed an important point, but not enough to turn me from my new-found fortune. I thanked him for everything, assured him he was the best driver on the road, and gave him a few *yuan* for hot boiled peanuts. The following day, basking in the comfort of a cushioned sedan, I sighted the truck pulled off the road. Yung was carrying water from a nearby stream to fill the radiator. He didn't see me, but I mentally wished him better luck with the brakes than with the radiator.

The rest of the trip was so mundane I almost felt I was cheating. The presence of a representative of the Bank of China, which was sponsoring Hall's feasibility survey of a proposed pipeline, assured us VIP treatment whenever we stopped, usually at the home of another bank official. Our driver was not Yung Chu-tsin, but neither was our transport an overloaded, overheated, brakeless Dodge truck. We were able to weave our way through the many traffic jams at a fair rate, while the splendor of the Yunnan mountains increased at every curve.

Mountains weren't the only obstacles to be conquered when the road was built. Two of Asia's greatest rivers, the Mekong and the Salween, posed formidable barriers that had to be spanned. The problem was solved by the construction of the two huge suspension bridges that looked as sturdy as the Golden Gate from a distance but proved to be something less. Both were described as "free suspension" bridges. Great stone towers carried the heavy cables which in turn supported the roadway, nothing more than heavy wooden planks placed transversely across the cables and lashed into position. When a truck or car made the crossing, always single-file, one way, the roadway would sway and undulate fearsomely, like a hammock, but apparently it did the job. After watching several vehicles sway their way across, both Hall and I decided to walk.

The Mekong bridge, known as the Kungko, appeared to be a bit the larger, but that was only an estimate. No specifications were available, no cameras were allowed, and military units provided the only organized guard units on the entire road. Regardless of size, there was no doubt the Salween span had the greater and more spectacular visibility. We first sighted it from the top of a pass while it was still some twenty-five kilometers (fifteen miles) distant and more than a mile below us. The descent was magnificent as we watched the the span appear and disappear dozens of times, always growing in size, during the more than an hour it took to wind our way down.

The bridges were outstanding examples of the innate engineering skills, rudimentary but effective, that have distinguished the Chinese down through the centuries, the same genius that has enabled them since the days of Confucius to move water up the steepest mountains to irrigate rice fields high above the clouds.

As we moved west and southward after a night in Paoshan, there was greatly increased evidence that the road was still under construction. Conscripted peasants of every age, from tiny children to their eldest elders, worked side by side with volunteers imported from neighboring provinces in large crews, breaking stones by hand and carrying the resultant rubble in wicker baskets to widen and improve the grade. I had been told that the tradition of binding women's feet had long since been abandoned in China, but I saw scores of small girls with bound feet hobbling along beside their elders, many of whom had their feet bound also, each with a tiny basket to add a few stones to the total. It is impossible for me to judge the age of senior Chinese with any accuracy, but at least 20 percent of this work force of thousands appeared to be well above their three-score years. Only the rice farmers were exempt, and they only during the planting and harvest seasons.

We spent our last night in China as guests of the *sawbwa* of Mangsheh, a local potentate who headed the district of that name, levied his own taxes, printed his own money and ran his own *"sawbwa-dom"* without question. His residence was a large frame house, not unlike a midwestern American farmhouse. The *sawbwa* was a genial host, very proud of his meager stock of English words. In response to his question, I asked for a bath, a request that seemed to please him. A few minutes later a boy appeared at my door and motioned me to follow him. The bathroom was a large room, similar to my bedroom, and in its center stood a gleaming white porcelain tub on its four feet, filled with enticingly warm water. I lost no time stripping and getting myself into a luxuriant situation. It was the first bathtub I had seen since leaving Hong Kong. When I finished, I reluctantly stepped out of the tub and turned to pull the plug and drain the now discolored water. That was a mistake! The tub was just another piece of furniture, like a chair or table, and I had to act fast to replace the plug and avoid a flooded floor. The tub had been filled by hand and it would be drained the same way.

The district of Mangsheh was notorious as the worst malarial area on the whole Burma Road, and the disease had claimed the lives of many workers. I had been warned to double my daily dose of quinine (which I usually omitted) and to make sure my mosquito net was firmly in place over my bed any time I found myself in Mangsheh. Now I was actually in Mangsheh and couldn't plead ignorance. What I hadn't been warned against was the hospitality of the *sawbwa* and his lovely wife, the *sawgan,* who provided their guests with a festive evening marked by a truly fine dinner and plenty of opportunity to propose *kan pai!* When I finally did retire to my room, I forgot the quinine entirely and was careless with the mosquito net. The next morning I was covered with mosquito bites, obviously a certainty for malaria. It was a stupid thing to do, but the only reaction was an irritating itch. This gave me my first hint that perhaps I was one of those rare individuals who are immune to malaria, a fortunate fact that would be borne out time and again in the long months ahead, in tropical climes.

The Burma Road crossed the Sino-Burmese border at Wan t'ing, a Chinese village that looked across the imaginary line at Kyuhkuk, a border station and nothing else. Here I left Hall and Mr. Hu, who were heading for Bhamo some miles to the west, and arranged a ride to Lashio in a station wagon that had something to do with the bank, although it carried Burmese licenses. The remaining miles to Lashio would not be difficult with the Yannan mountains behind me, I was told. From Lashio I could get a CNAC plane to Rangoon. I said good-bye to my friends and headed for Burmese customs to have my passport chopped. As far as I was concerned, the headaches were over. I was home free.

After nearly an hour, the passport officer returned with my passport. He was very sorry, of course, but my visa wasn't valid and I could not enter Burma! I was stunned. He said I would have to go back to Kunming and get a valid visa. I was talking to a native Burmese and thought perhaps I just hadn't understood. But the officer made it very clear that he would not accept my visa and that there was no place nearer than Kunming where I could get another.

Two weeks before, I had been eager to see firsthand this modern engineering miracle they called the Burma Road, but I had no wish at all to see it again, particularly when I had no idea where to look for transportation. I asked if I could wire Rangoon, but the officer assured me it would take at least a full day to get an answer. Then I inquired about a telephone. "Yes, there is a phone, sir, but you can't use it." "Why not?" "It is too expensive."

That gave me a little hope. I had some dollars, "gold" and "Mex." After I assured him I would pay whatever was necessary, he finally relented, and before too long I was talking to his superior in the capital. I explained that my visa had been gotten for me by the British press attaché in Chungking and that I had no idea it wasn't valid. (To this day I'm not sure what was wrong with it.) He finally agreed I could come as far as Lashio if I would report to immigration as soon as I arrived and would promise to take the first plane back to Kunming if the matter couldn't be straightened out. I would have agreed to anything to escape a return trip. The cost of that phone call was something less than three dollars, hardly an amount that would agitate Sam Dean, my contact in the CBS treasurer's office.

The passport officer in Lashio proved to be a naturalized Burmese, born in the Philippines. When he saw my passport had been issued in Manila, we became instant buddies, and CNAC lost a fare back to Kunming. I had to remain in Lashio several days waiting for a plane to Rangoon, but thanks to Shell, Caltex, Socony, and Jack Hall, who finally caught up with me, there was plenty to do. The oil companies dominated the foreign population of the towns along the road, and their representatives formed a close circle.

During the trip I had scribbled a parody of Kipling's "*Mandalay*," outlining a few of the headaches encountered on those more than seven hundred miles. When I showed my effort to one of the men who lived the road, he immediately demanded a copy. Unfortunately I had no carbon paper in my gear, and none was to be found in Lashio. There was no way except to type a fresh copy, which led to another demand. By the time I had typed, by request or demand, about a dozen copies, I had little time to be bored in a village where there was absolutely nothing for a transient to do except eat and drink, and the ballad was engraved indelibly on my mind.

Rangoon's Strand Hotel seemed lavishly luxurious when I checked in on the evening of November 29, 1941. It was not the Ritz or the Waldorf, but it was light years ahead of the Chai-ling House and any of the so-called guest houses that had been my abodes for the previous two months. Best of all, it had hot and cold running water with all the gleaming, immaculate furnishings expected of a modern hotel bathroom. As soon as the room boy stowed my gear and left, I stripped, entered the bathroom, turned on all the taps in the tub and the wash basin, then flushed the toilet just to hear the music! Next I took a warm shower to get the worst of the Burma Road off my exterior and, finally, drew a tub and soaked for a beautiful half-hour. Life holds few luxuries more taken for granted, while contributing so richly, than hot and cold running water!

The following week was spent in the futile attempt to locate any broadcast facilities capable of reaching either Manila or Batavia, the two cities south of Tokyo able to relay a broadcast signal across the Pacific. Rangoon Radio officials cooperated wholeheartedly but without success. There would be no broadcast reports from Rangoon.

The only city remaining on my original itinerary was Bangkok, which, although only 360 air miles distant, was completely inaccessible by air at that time. The only alternate route was by ship around the southern tip of the Malay Peninsula, probably with a change of ships at Singapore. Inasmuch as my friends at Rangoon Radio were certain I would not find the needed facilities in Bangkok, I was about to wire my recommendation that we forget about Thailand, but that message was never necessary. Three days after my arrival in Rangoon, the government decreed a one-week practise blackout. By the end of the week, however, the blackout was permanent, and we had quit pretending.

S-P-E-C-I-A-L   R-E-P-O-R-T

Ballad of the Highway

As my journeying carried me southward toward Burma and Rudyard Kipling's Mandalay, the words of his famous ballad kept moving through my mind, together with the thought that those words might well be adapted to this tortuous highway. There were no flying fishes along the highway (as a matter of fact, the flying fishes closest to Mandalay are four hundred miles away), but we did have "yellow fishes" in profusion and the proud stone towers of the great Kungko suspension bridge were as intriguing as any pagoda in Moulmein, where the temples in fact face westward, not "eastward toward the sea."

Over a period of several days, I scribbled my own version of *Mandalay*, more accurate geographically than the original, if less amorous. I shall never forget it because it was engraved indelibly on my mind as I ground out innumerable copies (in the absence of carbon paper) for my friends in Lashio whose careers at that time were tied to the road.

'Cross the old Kungko suspension
Where it spans the broad Mekong,
There the Burma Road goes winding
And the gas trucks roar along.
O'er the mountain tops from
    Mangsheh,
Through the gorge of Ipingling,
Come along you yellow fishes,
Hop a ride to old Kunming,
    Hop a ride to old Kunming!

Chorus:
On the road from Mandalay,
Where the yellow fishes play,
Where the pigeon flows unceasingly
Clear up by Chungking way;
On the road to Lashio
Where a thousand truckmen go,
Their horns forever screechin'
From Kunming to Lashio.

There's a million sweatin' coolies
In the land of tea and jade,
Making small ones out of big ones
To improve the Burma grade.
There's a thousand peaks and valleys
Just to try the soul of man;
There's a hundred dingy *pen-kwans*
Like that one in Paoshan,
    Oh, that one in Paoshan!

As the convoys pound the highways
With their stores for China's aid,
All those stinging yellow dust clouds
Overhang the Burma grade.
They will choke your burning nostrils
And clog your skin and hair
'Til you'll thank the great Almighty
For a breath of pure, fresh air,
    Just one breath of pure fresh air!

First you climb the highest mountain
And attain the steepest pass,
Then you freewheel down the valley
To conserve the driver's gas,
And the only thing that saves you
From a glimpse of Heaven's goal
Is a narrow strip of brake-band
And a prayer that's from the soul,
    Oh, that prayer that's from the
    soul!

I probably should have mentioned the traffic jam, gun fire, hot boiled peanuts, leaky radiators and non-existent brakes, among other things but the ballad gives you a fair idea of what a nation can do when its back is against the wall.

The fact that the Burma road ever existed is a tribute to all the people of China.

PART 2

CHAPTER 10

"It's Impossible"

My first instinct was to ignore the knocking, and I burrowed deeper under the pillow. But the annoyance continued, quietly insistent, so I forced myself awake, pulled on a robe, and opened the door. A room boy who looked as sleepy as I felt was proffering a cablegram on a salver. That in itself was not surprising. Cables and radiograms are everyday fare for reporters overseas. What was unusual was the "Urgent" stamp that explained my rude awakening. Instantly intrigued, I took the envelope, perched on the edge of the bed, and tore it open. The message was brief and completely baffling: "Please file all newsworthy material continuously unless otherwise directed."

It was signed by Paul White, and I studied it with complete disbelief. Why would anyone spend good money for an urgent cable directing me to do exactly what I had been sent to the Far East to do in the first place? White was one of the greatest news executives I ever knew, but he was not without his human frailties. I finally decided the message had been prompted by an overlong visit to Louis and Armand's, his favorite spa, and went back to sleep.

I had retired quite late the night before after a Sunday evening dinner with Lt. Gen. D. K. McLeod, the general officer commanding (GOC) in Burma, in his Rangoon quarters, an evening shared with two colonels from Britain's Indian army and General McLeod's aide. It had been a stimulating evening. General McLeod's quarters were tropically comfortable at a time when air conditioning was a novelty and in a city where it could be extremely hot at any time. The high-ceilinged drawing and dining rooms were cooled effectively by lazy ceiling fans—*punkahs*—and the broad, screened verandah where we concluded the evening could have been a setting right out of Somerset Maugham. Our host, a ramrod six feet with brown hair just starting to turn, was soft-spoken but decisive and the conversation was briskly paced and wide-ranging. Nothing suggested that this would be the last dinner party ever hosted by a British GOC in Burma.

Still, there was a keen awareness of the menace to the north, and the Japanese figured importantly in our conversation all evening. As we moved to the verandah for coffee and cognac, the general turned to me and asked, "Mr. Dunn, how can it be possible for your country to get into this war—as it has to before long—on a unified basis, without dissension among your people?" I probably laughed, but not from mirth. This was the question that had dominated every rap session I had joined from one end of the Orient to the other, always without solution. "Sir, I've got to admit I can't answer that. As you know, a large and sincere portion of our population believes we should let Europeans fight their own wars, in Europe or in Asia, and opposes any type of intervention. That is the big problem."

"What if Japan were to attack the Philippines?" That came from one of the colonels. "Such an attack would certainly bring us into the war but not necessarily as a unified nation. We've promised the Philippines their early independence, and a lot of Americans no longer consider it American soil. There could still be a lot of dissension."

General McLeod left no doubt that in his opinion Great Britain would soon need all the help it could get in the Pacific, and his guests agreed. Further, he indicated deep concern about the probably hostile attitude of the Burmese people toward the British if their country were invaded. Events would quickly prove him correct.

Shortly after seven I dressed, took another look at White's perplexing cable, and went down to the dining room. The rear echelon of the American Military Mission to China, whose job it was to expedite war materiel and supplies up the Burma Road, was headquartered in Rangoon. Members of the command staff, under Col. E. M. Twitty, also were billeted at my hotel, the Strand, and I usually joined them for breakfast. For some unexplained reason it was never possible to buy a copy of Rangoon's single English-language newspaper at the hotel cigar stand. Consequently, it was my habit to eat breakfast before setting out in search of the printed word, and my military friends knew it. They were well prepared for me when I joined them.

"Have you seen the paper?" someone asked casually. "Of course not," I replied, pulling out a chair. "Anything happen?"

"Nothing much," shrugged Colonel Twitty. "The Japs bombed Pearl Harbor." I was not to be taken in. I had been to Pearl Harbor and had been briefed on the impregnable defenses. I'd never swallow that one. I shook out my napkin and took a sip of water. "Anyone hurt?"

"There must have been. They sank a flock of ships and apparently blew the hell out of everything else." There still was no sign of emotion from anyone. Obviously my military friends were having me on.

The banter continued through the toast and coffee, strictly low-keyed and masterfully conducted by Maestro Twitty to prove that an otherwise reasonably intelligent reporter could listen to the truth and not believe it. They were successful.

More important, they were also successful in illustrating the attitude of most Occidentals in the Orient in December, 1941: "Don't take the Japanese too seriously. If they start anything we'll teach them a lesson, and damned fast!" If the strike had been made by Germany, there would have been no levity. It was an attitude the Japanese had counted on.

When I finished my coffee, I excused myself and left the hotel in quest of a newspaper that would tell me what, if anything, actually was happening. I turned right down the Strand, but only a few steps from the hotel I met the American consul striding toward me, probably looking for Colonel Twitty. He had a newspaper clutched in one hand and stark tragedy etched on his face. Instantly I understood Paul White's cable. I reached for the consul's paper, but the first look at his face had told me the story. My God! Those bastards weren't kidding!

Those two weeks following Pearl Harbor were the most frustrating of my career. Rangoon had never figured in my itinerary as more than a brief stopover. I needed only to check out facilities for intercontinental broadcasts (nonexistent), pinpoint news sources, and learn what was being done to expedite vital war supplies to China. I had completed most of my agenda by that fateful Sunday evening and had booked sea passage for Bangkok two days later.

At exactly the time that General McLeod, his military guests, and I were debating how the United States might enter the war as a solid, unified nation—between midnight and 2:00 A.M., on Monday, December 8, Rangoon time—the enemy at Pearl Harbor was supplying the one answer no one of us had ever dreamed. A few hours later Adolf Hitler settled the question beyond challenge with his own declaration. My country was at war! I was no longer a *foreign* correspondent, I was a *war* correspondent, half a world away from home and completely outside the protective arm of Uncle Sam. It was a sobering realization.

The Japanese attacks on Pearl Harbor, Manila, and Singapore in quick succession had cancelled all normal transportation instantly.

I found myself sequestered in a colonial backwater of the infant Pacific war, minus a viable microphone and with little "newsworthy material" to file by cable.

I wanted desperately to reach either Singapore or Java, both but a
few brief hours to the south, but the only air carrier that made any
pretense of operating in that area at that time was KLM (KNILM in
the Indies). The men at KLM were understanding but told me bluntly
that because of their limited facilities and intermittent service, I
would have to accept any space they cleared, regardless of destination, or remain in Burma. That might well have taken me to India,
completely out of the Pacific war, but I closed no options.

It immediately became almost impossible for a reporter to locate
what little news there was in Burma at that time. Waiting for Japan
to move in their direction, the British were getting jittery because
the enemy was not reacting as anticipated. The British had expected
the enemy to be halted short of Burma by the "impregnable" fortress
of Singapore, just as we Americans had known beyond question that
Pearl Harbor was invulnerable. Consequently, there was no need for
important defenses within Burma itself. But the Japs bypassed Singapore. Instead, through the treacherous collaboration of the Thai premier, Pibal Songgram, the Japs were in Thailand only 350 miles to
the southeast, in perfect position to strike the vulnerable Burmese
border. There soon would be a real story in Burma, but not for a radio
reporter. I had to be where my mike was operational.

The officers with whom I had to work were cordial, even friendly,
but rigidly correct, obviously uncertain of me because I was the only
correspondent in Burma at the moment and they had had no experience with the breed. I don't think they really mistrusted me, but
they were taking no chances. For example, it took three days to clear
a story on my trip down the Burma Road, a story which had nothing
in it directly pertaining to Burma or the British.

A better indication of the brittleness of the situation came in an
exchange of cables with White, who was urging me to move anywhere,
but quickly. In one wire he completed his business message and,
knowing that South Bend, Indiana, was my hometown and that I had
always been an ardent Notre Dame fan, he concluded, "NOTRE DAME
FINISHED SEASON UNDEFEATED TIED ARMY." That was cheering news for
me at a time when good news was almost nonexistent. I answered
the query and concluded, "HURRAH FOR THE IRISH."

The next morning I received a surprising and urgent summons to the office of the chief censor. I had filed no copy in the preceding twenty-four hours, but I reported promptly to the secretariat to find the colonel in an unsmiling mood. As I entered his office, he picked up a sheet of paper and without rising, an ominous deviation for a British colonel, pushed it across the desk to me. It was my wire to White, and the colonel pointed an accusing finger at the bottom line. "Will you please explain what this means, Mr. Dunn, 'Hurrah for the Irish'?"

I wanted to laugh, but the colonel's expression warned against even a smile. He was in no mood for levity, nor was he going to condone support for the Sinn Fein or the IRA, even at a distance of some ten thousand miles. I brought out my copy of White's previous wire and indicated the reference to Notre Dame. Then came the incredible task of trying to explain to an officer in Great Britain's colonial service just how a college in Indiana bearing a French name that was always mispronounced had come to be known as the Irish. I didn't mention *Fighting* Irish lest he misconstrue that as well. Finally, I gave up. "Take it out," I told him. "It has absolutely no importance." At that he unbent a bit. "Do you mean you don't care if it moves or not?"

"I don't care at all. Kill that sentence completely, but move the rest of the message, please." That seemed to satisfy him, for he then okayed the entire message, "Irish" and all. Under normal circumstances the questioning could have been funny, but no one in official Rangoon was in any mood for jest or jollity at that nervous moment.

Then came the news, only two days after Pearl Harbor, that the two vaunted British warships, the battleship *Prince of Wales* and the battle cruiser *Repulse,* had been sunk by enemy aircraft off the coast of Malaya as they moved north to meet the enemy. It was still possible for us to rationalize the attacks on Pearl Harbor, Manila, and Singapore as lucky blows against careless and unprepared targets (we had almost no real information), but only superior power, expertly administered, could account for the swift destruction of those two dreadnaughts. The Japanese were tough and they were powerful. It was going to be a long and bitter war.

Twenty-four hours later I learned that Cecil Brown, the reporter White had hired in Europe to backstop me in Singapore, had been aboard the *Repulse* and had survived to supply the network with a "world beat," the first eyewitness story by any media. I was happy, of course, for CBS News and for Brown, but I would be less than honest if I didn't admit a little salt in my own wounds. There can be no situation tougher for a reporter than to find himself just barely out of reach of the most important story of his career. I became a major nuisance at the KLM office.

Actually, there were a couple of good stories in Burma at that time, but both were completely off the record. First was the appearance of a contingent of Flying Tigers to cooperate with the Royal Air Force (RAF). I had encountered the American Volunteer Group previously in China and I knew they were chafing for action. But I could report nothing until they were actually engaged in combat. This news blackout also blanketed the second potential story: the tens of thousands of tons of war materiel that lined the banks of the Irrawaddy and Rangoon rivers, and the efforts being made to transship it up the Burma Road to China. This constituted one of the biggest military targets in Asia at that moment but it, too, could not be mentioned until the enemy had actually attacked it. Surprisingly, the Japs didn't seem interested; they had their own timetable.

It was frustrating, of course, but not as frustrating as it would have been if I had had a microphone they could hear in San Francisco. There is minimal satisfaction for a radio reporter in filing even the most "newsworthy material" for someone else to voice.

Meanwhile, the few refugees trickling across the Thai border reported a complete lack of resistance to the Japanese, who were reinforcing in strength. On the seventeenth, nine days after Pearl Harbor, Darrell Berrigan of the United Press arrived from Bangkok with Harold Standish of the *Sydney Herald*, and I was no longer the only correspondent in Burma. They had covered the more than four hundred miles in just over a week, mostly on foot, and they, too, reported no Thai resistance. The arrival that same day of Leland Stowe of the *Chicago Daily News* from Chungking brought the total foreign press in Burma to four eager reporters, eager to move to another destination fast.

Haunting the KLM office paid off just a day later on the eighteenth when I was told that a plane was due from Calcutta on Saturday the twenty-first to depart for Java the following morning. There would be room on board for all of us. It was improbable, KLM reported, that we would stop at Singapore, almost directly on our southward route, because of the war situation. We likely would go directly from Medan on the north coast of Sumatra nonstop to Batavia. I cabled White the good news and notified Brown there was an outside chance I might see him and, if so, I probably would remain in Singapore to give him a hand.

That night the entire foreign press corps, all four of us, gathered at the Silver Grill, Rangoon's only night spot, and decided almost unanimously to accept KLM's hospitality. Only Lee Stowe decided to take a longer look at the local situation and then return to China. Burma would soon be a major story, but there was action right now in Malaya and the Indies to the south, and in both China and the Philippines to the north and east. We were ready to move.

Berrigan, Standish, and I arrived at the Rangoon airport just at the break of dawn on Sunday morning to find the big DC-3 warmed up and ready to go. We wasted no time. As we rolled down the grassy runway and lifted clear of Burmese soil, the sun broke over the eastern horizon to bathe the towering Schwe Dagon pagoda, Rangoon's greatest glory, with a sheen of purest gold. It was a breathtaking finale to a frustrating fortnight.

Approximately an hour after our takeoff, we learned later, the overdue Japanese paid their first bombing visit to the Rangoon airport and docks, leaving considerable devastation. I had missed my first real "newsworthy material" by a brief sixty minutes.

CHAPTER 11

No Doubt of Japan's Intentions

I left Rangoon with mixed emotions, happy to depart a theater from which radio reports were impossible but seeing little in the far prospect to please. The successes of the Japanese in that first fortnight were frightening.

The Germans gave us the term *blitzkrieg* early in the war, but Hitler's hordes never dreamed of lightning territorial conquest to equal what Japan had accomplished in those two brief weeks. In the time I was isolated in Burma, the Japs had moved into the Philippines in force and were perilously close to Manila. Ignoring Singapore, they had invaded the Malay Peninsula at its lightly defended northern border and were moving steadily to take that stronghold from the rear. Their troops were in Thailand, almost as the guests of Premier Song-

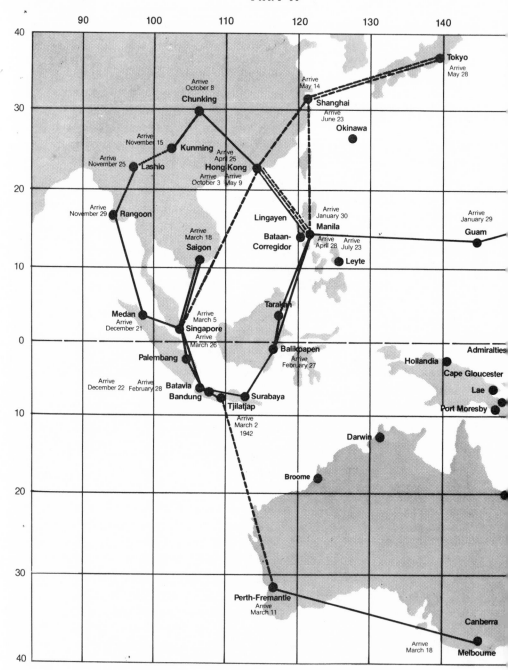

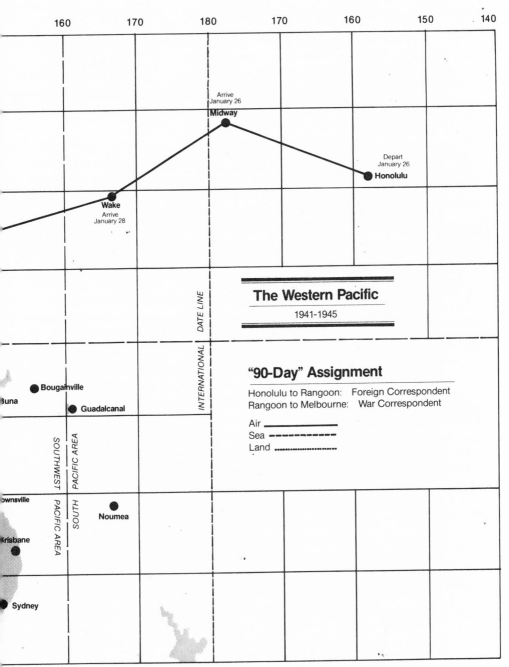

160   170   180   170   160   150   140

Arrive
January 26
Midway

Depart
January 26
● **Honolulu**

Wake
Arrive
January 28

INTERNATIONAL DATE LINE

The Western Pacific
1941-1945

"90-Day" Assignment

Honolulu to Rangoon: Foreign Correspondent
Rangoon to Melbourne: War Correspondent

Air ——————
Sea
Land ••••••••••••••••••

● Bougainville
Buna
● Guadalcanal

SOUTHWEST PACIFIC AREA

SOUTH PACIFIC AREA

ownsville
● **Noumea**

risbane

● Sydney

gram, ready to strike into Burma, while the troops they had stationed in Indochina were being reinforced, without opposition, for complete occupation. The fall of Hong Kong we knew was only hours away, and Guam already was the first American territory captured. Wake Island was immediately threatened. The swift destruction of the *Repulse* and the *Prince of Wales*, probably the bitterest single blow, erased the last doubt as to Japanese strength.

I questioned hard the sanity of following any route that didn't lead directly to Madison Avenue. Still, I wasn't ready to quit before I had really begun. Besides, there was one bright spot ahead, the excellent transpacific communications I knew I would find in Batavia.

This was my frame of mind as I returned once more to the Netherlands East Indies, and if the previous two weeks had marked only utter frustration, the following two weeks certainly did not. I wanted a story to report and I found one. I wanted radio facilities to reach CBS and the American public, and the Dutch in Java gave me facilities as fine as could be found anywhere in 1941. What I did not want to do was to report the defeat of a valiant people abandoned by their allies in the face of overwhelming odds. But I did just that.

Of all the people I visited in the Far East in that year before Pearl Harbor, only the Dutch seemed to have no doubt of Japan's intentions. With the exceptions of China, already locked in a death struggle with Japan, and of Japan itself, it was business as usual throughout the Orient with only a few token gestures toward preparedness. Only the Dutch were leaving nothing possible undone in preparing for the blow they knew was coming, refusing to let the staggeringly adverse odds discourage them. With their native Netherlands already in Nazi hands, these people were determined to make a do-or-die stand in the one place left to them. Obviously they were praying for a miracle and determined to be ready if a miracle did materialize.

Our first stop out of Rangoon was the island of Sabang, about 365 miles due south, just off the northern tip of Sumatra. It was a refueling stop, a Dutch air base, and defense preparation, everywhere evident, was primitive and sadly inadequate. Even to my then inexperienced eyes the base was untenable if confronted by real force. The same was true of Medan, facing the Strait of Malacca on the northwestern coast of Sumatra, where we spent the night. Within a week Medan would be the first city in the Indies to feel the fury of Japanese bombs. Although security was tight (our native taxi driver was not allowed on the base), it was obvious that wooden abatis, slit trenches, and bamboo obstructions would prove little more than a nuisance to a well-equipped enemy. Still, it was the best the Dutch could do with what materiel was available. They didn't lack funds, but they could purchase only what their allies didn't want or couldn't use.

During the evening word came that we would, after all, be able to land in Singapore the following morning. I wired Cecil Brown to meet me and again indicated my intention of joining him there if needed. Singapore was only a few miles east of our direct route to Batavia. Brown met me at the airport, but he was emphatic in his recommendation that I continue to Java. Transportation out of Singapore was becoming more difficult by the hour, but I would have no difficulty returning if developments warranted. Harold Guard, an old friend representing the United Press in Singapore, had come out to meet Berrigan, and he seconded Brown's recommendation. I returned to my plane.

The approach to Batavia by air was, as always, a beautiful sight, a sprawling community of vivid colors, of immaculate white houses with red tile roofs nestled in a sea of tropical green, a verdancy not often found in the more temperate zones. Not all the houses were white, of course, but that was the impression you got as your plane came in low for the landing, and when you left the airport you found yourself in a city of spotless streets and friendly people. Even the canals in which the Javanese housewives washed their clothes, and themselves under their clothes, had to be cleaner than they appeared. The whole ambience was one of cleanliness and absence of visible poverty. Your plane had just landed you in what was probably as close to an earthly paradise as could be found anywhere.

Jack Raleigh, the American writer I had signed as a stringer on my previous visit, was at the airport to escort me to the Des Indes Hotel. Once settled, we went directly to the government information office (formally termed *het Regering Publieteits Dienst* in Dutch but mercifully shortened to RPD) to renew my acquaintance with Dr. J. H. Rittman, the director. As usual, the good doctor was extremely helpful, as were all his aides. "Papa" Rittman, as everyone called him, was a cheerfully rotund man of medium height with a wiry thatch of dark, graying hair above his all-observant glasses. Correspondents would be arriving from all points of the globe in the next few weeks, and they wouldn't hesitate to ask for help far beyond the normal call of duty, but nothing seemed to ruffle him.

He took me first to see the new overseas broadcast studio, enlarged since my previous visit, still modest but completely adequate. Actually there wasn't much to see in the studio, which was designed for voice transmission only: a table desk with the microphone, headphones and talk-back speaker for communication with the monitoring engineer and finally a clock and a muted fan for ventilation. The most important equipment, of course, was out of sight, miles away in Bandoeng in this instance, the great transmitter-receivers that provided the bridge across the Pacific to link with the network at San Francisco. Visible or not, you knew they were there and they were good. (Not long after my arrival in Batavia one of the studio engineers suggested that we could put a better signal into San Francisco if we had a better microphone. I had no knowledge of transmission techniques but I agreed that anything looking toward improvement would be welcome. Accordingly, Dr. Rittman made a search and produced a new microphone of the latest type which, he explained, had been "borrowed from the governor general." The mike stayed with us as long as the NEI held out, doing yeoman service. I have always doubted, however, that it ever found its way back to its rightful owner.)

Next the doctor introduced me to the three gentlemen—I use that word advisedly—who would be my censors. Unlike many censors I would confront in the years ahead, these were professional men, attorneys and educators, chosen for their erudition and judgment. I would find them completely fair but totally incapable of reversing a decision once made. You could reason with them on any point as long as you kept your cool and didn't try to force the issue. But if you raised your voice even to a junior grade shout by way of emphasis, you were finished, a fact many correspondents to their sorrow were slow to learn.

I didn't have long to wait to try both the radio facilities and the censors. Almost simultaneous with my arrival, Raleigh received a message from New York scheduling me for a live report the next day. The news in the Pacific at that moment centered to the north in the Philippines, where the Japanese had to be checked if their drive to the Indies was to be slowed. With the enemy in those islands in force, however, the situation was growing desperate, as was the situation in Malaya. The next morning I studied all the official reports from Manila, talked to the Dutch military spokesman, added some observations from my trip south, and got my first clearance from the censors. Thus equipped, I made my first official visit to the new studio. It would be my first live report to the networks since I had left Chungking six weeks earlier. There was nothing wrong with the facilities I had coveted for so long, either in the studio or in the distant Bandoeng hills, but I hadn't figured on the vagaries of atmospherics, those pesky "circumstances beyond our control." We couldn't raise San Francisco.

S-P-E-C-I-A-L   R-E-P-O-R-T

Blind Broadcast

It was, perhaps, prophetic that my first live report to CBS News after the outbreak of hostilities was a blind broadcast, a method of transmission that would prove invaluable many times in the ensuing four years. The blind broadcast was a procedure whereby we radio reporters would shoot our arrow into the air and pray it might come to earth on an invisible target some ten thousand miles, or more, distant. Surprisingly, the strategy worked with encouraging frequency, and the public was never aware of any difficulty.

The fact that our Pacific transmission point was sometimes unable to contact San Francisco, always our West Coast control point, didn't necessarily mean that the reverse was true. San Francisco could often receive an acceptable signal from our part of the world when we were completely unable to read their transmission.

When that happened we would talk ourselves into the schedule so our report, if technically acceptable, could be fed live to the network news program. This procedure was possible because all intercontinental broadcasts were scheduled on Greenwich Mean Time (GMT), the exact time recorded at Great Britain's Greenwich Observatory east of London on the

Thames at longitude zero. Instead of trying to determine the local time at the various broadcast origination points, New York would forward all schedules in GMT, usually a week's schedule at a time but subject to change. It was then up to the correspondent himself to determine the *exact* differential and conform.

Your local broadcast studio, whether in Batavia, Sydney, New Guinea, or London itself, always had a clock synchronized with GMT. You always checked your watch and your stopwatch against that clock. The "talk" routine, always basically the same, would start about three minutes before your scheduled go-ahead time, while the network news program was already in progress. You would begin:

"Hello, San Francisco. This is Dunn in Batavia and I am unable to read you. I shall, however, make my report exactly on schedule, from 22:21 and 15 seconds to 22:25 zero. I will begin my transmission in exactly three minutes from . . . *now!*" After 30 seconds you would repeat: "This is Dunn, I will begin my transmission in exactly 2 minutes and 30 seconds from . . . *now!*" Other repeats would follow at 30-second intervals until the final 30 seconds, which you introduced, "I shall count each 5-second interval down to 10, then start my report after 10 seconds of silence ... 25 ... 20 ... 15 ... 10." Then 10 seconds of silence and, "This is Batavia, quietly awaiting further word on Japan's all-out attack on the Philippines, an attack that undoubtedly will ..."

In New York the program director would take his cue from San Francisco. If the signal was good and the timing correct, the director would cue the anchor man, who would make the normal introduction, and the program would switch to the West Coast and beyond. If the signal or timing was not acceptable, the anchor man, on cue, would introduce a standby point, and the listener would never be the wiser.

Once your arrow was on its way you had to wait until atmospherics cleared and San Francisco could give you a report on whether you had hit your target, usually on your next scheduled contact. It was several hours before I learned that my report had indeed been heard on the entire network with a transmission rating of "good." It was to be a not-too-infrequent routine in the years ahead.

CHAPTER 12

Bittersweet

I had hardly unlimbered my typewriter before I was summond to the RPD by a phone call from New York. Paul White wanted me to charter a plane and get back to Manila as quickly as possible. Ford Wilkins, managing editor of the *Manila Bulletin* and CBS News's representative during my absence from what was to have been my base, had found it impossible to handle both jobs with a war erupting around him, and the only other reporter available was proving barely adequate.

I promised Paul I'd try but gave him little encouragement. The chances of a civilian transport plane reaching a distant capital already under siege looked to be nil, and I got quick confirmation. KLM (KNILM) had planes and crews available but flatly refused to consider a flight they were sure would cost them both the plane and crew. They voiced no concern for the probable fate of a reporter they felt was obviously retarded for even posing the idea. If by some miracle the flight had succeeded, however, I would only have found myself in a besieged city less than ten days before it fell, my value to CBS News soon terminated.

As events developed, there could have been no better place than Java to observe and report the last few weeks of the Japanese blitz on the whole of Southeast Asia. At the time of KLM's refusal, the fall of the Philippines was certain, although concerned observers were still praying for the impossible. The British were muddling badly in Malaya's jungles but there was still faint hope they would finally make a stand, at least long enough for their allies to reinforce the NEI.

But there would be no important reinforcements. That decision, unannounced, had been reached only a few hours after Pearl Harbor when Winston Churchill suddenly appeared in Washington for talks with Franklin Roosevelt. It was then and there decided to concentrate our primary effort on the Axis powers, a decision that spelled the doom of the Indies. Consequently, with the exception of the far too few long-range bombers that were flown into Java and a few fighter planes being routed through Australia, most of which never arrived, Allied forces in the Indies would have to do with war materiel and personnel already on hand, not nearly enough even to slow down the Japanese juggernaut.

Although no one would admit it at the time, the full force of the Japanese thrust was moving inexorably toward that symbolic "governor's microphone" in the modest RPD studio. When we lost that mike, we would be out of the western Pacific with only Australia remaining!

Of all the Occidentals in the Far East at that time, the Dutch had by far the most to lose, and they lost by far the most. The United States already had announced its intended withdrawal from the Philippines. The vast majority of British in Malaya and Burma, as well as the French in Indochina, were true colonials, men serving their countries to the best of their abilities while on foreign soil, but always looking forward to that ultimate return to their homeland. That was not true of the Dutch, who, unlike the true colonial, actually lived in the islands. They had come to the Indies before the Pilgrim Fathers ever set foot on Plymouth Rock and nearly 170 years before the British founded their first settlement, a penal colony, on the present site of Sydney.

When the Japanese moved against the NEI, most Dutch families had been there for long generations, without ever having visited Holland, and knew no other home. The Dutch attitude toward the native population was entirely different from that of our forefathers or the Australian settlers. They established their rule firmly but with minimal bloodshed, and they maintained an unswerving policy of respect for native property rights. They never required the Indonesians to learn a foreign tongue, but instead taught themselves to speak Malay. They adapted their lives to that of the indigenes rather than trying to superimpose European mores. Most important, despite a population that averaged more than thirteen hundred human beings on every square mile of Java alone, an island roughly the size of Louisiana, the Dutch and the Javanese had evolved an economy that minimized poverty almost to the vanishing point, where work was plentiful and the cost of a comfortable life was within the reach of everyone, and which not only fed its millions but produced surpluses for export.

Finally, whenever an Indonesian married a Dutch citizen he or she automatically acquired Dutch citizenship with all the perquisites. The Indonesians as a race are a handsome and intelligent people, and interracial marriages were not uncommon and usually successful. My friend Dr. Rittman, for example, had a charming Indonesian wife.

The Dutch swore to defend the islands to the last man because they were facing the conquest of their homes. But of course they were far too few, and their "allies" had more important priorities. Most of us observers understood this situation, but, like the Dutch, we probably were praying for a miracle.

The 1941 holiday season in Batavia was anything but festive. All attention was turned north of the equator where the Japanese celebrated Christmas by occupying Hong Kong, on the Philippines where the enemy was closing in on Manila, and on the Malay Peninsula where the British were mired in a new brand of jungle warfare.

Jack Raleigh, whom White had recently elevated from stringer to staff correspondent, had been extremely helpful in getting me settled when I arrived from Rangoon. His wife, Betty, was doing string assignments for Mutual Broadcasting System (MBS). They had a house only a block from the Des Indes. Realizing this would be my first Christmas away from my family, they planned an all-out effort to inject a bit of Christmas spirit into the season. Unfortunately for their Christmas plans but happily for Betty's well being, a U.S.-bound freighter put into a Java port and the skipper offered Betty transportation. It took some convincing by Jack and me, but there was only one decision she could make. As a result, Christmas Day was celebrated with restaurant fare and a futile effort to get a call through to my family.

The transpacific facilities provided by the Dutch were excellent, but this was long before the age of satellites and there was no way to best adverse atmospherics. White's call concerning the impossible charter flight to Manila was the last communication we had with San

Francisco for four days. There was nothing to do but be patient, a tough assignment for a homesick reporter. It wasn't until the following week, on the twenty-ninth, that the circuits cleared and I was able to complete my Christmas call, four days late but still a welcome link with my two girls.

The only bright spot in that period actually came on Christmas Day, but had nothing to do with the holiday. An announcement came from Chungking Radio, immediately confirmed from the States, that the Flying Tigers, whom I had been forbidden to mention in Rangoon, had teamed up with the RAF on Christmas Day to repulse an enemy air raid and score the first Allied victory of the Pacific war. In an air battle over Rangoon the combined forces had shot down seventeen Japanese fighter planes and bombers at a cost of only three Allied planes. Many of those engaged had to be men I had met in Kunming, Lashio, and Rangoon, and I could understand how elated they were to be in action after long months of standing by in China.

The abrupt departure of Betty Raleigh left Mutual without a representative in Java, and while that would hardly seem the concern of a CBS correspondent, it wasn't long before I found myself involved. Shortly after my arrival in Batavia, I had met Frank J. Cuhel, an American on leave from a major New York concern who was managing a local import-export firm. Frank was a handsome six-footer who had been an all-time football great at the University of Iowa and a medal-winning hurdler on the American team at the 1928 Amsterdam Olympics. He had been in the Far East for several years and spoke Malay, a real asset in Java. Betty was on her way before Frank learned of her plans, so he came to me and asked if I thought Mutual might be willing to give him a chance at the assignment. I thought it was a great idea and gave him the name of Johnny Johnston, who headed MBS News at that time.

The next day Cuhel came rushing into the RPD, brandishing a cable. "I got the assignment!" he shouted at me in great glee. "Where's a typewriter?" This had to be urgent, so I told him to use any of the machines in the newsroom and asked how soon he was to go on the air. "Day after tomorrow," he replied breathlessly, and everyone howled. It wasn't long, however, before Frank Cuhel, who proved to have a natural flair for news, was crowding his broadcast deadlines with all the nonchalance of a seasoned veteran.

Just six days after my brief stop at Medan on the twentieth, the Japs staged a heavy air attack on that city and its airport, inflicting many casualties and heavy damage. It was the first direct strike on NEI soil, and, although Medan was still a thousand miles northeast of my microphone, we knew the next strike would be closer and each succeeding day would narrow the gap.

It was on New Year's Eve that I made one of the most inaccurate forecasts of my career. I opened my broadcast with the words, "In less than two and a half hours we will bid farewell to 1941, and the farewell will not be an occasion for tears." Exactly two hours and twenty minutes later I stood with friends in the Box, Batavia's cricket club, to watch while those assembled there joined hands for a tearful rendition of "Auld Lang Syne." Most of them were Dutch, but several English were present and a few Americans, all viewing the advent of the new year with trepidation.

My prediction, of course, was founded on the premise that no one could possibly mourn the end of a year that had spawned the tragedy of Pearl Harbor and loosed the Japanese Juggernaut to ravage the western Pacific and Asia. The tears of these people were, certainly, tears of apprehension for a new year that held almost no hope for a brighter future. Their world was visibly crumbling. Their not-too-distant neighbors to the north were immediate victims and their own turn would follow. They knew they were on the threshold of a year that could hold only anguish for them.

We were a long distance from Guy Lombardo and the Roosevelt Grill.

The worst blow to us Americans came at the end of the unhappy season, on the third of January, when the word came by enemy radio, immediately confirmed by American sources, that Manila had surrendered. Many of the Americans living in the NEI had once lived in Manila, and almost all had friends in those islands, friends who would now be prisoners of the Japanese. More tears undoubtedly were shed, if not openly.

Sentiment aside, the most ominous significance in the fall of Manila from where we stood was that the enemy had cleared another barrier between themselves and the NEI. It was reported that a sizable force of Americans and Filipinos had withdrawn to the Bataan peninsula across Manila bay to the west, under the command of General Douglas MacArthur.

This peninsula, extending south from the westernmost mainland of Luzon, was obviously a defensive position and it was certain that this force, sequestered and committed to its own defence, could mount no threat to the enemy flank as the Japs moved toward the Indies. Only Singapore and Malaya remained as doubtful obstacles.

Soon after I moved into the Des Indes I had a short-wave radio receiver installed in my room so I could monitor the enemy's broadcasts from the north. Immediately after Manila's capitulation the Japanese began a series of "newscasts," mostly blatant propaganda, probably using the same transmitters and studios I had used in my own reports from Manila.

We could not credit Japanese reports unless they were verified from other sources—as was the report of Manila's surrender after MacArthur had declared it an open city—but it was possible to get some idea of what the enemy was thinking by listening to his words. It was a technique White and I had developed early in the European war when we set up the CBS "listening post" on Long Island. The engineering department equipped it expertly, and we hired a full staff of linguists to monitor the Axis twenty-four hours a day. Every word uttered publicly by Hitler, Mussolini, or any member of the Axis hierarchy was recorded, translated, and studied carefully. If anything of significance, no matter how minor, was detected it was immediately passed on to the New York and national media. The basic idea was to keep ourselves informed on what the enemy was talking about at any particular time. My own Des Indes monitor was infinitely more modest, but it served a purpose.

There is very little humor to be found in wartime propaganda, but the Japanese did provide us with one hearty laugh at this time. I was sitting at my desk on the screened veranda of my room, listening to the enemy broadcasting from Manila. Their lead story told of the capture of Adm. Thomas C. Hart, commander of the U.S. fleet in the western Pacific, together with his entire staff. As I listened I looked out over the deer park that was a feature of the hotel. Along the path, hardly a dozen yards distant, came Tommy Hart and three of his staff, apparently on their way to the dining room. Obviously no one had bothered to tell them of their capture.

My memories of those critical days in Java can best be described as bittersweet. It was a distinct pleasure to enjoy this island paradise even for a few brief weeks, but it was painful beyond measure to have to report the relentless approach of the Japanese, nearer every day, with no hint of effective help from any source.

Batavia was a delightful city, immaculately clean, well provided with the amenities of life, and expertly designed to cope with the tropical heat that blankets any country less then eight degrees below the equator. The heart of the city for the visitor was the great, sprawling Des Indes Hotel, situated in the midst of a many-acred park lush with tropical foliage and populated by miniature deer. Air conditioning was almost unknown in prewar Java or elsewhere in the Far East, but it really wasn't needed at the Des Indes. Each individual room had its own screened verandah facing on the deer park and was open front and back to welcome any passing breeze. If the breeze was reluctant, great ceiling fans kept the air moving and the room comfortable.

The bathrooms in the hotel, designed especially for the tropics, were unlike any I have ever encountered elsewhere. Each bathroom had a large drain in the center of the tiled floor—no tub nor shower —and was equipped with a ceramic reservoir filled with water that dripped from a special tap, always at room temperature. To bathe, you stood in the center of the room and used a large bucket-shaped dipper to pour water over your body. Then you soaped yourself and rinsed with more dippersful. Water at room temperature is incomparable for tropical bathing.

Another amenity was the laundry service, also unique. Batavia in 1941 was not an informal city, and everyone, including visitors, wore business suits complete with coat and tie, but always of washable materials. You usually changed completely and bathed every noon and evening, which meant wearing three suits every day! At the Des Indes you could wear the same suit twice every day, immaculately laundered and pressed, and you often did.

The dining room was large and airy—plenty of fans—and flanked by a broad verandah ideal for preprandial relaxation. The food was excellent with either a Dutch or Indonesian accent, but the *pièce de résistance* was *rijsttafel* (literally, "rice table"), undoubtedly the most spectacular presentation of food since the days of the Caesars. It was served only at noon, probably because you needed a good siesta afterward. When you ordered *rijsttafel*, a waiter wearing the distinctive Javanese livery would come to your table bearing (that's the only verb for it) a huge silver bowl piled high with snowy white rice. He would be the *mandooer*, or captain, and immediately behind him would come a line of anywhere from eighteen to two dozen waiters also in ethnic garb, each bearing two to four serving dishes for a total of from forty

All correspondents arriving in Java were duly accredited by the Dutch government, but uniforms were not specified and not worn except by arrivals from other theaters. This missing regulation was an obvious boon to me as I braved Java's tropical heat in front of the Des Indes Hotel.

to sixty different foods. Included would be every type of meat and fowl cooked in exotic sauces, hot and cold, fish and shellfish in a dozen forms, curries, vegetables cooked, pickled, or raw—the list was endless.

The Dutch used to enjoy watching the uninitiated come to grips with their first *rijsstafel* because the neophyte invariably would try to take a little of everything, and the result, of course, was a heaping plate that a team of hungry men couldn't consume, much less one bedazzled newcomer. The proper way to enjoy this Lucullan repast, I quickly learned, was to be *very* selective. Of the dozens of offerings, one should choose only a few of compatible flavor to blend with the rice. Most of the dishes should be smiled upon but deferred to another day. In this way one could sit down to a *rijsttafel* and enjoy a completely different meal each time. Today, for example, you might favor the curries; next time you might concentrate on the seafood or perhaps the meats in their various sauces—the variations were inexhaustible. In this way *rijsstafel* became a civilized and very intriguing experience.

Batavia had one refreshment spa I'll always remember, and I don't refer to the Black Cat, the city's only night club. Still vivid in my memory after more than four decades is a modest little bistro that bore the name of its proprietor, *Oom Dolp*. Uncle Dolp's specialty, for me at least, was a magnificent ham sandwich on a soft roll, *broodje met ham*, washed down with full-liter bottles of Heineken's best brew.

During my years as an overseas reporter, my best friends were correspondents in my own media, in other words, my competition. In addition to Sid Albright of NBC, one of my closest friends was Frank Cuhel whom I had helped to sign with Mutual and who developed into a formidable competitor almost immediately. Night after night Sid, Frank, and I would meet at Oom Dolp's after our reports to the networks were ended to discuss transpacific circuits and outline our own brands of Pacific war strategy over *broodjes en bier*. I still believe that if the Allied high command had had access to some of the strategy we formulated during those sessions, Oom Dolp might have had to wait a bit longer for the Japanese clientele he was about to acquire.

It was clear to all of us that the only hope for these islands lay in massive Allied reinforcement. The Dutch were at sea with their allies, fighting valiantly with their inadequate fleet, but the fate of the *Repulse* and the *Prince of Wales* had proved beyond question that sea power alone could not succeed. What was needed was air power, and that power was almost entirely lacking.

The fighter arm of the Dutch Air Force was equipped with an American plane called the Brewster Buffalo, probably the most inadequate combat plane ever designed, certainly hopeless against the Japanese Zero. The Dutch were using these abominations strictly because they were the only planes we would sell them. One evening, on the verandah of the Des Indes, I dropped into a chair beside a Dutch fighter pilot whom I had met before. He was sipping a glass of Holland's ubiquitous Bols gin and seemed completely preoccupied. We exchanged brief greetings while I signalled for a waiter. Suddenly, in the precise English learned only from textbooks, he solemnly advised me, "Tomorrow I am going to die." I looked at him quizzically, half expecting a macabre joke, but he was completely serious. "We have a mission tomorrow, and I know what will happen. Our planes are no good." Actually my friend did survive that mission, but his death was not long delayed—the fate of most Brewster Buffalo pilots sent into combat. If the Buffalo ever scored a victory, it was never reported to this observer, and Holland's allies had no better planes they were willing to part with. The American bombers the Dutch were flying were excellent planes, and the Dutch used them effectively in the early days of the war, but without good fighter escort the effectiveness and the life of any medium bomber is limited.

Early in January a rumor got started that the great French liner, the *Normandie*, had been converted into an aircraft carrier and was headed for the west coast of Java (it was never clear just where it was coming from) loaded with the planes we had to have. It was a ridiculous rumor, of course, but the civilians wanted so desperately to believe that it gained credence for three or four days. Then, like a blast from Antarctica, came the shattering word of the great ship's burning at her pier on the New York waterfront. That was only one incident, but with us at all times was the sobering realization that these brave people, facing the future with such hope and optimism, were moving inexorably toward certain and total disaster.

CHAPTER 13

Left Alone

After the fall of Manila, the lull in Japanese air activity over the entire Indonesian archipelago only led to the belief that the enemy was regrouping in preparation for another major offensive. The NEI was the obvious target. The situation in Malaya and Singapore wasn't entirely hopeless, at least in official pronouncements, but the Japanese appeared to have the forces they needed on that peninsula, and with the Philippines neutralized there would be little reason to delay the anticipated drive on the oil of the Indies.

In January, 1942, a new command was announced to include all southwest Pacific territory not already in Japanese hands. The new commander in chief would be Gen. Sir Archibald Wavell, operating from an unannounced headquarters. Second in command would be Maj. Gen. George Brett of the U.S. Army Air Corps, while Rear Adm.

Thomas Hart would command the Allied naval forces. Both Brett and Hart were to be given another star, but the latter would still be out-ranked by his second in command, Vice Adm. C. E. L. Helfrich, com-mander of the Royal Netherlands Indies Navy, who had been longer in rank.

Personally I liked Admiral Hart, whom I had known in Manila, but I have always believed that Helfrich would have been the better choice. He was the one man in the world who had anticipated the timing of Japan's initial attack and had ordered his own fleet to sea on No-vember 30, eight days before Pearl Harbor. He knew the waters of the archipelago like those of his own bathtub, and, most important of all, he was fighting in defense of his own island homeland. Nevertheless, the choices weren't that bad and, as we soon discovered, were of no more importance than the top-secret location of headquarters. No command staff could ever succeed, whatever the qualifications of its chiefs, without men, ships, and planes.

Meanwhile, in Singapore, Cecil Brown faced a situation too diffi-cult to handle. Because of technical limitations, the British were un-able to provide him a closed circuit to San Francisco, and as a result every word of his broadcast reports was also carried by Radio Singa-pore to the entire civilian population of the colony. The censors re-fused to allow him to report bad news that might upset the people. The result was inevitable: a constant battle between Brown and the censors that required more tact than Brown was prepared to use. In the ensuing verbal conflict he was finally disaccredited and his broad-cast privileges revoked. There's no question that the situation was difficult, but Martin Agronsky, sent by NBC from the Middle East to Singapore, managed to keep his cool and his accreditation as long as there was anything to report. Brown's disaccreditation came on January 8, and from that time up to the final surrender five weeks later CBS was without radio coverage in Singapore. There was no sol-ace in the fact that Agronsky was a top-notch reporter who knew how to take full advantage of a situation.

When I learned what was happening, I called White and suggested sending Raleigh to Australia and bringing Brown to Batavia to work with me. Paul agreed but decided not to send a replacement to Singa-pore. He didn't think it would hold out as long as it actually did. Ac-cordingly, I sent Raleigh to Port Darwin, northernmost settlement in Australia, with orders to continue to Melbourne if there were no fa-cilities for reporting the activities of an American fighter group reportedly being organized there. As expected, getting out of Singapore was not easy, and it took Brown two weeks to join me. Immediately we encountered an impassable road block. Dr. Rittman greeted Brown cordially when I introduced him but immediately informed us that he would not be allowed to broadcast from the NEI!

As a member of the faltering alliance that now included only Singapore and the Indies, the Dutch government considered itself bound to honor any disaccreditation imposed by the British. Rittman promised to intercede personally on Brown's behalf, but to no avail. A brief talk with Comdr. John Proud, British press officer who had just arrived from Singapore, indicated the British would remain adamant as far as Brown was concerned. I was given the distinct impression he had stepped on too many toes in his censorship fight, possibly with prior intent. In the meantime, despite handicaps and headaches, Agronsky was using what facilities were available in Singapore to keep NBC's presence on that front very evident.

There was nothing to do but to send Brown on his way, and he left for Australia as soon as transportation could be arranged. White wanted him to stay in Australia, which was almost certain to be the next theater in the Pacific war, but he continued on to the United States and a desk on Madison Avenue. I was left with a war on my hands, strictly on my own.

The January lull in Japanese air operations was brief and did indeed mark the start of Tokyo's final drive for the greatest prize of the southwest Pacific, the oil of the Indies. Almost directly south of the Philippines at the upper end of the Macassar Straits lay the little island of Tarakan, third in importance of the major Indonesian oil fields but geographically likely to be the first target. Next came Balikpapan, second in size and importance, further south through the straits on the east coast of Borneo. Finally, Palembang, largest and richest of the three, was situated in southern Sumatra almost due north of the eastern tip of Java. Possession of Palembang would give the Japanese not only the richest oil fields in Asia, but also a clear sweep of the NEI archipelago, within easy fighter and bomber range of the governor general's microphone.

We braced ourselves for the first blow, and it wasn't long in coming. On the morning of January 11, shortly before Raleigh left for Australia, a message arrived from the RPD advising us to report to that office as soon as possible for "information of grave importance." Jack turned white, certain that the entire United States fleet had been destroyed. If pressed, I would have guessed a Japanese landing on some part of actual Netherlands Indies soil, and a special communiqué proved me correct. The Japanese had landed in force on Tarakan Island just at dark on the preceding evening, and the battle for the oil of the Indies was definitely under way.

There was no element of surprise. The Japanese had been pounding Tarakan from the air for two days, a tactic that usually preceded a landing attempt. The Dutch had anticipated the blow, and the utter demolition of the fields and installations began even before the first enemy troops came ashore. A complex system of mines and demolition charges had been installed months before—further evidence that the Dutch understood and respected Japan's intentions in the Pacific better than their allies—and the moment the invasion was certain, they threw the switch. According to survivors of that bloody battle, the raging fires fed by the flood of oil from ruptured storage tanks created an inferno in which heat took a greater toll than bullets.

The Dutch did a good job of demolition but the fact that the crude oil of Tarakan is one of the highest grades in the world—requiring no refining and thus no additional time to rebuild refineries once the wells were replaced—made it doubtful how long the fields would remain useless to the enemy.

Almost unnoticed in our intense concentration on Tarakan were simultaneous Japanese landings on the north coast of Celebes, third largest island in the NEI, near its capital city of Manado. Here, again, the Dutch put up a fierce defense for several days, but the end result was never in doubt. The ring was constricting rapidly.

About this time, in mid-January, 1941, a new voice began to come in on my short-wave receiver, obviously beamed from the Philippines but giving no hint of its exact location. It identified itself as the Voice of Freedom and broadcast news from the Allied-American point of view. Americans in Java began listening for its reports with keen interest. I guessed it was coming from General MacArthur's forces in Bataan and later learned that it did indeed operate from Corregidor.

The enemy attack on Balikpapan was signalled by air raids, and on January 23 we learned that a large enemy convoy was forming in the Macassar Straits below Tarakan. Allied air and sea forces lost no time putting the convoy and its escort under concentrated attack. A bitter three-day battle ensued, with both sides taking heavy losses, but inevitably the Japanese continued southward, slowed only by the punishment they absorbed. They were moving slowly toward a demolished objective, however. In the biggest surprise of the year the Dutch had totally demolished the Balikpapan installations two days before the convoy had begun to form in the straits, before the enemy had made his first move in their direction, and thus before invasion was even certain. The total investment destroyed was estimated in the scores of millions of dollars, and military observers could compare the action only with Russia's earlier destruction of the great Dnieper dam in the face of onrushing Nazis. Staggering as they were, the Balikpapan destructions were dwarfed when the much larger installations at Palembang were blown out of existence a few days later. The Dutch meant what they said when they promised the Japanese would capture little of value in the Indies.

While the enemy was establishing himself firmly in Borneo and Celebes, the situation in Malaya-Singapore was disintegrating swiftly. Every day brought to Batavia more refugees from the north who reported constant reverses, crumbling morale, and general disarray. Among them were numerous correspondents, mostly British and Australians, intent on moving on as quickly as possible to India or Australia.

When Til Durdin of the *New York Times* walked into the Des Indes one morning, I decided the end was near. Tilman Durdin was an old China hand and a fine reporter. He had seen the Japanese in action against the Chinese during his term in Shanghai and understood their capabilities better than most. Til also was a calm observer who would never panic. When he told me there was no hope for the British in their immediate situation, I accepted it as gospel. "Chaos" was the word he used to describe the colony when he left, a departure prompted by the fact that his wife, Peggy, herself an old China hand, was with him in Singapore and he had to get her to safety. He held no brief for the future of the Dutch in the NEI, but, unlike many of the arriving correspondents, he had no intention of leaving until the last chapter was in his typewriter. He found Peggy transportation to Australia, then settled in to check the finale.

The British were sharply criticized for their poor showing in Malaya, and the harshest words came from their own nationals. Harold Guard, who had been UP bureau chief in Singapore when the Japs attacked, was a veteran of World War I who had already lost two sons in the European theater of World War II. He was particularly bitter.

To him the Malay debacle was the direct result of a spirit of defeatism that started with and paralysed the high command. The front-line soldier, Guard maintained, was brave, confident, and perfectly capable of holding his own with the enemy, but a continual series of unexpected and unexplained withdrawals prompted by contradictory orders finally destroyed even his morale. Guard didn't believe for a moment that Malaya was indefensible, and because of that conviction he swore he was going to the United States as quickly as possible and apply for American citizenship! (He changed his mind long before the war ended after he had had a chance to witness some SNAFU decisions by American brass.)

On February 1, the British abandoned the Malay Peninsula and announced their determination to concentrate their forces on the defense of Singapore Island. The simultaneous transfer of their press headquarters to Batavia and the enforced exodus of all that was left of the press corps, however, was hardly a vote of confidence in the immediate future. The British press headquarters was set up in Batavia not far from the RPD under the direction of Comdr. John Proud, who had been press chief since before my first trip to Singapore nearly a year earlier. He was not only a competent officer, but also a realist who devoted most of his time to helping correspondents find means of removing themselves to other destinations, much to the displeasure of Papa Rittman.

Reversing the southbound tide temporarily, Joe Harsh of the *Christian Science Monitor* and H. R. ("Red") Knickerbocker of the Hearst newspapers, arrived in Batavia from Australia, having been helped with their transportation by Dr. Rittman. Their first question upon meeting the good Papa in person was, "How can we get out of here?"

Right in the midst of the general exodus from Singapore General Wavell issued a special order urging his men to hold on in Singapore because of the great reinforcements the United States and Britain were rushing to the Pacific theater. The order, coming on February 5, contained not one word of truth and had the negative effect of raising new false hopes in the hearts of the beleaguered NEI civilians. The Dutch command knew better, but I was not allowed to express my personal doubts. I gave the order a secondary paragraph in my report that evening.

At this time the Southwest Pacific Command announced that Admiral Hart had been replaced by Admiral Helfrich. It was an appointment that should have been made when the command was formed, and now it came too late. The Battle of Macassar Straits, while costly to the enemy, had cost us heavily too. The inadequate fleet Hart had led into battle was much more inadequate when Helfrich took over. He never had a chance.

It took the Japanese just fifty-seven days after Pearl Harbor to put themselves into position to drop bombs on Java. On the third of February a large group of Japanese bombers with fighter escort struck at Surabaya, seat of the NEI naval base, but for some reason (they probably didn't want to destroy unnecessarily facilities they intended to use) the city rather than the shipyards was the primary target. Some thirty civilians were killed and four times that number were seriously injured.

After the intensity of the Surabaya raid, the long-anticipated first strike at Batavia was almost an anticlimax. On Monday, February 9, a group of correspondents were having lunch at the Des Indes, discussing reports that the Japanese had made a successful landing on Singapore Island the night before. As we talked, the air alert sounded, but after long weeks of false alarms, no one paid much attention. About thirty minutes later we heard the sound of planes obviously not our own. We rushed to the verandah just in time to see a half-dozen planes pulling up sharply over Kemajoran airport some two miles distant. Even at that distance we could see the soon-to-be familiar red meatball that spelled Hirohito on the under surface of their wings.

Albright and I joined Cuhel in his car, and like a trio of damned fools we raced to the airport to see what had happened. We found the strike had been a reconnaissance-strafing mission delivered by a flight of Zeros (we called them Mitsubishi navy-naughts or "navy-O's" at that time), coming in from the east at treetop level. The flight continued to Tandjong Priok, Batavia's port, where the anti-aircraft fire kept them at a distance. Damage was minimal at both places, and the harbor gunners did shoot down one plane. As for the three of us, we were lucky there was no follow-up to the raid. It didn't take long to learn never to go to any airport when enemy planes were in the area.

General Wavell's special order to the Singapore troops had had little effect. When we returned from Kemajoran that afternoon, official sources informed us that the Japs had indeed made a successful landing on Singapore Island the night before. One week later Gen. Arthur Percival (Wavell had already departed) surrendered his entire command—sixty thousand men and ordnance—unconditionally.

It isn't easy to avoid personal panic when everyone around you seems determined to force on you his own decision to leave the theater. Almost every correspondent who left Java in those hectic final days tried to talk me into going along, not, I am sure, out of concern for my well-being but because he wanted his own decision endorsed. Incredibly, I had in just two months become the dean of the foreign correspondents in Java and, more important, I was the only radio reporter who was actually a staff correspondent. The transpacific circuits were excellent, and CBS News was scheduling me twice a day. For those reasons I felt I had a special obligation to the network. Paul White gave me no advice except to be careful, but he did promise that CBS would take care of Catherine and Patricia if I were taken prisoner. The thought of getting killed never entered my mind.

Meanwhile there was no dearth of news to report, but there certainly was a dearth of good news. On February 13, the Japanese had dropped paratroops on the Palembang installations in an effort to secure them intact, but Dutch and Malayan troops quickly contained and wiped out most of this force and held off reinforcements pouring ashore for the nearly four days necessary to complete total demolition. On the following Tuesday, the sixteenth, I learned that L. W. Eliot, Standard Oil's top NEI executive, had escaped from Sumatra after supervising the destruction, so I rushed to his office for an exclusive interview.

"Shorty" Eliot was anything but short. In his mid-forties, he stood nearly six-foot-six, carrying some 225 pounds without an ounce of fat. (I came to know him well when he later became a colonel on General MacArthur's staff.) He had been in the Indies for many years and had built much of what he had helped blow off the map. I'll never forget this hard-as-nails giant telling me, "I'll admit I shed some tears, Bill. You just can't see your life's work go up in smoke without weeping."

As Eliot told the story, the first paratroops landed on Saturday afternoon near the Standard plant and inside the Shell refinery area and were at once engaged by the Dutch. Immediately the plants shut down, and all nonessential personnel were evacuated. At that time there were approximately 670 employees on duty, including 70 Americans, 300 Europeans, and the same number of Malayans. All were evacuated safely despite the fighting. That accomplished, final preparations were completed and at two o'clock on Sunday morning the army experts went to work. In one hour they destroyed all vital instruments, machinery, and loose equipment. Dutch and Malay troops, still holding the enemy at four key points, were allowed to withdraw to safety before the fire bombs, released simultaneously by a complex electrical system, set the entire refinery stock ablaze with a deafening roar. Millions of barrels of gasoline, crude oil, priceless aviation fuel, and other petroleum burst into immediate and inextinguishable flames.

This inconceivable inferno, however, was not the finale. There still remained 81 miles of subterranean pipeline and the great oil fields themselves to be destroyed. The death of the pipeline, Eliot said, was an awesome accomplishment. Malay crews, working by hand, ignited fuses that set off previously placed dynamite charges every few hundred feet for the entire 81 miles and, in record time—81 miles of complete and utter destruction! Eliot was forbidden to reveal the method used to cut off permanently the flow of oil from the hundreds of wells in the surrounding fields, but he swore the enemy could drill three wells from scratch in less time than it would take to open one of the sealed shafts.

With the Japanese in possession of burned-out Palembang, their immediate invasion of Bali, directly east of Java, followed as expected. Again there was only token resistance. The enemy now controlled all the NEI except Java, and the fate of the governor general's microphone was strictly a question of When.

Coincidental with the fall of Bali, Dr. Rittman advised us that all RPD facilities, including the GG's mike, would be transferred to Bandoeng, a mountain resort about sixty miles south of Batavia, on the following day, February 21, a Saturday. By this time the number of reporters had thinned until there were little more than a score remaining of the dozens who had flooded Batavia only a few days earlier. Rittman's announcement spurred the exodus.

On the same day Commander Proud called a press conference to advise us that at the same time the RPD made its transfer the M.S. *Klang* would leave Tandjong Priok, Batavia's port, for Australia. Proud urged us all to join him. His move badly upset Dr. Rittman and his staff (and probably the NEI government), for this was an admission of defeat they were not yet prepared to make.

I met Harsh, Knickerbocker, and Al Raymond of the *New York Herald-Tribune* in Proud's office, and they went immediately to work on me, even following me back to the Des Indes, urging me not to be a damned fool and to join them on the *Klang*. I still was adamant.

As the Dutch government prepared to move its base from Batavia to Bandoeng, Comdr. John Proud called together more than a score of correspondents and urged us to board a military transport, the M.S. *Klang*, leaving the following day for Australia. Most of the group heeded the warning. Among those present who did not leave then were Witt Hancock of the AP (extreme left in dark suit), Winston Turner of the Australian AP (tenth from left), and myself (on Turner's right). *Courtesy British Army*

(As a matter of fact, both Knick and Raymond charged their minds at the last minute.)

Frank Cuhel, a long-time resident of Java, had his own car, and we had already decided to stick together and, when the time came, head for Malang where the American B-17's were based, or for Tjilatjap on the south coast, which, we were told, probably would be the last port to close. We admittedly had no idea how we would recognize that critical time when it actually did come, but the car was our ace in the hole. It nearly turned out to be a joker.

Later at the RPD Albright took me aside and told me he had decided to leave with Proud. I said I would do the same in his position. He, too, had a family waiting for him, and NBC, for whom he had done a good job, had hired him in Java and so had no investment in him. He had earned what they paid him, and the books were balanced. On the other hand, CBS News had invested quite a few thousand dollars in my assignment, and I felt a real obligation to continue as long as possible.

The next morning, as I was sorting out the gear I would take to Bandoeng, Sid came to my room to say goodbye. "Bill," he asked, "do you have a good map of Java?" I assured him I did. He then brought out a small pocket compass and handed it to me. "Here, take this. If you have to head for the hills, it might come in handy." Although his departure left CBS in sole possession of the story (Mutual called on Cuhel only a few times), Sid Albright was one of the very few who didn't try to talk me into leaving.

Shortly after Sid's farewell that Saturday morning, I made my final report from Batavia. I tried to give New York some indication I was moving to an unnamed destination (we were never permitted to identify Bandoeng by name), and I concluded with a plea for the assistance I knew would never come, strictly as a salute to the Dutch and their valiant stand in the face of indifferent allies and overwhelming odds: "There has been no formal evacuation of any sort from Batavia, but voluntary removals to other parts of Java are not being discouraged and some government departments are being transferred to new quarters to enable closer contact with the defending forces. Above all, Java is still waiting for news of Allied aid in force, the aid Java believes it has earned by the heroic work against the enemy on behalf of itself and its allies in the first ten weeks of this war. This is William J. Dunn in Batavia."

CHAPTER 14

Invaded

The fourteen of us who went to Bandoeng had to arrange our own transportation. Train service, limited at best, was not to be trusted, and every plane in Java had joined the defense corps. Cuhel had to stay in Batavia a day longer to clean up some personal business, so

I joined Harold Guard, who had promoted a miniature Peugeot complete with driver, and we started south shortly after noon. Java's rolling countryside was beautiful and deceptively calm. The people in the fields and villages through which we passed were going quietly about their daily routines, seemingly unaware that they were on the eve of an enemy occupation that would change their lives forever. One had to wonder if any of them had any understanding of the menace of the situation.

We reached Bandoeng early in the evening and found the lovely little city in complete disarray. The principal hotel, the Hohman, and all other hotels and hostels were filled. No one had any idea where the RPD might be found, not even the cable office, which I did find in time to send CBS an urgent message cancelling my report for that evening. I still needed a mike, GG's or not, to reach the network.

In a dormitory of a nearby school, I eventually found an empty cot in a crowded room that admitted neither electricity nor water. Fortunately the exodus from Bandoeng rivaled that from Batavia, so a return to the Hohman at daybreak provided me with a room. Amenities included an air alert about twenty-five feet above my window, a doubtful asset of which I became acutely aware even before I finished unpacking my gear. That was a false alarm, but most of those which followed in the ensuing days were not.

That night, Sunday, February 21, I made my first broadcast from the anonymity of "Java." I had finally located the RPD, nearby, of course, and found the governor general's microphone awaiting my arrival. The news centered on an obvious enemy air campaign against the island's airports. The Japs now had the whole of Java within easy range of both their fighters and bombers and were concentrating on wiping out our rapidly dwindling Allied air force on the ground. Bill McDougall, another Unipresser who had arrived in Java from Chungking a few days earlier, made a quick trip to Malang and came back to report American morale at that base extremely low. The enemy had destroyed three B-17 Flying Fortresses on the ground two days before, and both pilots and crew members felt helpless without the fighter protection they never got.

On Tuesday morning, awakened as usual by the nervous siren, I went down to join Guard, McDougall, and John Morris (another Unipresser) at breakfast. Just as I pulled out a chair, I glanced out the window and saw six Zeros heading directly at us at an extremely low altitude. The crackle of machine-gun fire followed immediately.

I ducked behind a convenient wall while Morris and McDougall jumped through the window into a slit trench. The Japs made one pass with minimal results and disappeared. After a long moment I cautiously emerged from behind my wall to see what had happened to Guard. "Pop," as we called him, had no joint in his right knee, which a shell fragment had shattered during World War I. Consequently he wasn't as agile as his juniors, and he hadn't bothered to duck. Instead, I found him hobbling nonchalantly around the otherwise empty dining room, helping himself to whatever looked appetizing on the hastily abandoned plates!

On Wednesday morning several of us set out to see for ourselves what damage the enemy was doing at nearby airfields. About four or five miles from the Kalidjati airport in western Java, we sighted a flight of enemy planes attacking the very field we had planned to visit next. From our hilltop vantage point we had a good view of the action and congratulated ourselves on our perfect timing. We reached the field a few minutes after the attack ended. There hadn't been many planes on the ground, and material damage was limited to one Martin bomber destroyed, a defending Hurricane forced down, minor damage to a couple of buildings, and a series of small craters that pockmarked the field.

With the stupidity that often accompanies ignorance, we walked across the field to inspect the smoking wreckage of the bomber. Just as we reached the middle of the field, Jack Findon of the *London Express* shouted, "Here they come!" I looked where he pointed and saw a flight of sixteen meatball bombers coming directly at us from the northeast at an altitude of some ten thousand feet. As we looked, we could see the first stick of bombs chipping the far side of the airport, about a half-mile distant but heading our way. Few places offer less cover than the center of an airfield, but we plopped headfirst into the only declivity within reach, a shell crater about three feet deep, and lay face down while the explosions came closer and closer. After what seemed an eternity, probably about ten seconds, we heard explosions behind us, and Findon, a veteran of the London blitz, calmly informed us it was all over. The nearest bomb had burst about twenty yards distant.

As we made a dash for the nearest sidelines, we spotted another bomber, alone, coming directly at us at treetop level, perfectly positioned for a strafing run. It was too low for us to see its markings, and I doubt that we tried. We just hurled ourselves into another crater and prayed. But the apparent menace proved to be a wounded Dutch bomber limping home with absolutely no interest in a trio of scared correspondents. In the more than three years of war still ahead, I never again took a stroll across a military airfield. In fact, I would be nervous today in the center of the J. F. Kennedy terminal.

About this time we began to get reports of a major naval battle in the Java Sea to the north involving much heavier fighting than the Battle of Macassar Straits, probably Admiral Helfrich's promised all-out effort to disrupt the enemy's plans. This battle, which was quickly confirmed, must have been launched on Helfrich's own decision. The so-called high command of the Southwest Pacific Command was even then and without ceremony leaving Java for India and Australia. Gen. Sir Archibald Wavell, C-in-C, Lt. Gen. George Brett, second in command, and Maj. Gen. Louis Breherton, air commander, and their staffs were on their way under conditions that bordered on panic, not even standing by until a decision was reached in the Java Sea.

At noon on Friday, February 27, Durdin, Knickerbocker, and Raymond called me out of the hotel dining room to tell me that we definitely were losing the Java Sea battle. They had nothing except rumors, but insisted the United States would not be able to help prospective refugees like us after another twenty-four hours. I promised to check my own Dutch sources but refused to commit myself. I was still determined the final decision would be my own. (A note in my diary on that date expressed the hope I was not being "all kinds of a damphool.")

The Battle of the Java Sea was officially confirmed in a late Friday communiqué with no information on how the Allies were faring. Both sides, according to the communiqué, were sustaining heavy losses. Although I devoted my next two broadcasts to the battle, using information from my military and naval sources, I was not allowed to report my firm conviction that we were taking a monumental beating. We all knew the overwhelming odds against Helfrich, and most observers believed a more conservative commander would have avoided the confrontation. Helfrich was fighting for his homeland, however, and not for some remote colony. He knew that reinforcements, if they arrived at all, would never be in time to challenge the great enemy convoy that was moving southward toward Java. He had to strike immediately or concede the island to Japan, and Helfrich was not a man to concede defeat without a fight.

White wired me that I had beaten everyone, including the wire services, with the first news of the Java Sea battle, and that little pat on the back made up to some extent for the extreme fatigue that had gripped me since my arrival in Bandoeng. The work involved in collecting information, preparing two extra long broadcast reports on six consecutive days that invariably started at four thirty in the morning, as well as the mental stress of trying to decide whether to go or not, was having its effect. I found myself dozing at meals, and the drink that should have been relaxing I feared might knock me out. Fortunately, I was in perfect health and excellent physical condition thanks to my recent and vigorous sojourn in Chungking, so I bounced back.

On Sunday morning, March 1, I awakened as usual at four thirty to the sounds of very unusual air activity. There had been no alert, or my overhead siren would have awakened me instantly, so the aircraft had to be our own. I was surprised that we had that many planes still flying, but I understood it could mean only one thing. Java had been invaded. I dressed quickly and hurried over to the RPD to find it deserted except for one censor who was doubling as press officer. "Is this it? Are they landing?" I had hoped for confirmation, but the officer was noncommittal except to tell me that I couldn't mention the air activity.

There was no late communiqué, but I still had a 6:21 schedule to meet, and there was nothing to do except to stall. I would put together a report rehashing events of the previous twenty-four hours, using information that had already been cleared to meet the deadline, then stand by the mike until I could get clearance for what I knew was happening. To my utter surprise, the censor flatly refused to clear the script. I protested strongly, showing him that the same material in an earlier report had been cleared by Dr. Rittman himself. The answer was still no and, prompted by utter frustration, fatigue, and probably a touch of nerves, I blew the cork. In a few choice words, some of which may not have been too intelligible to a Dutch censor, I expressed my opinion of censors in general and this censor in particular. I explained I would have to cancel my report with no time to write another. He merely shrugged and turned his back to pick up his phone.

I stormed into the studio, contacted San Francisco, cancelled my report, and tried to express my opinion of censors, only to be censored by the San Francisco censor. I signed off and sat there in front of the governor general's mike for a few minutes, trying to compose myself. The biggest story of my life was breaking around me and I was gagged! When I returned to the press room, the censor looked up from his telephone and asked, "How soon can you get San Francisco back on the pipe?" Instantly I realized I was saved. He pointed to the notes he had been taking. "I have a communiqué I'll give you as soon as I type it. Java has been invaded at three points." That squared the account. He couldn't tell me when the release would come, because he didn't know himself, but he saw no point in my going on the air with no news when the big story would be available very quickly. (I later apologized for blowing my top and revised my opinion of censors, at least temporarily. His only comment was, "Mr. Dunn, you are very funny when you are mad.")

I rushed back into the studio and tried to reopen the circuit. The Dutch technicians, operating from a different location, made a determined effort to help while I translated the communiqué into a broadcast report. Finally word came that the circuit was ready, and I returned to the mike. The voice from San Francisco asked what I had, and I told him I had a report for CBS that Java had been invaded at three points. "But Mr. Dunn, this is NBC. Why are you calling us?" My heart hit the floor. Here I was with a completely exclusive story of "transcendental importance" (one of Paul White's favorite expressions), and through a technical foul-up in San Francisco I had tipped it to the opposition. I was sure NBC would at least air a bulletin on the basis of my tip, and I would find myself scooped by a network that didn't have even a stringer in the entire archipelago.

Almost immediately, however, CBS came on the pipe and advised me that two minutes had been cleared for me on the Elmer Davis report at 8:55 P.M., New York time, only a few minutes later. This time I didn't tell even CBS what I had, although they doubtless knew. They all knew I would never demand immediate prime time without good reason.

Meanwhile, I stood by as instructed, my fingers crossed, expecting momentarily to be informed that NBC had beaten us. To my great relief, nothing happened and I started on cue. "This is Java, where Japanese troops have effected landings at three points on the northern coast. During last night—Saturday night in Java—landings were made in the northwest section of the province of Bantam, west of Batavia and directly opposite the lowest point in Sumatra, and in the bay west of Indramayu, which is east of Batavia and northwest of the coastal city of Cirebon. Early this morning a strong fleet started landings over an extensive coastal frontage about nineteen miles east of Rembang, at a point halfway between Semarang and Surabaya . . ."

When I finished, San Francisco read me a brief but welcome message from New York congratulating me on having scored a world beat on the actual invasion story. To be the first, worldwide, with a story of this importance is the ambition of every correspondent-reporter (Bill Downs, one of the great CBS-ABC correspondents, used to call such a beat the poor man's Pulitzer Prize), so my elation, leavened by fatigue, is easy to understand.

I never did tell White about my inadvertent tip to NBC, and to this day I can only assume that this particular technician, like many of his brothers, was more interested in the transmission quality of his circuits than in the news that passed over them.

This, then was *it!* I had stayed with the story to its climax, and now I was ready to start running!

CHAPTER 15

Flight

Back at the hotel I got hold of Frank Cuhel and suggested that the time had finally arrived to pack our meager gear and bid adieu to the governor general's microphone. I was a bit worried that Frank might be upset at having been beaten on the actual invasion story, but his only pique was with Mutual for having left CBS virtually in sole possession of the broadcast news out of Java during that hectic final week.

Maj. Tom Harrigan of the U.S. Air Corps was in command of a small contingent of ground crewmen who now had no planes to service. He told me that all American planes had left Malang and Jokjakarta for Australia, but that George Eubank, the major general who had commanded the group in Java, had promised to send a B-17 back to pick up the remaining men either late that afternoon or early Monday. Tom proposed to take all the correspondents still in Java along with him.

This was really good news. I briefed him in detail on how to reach me at all times, then breathed a little easier. We now had two aces (or so I thought), and I passed the word along to Cuhel. George Weller of the *Chicago Daily News* was with him, and both agreed Tom was our best bet. Guard and McDougall had left Saturday for an unidentified air field to board a plane for Australia. Guard boarded as scheduled, but McDougall changed his mind at the last minute. He had just learned that Witt Hancock of the Associated Press was still on the island and, refusing to leave his competition in sole possession of the story, he returned to Bandoeng.

Of all the correspondents I have known, Witt Hancock was by long odds the last who should have been sent to a combat zone. He was a diabetic on a strict insulin regime on which his very existence depended. For that reason alone he should have been the first to take off for saner territory. But Witt was a determined person who felt very keenly his obligation to the Associated Press, and he remained.

The number of correspondents had dwindled to six or seven now, all ready, with one exception, to dash as quickly as possible. The one dissenter was a Reuter's correspondent, Myron Selby-Walker, a tall cadaverous Englishman with a heavy black beard, habitually clad in khaki shirt and shorts and a badly battered, full-brimmed black hat. Selby-Walker swore he was not going to run any further. The Japs had run him out of Shanghai, Hong Kong, and Singapore, and Java would be the end of the line for him. He announced he was going to the hills to join the guerrillas and disappeared immediately. He must have been a casualty because I never heard of him again.

Meanwhile, New York was taking full advantage of my presence on the island and scheduled me for four and a half minutes on Sunday evening. I had heard nothing from Harrigan, and nagging doubts were beginning to build. Eccentric atmospherics provided additional headaches, and I had to stand by at the RPD until after midnight before I could clear the report. When I finished, CBS came right back with a request for another nine minutes (the normal broadcast report at that time ran from one and a half to two and a half minutes) at 7:31 Monday morning (6:31 P.M. Sunday evening in New York), so I stayed up all night, catching a few winks on top of a desk. When I finished my second report, I headed back to the hotel and passed out for about four hours. Before I turned in, however, I was able to get an excellent telephone circuit through to Catherine and Patricia and lied to them like a gentleman. I assured them that although I might show up missing for a few days, they had nothing to worry about, I knew exactly what I was going to do. I don't think Catherine believed me, but I couldn't tell her that my two aces were starting to look like one-eyed jacks, wild!

The blow fell shortly after I wakened. I dressed and went to find Harrigan. He was in the lobby, a very dejected air corps major. "Bill,

I'm getting no answers from Eubank, and I'm finally convinced he has no intention of sending a plane. I'm going now to tell my men to prepare to be prisoners of war. We've been written off." He was obviously bitter as we shook hands and wished each other luck. I didn't blame him.

Cuhel and Weller were in the dining room and agreed we should start for the coast as quickly as possible. The southern port of Tjilatjap was about 150 miles distant and the driving wouldn't be easy, but we had been informed it was the only port still open. As far as we knew only McDougall, Hancock, and Winston Turner of the Australian AP were still in town besides ourselves, and we went out to round them up. We located only Turner.

The four of us stowed our scaled-down gear (refugees travel light) in Cuhel's car and drove to the RPD to say *vaarwel*. Farewells in Rangoon had not been easy, but these were infinitely more difficult. These men had become valued friends in the short span of ten weeks, and I somehow had the nagging feeling that I was letting them down. We could try to escape, perhaps to return eventually to our own countries, but Papa Rittman and his staff could only stand by in the country of their birth and await the inevitable. Nevertheless, they all came out to the car to wish us godspeed.

Only a couple of blocks from the RPD we met Hancock walking toward us and stopped to pick him up. Much to our surprise, he flatly refused, and I got out of the car to reason with him. Like McDougall, however, he was determined not to leave the story to the competition. I cited his diabetes and his dependence on insulin, but he would agree only to find McDougall and join forces. With Bill's car they could follow us to the coast, and we'd all make a joint attempt to leave. Even then Witt rejected my suggestion that he buy up all the insulin he would carry. "You have to have a prescription," he insisted, although the Dutch had relaxed all regulations on anything that might be of value to the enemy, and Rittman would have procured insulin for him without cost. Finally and reluctantly we moved away and started for the coast, leaving him standing at the curb, a gaunt, rather forlorn figure, rather like a blue heron in his dark, nontropical suit and white sun helmet. None of us would ever see Witt Hancock again.

Our own headaches were only beginning. Before we left Bandoeng, we heard that the Japs already had taken Tjilatjap, but there was no other port open on the entire island as far as we could learn, and we had to make the attempt or submit to automatic capture. We all agreed that if we were to be taken it would be while we were at least making an effort to escape. We wouldn't submit without giving it a good country try.

It was a decision we had to reaffirm many times in the next seven hours. We left Bandoeng a little after five, and it quickly became apparent we were bucking a trend. Traffic wasn't too heavy, but what there was was coming our way. Although we were driving as fast as was consistent with the road, we never overtook a single vehicle. Several times we stopped oncoming cars and asked for information. It was never good. Everyone told us they were fleeing just ahead of the Japs, but no one ever claimed to have seen one.

It was getting dark when we pulled into Tasikmalaya, a fair-sized city that seemed to be in a state of suspended animation. Lights were shining brightly, surprising after long weeks of total blackouts, and there seemed to be none of the agitation so apparent on the road. We found a restaurant and a filling station that topped our tank with no mention of rationing. The Dutch citizenry that filled the large room, more a cafe than a restaurant, seemed utterly unperturbed by the situation. That old Dutch standby, Bols gin, was very much in evidence, but no one was drinking heavily. Only men were present, apparently just waiting for the inevitable. As Weller remarked, it was eerie to see them so resigned. It was almost with a feeling of relief that we returned to the car. As we paid for the fuel the attendant, speaking with a heavy Dutch accent, assured us that the Japanese were at Wangon, a tiny village about fifty kilometers ahead, where the road turned south to Tjilatjap. He had his information from people "who had just left there." His report disturbed us, but we unanimously decided to keep moving.

By this time it was completely dark, and traffic was almost nonexistent. We had hoped that Hancock and McDougall would catch up with us at Tasikmalaya, but it was obvious they were still far behind us if in fact they were coming at all. We passed a couple of military guard posts where Cuhel's command of Malayan was useful, but the information was always the same: the Japanese were just a few kilometers ahead. We approached the Wangon crossroads cautiously and with more than a little trepidation, but all we found was another guard post. Here the sentry told us there had been no enemy in the area, but that the port, still twenty-five kilometers to the south, had been occupied several hours before. This time we didn't believe him. By now we were sure we had made the right decision. Every rumor so far had proved false, and we were convinced we would find Tjilat-jap still in operation. We drove on with rising spirits. We were right as far as the port was concerned, but we encountered a completely unanticipated development: The harbor was absolutely empty.

I can't describe that moment. We had resigned ourselves to the possibility we might never reach Tjilatjap or that the Japs might be waiting for us if we did, but deep in my own heart I had been certain that if only we could avoid the enemy en route, we would find something afloat to carry us on our way. Not only was the harbor empty, but the dock area seemed deserted as well. We drove around aimlessly for a couple of minutes until Turner noticed a guard post in the shadows at the rear of the dock with a Javanese sentry on duty. Again Cuhel conducted the interview and returned to report that the last ship had sailed about an hour earlier. He did, however, learn where the naval commandant of the port lived.

We found the commandant very much awake and quite sympathetic. He told us that he was expecting another ship at daybreak, an interisland freighter bound for Fremantle on Australia's west coast. If we would return at 6:00 A.M., he would put us on board. We thanked him and left in quest of sleep. Things were looking up again! In less than fifteen minutes we had been lifted from the very depths and now were as optimistic as ever.

The only hotel we could find was completely booked, but the receptionist politely informed us we would be welcome to sleep on a pair of billiard tables in a room just off the lobby. Four hours later we were at the naval commandant's office. As we drove from the hotel to the port we saw not one but *two* ships lying at anchor in the bay. It was a beautiful sight. True to his word, the commandant authorized us to board a naval cutter to be taken to the M.S. *Janssens*, a Dutch interisland freighter.

Just before we boarded the cutter, Cuhel performed a ceremony seldom seen in modern society. As soon as we cleared our gear from his car, he headed it toward the end of the jetty, moving in low gear. Just before he reached the end, he stepped out and watched as the car plunged into Tjilatjap Bay. He stared at the swirling waters for a long moment, then turned back to us with a wry smile. "At least the little bastards will have to dive for it!"

There was no question of finding accommodations aboard the ship, which would be carrying Dutch naval personnel to Australia. All we

could hope for would be a bit of deck space to stow our gear. Fortunately we were among the first to board and were able to claim a
small area on the port side of the main salon for our scant belongings.
Sleep would come where we found it, usually on the bare deck.

While we were trying to get settled the captain of the *Janssens*,
Jan Praas, appeared and demanded to know what we were doing on
his ship. We explained that the naval commandant was our authority,
but he shook his head. "No. He makes mistake. You should be on that
ship." He pointed to the second vessel, about a half-mile distant. "Go
now to that ship." With that he made off. All our instincts told us
to leave well enough alone. We were aboard this ship. That was a solid
fact. We might be barred from boarding the other ship. After a brief
conference, we decided to leave our gear where we had stored it and
keep out of sight until we sailed. It worked. We had no trouble avoiding the captain, who had much more on his mind that four stowaway
reporters, and no one else gave us a glance.

All that day the tenders shuttled back and forth between ship and
shore, bringing more and more naval personnel to compete with us
for the limited deck space. We watched carefully for any sign of Mc-
Dougall and Hancock, but the day passed with no sign of them. We
had no way of knowing, of course, who was boarding the other ship.
Throughout the day everyone also watched tensely for any sign of the
Japanese, by air, land, or water, but our luck held. As the only port
still operating, Tjilatjap should have been a prime target, but the Japs
apparently were ignoring it just as they had ignored the Rangoon
docks for two whole weeks. Actually, the enemy was paying closer
attention than we realized. The Japanese did have submarines operating just off the coast, we learned later, and were successfully destroying whatever came through the mouth of the harbor. Of four
ships that had left Tjilatjap the day before, three were sunk and the
fourth, the ship Captain Praas had ordered us to board, had escaped
by ducking back into the harbor.

Not all who joined us were Dutch personnel. Shortly before noon
we saw several wounded men being brought aboard, most on stretch-
ers. Weller went below to investigate and reported they were men
from the U.S.S. *Marblehead*, a U.S. Navy cruiser that had been badly
mauled in the Battle of Macassar Straits. Most were seamen but there
were two officers, Lt. Comdr. Corydon Wassell, a naval doctor in charge
of the group, and Comdr. William Goggins, the *Marblehead*'s executive officer, who had suffered severe burns over most of his body but

was now ambulatory. We went below to greet them. Some of the seamen were also ambulatory, but all were assigned cots on a lower deck protected from the elements. Wassell and Goggins shared a stateroom. These men, with Cuhel, Weller, and me, were the only Americans on board.

At about five the ship-to-shore activity ended and about six we weighed anchor and started toward the sea. Before we had moved a half-mile, however, we stopped and dropped anchor again. It was during this pause that we learned the fate of the ships that had preceded us through that entrance, information from radio reports relayed to us by one of the ship's officers. The news didn't cheer us, of course, but I still couldn't believe it could happen to me. Stupidity can be a great blessing sometimes. We started moving again at about midnight, this time through a heavy rainstorm I am sure the captain had been awaiting. In a few moments we were in the Indian Ocean, moving almost completely blind. The storm lasted until well after midnight, but long before that hour I had found a bit of empty deck space just behind the bridge and well out of the rain and was fast asleep.

Three things I brought aboard proved invaluable in ways their creators never intended. One was a bath rug I had purchased in Batavia and discarded in Bandoeng. Somehow the room boy had got it into my bag, and it proved to be a real asset. Of sturdy terry cloth, it measured about six feet by four and served me at various times as mattress, sheet, blanket, towel, and even pillow, although I soon learned I already had an excellent pillow. This was the second item, my briefcase, a plain leather envelope filled with my papers, which cushioned my head admirably whenever I found a place to stretch out.

The third item, quite improbably, was an atlas I had purchased in Batavia, an ordinary volume possibly a little more comprehensive than a high school geography book. I had brought it aboard strictly as a tray on which I carried a couple of bottles of White Horse and a few tins of cheese and potted meat. As soon as we got settled in our corner of the salon, I cached the food and drink in the bottom of my bag and tossed the book on a table. Immediately that atlas became one of the most sought-after objects on the ship. Our fellow passengers, most of them veteran seamen, passed it around and studied it by the hour. But most important was the use Captain Praas made of it. The *Janssens*, an inter-island vessel, carried no charts of the Indian Ocean, through which we were moving. As soon as the skipper spotted the atlas, he commandeered it and took to to the bridge, where he used it to draw up his own charts. Furthermore, he produced charts accurate enough to let him correctly predict our Fremantle landfall twenty-four hours in advance. The atlas stayed with the *Janssens*, but I still have the bath rug.

On our first morning at sea I awoke at daybreak to find we were still skirting the Java coast, hardly a half-mile off shore and moving in an easterly direction. The weather had cleared and it promised to be a beautiful day, although personally I would have welcomed rain and fog all the way to Australia. Breakfast consisted of a rather soggy pancake with a bit of musty jam, some tinned corned beef, and bread, all washed down with very milky (canned milk) coffee. It was hardly a Waldorf brunch, but it was filling, and we had already survived our first twelve hours, longer than the ill-fated ships that preceded us.

About nine o'clock we sighted a flight of nine bombers heading west about two miles north of us. They were too far for us to identify the meatball markings on their wings, but their engines were churning out that now-too-familiar "Mitsubishi moan," and there was no doubt they were Japanese. They paid no apparent attention us us, but a feeling of uneasiness spread over the ship. We knew the Japanese knew of our presence and location, and we also realized we were helpless if attacked—we were completely unarmed. Our one very slim hope seemed to be that the enemy, trying to consolidate his gains on land, would be too busy to waste a few sticks of bombs on a plodding old freighter. We were partially right.

More than two hours after the sighting, about eleven-thirty, I was standing beside my open suitcase at the gangway door of the salon, watching the Java coast. I had just dug a tin of cheese out of the bag and was preparing to enjoy a bit of informal hors d'oeuvre before the noonday fare of sausages, cabbage, and potatoes. Suddenly I heard planes coming in from the west, then the staccato bark of machine guns. I dropped my cheese and sprinted for a stateroom about ten feet away (it had steel walls) and dived under a berth with what seemed like a dozen seamen (and reporters) on top of me.

At last I believed it could happen to me!

It really never occurred to me that the *Janssens* might survive. I lay there measuring the distance to shore and wondering if I could clear the ship when she sank. I thought of Catherine and Pat and wondered if they ever would know what happened. After all, the only persons who knew where I was were on the ship with me. I probably did a bit of praying, and I remember thinking I had little right to ask help from the Almighty after having kept Him on hold for so long.

The attacks continued for several minutes, and I didn't realize that no bombers were engaged. A bomb exploding on the ground makes a hoarse coughing sound that can't compare with the terrifying thunder of 20mm aerial cannon shells bursting against the resonant steel hull of a ship. It took me several long minutes after the Japs left to realize they were gone, that we were still afloat, and that casualties and material damage would prove much less than might have been expected. Eleven persons had been wounded, but only one seriously, and none of the boys from the *Marblehead* had been hurt. There was no apparent crippling damage to the ship, and we might have continued almost immediately except for an incredible incident that changed the whole situation.

The ranking senior officer among the Dutch naval personnel was a captain, in full uniform, who stormed into the main sálon immediately after the attack, screaming tearfully, threw himself on the deck like a frenzied child, beat the flooring with his fists, and demanded to be taken ashore at once. I never really understood the meaning of the word contempt until I saw the look on Captain Praas's face as he confronted the sniveling officer. His decision was immediate. The craven officer would be taken ashore as quickly as a boat could be lowered, and anyone who wanted to follow his lead would be free to do so. That order included all Malayan crew members as well as the naval personnel and other passengers.

The attack had come just opposite the little town of Patjitan, which fronted on a small bay. We moved in immediately and began to lower the lifeboats excepting only the one to which our whole group had been assigned. The Japs had blown a sizable hole in the hull of that one. The Dutch captain, still whimpering, was the first to leave. He was soon joined by quite a few of the Dutch whose roots were in the island and all the Malayan crew except one Javanese cook.

Meanwhile we reporters, together with Wassell and Goggins, met on the deck behind the bridge, where I had spent the previous night, to make our own decisions. Before we could start, however, the door to the bridge burst open and Captain Praas came charging out. He had a clipboard bearing a single sheet of paper with something typed across the top in Dutch. I happened to be the nearest, so he thrust the board into my hands, barked out a few sentences in Dutch, and rushed back to the bridge. I looked inquiringly at the first officer, who had come from the bridge with Praas, and he did the translating. The captain had said that any of us who wanted to go ashore could do so, but that anyone who wanted to stay would have to sign the paper agreeing to accept any orders the captain might give.

It was by far the hardest decision I have ever had to make. I was still scared as hell from the attack, and the lovely green slopes of Java looked very inviting. Still, I knew that leaving the ship would mean automatic internment at best. Remaining aboard would mean the very real chance of another, perhaps more determined, attack. I looked at the others, but no one offered any word of advice, pro or con. They just stood there and waited for me to make up my mind. Almost in panic myself, I signed the paper quickly, fearful if I pondered my decision I might change my mind. I passed the board along to Weller, and he, Cuhel, and Turner added their names to mine. All of them told me later they didn't know what they would have done if I, forced to make the first decision, had declined to sign.

When the board was handed to Doctor Wassell, however, he did demur. "I'm going to take my men ashore," he said. "My orders are to stay in Java with my wounded, and that's what I'm going to do." At this point Commander Goggins intervened. "Wait a minute, Doc, I think we should give the men the right to make their own decisions. Let's take a vote." Bill Goggins, of course, was the ranking officer, and Doc agreed. They went below, and when they returned a few minutes later every man had signed. In all fairness to Wassell, I must say that none of us believed his first decision was based on his personal feelings. It was just that he believed his orders were to stay and that he had no right to take his men into more physical danger on his own whim.

Once we had the big decision behind us, we all started pulling for two objectives. First, we wanted as many as possible to go ashore to make more room for those who remained and to make fewer demands on the ship's provisions, obviously in short supply. Second, we wanted rain. We were sure the Japs would be back, and another concealing storm might save us. Months later in Sydney Prass told me he credited the storm for the cover that enabled us to avoid the blockade outside the Tjilatjap harbor. In my opinion, his intimate knowledge of the offshore channels in waters he had sailed many times was just as important.

There was to be no rain in our immediate future, however, and we spent the afternoon in Patjitan Bay, one eye on the departing passengers, the other on a few discouraging clouds, and our ears cocked for any sound of the Mitsubishi moan.

The ship's chief engineer recruited a new crew from among the Dutch seamen and organized them into an integrated unit that handled the *Janssens* with complete competence for the rest of the voyage. It was a remarkable exhibition of voluntary cooperation for the good of the whole. Our civilian contribution—Doc Wassell and Bill Goggins, too—of cleaning the main salon each morning and serving the daily sausage, cabbage, and potatoes dished up by our one remaining Javanese cook, was minor indeed.

Tension was still high when we finally weighed anchor at dusk and headed straight south into the Indian Ocean, intent on putting as much distance as possible between ourselves and the Java coast before sunup. When I awoke the next morning after a second night on my private deck behind the bridge, the ship was not nearly as cluttered as on the preceding morning, and there was a definite spirit of camaraderie among those still aboard.

Still thinking of fighter-bomber range, we speculated on how far we were from the coast, but the seamen-passengers agreed that the *Janssens* would be lucky to average twelve knots, so we probably were somewhere between 100 and 120 miles from the nearest airstrip as we faced the new day. No one ever thought of asking Captain Praas, who kept everyone at arm's length and made it very clear he had no interest in anything but getting the *Janssens* to Australia. I made a game of trying to find a time when Praas obviously had turned the command over to an aide (he had some good ones) in order to get some sleep, but I never succeeded. Every time I checked the bridge, day or night, I found him on duty, either there or somewhere on the ship. It was a mystery I never solved, and when I questioned him on the subject months later, all I got was a hearty laugh and the assurance that a good sailor doesn't need sleep.

On our fourth day out of Patjitan I came out on the deck in the middle of the morning and was astonished to see the sun on the wrong side of the ship. We were heading due north, apparently back toward Java. As I stared in total disbelief, I realized we were moving in a great circle. I rushed back into the salon and found that our steering mechanism had broken down. Again the chief engineer took over, organized a crew of experts from the Dutch navy, and went to work down in the hold, as well as overside. After a few anxious hours we were on our way again.

By this time we were well beyond the reach of any Java-based planes, but submarines presented a different and continuing problem. Everyone aboard the *Janssens* realized that even at her best, which she certainly was not, she had no chance against a healthy submarine; she was never built for speed. Still, the farther south we moved, the stronger our feeling of well-being.

Meanwhile the chief engineer took several of us down into the hold and showed us his makeshift repairs. First, he and his crew had contrived a wooden bearing to replace the one that had failed, then placed an intricate framework of wooden braces around it to hold it in place and keep it operational. This was the kind of Dutch skill and ingenuity I still hold responsible for our delivery.

As we moved into subequatorial waters farther south, the weather began to cool and I had to take my bath rug and briefcase and sleep inside the salon. As a matter of survival we all took impromptu naps whenever we found a suitable bench or cot, day or night. On the morning of March 12, a Thursday, I found a vacant settee in a corner of the main salon shortly after breakfast and immediately plopped down for a siesta. It seemed as if I had just fallen asleep, but actually it was close to eleven when Cuhel came running in from the after deck, shook me awake, and with some agitation told me we were being followed by a submarine. My first sleepy reaction was one of doubt, which one look at Frank's face immediately dispelled.

I ran with him back to the fantail where I found Captain Praas and several of his officers watching with glasses the conning tower and periscope of a sub not much more than a couple of miles astern. The craft had been sighted from the bridge about nine o'clock, and since that time, in spite of our best efforts, she had gained considerable distance on us. For once Captain Praas was speaking English under stress. He said he wasn't sure the sub was actually following us, even though it was on the same course (we were just off the northwest corner of Australia), but if it were, there wasn't much we could do. If we could maintain our lead until dark, he thought we might be able to take evasive action, but there seemed almost no chance of that, because we didn't have the speed. Although we were always hungry with our limited rations (I don't know what we would have done if so many hadn't debarked at Patjitan!), lunch was completely forgotten as we stood on that deck, watching and wondering. By this time the naked eye could mark the decreasing gap that separated us, and it was not a pleasant sensation.

Suddenly a shout went up as a big Australian PBY flying boat came into view, moving directly toward us from the southeast. We all cheered as the plane circled and, with flasher signals, ordered us to identify ourselves. There had been no arrivals from Java in nearly a week, we learned later, and the Aussies were clearly suspicious of us. Nevertheless, the plane was truly a welcome sight. Here at last was help we could call on if needed. We flashed back our identification, then asked the plane to check the submarine behind us. Apparently the PBY had not sighted the sub; it left us abruptly and headed toward the craft. We could see it circling and watched the flashes that marked an exchange of information, but we were too distant to read them. In a few minutes the plane returned with the welcome news that our tail was a Dutch submarine heading for Broome on the northwest coast of Western Australia, principally a pearl fishing port but also equipped to handle small naval vessels. Relief swept the M.S. *Janssens* from prow to stern like a summer breeze and we all relaxed, returning to the joys of normal discomfort.

The night before landfall I staked out slumber space under a table in the salon and lost no time in getting to sleep. Before daybreak I was awakened by the sound of cards riffling on the table above. I looked out and found Doc Wassell playing solitaire, apparently the only person awake besides myself. That surprised me because Wassell and Bill Goggins, who outranked mere correspondents, had their own berths. "What the devil are you doing up at this hour of the morning, Doc? Why aren't you in your berth?" He turned a pair of red-rimmed eyes on me and shook his head in obvious distress. "I can't sleep, Bill. I'm worried."

"Hell, Doc, there's nothing to worry about. We've made our landfall and we'll be in Fremantle harbor in nothing flat." He didn't relax. "Bill, don't you realize that I am facing a court martial? I have violated strict orders to stay in Java with my wounded."

"Don't be crazy, Doc. You were ordered to stay with your wounded and you did. You've got them right here with you. Nobody can fault you for that." He shook his head doubtfully. "Bill, you don't know this navy."

Within seventy-two hours Lt. Comdr. Corydon Wassell had been awarded the Navy Cross by President Roosevelt. The citation stated that the doctor had "taken virtual command of the ship and through his superior knowledge of navigation had managed to elude the Japanese fleet and bring his men safely to Australia." Doc Wassell was one of the finest men I ever met and evidently a very competent doctor, but I can attest personally that he never in his wildest dreams even considered taking control of the ship. It's just as certain that if he had tried, Captain Praas would have had him in the brig immediately.

Doctor Wassell was a retired, and aging, medical missionary who held a commission in the naval reserve, and he probably would have been retired from the navy as well if it hadn't been for the war. He took excellent care of his men, always, but if Bill Goggins hadn't insisted on polling the men, Doctor Wassell would have stayed in Java with his wounded, and I for one would not have faulted his decision. If that had happened, however, the world would never had seen Gary Cooper playing the part of the good doctor in that wartime movie, *The Story of Doctor Wassell*.

S-P-E-C-I-A-L R-E-P-O-R-T

Covenant

Not until after the war did I learn what had happened to Witt Hancock and Bill McDougall after we left Witt standing at the curb in Bandoeng. Information from the wire services and a letter from Bill, not too long after the *Missouri* surrender, told me he had survived an enemy attack that had sunk their ship but that Hancock had gone down with the ship. From the first, Cuhel, Weller, Turner, and I had assumed Witt and Bill were aboard the second ship in Tjilatjap harbor, which followed us out to sea at sundown on March 2 and was destroyed by the enemy the following morning. What actually happened was quite different.

After the four of us had left Hancock in Bandoeng, he did join McDougall. They were directed not to Tjilatjap, which Dutch officials had assured us was the only port still open, but to Wijnkoops Bay (now known as Pelabuhan Bay), where a ship was loading with top-ranking officers of the

NEI armed forces. Wijnkoops Bay was closer to Bandoeng and very probably would have been our choice if we had known we had a choice. The ship at Wijnkoops was the Dutch passenger-freighter *Poelau Bras*, and the Japanese, who already were swarming all over the island, may well have known it was being used to transport VIP's.

The question has been raised why the Japanese, if they did know of the loading activities at Tjilatjap and Wijnkoops Bay, didn't attack the ships immediately. I believe these omissions were deliberate. The Japanese knew they owned the Indies. If they allowed the fleeing ships, and there weren't too many of them, to move out to sea and *then* attacked, there were no clogged ship channels to be cleared or sunken ships to interfere with their own later use of these valuable ports. (It took years to clear Manila Bay of the Japanese ships we sank in that port on our return to the Philippines.) How well this policy, if it was a deliberate policy, succeeded can be measured by the fact that of the last five ships that left the island, only one, the M.S. *Janssens*, escaped. And the Japs had at least two ports they didn't have to clean up.

When Hancock and McDougall boarded the *Poelau Bras* they were assigned minimal space but did manage to spend a fairly quiet night. The attack, by both fighters and bombers, came the following morning. This is Bill's brief summary:

"Hancock and I were assigned a lifeboat that was immediately destroyed in the bombing. When the time came to abandon ship, we ran to the starboard rail. Below us in the water was a water-logged lifeboat which some men were trying to push away from the side of the ship. We decided to jump into the water and swim to that boat.

At that moment a Zero strafed the decks. We flattened out on the deck, against the rail. When the plane passed, I jumped up and went overboard. Witt did not follow. I was pulled into the lifeboat and in turn helped pull in one or two other men while we tried vainly to push the boat away from the ship. The *Poelau Bras* was sinking so rapidly our boat floated onto the deck at the level of the bridge. A woman at the rail called us for help, and one of the men got out of the boat to give her a hand. (All this time Hancock was not with me.)

On the roof of the bridge was another lifeboat still latched in position which he thought might be used. I said, "No, it must be damaged or it wouldn't be there." But one of the men climbed up and confirmed my opinion. By now it was too late to get the first boat free, so I took off my shoes and swam off the sinking ship, trying

to get far enough out to sea that I wouldn't be sucked under when the ship went down.

I turned around to see the *Poelau Bras* sink and saw Hancock standing beside the rail. He appeared to be smoking a cigarette. He still had on his sun helmet and seemed to be looking in my direction. I yelled at him, "Jump, Hancock, jump!" Whether he heard me, I don't know. He made no move. He was still standing there as the ship's bow disappeared beneath the waves.

Why he didn't jump, I do not know. There are several surmises. He could have been wounded by the machine-gunning plane and dragged himself to the rail where he would have seen, from his vantage point, there was only one lifeboat and one life raft, both jammed full, off the starboard. Also, he had diabetes and required daily insulin shots. He would have had no supply with him had he succeeded in swimming to the lifeboat and getting aboard. These, however, are only surmises. Only Witt and God know why he didn't jump."

Once the *Poelau Bras* disappeared beneath the waves, Bill McDougall's troubles began to multiply. He learned immediately that there was no room in either the boat or the raft; the occupants were willing to use force to prove that point. He spent several hours swimming and floating before another lifeboat from the *Poelau Bras* picked him up and carried him to Sumatra.

Early in the ordeal Bill became convinced his problem was too great for him to handle alone. In his prayer for divine aid he promised that he would, if he survived, devote his life to the service of his Creator, and Bill

McDougall is a man of his word. He made a covenant with God and he never forgot. Even in his Sumatra concentration camp he began preparing himself mentally and physically for a new career. Once the war ended, he returned home, fulfilled some assignments for United Press, wrote his own story of his own war, and entered a seminary. Today Bill McDougall, correspondent, author, world traveler and *Covenanter*, is climaxing a fruitful career of service to his Creator and his fellow man as the Reverend Monsignor William H. McDougall of the Cathedral of the Madeleine in Salt Lake City.

We arrived outside the Fremantle breakwater about eight-thirty on the morning of Friday the thirteenth and were greeted by a squadron of planes that kept us under observation until we dropped anchor inside the mine field about two hours later (maybe the Aussies were superstitious). I predicted we would be on dry land that afternoon, but I hadn't counted on the unbelievable suspicions of the Australian government, or its representatives. Even today, quite a few decades later, I find it hard to forgive them for carrying their doubts as far as they ultimately did, particularly in regard to a group of American seamen who had been wounded in the early defense of that continent. Arrivals from Java had ceased a week before we appeared off their shores, and the Aussies apparently couldn't believe any ship could move as slowly as the *Janssens*. (We actually had averaged a little less than nine knots for the nearly two thousand miles from Patjitan to Fremantle.) That's the only reason I can guess why they kept us waiting for twenty-four hours before allowing us to come ashore.

Once at anchor we waited until three-thirty that afternoon before the first officials came aboard—quarantine, customs, and immigration. We filled out the usual forms, expecting to disembark immediately. Instead, we were told they would "advise" us, and the officials departed without explanation, taking Turner and two other Australians with them. When it became apparent we would not be permitted to land that evening, Dr. Wassell asked permission to remove his wounded, at least the three who should have been in a hospital. He was not given the courtesy of a reply.

Rice, hard-boiled eggs, and a dubious soup were sorry substitutes for the thick, juicy steaks we envisioned on shore. Still, we swallowed our disappointment together with the unhappy chow and settled in for an evening of cards, Bols, and my last bottle of White Horse. I did manage to snare a nice, soft, wooden settee on which to spend my twelfth consecutive night without a bed.

A little before ten on Saturday morning we were given permission to move into the Swan River—Fremantle harbor—and a few minutes later the *Janssens* eased into a berth alongside a pier and permission was given to go ashore. We had, at last, completed our unforgettable voyage.

I went immediately to the bridge to thank Captain Praas for more than I could express, and I found that a great change had taken place. It was almost impossible to believe that this laughing, happy Dutchman was the same grim-faced martinet who had kept the whole ship in constant awe, bordering on genuine fear, of himself. He shook my hand heartily (I wondered if he had forgotten ordering us off his ship) and only laughed when I offered to pay for my passage. "All I want," he assured me, "is that you write something good about my chief engineer. He is responsible we are here." I promised kind words for all his men, thanked him again, and went to collect my meager gear. I was only sorry it didn't include the governor general's microphone.

It was almost eleven when I finally went ashore to try and regain my land legs. I found a bank only a few yards from the pier and was able to exchange my modest stock of Dutch guilders for Australian pounds. As I completed the transaction, the teller complimented me on my timing. At noon, he told me, a decree of the Australian government would forbid the acceptance of any more Netherlands Indies currency for the duration. Had I been delayed another half-hour, I would have faced a hungry weekend in a foreign country without enough cash to take the trolly to Perth six miles distant.

After that narrow squeak my first expenditures in £/s/d were for messages to Catherine and Paul White, my first in thirteen days. Next was a plate of ham and eggs at the nearest restaurant. I had almost forgotten how delicious freshly cooked food could taste and was glad I had declined the tinned *nasi goreng* (fried rice) that would have been my farewell breakfast aboard the M.S. *Janssens*.

Once in Perth, even though Australia usually grinds to a halt on Saturday, I was able to get in touch with officials of the Australian Broadcasting Commission. They confirmed what I feared—no transpacific broadcast facilities west of Melbourne, a full continent distant. Furthermore, it was impossible to transmit voice across the continent by phone with any degree of fidelity. I sent White another wire advising him I would try to reach Melbourne as quickly as possible. That too would prove difficult, however.

I am standing with Lt. Comdr. (later Admiral) John D. Bulkeley, PT boat commander who brought General MacArthur out of the Philippines in 1942, just before we left on a night cruise up the Vitiaz Straits from Huon Gulf in search of Japanese barges that didn't appear. *Courtesy U.S. Navy*

We had learned of the capitulation of Java from Japanese sources while still at sea, but the expected confirmation when we reached Australia still cast a shadow over what otherwise should have been a joyful weekend. In my ten weeks in the Indies I had come to know and respect both the Dutch and the Indonesians and had come to accept their cause almost as my own, certainly as far as the Japanese were concerned. Cuhel, with his long residence in the Indies, was particularly affected, for he had left a score of friends behind for every one of mine. Fortunately neither of us could foresee that events following the Pacific war would signal the end of Java as a homeland for thousands of Dutch who had lived there for long generations. Still, as almost always happens in such situations, it would be the native people—the Javanese, Sumatrans, Balinese, Moluccans—who would suffer most.

On these simple, industrious, and happy people would be imposed the bitterest, the cruelest scourge ever devised by misguided "humanitarians" of the twentieth century—the so-called right of self determination. Under the cloak of this deceptive shibboleth would spring a virulent disease, germinating in these islands and spreading throughout the world, freezing men's minds so they would license, through inaction, a few strong-arm men like Sukarno, Moamar Khadafi, Idi Amin, and too many others of their ilk, to spread terror, torture, death, and imprisonment on millions of innocents, all in its hypocritical name! Sukarno alone would heap more wholesale imprisonment, torture, and death on his fellow Indonesians in a quarter-century than the Dutch were charged with in their four centuries.

The final capitulation of Java, last island of the NEI to surrender, had come five or six days before we reached Australia. The Japanese, in less than three months of lightning warfare, had conquered the whole of the Pacific–Far East except for the interior of China, a few square miles of the Philippines, and the island of New Guinea. Even Hitler's most devastating *blitzkrieg* could not approach that record.

While we were still trying for our land legs and looking for any type of transportation eastward, word came that Gen. Douglas MacArthur and key members of his Bataan-Corregidor staff had arrived in Alice Springs, up in Australia's Northern Territory, and were en route to Melbourne, we were told, to take command of the Allied force whose job it would be to mount a drive against an enemy that had yet to taste defeat. A long and bitter war was just beginning.

PART 3

CHAPTER 16

Trans-Australia

The little city of Perth, resting quietly on the banks of the Swan River, was a welcome haven after eleven nights on a wooden deck and twelve days on iron rations, but charming as it was, the capital of western Australia was hardly prepared for the tide of fleeing refugees that engulfed it after the collapse of Southeast Asia. The M.S. *Janssens* finally berthed in Fremantle, at the mouth of the Swan, on Saturday, March 14. The first arrivals, even before the actual surrender of Java, had been greeted almost as conquering heros, and Perth had extended itself to make them welcome. By the time our group disembarked, however, refugees were an old story and the city was strained to its limited capacity.

Hotels were the biggest problem. Rooms were available only as vacated, and vacancies were retarded by the near-impossibility of getting to any other destination. Win Turner had given me the name of the Adelphia Hotel before he left the ship, and I checked in shortly after noon, getting the promise of a room "when available." That proved to be only a few minutes before midnight, just as I was resigning myself to another night on the "deck" of someone else's quarters.

The local head of the Australia Broadcasting Commission had promised to set up a trial short-wave circuit to Melbourne in the hope that an acceptable relay might be effected at that point, but he had not been very encouraging. Such an experiment had never before been attempted. The ABC operation in western Australia seemed to be physically independent of its operation in the east.

I was never able to decipher the schedules of Australian National Airlines (ANA), the only air link to the continent's eastern cities. The airline operated a small fleet of Douglas DC-2's on a now-and-then basis two or three times a week. It could give me no hint of when I might rate a seat, as the waiting list was understandably long and I had nothing in the way of a priority.

Still, if the schedules of ANA were baffling, those of Australia's only transcontinental railroad were worse. Ian Morrison of the London *Times* joined Win Turner and me on a Monday morning visit to Perth's only railroad station and found it nearly deserted. We did eventually locate an agent who told us the next departure would be on Friday, four days hence. We could pick up our tickets and learn the actual departure schedule at that time. Further, there would be no food or sleeping accommodations on board. We might be able to eat at intermediate stations, as was the custom on trains north of Melbourne, but there was no guarantee that any of the small station restaurants would be open when we passed through. We would be best advised, he said, to stock up on canned goods and nonperishables sufficient for three to four days.

It was not an encouraging prospect, but the train seemed our only hope of reaching the east coast, so I invested in a dinner knife, fork, and spoon, a plastic cup and plate, and a pocket knife that had a can opener as one of its many attractions. I wasn't too disturbed by the lack of a berth, having long since developed serious doubts that such a luxury would ever again be part of my life.

On Wednesday the broadcasting commission advised me that the short-wave tests with Melbourne had failed to produce a signal of broadcast quality. There would be no broadcast reports on CBS News from Perth. I wired New York a brief resumé of my fruitless efforts to reach either Melbourne or Sydney, apparently the only two cities on the entire continent with transpacific voice capabilities. White was having difficulty understanding my situation, and I couldn't blame him. I couldn't understand it myself.

When we returned to the rail depot on Friday to pick up our tickets and learn the actual departure time, we were told that that departure time had been postponed *ten days*. I gave my Woolworth table setting to the hotel maid and to this day do not know if the train ever left Perth.

Certainly we hadn't been otherwise idle while waiting for the reluctant Antipodal Cannonball to roar eastward. Several correspondents joined together with the idea of buying a used car (new cars didn't exist in wartime Australia) and driving the distance ourselves. Officials of the Liquid Fuel Control Board killed that idea instantly, however. We were told emphatically that the chances of a breakdown in the Australian desert were too great and we would not be allowed the fuel necessary for any such foolhardy venture.

Finally, after plane, train, and auto had been denied us, I decided to try the military. At that time, I had no official standing with any nation, including my own. The U.S. War Department had promised me accreditation while I was still in Java, where I had been fully accredited by the now defunct NEI government, but the Japanese had arrived first. When I landed in Australia, I was just another civilian refugee in full flight. But my options were running out, and it was no time to stand on protocol. I paid an unofficial call at the office of Maj. Gen. Martin Plant, the general officer commanding in western Australia, only to learn that the general would be absent from Perth for several days on a mission. His aide-de-camp proved to be a very understanding captain who promised to contact the general and see what, if anything, could be done. It had all the earmarks of a gentlemanly brush-off, and I returned to the hotel with little hope. Shortly after dinner that evening, however, the manager of the Adelphia located me in the hotel lounge and told me that ANA was trying to contact me. I dashed for the airline office to learn that General Plant had ordered priorities for Turner, Morrison, and me on the next flight to Melbourne, leaving the following morning, Saturday. Furthermore, the plane actually departed on schedule!

It had taken a full week to get away from that lovely little city, one of the most attractive in my long memory but like Rangoon a genuine *cul-de-sac* for a radio reporter in 1942. The three of us left for Melbourne with the unhappy realization that many of our fellow scriveners from Southeast Asia had been left behind.

CHAPTER 17

Melbourne Reunion

Our arrival in Melbourne put me back in direct communication with CBS News and the network, and for the moment at least there was plenty to report over the excellent transpacific facilities of Australia's Amalgamated Wireless. The immediate story was the arrival in Melbourne of Douglas MacArthur and his reception by the government and by the people. There was never a doubt as to what that reception would be. Every Australian from the capital in Canberra to the most remote outback station knew their nation had to have help in this, the first threat to their soil since 1788 when the first British colony (penal) was established on the site of present-day Sydney. If that help came under the aegis of one of America's most famous soldiers, the all-out support of the United States would be automatic, Canberra reasoned.

MacArthur became an immediate idol. People followed him on his infrequent ventures out in public, congregated outside his hotel, and cheered his words as reported by the nation's media. If anything else was needed to capture the public imagination, the General supplied it with a stirring speech before the parliament in Canberra, in which he pledged the unlimited resources of the United States. His message was the lead story the next morning in every newspaper and newscast in the commonwealth. He said, in part: "My faith in our ultimate victory is invincible, and I bring you tonight the unbreakable spirit of the free man's military code in support of our just cause. That code has come down to us from even before the days of knighthood and chivalry. It will stand the test of any ethics or philosophies the world has ever known. It embraces the things that are right and condemns the things that are wrong. Under its banner, the free men of the world are united today. There can be no compromise. We shall win or we shall die, and to this end I pledge you the full resources and all the mighty power of my country and all the blood of my countrymen."

The General's instant popularity extended to everyone who came from the United States, man or women, even to expatriate reporters with no desire to shed the blood MacArthur had pledged. Greetings of "Hi, Yank!" came from every side, for every American was a Yank regardless of whether his roots were in New England or South Texas. As far as the Australian was concerned, we were there to help him save his country, therefore we were his "cobbers."

Within a couple of days after his arrival, General MacArthur held a press conference for the announced purpose of meeting the correspondents personally. There wasn't much he could tell us about his command, which was not yet organized, so the session proved to be more of a classroom discourse than a question-and-answer conference. Most of the hour was devoted to an exposition of his views on the war in Europe in response to a direct question. He introduced Lt. Col. LeGrande Diller, who would be his media relations officer for the remainder of the war, and then greeted each correspondent individually. There were thirty or so present, British and Australians in addition to the Americans, many of whom had just arrived from the States. He started around the circle, hand extended, and exchanged a few words with each man (women correspondents would appear later). When he came to me, he did a pronounced double-take, looked at me in disbelief, and asked how I had escaped from the Philippines. I explained that I had "escaped" from Java, having left Manila several months before the Japanese struck. He then asked about my plans and I said I wanted most of all to get back to Manila. He smiled. "You stay with me, Dunn, and I'll take you back to Manila." It was a promise he kept, although it required the better part of three years.

It was good to have access once again to good transpacific voice facilities. The transmission studio was in the center of the city, a short distance from the building on Collins Street, Melbourne's main thoroughfare, that would house the new Southwest Pacific Command. The engineer in charge was an Englishman named Mason, a Londoner on loan who took a keen interest in the correspondents and our overall operation. He was always on hand to assist with any problem, eternally cheerful and distinguished by an exaggerated British accent reminiscent of Robert Morley. On the several occasions when we visited the nextdoor pub for a bit of refreshment, Mason would preface each drink with his own invariable toast, "Jolly good luck."

In the early days in Melbourne, we were forbidden by the censors to have any conversation with San Francisco. When asked for a voice level, we were supposed to read from a card that carried an innocuous paragraph about "scientists in their laboratories." On one of my first contacts I was wearing headphones but didn't have the card. When San Francisco asked for the level, I motioned for Mason to read it, and he did, in his very best Morley tongue. When he reached the bit about the scientists he placed them in "la-*bor*-a-trees", and the San Francisco engineer let out a whoop that would have carried a good distance across the Pacific without a microphone. "Hey! That's terrific! Read it again." Mason did so, with the same inflection, then turned to me with a rueful smile. "I suppose I must sound bloody strange to those chaps." The restrictions on voice-level conversations died quickly as the censors decided we could be trusted, and to this day I consider the circumstances that placed us in the care of a really dedicated engineer a perfect example of "jolly good luck!"

Australia to the Yank was a land of paradoxes, from the winter that appeared in the summer months to the traffic that moved on the wrong side of the street. By the time I arrived from the Indies, four months after Pearl Harbor, there were a number of Americans on hand, including a contingent of army nurses as well as GI's and airmen. Almost all of them had left the West Coast in the middle of an American winter and, after four to six weeks on the water, had reached the island continent just in time for the onset of the Australian winter.

Summer in Australia provided the only weather in the Southwest Pacific theater chilly enough to call for a sweater.

Although the Australian winter is milder than the American, two winters in a row just didn't seem fair.

But the biggest surprise was the discovery that Melbourne, in particular, really took seriously the biblical admonition to keep the Sabbath a day of rest. There was nothing to do but rest. Every Sunday Melbourne came as close to going out of business as it possibly could and still keep the spark of life burning. All restaurants closed for the day, and hotels served only registered guests behind locked doors. Theaters and movie houses were locked, all sports were banned, and tramway cars remained in their barns. A drink was impossible. There was nothing for Americans on duty in Melbourne in the way of Sunday recreation unless they were fortunate enough to be invited to a private home. The burden of this custom fell just as heavily on the Australian Digger back from North Africa and the Middle East as it did on the alien Yank. It was almost impossible to walk down Collins Street on a Sunday without being stopped by a Digger in uniform asking if you knew where he could get something to eat.

The correspondents had their own problems. Those who came directly from the States arrived in the regulation army officers' uniforms we were required to wear. But those of us who had come down from Asia had nothing but the nonregulation clothes we brought with us, certainly nothing in our tropical wardrobes suitable for Australia's oncoming winter. No regulations were issued by the command or from Washington except that we were to wear the uniform of a commissioned officer. Melbourne's tailors were put to work, and some of the results were a bit startling. We were also required to wear insignia identifying us as correspondents, noncombatants, but no insignia was specified. Virtually all of us settled on collar/shoulder pins reading "War Correspondent." At first gold was preferred, and the jewelers did a brisk business. Then someone pointed out that silver outranked gold in the American military, so the jewelers went back to work, duplicating their original creations in silver. Nothing but the best for the scrivener!

Another difficulty was the question of salutes. A noncombatant doesn't rate a formal salute, but if he is wearing an officer's uniform (or a reasonable facsimile thereof), he is bound to have salutes tossed at him. We had no regulations to tell us when to respond or whom to salute in return. Most of us adopted the custom of returning all salutes as a matter of simple courtesy but to originate none of our own, a rule generally suspended when challenged by a bevy of stars.

Not long after the Southwest Pacific Command was organized, all correspondents received memos from the press office informing us we had been granted the simulated rank of second lieutenant. If we were taken prisoner of war, our government would guarantee our salaries up to that rank. Inasmuch as I expected CBS News to be much more generous if I were captured, I was not impressed, nor were my

The lack of regulations governing the uniforms correspondents were required to wear in the SWPA produced some wide variations. Here are Frank Cuhel of MBS and George Folster of NBC strolling the streets of Melbourne in uniforms they designed themselves (with help from the local tailors). Behind them is Ed Angley of the *Chicago Sun-Times,* wearing a completely different version.

fellows. It was a blow to our collective pride that our government considered correspondents deserving of no more compensation than the lowest ranking officer just out of candidate school. Apparently someone agreed with us, because not long afterward orders came from Washington overruling the theater press office. We were instructed to return our second lieutenant memos and receive, in return, new ones specifying our simulated rank as that of captain. By that time, however, I had developed an affection for the idea of being a shavetail, simulated or not, and I declined to return my memo even though the new rank could not be granted unless I did so. Actually, I took a rather perverse pride during the remainder of the war in my conviction that I was the lowest-ranking correspondent attached to any of Uncle Sam's armed forces.

CHAPTER 18

A General in Search of a Command

In spite of its location on the southeast corner of Australia, about as far from a combat zone as possible, Melbourne did hold some advantages for the network war reporter. First, of course, were the excellent audiotransmission facilities, without which you were back in Rangoon. Of equal importance was its designation as the seat of the embryo Southwest Pacific Command, giving the reporter first-hand access to pertinent information that had to pass through that headquarters.

It also meant that the reporter had the opportunity to develop his own news sources inside GHQ, a fact that distressed some members of the staff who liked to control dissemination of all important information. But it was a matter of great importance to the enterprising correspondent. Here I had a slight edge on some of my contemporaries who had just arrived from the States. I had known several of the key officers on General MacArthur's staff in Manila, all of them advanced one or two grades in rank since I first met them. Although I had known none of them intimately, they, like me, had just arrived in an unfamiliar land, and in a nation of strangers even a casual acquaintance seems like a message from home.

Richard K. Sutherland, MacArthur's chief of staff and a major general, had been a lieutenant colonel when we first met, both residing in the same hotel in Manila. Sutherland was a rather dour (one of the kinder adjectives applied to him at GHQ) individual who had succeeded Dwight D. Eisenhower on MacArthur's staff the previous year, but he had been all smiles that morning in July, 1941, when he greeted me in the hotel elevator, wearing the silver star of a brigadier general. He gained his second star on Corregidor and never heard the wing-beat of a colonel's eagle.

Charles Willoughby, MacArthur's G-2 (intelligence), had advanced from colonel to brigadier since I had first met him at a Manila cock-tail party given by Clare Booth Luce, his long-time friend. "Sir Charles," as he was known around GHQ, was born in Germany but had an accent that was more Oxonian than Teutonic. His military bearing, however, was strictly continental. After "Sir Charles" decided I was to be trusted, not long after we met again in Melbourne, he proved an excellent source of mostly off-the-record information that helped me understand the overall picture.

A third helpful staff member was Sidney L. Huff, a lieutenant colonel who attained that rank after long service in the U.S. Navy. Sid had been the General's chief A.D.C. on Corregidor, charged with the welfare of Mrs. Jean MacArthur and the son, Arthur. Before Pearl Harbor, however, Sid was in charge of the "Philippines Navy," three PT boats that were to have been the nucleus of a fleet. The boats were officially termed "Q-Boats," possibly in deference to President Quezon. I first met Sid when he took me for a trial run in one of his "ships" around Manila Bay. The General had Sid transferred from the navy when he joined the staff officially, and he was always a good source of information about the General's family and personal activities. All staff officers lived in the same Melbourne hotel, and through those I knew, it didn't take long to get acquainted with the others.

LeGrande A. Diller, universally known as "Pick," was a lieutenant colonel soon to wear an eagle and eventually the star of a brigadier. I had not known him in Manila, but when he arrived in Melbourne as the designated press officer, we became instant *amigos.* I would work closer with him in the next four years than with any other officer. We had our occasional differences, some of them beauties, but we always reached an understanding based on mutual respect.

One source of trouble was Pick's determination to act as chief censor as well as chief press officer, something like the district attorney deciding also to head the defense. In theory, at least, the press chief

The press officers and censors who worked with correspondents accredited to the Southwest Pacific theater. In the front row, second from right, is Col. (later Brig. Gen.) LeGrande A. Diller, MacArthur's chief press officer during the entire war, and to his right is Lt. Col. Philip LaFollette, his assistant. The others, all majors (or willing to be) are (front left) Norman Myers, (right) Jerry Baulch, (rear left) Selwyn Pepper, Edmund C. Hughes, Frederick A. German, John L. Cross, Jr., and Charles J. Arnold. *Courtesy U.S. Army*

is the reporter's best friend, helping him gather necessary information, providing him advance tips and important contacts, and, of course, being constantly aware of the creature comforts, able to produce command facilities when the reporter finds no motels or sidewalk cafes in jungles or other combat areas. Equally important, however, the press chief should act as a buffer between the correspondent and his natural enemy, the censor. The censor's duty is to see that no script or story is approved for release that might prejudice the command or the commander. This can be as important as avoiding "aid and comfort to the enemy."

Like all of those who accompanied MacArthur from Corregidor, Pick Diller was intensely dedicated to his C-in-C and declined to surrender the red pencil to any other officer, no matter how well qualified. There was always a chief censor at press headquarters, but all members of the correspondent corps knew that his decisions and those of his assistants were ever subject to review, revision, even reversal by Colonel Diller. Holding both sets of reins in one hand had to be a headache, but Pick Diller managed to live with it.

The arrival of Douglas MacArthur in Melbourne with his cadre staff was supposed to signal the birth of a new command, the organization of a powerful force that would finally halt the Japanese juggernaut and begin the northward drive back to the Philippines, then on to Tokyo and ultimate victory, the force he thought was assured him when he was ordered to leave his Philippines command.

Instead, the General met with one of the most severe shocks of his long career. There was no mighty force and there was actually no command. What he found was little more than one American division completely without combat training, the first contingent of three Australian divisions being returned from North Africa over the protests of Winston Churchill to defend their homeland, one American air attack group, also untrained, to coordinate with minimal Royal Australian Air Force (RAAF) units, and the few U.S. bomber units flown down from the Indies. These meager forces, together with a few supply troops, were just about the lot. Just as distressing, no command awaited him. Washington, having determined that MacArthur was more valuable to the overall war effort away from the Philippines, spent more time trying to define his command than the enemy had taken to occupy both Hong Kong and Manila. MacArthur arrived in Melbourne on March 27, 1942, and the Southwest Pacific Command was finally defined on April 28, thirty-two days later. It had taken the Japanese just eighteen days to occupy Hong Kong and twenty-seven days to move into Manila, but it had taken Washington four and a half weeks merely to make up its mind.

The reason for the delay, of course, was interservice rivalry. Although he had decided the Pearl Harbor disaster made it impossible for the navy to go to MacArthur's aid in the Philippines, Adm. Ernest J. King, chief of naval operations, insisted the navy should have the overall command in the Pacific. He had some powerful support, sufficient to delay the decision for the long month. Even at our distance, the members of the correspondent corps knew what was going on. Those who had left Washington only weeks before were well aware of the interservice struggle, and those who had been in the Pacific from the beginning had friends on the cadre staff who kept us informed. Apparently MacArthur didn't want the situation to erupt into a public dispute, however, and we were not allowed to voice our disapproval at the delay.

After nearly four weeks of waiting, most of the correspondents, including representatives of the Australian media, met with an unofficial GHQ spokesman on April 15. In the two-hour session, we made it plain we thought the time had come for the media to raise its voice in the States. The Australian press and radio already was remarking on the delay and calling for action. Our efforts brought only partial results. We could release a four-point statement that allowed us to admit the situation existed but offered little clarification. I led my April 15 broadcast report with that statement, which merely confirmed that the command had not yet been defined; that General MacArthur was still commander of the United States Armed Forces Far East, as he had been since the preceding July; that the only physical change had been the transfer of his headquarters to Australia; and finally that discussions were taking place in Washington but no decision or directive had been received. We still were not allowed to comment pro or con, but I did quote an editorial from the *Melbourne Herald*, one of the foremost Australian newspapers, which made clear Australia's firm support of General MacArthur and warned Prime Minister John Curtin, as well as Washington, against anything that might deny the General full powers to do the job for which he had been chosen and on which the future of Australia depended. Other correspondents filed similar reports, which were given good play in the American press. The directive came through just three days later, on April 18.

To the surprise of no one, the final decision proved to be a compromise. At the insistence of King and others high in the naval hierarchy, the Pacific was divided into two sections. MacArthur was given command of the Southwest Pacific Area (SWPA), which included Australia and all territory west of longitude 159° east, including the Indies and New Guinea. The Pacific Ocean Area, which included everything east of that longitude, was placed under the command of Adm. Chester W. Nimitz, who had been King's candidate for the overall command. In this area were the Solomon Islands with Guadalcanal.

News of the directive, although of utmost importance to us in the theater and to Australia with the Japanese menacing her northern shores, received secondary play in the American press. On that very same day Jimmy Doolittle and his squadron of B-25 bombers bombed the city of Tokyo, the one thing the Japanese knew could never happen. No one in the newly established Southwest Pacific Command begrudged those lads their headlines.

Once the status of the new Southwest Pacific Command was officially established, the correspondent corps began to take stock of its own concerns. Most of us were in excellent interim hotel accommodations, but I for one wanted to be more comfortable for the long term. Frank Cuhel had the same idea. A day or two after the SWPA command had been formalized, Frank came galloping into my room in the Australia Hotel (he had been a hurdler in the Amsterdam Olympics and the instinct was still there), all out of breath and obviously excited. "Come on, Bill, quick. I want to show you your new apartment!"

"What the devil are you talking about? I don't have an apartment this side of Forest Hills, New York."

"Oh, yes you have. I just signed up one for you, and you owe me the down payment."

Calming him with a bottle of Cascade lager, I finally got the story. One of his new-found Australian friends had told him of a new furnished flat not far from the center of the city, and he had rushed out to see it. It was an excellent little flat with a living room, sleeping alcove, and modern kitchen-dinette. Frank signed up immediately. When he learned there was a duplicate on the floor below, he signed for that one too, in my name. He explained it wasn't a lease and I probably could get out of it if I didn't like it, but he wasn't taking any chances of losing it.

It was the only time in my life I had ever rented a residence not only sight unseen but without even knowing it. I lost no time checking it out and ended by thanking Frank for acting on my behalf. It was ideally located in relation to GHQ, and the broadcast studio, modestly but adequately furnished, and the dinette made a perfect setting for my typewriter, notes, and the stack of daily papers I always accu-

WAR CORRESPONDENTS LINE UP FOR A CONFERENCE

1. Col. L. G. Diller.
2. Lt.-Col. L. Lehrbas.
3. Yates McDaniel (Associated Press).
4. Joseph C. Harsch (Christian Science Monitor).
5. Patrick Maitland (News Chronicle, London).
6. Martin Barnett (Paramount News).
7. Ian Morrison (The Times).
8. Jonathan Rice (Acme News Pictures).
9. Bynon Darnton (New York Times).
10. Lewis B. Sebring, jun. (New York Herald-Tribune).
11. "Newsreel Wong" (News of the Day).
12. Ralph Jordan (International News Service).
13. Jack Turcott (New York Daily News).
14. Wallace Kirkland (Life and official U . Army photographe
15. William Dunn (Columbia Broadcasting System).

How the flood of American war correspondents appeared to their Australian counter-parts. This cartoon by James Wells appeared in the Melbourne *Herald* in early 1942 and really caught the mood of the moment. Pat Maitland and Ian Morrison were Londoners, however, who ranked as refugees from Southeast Asia, as did I. Furthermore, I deny ever having had an affair with a Koala bear!

mulate. Finally, the landlady (the landlord was off to war) agreed to visit the premises daily and make sure they didn't become too bachelorized, although she drew the line at washing dishes.

Mutual Broadcasting was in good hands with Frank Cuhel. Martin Agronsky had come directly to Melbourne from Singapore to give NBC good representation. Sid Albright was still a stringer for NBC, but his first obligation was to United Artists, the Hollywood producers who had sent him to the Far East several years before as a business representative. He continued northward to U.A.'s Australian headquarters in Sydney.

Paul White called Jack Raleigh home for reassignment soon after my arrival in Australia, and I again was left alone with a war to cover.

Our only other remaining reporter was Jim Stewart in Chungking, and I had no direct contact with him any longer. Our men in Tokyo and Manila, W. R. Wills and Ford Wilkins, had been interned and all of Asia except parts of China, Burma, and India, was in enemy hands.

There now remained only two points in the entire theater, Melbourne and Sydney, from which we could put an audio signal into San Francisco and the network, and the new GHQ SWPA was located in one of those two cities. A reporter tied to the Melbourne or Sydney microphone was more a *foreign* than a *war* correspondent. Instead of moving regularly into the combat areas, two to three days distant by available transportation (you had to leave your mike for at least a week), we concentrated on news sources within MacArthur's headquarters and the Australian government, always alert for personnel moving between New Guinea, Japan's farthest thrust into the Southwest Pacific, and our base.

Quite a few of the correspondents who had come down from Southeast Asia, as well as some of the newcomers from the States, became restless when they realized how long it would be before MacArthur could launch any real offensive, and a number of them applied for transfers or a return home. I was more unhappy about the way the Japs had run me out of the Indies and more disturbed about the probable fate of my many friends in the Philippines and Southeast Asia who were now in enemy hands. I determined to stay with the SWPA command, and although he never told me, I'm sure that's what Paul White wanted.

From the day of our arrival in Australia it was certain that the fall of the Philippines was imminent. Our forces were trying to hold out with only what was left of the men and materiel they had on Pearl Harbor Day. The same navy that wanted to take full command in the Pacific still protested its inability to move any type of reinforcement through the Jap-infested waters. All the islands were for practical purposes in enemy hands, except for part of the Bataan peninsula on the western shore of Manila Bay, Corregidor Island at the southern mouth of the bay, and a few isolated pockets in the southern islands.

Bataan didn't last until the confirmation of MacArthur's new command, surrendering on April 21, and when Corregidor surrendered exactly twenty-seven days later, more than a few furtive tears were shed at 401 Collins Street, the new GHQ. I got the very strong impression that the emotions of these professional soldiers whom MacArthur had brought with him reached beyond military pride. Most felt real affection for the islands and the Filipino people, and all had service associates of every rank now at the mercy of a merciless enemy.

I suppose it would be a cliche to say that happiness and heartbreak go hand-in-hand in time of war, but it is also a bitter truism. Just at the time that MacArthur's command directive arrived from Washington, two reporters and a bride arrived in Melbourne from Corregidor, having eluded the entire Japanese armed forces to establish an unparalleled record for hitch-hiking under extreme difficulty. The reporters were Melville Jacoby of Time-Life and Clark Lee of the Associated Press (later the INS), and the bride was Annalee Whitmore Jacoby, the girl to whom I had delivered a lovely jade engagement ring in Chungking about six months before. Annalee had joined Mel in Manila, and they had married just before the first bombs dropped on that unhappy city. All three were able to get to Corregidor, no mean feat in itself, and when the fall of that bastion was inevitable they took off with the help of Filipino boatmen and started south to Melbourne some three thousand miles distant. Now here they were, all their perils behind them. Two weeks later, on April 29, Mel accompanied Brig. Gen. Harold George, a top air corps commander he had known in Manila, on an inspection tour of a nearby military air base. As they stood talking on the airport apron, a taxiing plane suddenly lurched out of control and crashed into them, killing both instantly.

In any war the loss of a close friend to enemy action in the line of duty is painful, but not as painful as to lose that friend in a senseless accident you feel sure could have been avoided or through the inadvertence of your own forces, as with Barney Darnton of the *New York Times*, who died when the boat in which he was an observer was sunk by American planes who mistook it for an enemy craft.

Only two other correspondents made it to Australia after the fall of the Philippines, Frank Hewlett of the United Press and Dean Schedler of the Associated Press. Dean was "home free and living on borrowed time," as he often exulted, but Frank was less fortunate. Both had miraculously escaped from Bataan, but Frank's wife, Virginia, had had to remain in Manila and presumably had been interned by the enemy. He would have no accurate information for three years.

S-P-E-C-I-A-L   R-E-P-O-R-T

Corregidor

I had interviewed Annalee Jacoby for CBS News on April 20, soon after she and Mel arrived from Corregidor. Annalee was now a correspondent for *Liberty* magazine, the only woman war correspondent accredited to the Southwest Pacific Area command. Her account of the last days in Manila and Corregidor was vivid and perceptive.

AJ: Well, [Corregidor was] not the best place in the world for a honeymoon, but we were so glad to be alive and still free that it didn't matter. Corregidor is a very small island, and there were a lot of people crowded on it. Any conversation involved at least twenty other people. My only chance to talk to Mel alone for the whole first week lasted just two minutes—then a bomb landed and we had to dash for cover along with everyone else.

WD: Why was it so comparatively few correspondents went to Corregidor or Bataan?

AJ: Everyone's asked us that. They just can't realize how Manila was toward the end. No other correspondents came, because they didn't want to ... they thought there was no chance to get out ... that waiting in Manila and spending the war in a Japanese concentration camp was the only way to come out of this war alive. None of us knew about the Bataan maneuver until New Year's Eve. By that time Manila was an open city; all the guns and troops had left days before. Bridges were being blown up on every side ... Japanese patrols had come down some of the roads to within a few miles of the city. We

couldn't get away by sea . . . the Japanese were just outside the bay and on every side. We knew it would be impossible to drive to Bataan by land . . . most of the roads were gone. All the correspondents met in our room, and over twenty-five decided there was nothing to do but stay. Only three of us wanted to take any chance whatever to get out. Clark Lee, Mel, and I got on about the last rickety little boat left in the harbor and went through the mine fields to Corregidor. Five minutes after we left the dock, it blew up with a tremendous explosion . . . sparks showered down on our heads, and by the time we reached the middle of the bay the whole waterfront was burning. If we'd been sensible, we would have stayed in Manila. But we were lucky. We got to Corregidor, and now we're in Australia!

WD: How was life for a woman on Corregidor? Were there many other women?

AJ: No, not many. There was Mrs. MacArthur, of course, and she was completely wonderful. When a raid started, she would look about very calmly to be sure her four-year-old son, Arthur, was under shelter. Then she would come in herself, as slowly as if nothing were happening. She did a tremendous lot for morale ... every soldier felt that he could stop and talk with her and go away feeling cheerful and matter-of-fact. Almost the only other women on Bataan and Corregidor were the nurses.

WD: How were their living conditions?

AJ: In the Bataan hospitals nurses were living in the jungles without any canvas over their heads. They slept on army cots on the ground. Most of them had lost their uniforms, so they wore air corps coveralls, several sizes too large. They bathed in a creek and waded out to rocks in the middle of the stream to wash their hair and their clothes. They made their way around the huge open-air hospitals in the dark, lived on two meals a day, worked long hours with hundreds of badly wounded men, and still made it all seem like fun.

WD: Sounds like the morale was high, despite the dangers.

JA: It was, Bill . . . everyone from General MacArthur on down. He was always the last to take shelter when shells began whistling overhead or when the siren sounded for a bombing raid. It made the rest of us have a lot less intestinal flip-flops when the explosions started. And the private

soldiers were the finest people I've ever met. Mel and Clark and I came onto Corregidor carrying one knapsack. We hadn't been able to bring any more. We had only a camera, a bar of soap, and a change of socks and shirts apiece.

Every soldier who saw us stopped, partly to talk to someone from outside and partly to ask if we needed anything. By the end of that first day, despite almost constant bombing raids, soldiers had brought us blankets, drinking water, sandwiches, a blue denim fatigue uniform for me, and one soldier even offered to walk two miles to get us some coffee. I never heard a man complain about anything except for a few who wanted to get to the front and fight. Japan can't win against the kind of spirit they have on Corregidor, Bill.

CHAPTER 19

War Correspondents in Search of a War

If the status of the radio reporter tied to the Melbourne microphone was that of a foreign rather than a war correspondent, it was doubly true when we transferred to Sydney. Despite its distance from any combat zone Melbourne did have its advantages as long as the theater command remained on Collins Street. All pertinent information from the entire Pacific gravitated to that headquarters, and the enterprising reporter could learn a lot more than was handed him routinely in the official communiqué. Daily press conferences were structured around the communiqué, but we usually gleaned more from the questions it prompted.

At each of the conferences every press association had a man poised like a yearling at the starting gate to grab the communiqué as soon as it was released and sprint to the nearest cable office in hopes of beating the opposition. Consequently it was usually on the New York network desk within minutes, certainly not to be repeated verbatim in our later broadcast reports. I always felt that my value to a specific news program rested in my interpretation of the official release, if it was important, in light of background knowledge of the overall situation, plus any other pertinent information not directly related to the GHQ release.

All this changed in early August, 1942, when MacArthur transferred his headquarters northward to Brisbane, a city much closer to actual combat areas but with no facility for putting an audio signal into San Francisco. The transfer of GHQ automatically meant a wholesale transfer of the press corps to the north. We radio reporters, however, could go no farther than Sydney, the only other Australian city with intercontinental audio capability. There we were anchored, and our easy access to unofficial GHQ sources no longer existed. Even telephone communication was impossible because a call from Sydney to Brisbane could easily take more than twenty-four hours, and no responsible individual, civilian or military, would discuss vital information over an open line in any event.

Pick Diller set up a rear echelon of the GHQ media office in Sydney, manned with press officers who doubled as censors. The Australian government, of course, had its own censors, and all current information had to be cleared through both. This was when we really reverted unofficially to the status of "foreign" correspondents. We still had to wear military uniforms and were subject to military regulation (we carried no passports), but there was no war in the neighborhood and we had to keep a close liaison with Australian sources for information to supplement what was relayed to us by GHQ.

The Cable and Wireless offices and studios were located in the heart of the city, on York Street facing Wynyard Park and just a block from the large apartment hotel, Martin Hall, that was to be my residence for more than a year. The press censors' office was about halfway between the two, and Base 7, the U.S. Army's local headquarters, was less than a half-block from the studios. It was an ideal situation, geographically at least. Still, what we needed most and couldn't achieve until we left Sydney was direct access to GHQ SWPA.

By the time we were settled in Sydney there had been a readjustment in the radio corps. Cuhel and I still reported for Mutual and CBS News, respectively, and Albright was still stringing for NBC. But Martin Agronsky had returned to the States, and NBC had hired George Thomas Folster to replace him. Folster, like Cuhel, had had no previous experience but did have an instinctive flair for the assignment.

Australia's transpacific link with the United States and the CBS network was based in the tall building on the right with the antenna on top. This view of Sydney's Martin Place was taken from my billet in Martin Hall. The American military base, Base 7, was located in the building to the left of the PLUME billboard and placed the censors just across the park from the studio.

There's not much to be seen in a news broadcast studio, but what there is, is important. This studio, in the headquarters of the Amalgamated Wireless of Australasia, in Sydney, was the final news studio that wasn't makeshift until the broadcast ship *Apache* came into being in 1944. By the way, I haven't smoked a cigarette in thirty-five years. *Courtesy AWA, Sydney*

Actually, I had hired Folster to string for CBS news more than a year before, by telephone from Manila. I had not met him personally until I arrived in Melbourne, but by that time White had let him go to make room for Jack Raleigh. With no reflection on Jack, it was one of White's major mistakes. Folster proved a big asset to our competition during the remainder of the Pacific war, served as Tokyo bureau chief during the occupation, and directed coverage of the Korean conflict.

Folster, who had come to Australia on an expedition for the American Museum of Natural History only to be ship-wrecked on the Great Barrier Reef, had rented a house in nearby Double Bay facing the harbor, while Cuhel, Albright, and I moved into Martin Hall together with a number of Americans, mostly military. Norman Alley, an old

It didn't take American correspondents long to adopt the Australian fondness for tea (as well as Australia's fine brews). Here I am playing host in my Sydney billet to Frank Cuhel (left) of MBS and Sid Albright and George Folster of NBC, my principal competition.

China hand who was head of the Hearst Metrotone/Newsreel coverage in the Pacific theater, was already in Sydney when we arrived, comfortably ensconced in the Martin Hall penthouse he had shared with another photographer just returned home. I had known Norman in Asia. When he offered to share his quarters with me, I accepted with alacrity and Cuhel later joined us.

The Martin Hall penthouse still stands out as the best accommodation I have ever enjoyed. The apartment occupied most of the top floor of a twelve-story building and included two double bedrooms, baths, a huge living-dining room, a complete kitchen, and a roof-top terrace overlooking the harbor. All this plus daily maid service for less than the two of us would have paid for standard hotel accommodations.

Almost immediately we organized a series of Sunday brunches that brought together a dozen or more military and civilian personages each week for pancakes, fried chicken, and conversation. The military included Americans and Australians of every rank (all ranks were suspended while they were our guests), while among the civilians were representatives of both governments, Australian newsmen and women, and fellow correspondents who happened to be down from Brisbane. No phase of the war escaped examination and discussion, and the seeds of many reports to CBS News were planted during those gastronomic conclaves that often lasted all afternoon.

The idea of *frying* chicken was almost unknown in Australia at that time, but our Aussie guests caught on fast. It was not possible to buy a "fryer" in a Sydney market, but I did locate a dealer who sold "broilers," young poults trussed for the spit, which we untrussed and sectioned for the frying pan quite successfully. American-style pancakes also were a novelty to most Australians. By "American-style" I refer to the old-fashioned flannel cakes, as thin as crepes but with beaded, crispy edges. Alley's preference was for this type of pancake made with sweet milk, a recipe his mother had given him years before. *My* mother taught me to prefer a sour-milk recipe (and I still do.) So we took turns, serving sweet-milk pancakes when Alley manned the griddles and sour-milk cakes when I ruled the kitchen. The griddles, incidently, were a pair of genuine American cast-iron utensils, practically a gift from a Melbourne merchant who didn't know what they were designed for and couldn't sell them to his Bourke Street clientele. If our guests had any preferences, it wasn't obvious. They all seemed content with whatever type of pancake flipped off the griddle, sweet or sour, and before Alley finally moved on to greener newsreel pastures, we had old and new friends coming all the way from New Guinea to share our table and bring us word of what was happening up north.

The Japanese did, in fact, make several attempts to bring the war to Sydney, fortunately with minimal success. The first came on May 31, while I was still based in Melbourne but was in Sydney for a meeting with Prime Minister John Curtin. I was having dinner in a restaurant not far from the harbor with two officers from the cruiser U.S.S. *Chicago,* which was in port for an unspecified stay. Suddenly loud detonations obviously from the harbor interrupted our conversation. Both men jumped to their feet and one exclaimed, "Those sounded like depth charges!" With that, they were off, just in time,

This shows me in Melbourne, displaying my culinary skills to Al Noderer of the *Chicago Tribune*, Bill Courtney of *Colliers* magazine, and Lt. Julie Mramor of the American nurses corps, almost hidden behind the chef. *Courtesy Melbourne Herald*

I learned later, to board their ship before it weighed anchor and headed out to sea. Immediately there were rampant reports of enemy action in the harbor, but once the detonations ceased nothing more happened. After several hours the government spokesman informed us that three (later amended to four) midget submarines had indeed entered the harbor at nightfall, but had been immediately detected and destroyed. They undoubtedly had come from a "mother" ship not far off the coast of New South Wales. Each apparently had been manned by two persons, and only one survived long enough to inflict minimal damage on one small harbor craft.

I spent the next three days on the harbor with the crews striving to salvage at least one of the four for naval study. On the third day they partially succeeded. Soon after, I made my report to the network.

Today I saw the job completed and the battered steel cylinder that had once been a menacing weapon deposited on dry land. Although it was previously indicated that this particular midget was probably identical with those used at Pearl Harbor, when the craft was lifted out of the water it was found to be slightly larger type.

Only two-thirds of the submarine was raised, the tail section having been torn away by the force of the depth bombs or by salvage operations which followed. The sub, intact, would probably be close to sixty-five feet long. It is almost needle-like in its proportions, being barely five and a half feet in diameter at its thickest point, capped by a conning tower probably two and a half feet tall.

As it rose from the water in the arms of a huge crane, the marks of its terrific beating were apparent. Steel plates were battered badly, and water poured from several seams as well as the open section at the rear and a hatch cover on the bottom which had been warped open. Below the conning tower it carried two numerals, but there were no Japanese characters of any kind in evidence.

From the battered nose peered the shining tip of a live torpedo, as though it had been jammed in the act of firing. Actually naval observers doubt that the tube had been fired, because closer inspection indicates its cover probably had been blown away by the blast which had obviously crushed the covering of the second torpedo directly below it. On both the nose and the conning tower were steel cutting edges designed to aid the craft in getting through antisubmarine nets.

The entire craft gave the appearance of great flimsiness and could not be compared in careful construction with its larger brothers.

The question of whether either of the probable two-man crew is still aboard is not yet answered. Naval officers who inspected the craft briefly through the open hatches reported the first object they were able to identify through the mud and water was a neatly folded umbrella!

The "neatly folded umbrella," which caused so much comment and head-scratching among the inspecting officers, was later discovered to be, instead, a samurai sword. After all these years, I still wonder which of the two items would be the biggest asset in an underwater sortie into enemy territory.

One week later one or more submarines lobbed a few shells into the area surrounding the Heads, the entrance to Sydney Harbor, and onto the coast at Newcastle about 165 miles north. There was almost no damage, and that was the last enemy attempt to harass Sydney by water.

John Curtin was not an imposing man at first meeting; slender, medium stature, clean-shaven, with rimless glasses and a crop of dark hair in which the gray would soon predominate. He reminded me at first of a college professor, but when he spoke no one would think he was delivering a classroom lecture. I had not encountered him on any of his infrequent trips from Canberra to confer with General MacArthur, so when I learned he was to address a large Empire Day luncheon in Sydney, I made the trip north to evaluate for myself this man who governed our largest remaining ally in the Pacific.

As it turned out, this was one of the last observances of Empire Day, although the ultimate demise of Britain's empire was then only faintly indicated. John Curtin's talk was invaluable to a reporter not too long in the country. For the first time, I heard a precise statement of Australia's position, as a loyal member of the empire, on a war that threatened not only that continent, but all member nations of the empire and their allies.

The prime minister spoke for about forty-five minutes without a written note, but the speech could well have been read from a thoughtfully prepared script. He made it clear that Australia expected the help due it as a member of the empire and as an ally whose stake in the conflict was as vital as any. In return, he said, the vast natural resources of his nation would be dedicated to the worldwide effort, and the people of his nation would make any sacrifice necessary. There was no verbal fireworks, no tub-thumping, just a straightforward statement of Australia's position, forceful without being blunt.

It was not difficult to understand how this quiet man, with his mild appearance, had been able to stand up to Winston Churchill, not once but twice, bringing his men back to their homeland where they were sorely needed. Churchill had convinced Roosevelt that the defense of Europe should take precedence over the struggle with Japan, despite our pledge to the Philippines and despite the urgent needs of the Americans in those islands trying to fulfill that pledge. But Churchill could not persuade John Curtin that Australian troops would be more useful to the overall cause in North Africa, where most of them were fighting when Japan struck, or in India, which he feared might be Japan's next target. As far as John Curtin was concerned, Australia's overseas divisions were coming back to defend their own soil, and subsequent events, particularly in New Guinea, proved his decision the right one.

Much has been said about the valor of the Australian soldier, but not too much. The Digger, the Australian fighting man, was brave almost to the point of foolhardiness, sometimes lacking a bit in military spit-and-polish discipline but ready to tackle any assignment without question and with the ability and confidence to complete that assignment. One story current in combat areas was probably apocryphal but illustrates the regard his allies had for Digger fearlessness. A contingent of Digger infantrymen were being briefed before their first parachute jump. "You'll pass over the target at about two thousand feet," the colonel told them, "at which time you'll be given the signal to jump." One Digger raised an inquiring hand. "Sir, why can't we fly over at a hundred feet?" "Impossible," the colonel protested. "At a hundred feet your parachute wouldn't have time to open." "Good-oh!" exclaimed the Digger to his cobbers. "We're gonna have parachutes!"

Although comparatively small, the Royal Australian Air Force had been combat-seasoned alongside its English cousins in the Battle of Britain as well as in North Africa, and it proved one of our most effective weapons to counter Japanese attacks on New Guinea and northern Australia during those early months of 1942.

Over those many months in Sydney, I came to know the Australian people well and developed a respect and affection that has never left me. The more I saw and associated with the civilian population, the easier it was for me to understand the valor of the Digger and his RAAF brothers and the firm but quiet leadership of the prime minister. This was Australia at its best.

The Australians fortunately suffered fewer hardships of war than many of their allies. The nation lay just beyond the effective reach of the Japanese, and the Nazis were a full half-world away. Moreover, in spite of almost continuous lack of proper rainfall and resultant water shortages, Australia produced more food and raw materials than she could ever use. Only petroleum products had to be imported. Rationing, except for gasoline and oil, was largely a token gesture and not a real hardship. But the Australian would have taken the sternest restrictions chin-up had it become necessary. Australia was, is, and probably always will be a nation of intense political convictions and rivalries, probably more fiercely contested than in the average democracy. But those rivalries were very much muted during the war years as almost the entire country united in the face of an enemy whose goals were all too evident.

I say "almost" because, unfortunately, the record of organized labor in wartime Australia was shameful, particularly when measured against the all-out contributions of the populace as a whole, military or civil. The situation was a constant source of embarrassment for John Curtin as head of a Labor Government. From the first, the unions flatly refused to suspend the right to strike for the duration or to grant other concessions. It was to be "business as usual," the pretext being —and it was only a pretext—that they were protecting the rights of their cobbers who had gone off to fight. The fact that their cobbers in uniform didn't want that kind of protection and said so, loudly and often (I never met a Digger who wasn't opposed to wartime strikes), made no difference. Unfortunately for the war effort, the "protection" program took the form of innumerable work stoppages. The eternal desire for higher wages prompted routine strikes, of course, but petty grievances such as dirty washrooms, poor canteen food, or disagreement with the super would also send the cardholders scurrying for the exits. The policy seemed to be to strike first, then negotiate.

In 1942, shortly after MacArthur arrived in Melbourne and while the new command was being organized, a major strike gripped the coal fields of New South Wales, a strike that threatened the war effort. In a land without petroleum, coal was absolutely vital as the fuel that stoked the nation's industrial complex. Without coal in ample supply, the heavy industry that armed the men in the field and supplied them with the materiel of war would come to a halt.

Despite pleas from a Labor government and appeals to patriotic duty, negotiations went nowhere until the Labor prime minister finally announced a program whereby miners who refused to return to work would be conscripted for military service. It was a revolutionary move because the Labor party in Australia traditionally opposed military conscription. But it was one of John Curtin's finest hours, and he had the near-unanimous support of the public and the media.

CHAPTER 20

Japan Threatens from New Guinea

While Douglas MacArthur was moving his command headquarters north to Brisbane, the Japanese were advancing south toward the Solomon Islands and New Guinea, both calculated steps along the

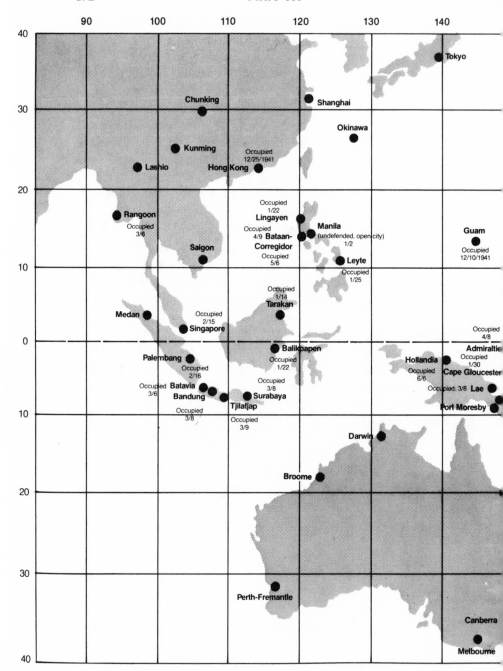

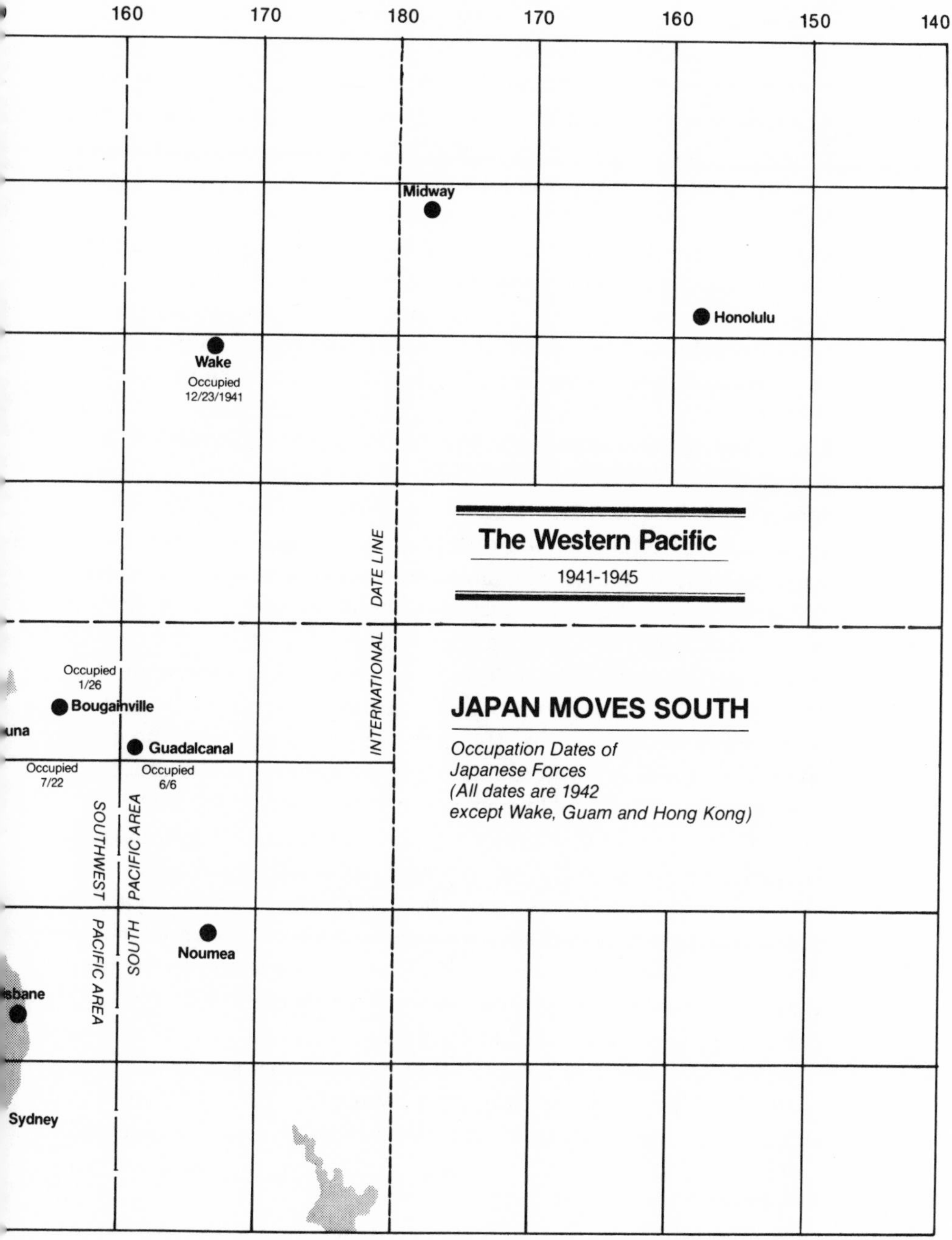

160　170　180　170　160　150　140

Midway

Honolulu

Wake
Occupied
12/23/1941

DATE LINE

INTERNATIONAL

The Western Pacific
1941-1945

Occupied
1/26
Bougainville

una

Guadalcanal

Occupied
7/22

Occupied
6/6

SOUTHWEST PACIFIC AREA

SOUTH PACIFIC AREA

JAPAN MOVES SOUTH

*Occupation Dates of
Japanese Forces
(All dates are 1942
except Wake, Guam and Hong Kong)*

Noumea

sbane

Sydney

road to Australia. Within just over two weeks, in early July, 1942, the enemy made his first landings on Guadalcanal Island at Lunga Point, then occupied Buna and Gona, two tiny but strategic villages on the north coast of New Guinea about a hundred miles northeast of Port Moresby, our only major base on New Guinea at that time.

Guadalcanal and the remainder of the Solomons lay in the South Pacific Area and were the responsibility of Adm. Chester W. Nimitz, but the whole of New Guinea lay in the Southwest Pacific Area and was of immediate concern to General MacArthur. Both targets were many hundreds of miles from our Sydney microphones, and Folster, Cuhel, and I never lessened our campaign for transmission facilities in New Guinea, but we received little in return except conversation.

Three months before the Japs hit Guadalcanal, American forces had occupied New Caledonia, the French island colony directly between the Solomons and Australia's most eastern point in Queensland, just below Brisbane. Here the U.S. Navy was building a base, naval and air, from which to protect our main shipping lanes between Australia and the States. The naval liaison officer in Sydney informed me (and probably my colleagues of the mike as well) that there were plans to develop a communications center in Noumea, capital of the island, to provide a direct link with our bases on our own mainland. He suggested I might be interested in transferring my personal base to Noumea and assured me the navy would welcome a radio correspondent. It was not an official suggestion, more on the order of a scotch-inspired idea, and I never gave it serious consideration because I couldn't see how it would solve my present transmission limitations. Guadalcanal was developing into a brutal conflict with the fate of Japan's southward progress very much on the line, but a brief glance at the map showed Noumea almost as far from Guadalcanal as Sydney was from New Guinea. Besides, I had already made up my mind that the real action on our road to the Philippines and Tokyo would come from the Southwest Pacific Area.

Japan's occupation of Buna-Gona provided immediate proof of John Curtin's wisdom in refusing to allow Winston Churchill to send the Australian troops anywhere but home. Several thousand Australians were lost as prisoners when Singapore surrendered, and those who had been in the Middle East and North Africa saved the bacon for the Allies while the United States, none too swiftly, brought up its own troops.

Within a week after landing at Buna, the enemy had moved inland about thirty miles to another native village, Kokoda, from which a tortuous "trail" extended over the rugged Owen Stanley range, east of the 13,350-foot Mount Victoria, leading directly south to Port Moresby.

Japan's original plan for denying New Guinea to the Allies ended in disaster for the enemy and our first victory since the start of the war. Port Moresby lies on the south coast of eastern New Guinea, facing the Coral Sea where it meets the Torres Strait. The Japanese proposed to send a task force from Rabaul, its newly acquired base on New Britain Island, around the eastern tip of New Guinea to attack Moresby from the sea. At the same time they hoped to flush out the main body of the Allied fleet so a larger force from the Solomons could engage and destroy it, obviously underestimating our recuperative powers.

The result, May 4–8, was utter defeat in the battle of the Coral Sea, the first naval battle ever fought entirely from the air. No ship engaged ever sighted an enemy ship, and not a single shot was fired by any ship's battery. Carrier-borne planes did the fighting and, except for the loss of the carrier Lexington with sixty-nine men and a tanker, the battle was one-sided. What the enemy didn't know was that we had broken their code and knew their plans in advance.

The Japanese retired after the loss of one carrier, severe damage to a second, and hits on transports and smaller craft. Of the 125 planes that launched the attack, 69 (or 70 percent) were lost, with pilot casualties over 50 percent. Our losses were largely confined to the Lexington, which was struck by two air-borne torpedoes and suffered internal explosions after the conflict ended. The Japanese had finally learned that the U.S. fleet, although crippled, did not die at Pearl Harbor.

Apparently convinced by their failure in the Coral Sea battle that Moresby could not be attacked successfully from the south, Japan determined to march across the intervening range and take that base from the rear. It was a wild idea from the first, but it just might have succeeded if Gen. Sir Thomas Blamey's matchless Diggers had not been available at that time.

The Kokoda Trail, actually even less than a footpath, started climbing as soon as it left Kokoda village and continued to mount precipitously through tropical rain jungles for nearly half the remaining seventy miles to the goal, rising thousands of feet to clear the unrelenting ridge that was the Owen Stanley range. It was hard enough for a soldier on foot, and transporting supplies, munitions, food, over a trail that would stump a barefoot native was almost impossible. Many necessities had to be left behind, including adequate food supplies.

Only a few miles to the south, the Australians were also climbing the Kokoda Trail on the southern slope, but they had one big advantage over the Japs—Gen. George Kenney's air force. Transports supplied ground troops on a scale never before known in modern warfare. The DC-3's, which the army called C-47's, accompanied the Diggers overhead, dropping tons of food, munitions, medical supplies, everything necessary to fight a war, all the things the enemy was trying vainly to transport by Korean coolies and native bearers.

It was no match, and when the two forces finally met high up in the forbidding ridge, the Japanese were in no physical or mental condition to fight anyone. Most were half-starved and many badly ill from eating poisonous berries in lieu of normal rations. Jungle diseases were rampant because of the lack of medical supplies and even guns and ammunition were in short supply and in poor condition. The retreat was a rout, and on November 2, just three months after the Japanese had left their Kokoda base to start their ill-fated safari, Australian troops moved into the Kokoda town square and raised an Australian flag dropped to them by some thoughtful fighter pilot. There was no fanfare. The flag was raised, and the Diggers left immediately in pursuit of the fleeing enemy, now rushing pell-mell northward to the coast and Buna.

During their incredibly bungled trek up the brutal trail, the Japanese command had continued to move troops into the Buna-Gona area, probably realizing that that primitive salient would soon be under heavy attack. The Japanese clearly regarded the great island of New Guinea as the gateway to Australia, an eleven hundred–mile barrier across the northeast corner of that continent which they dared not leave behind them. Having failed to threaten Moresby from the Coral Sea and again over the Owen Stanleys, they were determined to make a do-or-die stand in Buna, a base vital to any renewed drive toward coveted Port Moresby and to the conquest of New Guinea. They were reinforcing and digging in for just such a stand.

Meanwhile our navy was having its troubles in the Solomons. Vice Adm. Robert L. Ghormley commanded the fleet that was to place the First Marine Division on Guadalcanal, Tulagi, and a couple of smaller islands to the north of Guadalcanal. Early results were encouraging because the element of surprise was nearly perfect. It was one of the few things that did go right in the early campaign. Two regiments swarmed ashore at Lunga Point and after a few hours of struggle with the swamps and jungles, their first objective fell almost without opposition. The airstrip on which the Japanese had been working for weeks was captured, almost four thousand feet of graded runway nearly 85 percent paved with coral and dry cement. It was a prize beyond measure, and the marines promptly named it Henderson Field after a marine officer who died at Midway. It would be the scene of much bloody combat in the months ahead, but the enemy never regained it.

On the beaches behind these men, however, things were not progressing smoothly. The business of offloading supplies was not moving on schedule, and by nightfall much less than half the cargo had been brought ashore. Darkness also brought the Japanese fleet with a surprise of its own. An enemy task force, apparently hidden behind nearby Savo Island, caught Ghormley's defending columns completely off guard, and in the brief but lethal battle that ensued, four American cruisers were sunk and a fifth damaged. Then for some incomprehensible reason the Japanese withdrew, ignoring the helpless transports that would have been sitting ducks.

As the Japanese moved away to the north, the remainder of the American force, transports and escorts, weighed anchor and sailed south, clear out of combat, taking all the critical materiel that had not been unloaded and leaving the two marine regiments strictly on their own, undermanned and undersupplied. Nothing like this had ever happened in American military history, but it apparently had been decided that the Savo battle losses were insupportable and the marines would have to be abandoned to save the remaining ships.

That was the situation when Vice Adm. William F. Halsey succeeded Ghormley and swore to support the marines if it cost every ship in the navy. It took time to rectify the situation, but Halsey wasn't known as Bull Halsey throughout a brilliant career without reason. Fighting ships were useless, he said, if they weren't willing to fight.

In the Southwest Pacific observers like me were watching these developments as closely as distance would permit. Although the SWPA was not directly involved, there was still only one Pacific war, and missteps made in either area had to have an effect on the other. My own broadcast reports, however, dealt largely with New Guinea and Buna, where a major campaign was developing, and with General Ken-

ney's air forces, which were rapidly gaining the air control so necessary to ultimate victory.

One development we regularly reported was Kenney's continual
air strikes on Japanese bases in the northern Solomons, which represented MacArthur's effort to support the beleaguered First Marines.
Buin, on the southern tip of Bougainville, and Faisi, a few miles south
on Shortland Island, were important enemy air bases and staging areas
for the southward movement of troops and supplies. Both targets were
just barely within the range of our heavy bombers, and MacArthur
ordered their continual harassment. Guadalcanal itself lay another
three hundred miles to the southeast, and at that time we had no
long-range bombers that could cover the extra six hundred miles for
that round trip.

There was no other way MacArthur could help the marines. His
too few troops had to reinforce the Australians in New Guinea, and
he had no bottoms in which to move troops had they been available.
Finally, he was never asked for assistance. Guadalcanal was a U.S.
Navy operation, and Adm. Ernest J. King, chief of naval operations
in Washington made no secret of his intention of keeping it that way.

It was therefore disconcerting to hear reports coming in from the
South Pacific blaming the plight of the First Marines on the "refusal"
of Douglas MacArthur to come to their aid. Obviously, a powerful
element in the navy was not about to tell the beleagured marines that
the decision to abandon them came from one of their own. Just as
obviously a whipping boy was called for, and Douglas MacArthur was
there, just across the Coral Sea.

The men in the Guadalcanal jungles had no access to intelligence
reports, only whatever scuttlebutt filtered down to them, and the
cover-up campaign was effective. It was even put to verse:

> Oh, they sent for MacArthur
>   To come to Tulagi,
> But General MacArthur said: NO!
>   He gave as the reason
> It wasn't the season.
>   Besides, there was no U.S.O!

Even after Admiral Halsey reversed the situation and brought the
marines the aid they had to have, the MacArthur myth persisted.
There probably are veterans of Guadalcanal who still believe it. Interservice rivalry can be ruthless.

CHAPTER 21

The Owen Stanleys

My first flight over the Owen Stanley range, on November 24, 1942, is still deeply engraved in my memory despite the passage of nearly half a century. During my years with American before the war, I was taught that altitude was one of the finest forms of aerial insurance, a theory bolstered by the edicts of the FAA or whatever the regulating body might be in any particular country. The nonpressurized transports of that time normally cruised at from two to eight thousand feet, which meant you could relax in your seat and look out the cabin windows at vast expanses of your part of the world.

The airlift over the Owen Stanleys, however, operated on the very sound theory that altitude was a hazard to be avoided at all costs. The higher you flew the better your chances of being spotted by an enemy plane, and such an encounter could be unpleasant for a completely unarmed and defenseless transport. Consequently, when you looked out the window of a C-47 — not an easy feat when you were hunched in a bucket seat with your back to that window — you were gazing at trees, foliage, or rugged mountain terrain, always within a few feet of your wing tips and seemingly much closer. You got used to it after a few trips, but that first one could shake you.

My destination was Buna, where the Japanese were still fighting fiercely to hold their one base closest to the Australian mainland. For long weeks I had been reporting that battle based on the official communiqué, interviews with combat pilots down from New Guinea on rest and recreation detail, and the local press, which included some excellent reporters ("roundsmen" to their Aussie editors), several of whom were friends dating back to Asia.

New York seemed satisfied with this coverage, but I wasn't. There's a saying among war reporters that the closer you get to the front, the less you know about the war, and it carries a lot of truth. The GI in the front line knows only what a few men on either side of him are doing. The horizons of company and battalion commanders extend a few meters farther, but regimental and division command posts provide the only real chance of viewing the whole picture.

Further, no first-class correspondent is ever content to cover his story at second hand. The ideal way is to keep moving from command to command, sector to sector, returning regularly to GHQ or the highest local command to see how what you've uncovered in the field fits into the overall picture. That was one of the handicaps the radio reporter had to accept in that era of limited facilities. It took at least two days each way for a round trip from Sydney to New Guinea via assorted civil and military transportation, and a third day was probable. The entire situation could change in that length of time, but I still was determined to see some action for myself.

The American Red Cross had a fine reporter, George Moorad, in its Sydney information office, who was more than willing to spell me for a couple of weeks. I scheduled a trial broadcast, and when White accepted him, I headed north. A day in Brisbane renewed contacts with some of the staff members from Manila, then I was on to New Guinea as one of three passengers on a beaten-up old DC-2 belonging to one of the domestic air lines and piloted by an English civilian flying for Australia. We had been in the air no more than a few minutes when he came back and told us we would make an unscheduled landing at Townsville, some six hundred miles north of Brisbane, because it had a very long runway. Our brakes, he reported, were shot, and we would need all the runway possible to avoid what he termed "a certain amount of bother." Four hours or so later, we coasted into the wind on Townsville's runway which fortunately did prove to be very long. After a few tense seconds we rolled to a stop with a few inches to spare but marking the loss of the day it would take to repair the brakes and the hydraulic system that controlled them.

To designate Port Moresby a combat zone in December, 1942, was to stretch the facts a bit. The nearest enemy troops were beyond the Owen Stanleys, and the little port was surrounded by a group of airstrips that based some of George Kenney's finest fighter and bomber units in such strength as to discourage random enemy air activity in their vicinity. It had been several weeks since the Japanese had made a pass at the area, and the evidence was strong that they were concentrating their air arm on targets less well protected.

Still, it was so designated, and the designation had its fiscal advantages. Many of the charges an officer incurred for normal billeting were suspended in a combat area, and cigarettes were free! Cynics even hinted that our own pilots were staging occasional mock raids at night in order to keep the Moresby combat rating intact. That, of course, will never be proved, but even the correspondents relished the idea of not having to put out the few pennies their smokes cost them in the noncombat commissary or PX. The idea of something for nothing is always attractive, even for broadcasters with expense accounts.

The only press accommodations in Moresby at that time, provided by the Australians, were a bit primitive but comfortable, and the press officers were completely helpful. Still, my interest in that base was minimal and I wanted to continue northward. The next morning I was boosted into a dilapidated old truck that predated the war by at least ten years but carried in newly painted colors the proud name, "Madonna of Moresby." The GI and the Digger both had a penchant for naming any vehicle in which they rode or flew, and some of the names were from way out in left field. Despite the halflight of early dawn, the airlift was well under way when we reached the airstrip. The Madonna dropped me off at the operations shack, where an Aussie lieutenant took my name and gave me the number of the plane to which I was assigned. Within minutes a sergeant pointed to it coming in, a white towel or handkerchief fluttering from the cockpit window to signal it was carrying wounded.

Ambulances rushed to meet it and the wounded, most of them ambulatory, were offloaded in minimal time by dedicated crewmen while another crew stood by to begin loading supplies for the return flight. This C-47 (all the planes I saw in this operation were C-47's) bore the sobriquet "Eager Beaver," and this time it was no misnomer. In fact, every one of the more than twenty planes moving on and off the airstrip with efficient precision could have carried that same name. I had never seen a plane loaded manually with greater facility, and having spent many years on American airports, I was fascinated at the sight. When the pilot, a youngster from my native Indiana, finally signalled, I climbed aboard and we left without ceremony.

Pausing briefly to rev the engines, we headed directly toward the forbidding mountain barrier that extends some six hundred miles along the length of New Guinea's Papua territory. We were climbing, of course, but only enough to barely miss the treetops. Being the only passenger, I arranged a perch atop the cargo so I could look out a window, and that was a mistake. I certainly didn't like what I saw. The crew chief was squatting alongside, getting a big kick out of my obvious discomfort. He explained what I already knew: with camouflage livery of green and brown paint, our plane was taking full advantage of nature's variegated background.

We flew through a pass, probably at about eight thousand feet, with towering cliffs on either side, then began "skiing" down the northern slope, again using the foliage as cover. I had one bad moment (actually, I never relaxed for even a moment) when I spotted a fighter plane coming head-on, directly at us. The crew chief saw my reaction and shrugged. "P-40," he grinned as the plane pulled up to pass over us.

As we moved with the terrain down toward the coastline, I frankly wondered where in all that vast expanse of wilderness, broken only by occasional fields of cunei grass, we were going to find a place to set down. We flew over a tiny strip carved out of that six-foot grass where another C-47 was being loaded but continued another few kilometers before we banked sharply and side-slipped into another small clearing that the FAA would never have approved for a Piper Cub. My friend from Indiana was *good* at those controls, as were all those youngsters from all over the States who were manning the greatest military airlift ever known to that time. I crossed the Owen Stanleys many times in the following two years, but even after the enemy's air threat had been minimized in Papua and our C-47's could fly as high as they chose, memories of that first flight kept me from ever again opting for a window seat.

Gen. Sir Thomas Blamey, who had commanded Australia's forces in North Africa and the Middle East, was the top field commander in this campaign, reporting directly to General MacArthur. Under him was the U.S. First Corps (I Corps) commanded by Lt. Gen. Robert L. Eichelberger and consisting of the Thirty-second and Forty-first divisions and incidental units. Lt. Gen. Edmund F. Herring commanded the Fifth and Sixth Australian divisions.

Long weeks of lethal fighting had forced the Japanese into a narrowing area between the neighboring villages of Buna and Gona, and a decision was near. Both sides had suffered heavy losses, but the enemy was hit the hardest and was having great difficulty in reinforcing and supplying his units. George Kenney's innovative airlift was MacArthur's ace and would make a considerable contribution to final success.

My primary target was I Corps headquarters which, like everything else in this unprecedented jungle, was hard to find. There was no casual transportation in the Buna area. Every jeep and truck moved only on official business, and it became immediately obvious that I would have to do a lot of walking unless I could hitch a ride with a driver moving for a reason. Fortunately, a GI who had brought a returning officer to the Eager Beaver heard my questions and offered to take me within walking distance of my objective because his next assignment took him in that direction.

There were no conference tables in the Buna jungles, so when General MacArthur's intelligence officer crossed the Owen Stanleys for a conference with the First Corps command, the talks were *al fresco*. Here Maj. Gen. Charles Willoughby, G-2 SWPA (second from right), chats with Brig. Gen. Clovis Byers, General Eichelberger, myself, and Col. Tom Hamilton.

My GI friend drove me along a series of jungle paths just barely wide enough for the jeep. The driver, a sergeant, was on his way to pick up ambulatory wounded who would be returned to Moresby. The field hospitals, he explained, were barely adequate to care for the seriously wounded, so every effort was being made to evacuate all who could be moved without complication as quickly as possible. We were still in the middle of nowhere, as far as I could tell, when the sergeant braked to a halt and pointed to a footpath leading into the thicket at the left. "In there," he said. "Just follow that path and don't wander away from it!" With that he was off, leaving me to explore on my own.

A jungle is never silent, day or night. Even without the man-made thunder of war, there is the ceaseless chatter of birds, the perpetual drone of insects, and those other, unidentified sounds that might indicate the presence of almost anything living, particularly to the imagination of the uninitiated. Fortunately, the I Corps command was only about a hundred meters from the jeep trail, but even in that short distance it would have been easy to take a few false steps and lose the path completely. I would do just that during the next several days.

The clearing in which I Corps was based resembled a cross between Hollywood's version of an African *kraal* and a Boy Scout encampment. A couple of jerry-built huts were surrounded by tents, large and small, and great clouds of camouflage netting overhead added to the partial concealment provided by lush natural foliage. I expected to be challenged, but no sentry appeared. (I learned later that my approach had been observed from the time I left the sergeant.) Instead, I was greeted by a man I assumed to be an officer, clad in jungle greens but wearing no insignia. That gave him the advantage, because I was wearing my correspondent pin on my fatigues.

He extended a hand and introduced himself as Brig. Gen. Clovis Byers, I Corps chief of staff, and asked what news service I represented. It isn't often that you are greeted by a general officer in the middle of a jungle, and I learned later that New York doubted me completely. When I mentioned the meeting in my first cabled dispatch, White promptly demoted the general to a colonel "to make it more plausible." He knew that general officers didn't wander around the jungles of New Guinea looking for reporters in need of a hand. What had happened, of course, was that word of an approaching stranger had reached Byers, and he had walked out to see who I was. Infinitely more bizarre things have happened in combat zones all over the world. Formal protocol eases in the presence of a hostile enemy.

We talked for a few moments while I showed him my orders. He told me that General Eichelberger already was inspecting one of the forward positions in the Buna area and mentioned the presence of two fellow correspondents, Tilman Durdin of the *New York Times* and Al Noderer of the *Chicago Tribune*, both old friends. Finally he turned me over to a corporal who took me to the supply tent and issued me a shelter-half (two of them make a pup tent, and the good earth is the mattress). At this time both Durdin and Noderer appeared and offered to show me the ropes. Neither was wearing his correspondent insignia because, as General Byers had explained, General Eichelberger had banned the wearing of any metal insignia and ordered that all dog tags be taped to prevent reflections of sunlight that might catch the eye of a sniper or any enemy observer. This rule, I found later, did not apply to the corps commander himself, who visited the forwardmost position regularly, always wearing the three silver stars on his collar. "I want these youngsters to know the Old Man is up there with them," he explained.

Noderer, who had arrived only a short time before myself, offered to join shelter-halves, and we had our pup tent in short order, but Durdin's idea wasn't so simple. We had been warned of possible enemy shelling of the corps area, and everyone was advised to dig a foxhole. Til wanted me to join him in digging a shelter large enough for both of us. He had occupied a foxhole alone during an enemy shelling in Guadalcanal not long before and described it as his most terrifying experience of the war. If he had to undergo another bombardment, he wanted company! Why he chose me as a partner in the venture, in view of my excess avoirdupois, he never revealed, but the result was that the representative of CBS News spent his first day in a New Guinea jungle wielding a spade in 100-degree heat, sweating to dig an oversize foxhole which happily wasn't needed after all.

With no audiotransmission nearer than Sydney, some two thousand miles to the south, the time I could spend in New Guinea on a single trip was limited. What time I did have was devoted to checking division and regimental command posts, visiting field hospitals both as a reporter and as a victim of the trots, an ailment almost inevitable in the jungle, interviewing dozens of GI's and officers, and filling a notebook with information that would prove useful when I got back to my microphone.

On my third day General Eichelberger asked Noderer and me if we would like to accompany him on his round of forward positions. We accepted with alacrity, and the trip was rewarding, particularly the opportunity to see a corps commander in action in the field. At each stop he would signal a halt at what he considered a safe distance for noncombatants and order the two of us to stay there. ("I don't want any dead reporters around here.") He would then proceed on foot, accompanied only by an aide or an orderly, an imposing figure topping six feet, his three silver stars sparkling in the sunlight. Why he was never killed or wounded only the Almighty can answer, for he rivaled Douglas MacArthur in his disregard for the enemy. A few days earlier one of his aides had been severely wounded by his side, and a couple

of days later General Byers was hit in the hand by a bullet undoubtedly intended for his chief. Noderer and I disregarded "orders" suffi-
ciently to keep him in sight, but frankly neither of us had any overwhelming desire to stroll leisurely through an area where everyone
else was either prone or behind barriers.

During a stop at a field hospital on the way back to I Corps, the
general spent considerable time with the commanding colonel, inquiring about the general condition of the wounded and asking about
several special cases. He was particularly concerned about punctual
arrival of medical supplies, but seemed satisfied with what he learned.
The supply line was functioning. Then he walked into the great can-
vas-covered ward and talked briefly with a dozen or more of the men,
asking sympathetic and understanding questions, obviously taking a
reading on the standard of morale. For most of these men combat had
ended. Morale seemed surprisingly high, possibly just for that reason.
Most, but not all of the men seemed to appreciate the general's personal interest. A couple of them were rather curt in their answers and
one, apparently recognizing the three silver stars, turned his face away.

I learned later that many of the men who fought at Buna-Gona felt
they had been called on for much too much, and, as the one American commander on their immediate horizon, the corps commander
became the target of their ire. Some GI's were even referring to him
as the "Butcher of Buna," as baseless as the "Dugout Doug" sobriquet
the GI's of Bataan fastened on MacArthur. Although General MacArthur was in Port Moresby during most of the Buna campaign, he never
crossed the Owen Stanleys until much later. The soldier on the front
line was hardly aware of his existence, but he was well aware of the
corps commander and Eichelberger thus became a natural target for
the unhappy.

I became a firm admirer of Bob Eichelberger, developing a friendship that lasted until his death long after the war. No commander
ever felt a deeper concern for his men, but he had his orders, directly
from the C-in-C: "Take Buna or let me know that your lifeless body
has been found on the field of battle." He took Buna, with the vital
assistance of General Herring and his Australian divisions, but the
cost was high on both sides.

Some critics feel that the Buna campaign was MacArthur's biggest
mistake of the war, that the base could have been neutralized at much
less cost and, once isolated, left to wither. If Buna really was a mistake, it was one MacArthur never repeated. From that time he spe-

cialized, expertly, in the island-skipping technique, profiting from the advice of Wee Willie Keeler, an oldtime baseball player he had admired in his West Point days, to "Hit 'em where they ain't!"

When the time came to return to my Sydney mike, General Eichelberger invited me to join him for breakfast. It was not as formal an invitation as it may sound, because I Corps had only one mess, a long table made of wooden planks placed over wooden sawhorses. Mess was served in relays until all personnel had eaten. We talked about our families, and he spoke of "Miss Em," whom he had married when he was only a shavetail just out of West Point and to whom he wrote a letter of at least a few lines every day.

"Bill," he said in parting, "in one of your broadcasts mention that you have seen me and that I and my staff are all in good health. Miss Em or one of the wives will hear you and spread the word to the others."

I looked at him in surprise. "General, I'd love to do just that but have you forgotten? You (and all units and personnel in the Buna campaign) are completely off the record." His face fell and he looked as dejected as the lad who couldn't go to the picnic. "That's right. I *had* forgotten." He shook his head in obvious disappointment. "What's the good of being a general?"

My too-brief visit to the Buna area merely underlined what I already knew. You can't be a war correspondent without a war! My fellows of the microphone were of course in full agreement, but it took us nearly ten months to convince GHQ that the time had come to break the electronic bonds of Australia.

S-P-E-C-I-A-L   R-E-P-O-R-T

Transport Plane

Back in December, 1935, I had stood on the apron at Clover Field, the company airport of the Douglas Aircraft Corporation in Santa Monica, and witnessed one of the greatest forward steps in the history of air transportation. It was the first test flight of the Douglas DC-3, a revolutionary new transport plane that would rewrite all existing ideas of commercial flying. What I didn't realize was that I was also attending the birth of a great new military weapon, a tool that would contribute, all out of proportion to its original concept, to Allied success in a future Pacific war and to the ultimate overthrow of the Japanese empire.

I was at that time publicity director of American Airlines (AA), and the DC-3 was then an AA exclusive, not because Douglas was being selective in its customers, but because, incredibly, no other airline would have anything to do with it. The basic idea of the DC-3 was obviously too advanced, possibly "radical" would be a better term, for acceptance.

The Douglas DC-2, immediate predecessor of this new plane, was a fourteen-passenger transport powered by two Wright Cyclone engines, F-2 or F-3A, each rated at 710 horsepower. It probably was the equal of any transport of that time and certainly the most popular, but it had the same deficiency as all commercial planes of the mid-thirties. It could not lift and carry a payload sufficient to enable an airline to make money without subsidies.

William ("Bill") Littlewood, American's vice-president for engineering, was trying to find a solution to this vital problem when the Wright Aeronautical Corporation advised him it was ready to introduce a new Cyclone, the G-2, which would deliver 1,000 horsepower. For the DC-2 this meant a potential increase in available power of just over 40 percent, and it also meant that a DC-2 powered with two G-2's would have considerably more power than it needed. That gave Bill Littlewood the inspiration that would transform the entire aerospace industry: why not split the DC-2 fuselage from nose to tail and widen it to accommodate another row of seats with a comparable increase in the overall payload capability? His slide rule and long hours of study and research told him the result would be the first transport plane that could actually make money.

C. R. Smith, only recently named president of American, bought the idea instantly. His faith in Littlewood was complete. If Bill said this was the plane they needed and vouched for its performance, that was good enough for him. It took some selling to convince his board of directors that a "stretch version" of an existing plane would be aeronautically sound, however. The idea of a "stretch version" had never been advanced before and was greeted with almost universal skepticism, inside as well as outside the corporation. But he got approval of the initial order, six planes in the sleeper-plane configuration to be known as the DST (Douglas Sleeper Transport) and fourteen, with an option for another twenty, in the twenty-one-passenger DC-3 configuration, basically the same plane. All this from a reluctant board.

Next came the task of selling Donald Douglas the idea. Douglas didn't question the merit of Littlewood's proposition, but he had an unprecedented backlog of orders for 150 DC-2's and was understandably reluctant to disturb his smoothly operating assembly line for American's relatively small order for a different plane. But again, C. R. Smith prevailed, and the plane went into production. Even then no one else in the industry showed any faith or genuine interest, and American had all six of its DST's in operation before Douglas got another order. Then came the deluge!

C. R. continued to encounter doubt within his own organization until the plane proved itself in operation. He had approved a publicity promotion I organized with the Columbia Broadcasting System whereby the network would install a transmitter in the first DST delivered and make a series of nationwide broadcasts from the air while the plane was making its first transcontinental flight. The CBS producer and announcer had joined me in Hollywood and the engineers were just leaving New York when C. R. called me from Chicago, then our corporate headquarters, abruptly cancelled the entire promotion, and hung up before I could ask any questions.

That was completely unlike C. R., and I sensed something beyond his control; he would never change his mind so abruptly without cause. We had discussed the promotion in great detail and he seemed enthusiastic. Sure enough, he called me later to explain that his first call was made from a conference room where the nervous directors were deciding that they probably had made a major mistake in approving the idea of such a plane originally and were determined not to be on a nationwide broadcast network if the plane crashed en route!

In view of the distinguished record of the DC-3 and its military versions in the past half-century, and they are still flying all over the globe, it is almost impossible to credit the skepticism and opposition to the DC-3 at the time of its introduction. "Stretch versions" of existing planes are commonplace today, of course, but fifty years ago the idea was unheard of and thoroughly distrusted. At that moment, it seems that only two executives in the entire air transport industry—C. R. Smith and Bill Littlewood—had the vision to believe in the airplane that would revolutionize air travel and provide immeasurable help in defeating a bitter enemy in a not-too-distant war. Douglas would have built the plane eventually but, in the face of almost universal skepticism, it might have taken a long time to happen—perhaps too long.

Finally I was given orders, directly from the board, not to disclose any movements of the plane in advance. That order nearly cost me my job. When the skeptical directors assembled at Chicago's Midway Airport to mark the arrival of the doubtful flying machine, one of the first persons they saw was Wayne Thomis, aviation editor of the *Chicago Tribune*, and, of course, Dunn was to blame. It took C. R.'s intervention plus the fact that the plane actually had *not* crashed en route to calm them down!

When I first arrived in New Guinea, I thought I knew quite a bit about the capabilities of the DC-3, having been present at its birth, having watched it move into universal acceptance, and having flown it as a passenger all over Asia and Australia. But it was in New Guinea that I learned what an airplane it really was.

The military version was basically the same as the DC-3 of Clover Field except for a much larger cargo door, bucket seats for an obvious overload of GI's, and its designation. The army called it the C-47 (it was the Dakota to the British and Anzacs) and treated it like a Mack truck. It thrived on overloads, unpaved airstrips, undertrained crews, and continuous overwork, and it obviously recognized none of its limitations as spelled out so meticulously at the time of its original certification by the FAA a half-dozen years before.

In October-November of 1942 two regiments of the U.S. Thirty-first Division were flown across the Owen Stanleys to Buna in the first mass movement of troops by air in history, and both the American and Australian divisions that fought that bitter battle were almost entirely supplied by the C-47 airlift, operating in all kinds of weather with loads that would never have been cleared from any full-length, perfectly paved runway in the United States. All this with crew members who only a few months earlier would have been proud to be trusted with the family tractor back in Iowa or Indiana. The first pilot who flew me over the big ridge was proud of having logged nearly four hundred hours in very few months. No domestic airline of that time would even consider an application for a copilot's seat unless the applicant could show a log of at least a thousand hours.

There were scores of stories of the feats performed by the C-47, but my favorite, which I didn't believe until I checked it out personally, was of the C-47 that landed on one of Moresby's cargo strips, due for a change of crew. The plane was scheduled to pick up a load of pierced plank, the steel airport matting used to surface dirt strips and as heavy as steel is bound to be. A full load of this matting (a gross overload by all FAA standards) would cover the floor of a C-47 to a depth of about four inches. After the departing crew chief ordered the plank onloaded and covered with a tarp, the plane still looked empty. When the relief crew chief arrived, he found the same loading order and had a *second* load of steel placed on top of the first, which neither he nor the pilot realized. When the time came for takeoff the pilot remarked that the plane seemed sluggish, but apparently he wasn't experienced enough to suspect the reason.

He moved the plane to the end of the field and, after a brief rev-up, opened the throttle and started down the runway. Fortunately it was a long strip, because he needed every inch of it, just managing to get the plane off the ground before running out of field. Airborne, barely, he was unable to climb and had sense enough to avoid a stall by not trying. Miraculously, he managed to inch the plane around in a great circle and get back on the ground. Taxiing, still with difficulty, back to operations, the shaken pilot told the major, "There's something very wrong with this plane!" A brief inspection brought the reply, "If there was anything wrong with this plane, you wouldn't be here talking to me." A double overload of steel matting may not have been the biggest load the C-47 ever lifted, but it certainly is sufficient to prove the incredible abilities of the airplane, the same plane most of the airlines wouldn't believe could fly!

C. R. Smith, called into the service, went on to wear the two stars of a major general and headed the Air Transport Command before the war ended, but I am convinced, based on my own experience, that his greatest contribution to the Pacific war came much earlier, when he challenged his board of directors and induced Donald Douglas to build the DST.

CHAPTER 22

Home

The year 1943 saw steady if unspectacular progress both in the Solomons and New Guinea as we gradually forced the Japanese northward. The year opened with the successful conclusion of the Buna-Gona campaign, and the intervening months, leading to holiday landings on Cape Gloucester, saw us clearing the enemy out of New Guinea's Huon Gulf area with the capture of Lae, Salamaua, and Finschhafen.

The key to the area was the native village of Lae, situated on the extreme northwest corner of the gulf at the mouth of the Markham River. The Japanese had built Lae into a base of considerable importance. Only a few miles west was Nadzab, one of their major strategic air bases, soon to become our principal air base north of the Owen Stanleys. Japan's determination to defend and retain control of this area led to our most spectacular victory of the year, a victory I was unable to report.

In March, 1943, with inadequate air cover, the enemy tried to run a large convoy of transports, supply ships, and naval escorts to Lae and the gulf. The route ran through the Bismarck Sea, which lies to the north of New Guinea and New Britain, and through the Vitiaz Straits, which separate the two islands. The Japs' need for reinforcement and supply was becoming critical. On March 1, one of Kenney's scouting planes sighted the convoy, and the Allied air forces took it under attack immediately. Within the next four days the entire convoy was either destroyed or turned back. The final score is still debated, but General Kenney later told me his personal investigation satisfied him that at least twenty ships of all types were sunk. The fate of the Huon Gulf had been sealed. All further supply communication had to be by barges traveling at night or by submarine.

The Battle of the Bismarck Sea was heralded as the first naval engagement in which the victors fought without the aid of any naval combat participants, but I remembered that dark day in Rangoon in December, 1941, when we learned that Japanese planes had sunk the *Prince of Wales* and the *Repulse* off the east coast of Malaya. That action had convinced me that no naval might could stand against air attacks without the protective canopy of comparable air power. The Japanese obviously had forgotten the lesson they themselves had taught.

At the time of the Bismarck Sea victory, however, I was heading east for my first home leave in twenty-five months. In February of 1943 Paul White apparently decided that my "three months" had expired and suggested I return for a change of scenery. I had experienced several attacks of homesickness in those months of separation from a too-patient wife and a daughter just moving into her teens and now that the suggestion had been made, I lost no time in complying. I was fortunate in having an experienced and completely competent reporter to take over the microphone. George Moorad had done an excellent job for us during my trip to New Guinea, and the Red Cross was willing to let him repeat. I was on my way in hours.

My return from the Pacific was in sharp contrast to my outward journey two years earlier. At that time I had made the trip from the Golden Gate to Diamond Head aboard the *Matsonia*, a luxury liner, and had completed the jaunt from Pearl Harbor to Manila in one of Pan American's big clippers, first class all the way. Returning, I took whatever accommodations flying freighters could provide on or among their more important cargoes of war supplies. At Pearl Harbor, along with a rear admiral and a marine corps colonel, I was promoted to a "converted" navy bomber. Passenger accommodations were limited to one seat, which of course was assigned to the ranking officer with his two stars. The colonel and I made ourselves as comfortable as possible on the floor—the bomb bay doors that happily had been sealed. The admiral offered to take turns, but the colonel and I demurred. Actually, we were a quite congenial trio. The colonel, a personable chap with the eagle pinned to his collar, was on his way to Washington for special assignment, although neither I nor the admiral was aware of it. The next time I saw the man who had shared the bomb bay floor with me, that eagle had been replaced with four silver stars: Gen. Clifton B. Cates, commandant of the U.S. Marine Corps. No NASA shuttle ever made a more rapid ascent.

In the armed forces, a brief respite from combat duty is termed R and R, for rest and recreation. That does not necessarily apply to a correspondent on home leave. In five weeks' absence from the Pacific, I found myself merely hoping for a bit of rest. Recreation, if you excepted luncheons, dinners, and cocktail parties, was completely out of the question. From the time I deplaned at New York's LaGuardia Airport into the welcoming arms of my family, the powers-that-be came up with endless ideas for things I might do for the good of CBS. Who could say no?

My plane landed about four in the afternoon, and White expressed disappointment at my decision to spend the remainder of the day in a home I hadn't seen in two years instead of rushing directly to our newsroom on the upper levels of Madison Avenue. During those weeks I divided my time, on the basis of suggestions that bordered on being

This is a somewhat backward view of the first three members of the newly formed CBS News. I, who was the first editor of CBS News, am pointing out the scene of the Pacific action to Matt Gordon and Henry Wefing during my first home leave. *Courtesy CBS News*

orders, between New York, Washington, and Chicago, managing a couple of days in South Bend with my parents. Catherine was able to be with me most of this time, but Patricia (who had grown six inches since I last saw her!) was tied to her classroom and had to settle for only occasional moments with her dad.

The first thing I had done was to shed my uniform and invest in some civilian clothes, but in Washington a Pentagon press officer chided me, "Are you ashamed of your uniform?" I didn't want to admit I was just plain tired of being told what I had to wear, but I did an about face and a new set of civvies was relegated to mothballs.

In Chicago the manager of WBBM, our top Midwest station, cajoled me into attending a dinner of the executive committee of the

Red Cross, a group of top-rank business executives whose primary qualification for the committee was a personal ability to dig down and help underwrite Red Cross programs. The guest of honor and speaker was to be Maj. Gen. Alexander Vandegrift, commander of the First Marine Division on Guadalcanal and one of the outstanding heroes of the early war years. I admired the general and really welcomed a chance to meet him and exchange impressions of the Pacific war. General Vandegrift acknowledged the toastmaster's introduction, then looked at his watch and apologized for not being able to postpone a plane departure that required him to leave immediately. He explained, however, that he had a qualified substitute, and he turned to me. "I have worked with war correspondents ever since this war began, and not one of them has ever let me down." With that and a quick handshake the commander of the First Marine Division on Guadalcanal was gone, leaving one astounded correspondent wishing himself back in the wilds of New Guinea!

Early in the leave I met with some of the best CBS engineers to ask for ideas that might improve our product from the Pacific, but the answers were negative. All they could do was to make sure all was perfect with the network, and that they did. I was in the hands of the Signal Corps and the Australian government.

It was wonderful to be with my family again, if only for a few hectic days, but we knew that another decision had to be made. This time White indicated that while he would like for me to return, the decision must be my own. It wasn't easy. We had already been separated for too long a time, and for two weeks after the fall of Java my girls hadn't known if they still had, or ever would have again, a husband and a father. There would always be the chance that agony might be repeated, without a happy ending. Still, Catherine knew the Pacific war was very personal to me. I had lived with it since before it began, had invested important years of my career, and had seen it claim the lives of very close friends. Furthermore, I still had many friends out there committed to seeing it through. Catherine agreed it would be fundamentally wrong to quit after having come so far. Only she knows how she reached her final resolution.

Getting back to the Pacific wasn't too easy this time, because my friends at the Air Transport Command gave me a flat turn-down. My orders from the War Department, they pointed out, didn't indicate any specific date when I was to report for duty, so there was no need to enlist the speed of a flying machine. I could swim or take a canoe as far as they were concerned.

As a matter of fact, for security reasons the orders specified no destination either, and theoretically at least I was the only passenger on my particular Liberty ship who knew we were bound for Australia. Our skipper, however, had a very definite idea as to where we might be going. Shortly after we moved westward under the Golden Gate span, he staged the usual boat drill. He summoned all passengers, among whom I was the only nonserviceman, and announced there would be no more boat drills. "We are carrying nothing below decks except explosives. If we ship a torpedo or a bomb there will be no need of lifeboats!" Despite that happy thought, my five hectic weeks of feverish activity were balanced by five weeks in a "dog house" on the deck of a wartime freighter where rest was unavoidable and recreation consisted of a nightly poker game, two-bit limit, in the ward room. I was a thoroughly rested and recreated reporter when I finally debarked in Brisbane.

CHAPTER 23

No Young Veterans?

Just before Christmas in 1943, word finally came down from Port Moresby that the Signal Corps at last had developed a transmitter that could span the Coral Sea with a broadcast signal capable of being relayed from Sydney to the West Coast. I never understood why it took so long to accomplish. It could not have been technical difficulties, because we definitely had the know-how, and I felt there had to be a political angle involved. For example, as long as we were operating on Australian soil, including Port Moresby, both governments had an equal say in the matter of nonmilitary censorship. Once we moved north of Papua (Port Moresby was its capital), the sole jurisdiction would rest with the American (Allied) command. But all my efforts to elicit an answer resulted only in double-talk.

The date set for our start of operations was most opportune, as it turned out. December 17 was only a week before the not-yet-announced landings on the Cape Gloucester beaches of New Britain Island, possibly the reason that particular date was chosen. But reasons were no longer important. What mattered was that (fingers crossed) we were going to have an operating microphone within accessible range of the combat areas. I left for New Guinea immediately, hopes high.

GHQ had, I discovered, created living quarters for the media far superior to those on my previous visit. The camp, known to all as the "Country Club," was situated in a palm grove on the shore of a small cove on the Coral Sea, just outside Moresby. A large headquarters building, a tribute to the talent of the plywood artists, was matched by a mess hall only a few yards distant combining more plywood with yards of wire screening and adjoined by a galley that really knew how to make the most of army rations. These buildings were surrounded by tents with wooden floors and comfortable cots, plywood and canvas structures with screened sidewalls that could be opened to the breezes wafting in from the sea.

One apparent drawback was the large number of palm rats that were in the grove before we arrived and showed no intention of leaving. I soon learned that despite their size, about that of an average kitten, they were harmless. At least I never heard of any untoward incidents. They seemed to be vegetarians, born and nurtured in palm trees, with no interest in the intruders. Still, it was a bit disconcerting to relax on a cot and watch the happy rodents racing up and down the electric wires that hung loosely from the peak of each tent.

I hadn't come two thousand miles from Sydney in search of comfort, however. My only legitimate interest was the studio and transmitter that was to link New Guinea and New York and the nation in between. Both were housed in what appeared to have been an old boathouse on a pier that jutted into the bay. To my nontechnical eyes, it seemed to be the answer. It was not.

On the morning of December 17, I sat down in front of a brand-new microphone for my report scheduled for the news roundup on the evening of the sixteenth in New York. I had an important story. Our troops had successfully landed on Arawe Island, just off the southwest coast of New Britain about 250 miles north of Port Moresby. It was the first move toward neutralizing Rabaul, located on the eastern tip of New Britain and Japan's most important base south of Truk. The tests went well, and I delivered the report with a great feeling of elation, which evaporated when I learned the circuit had failed after less than a minute. The technicians insisted the matter would be cleared quickly.

That evening I was scheduled for a second report, and again the

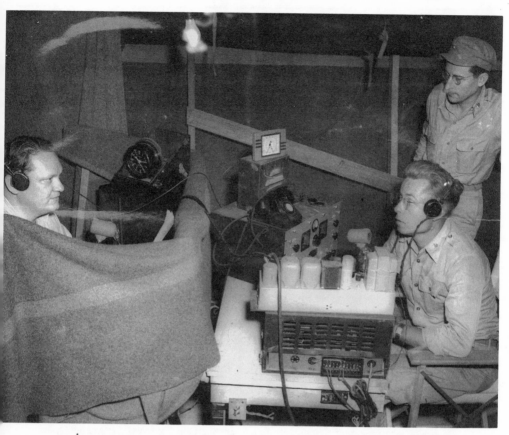

Broadcasting from a jungle holds its hazards, first of which are odds against getting your voice out of those smothering blankets and throwing it clear across the Pacific. But the Signal Corps never quit trying, and much of the news that reached the American public from the Pacific originated in such unlikely "studios" as this one in New Guinea. *Courtesy U.S. Army Signal Corps*

tests were encouraging. After disposing of the news from Arawe, I attempted to give the people back home some idea of what my change of base would entail:

> Tonight I am reporting to you directly from General MacArthur's New Guinea headquarters—from a small studio just completed in one of the numerous palm groves that sprinkle this great island. I am talking from the very heart of Allied activity in the Southwest Pacific, surrounded by airstrips and military installations. From time to time you undoubtedly will hear planes in the air above this microphone, but here's a tip: if you do hear planes during these reports,

Several makeshift studios were tried at Port Moresby before this masterpiece of plaster-board and plywood did the job. Here I made the first broadcast from the new facility while my colleagues looked on. To my right is Royal Gunnison of MBC and to my left is Col. Abe Schechter. Standing, from left, are Sgt. Don Campbell, Lt. Stanley Quinn, unidentified, Clete Roberts of NBC Blue, George Folster of NBC, Art Feldman of MBS, and Capt. Donald Weiss. The NCO at the right also is unidentified. *Courtesy U.S. Army Signal Corps*

you can be pretty sure they are Allied planes. This studio is well within reach of enemy planes from several directions, but our successes of the past few months have placed it pretty well beyond enemy ambitions.

It was also well beyond the reach of CBS News. The circuit had failed again, this time, according to Sydney, because of atmospherics across the Pacific. Two more failures followed in rapid succession. I wired White I was leaving Moresby to cover an important story in person, and then, if there was no marked technical improvement, I would return to Sydney. By this time we knew that the First Marines, having recuperated from Guadalcanal with an extended rest and rehabilitation period in Australia, were to be landed on Cape Gloucester, the westernmost tip of New Britain. The landings at Arawe had been a feint to mislead the enemy, and it had worked beautifully.

As usual, White accepted my decision with silence. He almost never answered my messages unless he disagreed. All he wanted, apparently, was to be kept informed. I had also learned that one of his weaknesses as a remote-control boss was his inability to read a map —and there were reams of maps in the New York newsroom—and visualize the actual distances involved. Early one Christmas season he had asked me to set up holiday broadcasts by service men and women in three bases as widely separated as Montreal, Key West, and Panama, all within a twenty-four hour period—and that with no jet transportation available! (This same geographer had suggested I might survey the entire Far East in three months.)

I prepared a broadcast for my December 24 schedule and left the script with an officer of Armed Forces Radio to be read in my absence. Then I left for Cape Sudest on the north Guinea coast, where Adm. Dan Barbey was assembling the amphibious task force that would put the marines ashore. I had yet to make an actual beachhead landing, and if I did have to return to Sydney it would have been hard to foresee the next opportunity.

The half-dozen correspondents accompanying the force all assembled in the admiral's quarters aboard his flagship for the briefing. As Barbey and his aides explained the objectives and proposed schedules for the operation, he was in exceptional spirits. "As you men know," he told us, "it is customary to keep correspondents under wraps after their briefing on any given operation. Actually, you will have no opportunity to fall into enemy hands, at least not until the operation is well under way, but I'll tell you frankly, it wouldn't make any difference. This operation has been so well organized and we are so well equipped, both on the sea and in the air, that there's nothing the Japanese can do effectively, even if they knew our plans in detail." I never heard another task force commander so outstandingly optimistic, but events proved him right.

The marines we were sending into action were a magnificent mix of veterans who had learned their jungle warfare in the Solomons and eager replacements not long out of boot camp, anxious to show the "old men" they could fight with the best. Early in my career as a reporter I was given a style book by the United Press that contained all the usual "do's" and "don't's." One of the "don't's" I have never forgotten, because I've seen it disproved too many times. We were told never to use the term *old veteran,* because it was obviously redundant. I hadn't spent many minutes aboard the destroyer-transport to which I was assigned before I knew that not all veterans are old! The company of marines we were carrying had a nucleus of veterans—all youngsters in their twenties. At that time, some two years after Pearl Harbor, Douglas MacArthur was heading an American and Australian force that boasted a priceless leavening of young veterans of some strenuous campaigns, both in the Pacific and North Africa. They were the backbone of the Allied effort. (My apologies to the United Press.)

The lads moving toward the Gloucester beaches were not only youthful veterans, they were *United States Marines* (the italics are theirs), and they never let you forget it. As soon as they learned there was a reporter on board, they demanded that I "tell the folks back home the marines did it," phrased in a dozen different ways. The company we carried was under the command of Capt. Marshall Moore, also a youngster with the whole of the Solomons campaign behind him. He was an upstate New Yorker from Geneva who believed wholeheartedly in his men and in the task ahead. He solemnly advised me it was no happenstance that his group had been picked to lead the assault, because his group "was the best in the unit, and the unit was the best in the entire marine corps."

It took thirty-six hours to reach the Gloucester target, and most of the men spent the daylight hours on deck, cleaning their rifles—taking them apart, oiling each part meticulously, then reassembling them, sometimes two or more times. Bayonets and machetes were sharpened again and again. The whole scene was marked by continuous conversation, much of it banter but also some serious words about what they had experienced at Guadalcanal and what they could expect on the morrow. Moore spent hours with his junior officers in the ward room, poring over maps and aerial photographs and making sure each man understood his assignment down to the last detail. We were scheduled to start the landings on the morning of the twenty-sixth, and on the evening of the twenty-fifth—Christmas evening—Moore advised me to keep an eye on his men. The eve of any landing, he explained, is when nerves begin to fray, if they are going to fray, and tension can begin to mount. As far as I could tell, there was no noticeable difference from the preceding night. If there was any unusual tension, it wasn't apparent to a reporter who spent most of his time with them. I took a lot of personal ribbing for being on a

combat mission without being ordered. No one remarked on my remarkable courage. The kindest words addressed me were variations
of "you must be some kind of a damned fool!"

Our destroyer was under the command of Lt. Comdr. V. C. Allen
of Burlington, Iowa (the U.S. Navy could not exist without the great
Middle West), and we carried the flag of Comdr. James Willis of West
Virginia (still far from any ocean), commodore of our division. He set
sail from Cape Sudest on Christmas Eve, and our marines spent Christmas Day cruising a tropical sea with the nearest Christmas tree some
thousands of miles distant. Thanks to our skipper, however, these
American youngsters got a genuine homestyle Christmas dinner. Allen took the situation very seriously. "This will be the last Christmas
dinner a lot of these boys will ever eat," he told me. "No one is going
to miss a Christmas dinner on my ship."

The ship's galley outdid itself. At midday the call was sounded,
and the warriors lined up for a repast most of them probably have
never forgotten: roast turkey and stuffing, baked ham, cranberry sauce,
mashed potatoes and giblet gravy, asparagus, string beans, carrots,
bread and butter, coffee, and plenty of pickles and olives on the side.
Portions were unlimited, and anyone could pass through the line as
often as he desired. Only the soup went begging because most of the
men reserved their mess cups for coffee. A full breakfast of ham, bacon, eggs, toast, coffee, and fruit juice was waiting at daybreak on the
twenty-sixth before the men left to hit the beaches. Captain Allen
repeated his vow that no warrior would ever leave his ship to meet
the enemy on an empty stomach. The skipper of any naval vessel from
a landing barge to a battleship is in complete command of that craft
as long as it is at sea, but not all skippers agree with Captain Allen
on the subject of food. Al Noderer, the *Chicago Tribune* reporter who
made the run on a neighboring destroyer-transport, told me the captain of his craft announced they were "not going on a picnic . . . this
is war!" And his gyrenes spent their Christmas Day and hit the beach
on iron rations.

As we moved in to the beach in early morning, Commander Willis
gave me a schedule of operations, and I positioned myself on a corner
of the bridge, watch in hand, to check the coordination. Everything
moved exactly as planned, and the instantaneous switch from almost
complete silence to deafening cacaphony was startling. First the screening cruisers, some miles behind us, began their bombardment of the
beaches. Blinding sheets of flame blotted out each warship from sight

momentarily, then an exact pattern of shells moving in a perfect parabola arced overhead to burst on the beaches. The bombardments at Leyte and Lingayen would prove even greater, but Gloucester was enough to make you glad you weren't on the receiving end. The great tracer shells, amazing in their deceptively lazy progress, moved overhead with all the apparent lassitude of a covered wagon. The marines, equipped for the shore assault, lined the decks to watch. Again on schedule, the bombardment ended as suddenly as it began. The startling silence was almost instantly interrupted, however, by George Kenney's bombers, heavy and light, moving in from the south and west to unload their cargoes into the target area with lethal accuracy.

Just as the cruisers ended their bombardment the order was given to lower the boats and barges, and as soon as the craft touched the water the marines began to swarm down the rope ladders to climb aboard. The last to leave was Captain Moore, who had been standing by the rail and checking his men as they went overside. I accompanied Captain (his command rank) Allen down from the bridge for a parting handshake with Moore, then watched the marines quickly disappear into the covering smokescreen that the light bombers had laid down. The continuing operation of the light bombers over dry land was so close to the beaches that the slightest error in their bombing and strafing runs would have been disastrous. But there were no mistakes. It was a precision operation, a revealing demonstration of what perfect coordination of land, air, and sea forces could accomplish.

Once the marines were firmly on land, fortunately with only minimal opposition, my own goal was to reach the nearest microphone as quickly as possible, and that meant Moresby. I would have an even break with AP and UP if my mike didn't let me down. All the wire service reporters were in this same task force, and my chance of reaching a microphone was just as good as their chances of reaching transpacific Morse transmission.

On the return, aboard ship, I wrote a lengthy report to file if my mike was still recalcitrant. At Cape Sudest the next morning I fortunately found a cargo plane heading for Moresby almost as soon as we moored, and I was back at the Country Club on schedule. I filed my report immediately and voiced a broadcast that did reach the network, if not too clearly. Still, it was good to get through at all, because Cape Gloucester was an important step toward Manila and Tokyo, a key move in MacArthur's overall plan for reconquest of our lost territories.

The Gloucester maneuver marked our first territorial occupation north of New Guinea and moved us another stride in the direction we had to follow. It also isolated Rabaul, Japan's most important base south of Truk and a thorn that had rankled ever since our arrival in the Southwest Pacific. Cape Gloucester lies on the exact opposite tip of New Britain from Rabaul, approximately three hundred miles to the west, and our occupation placed us squarely across the sea lanes that supplied that base. This was the first major example of the "island skipping" technique MacArthur was to perfect so profitably—isolating an enemy base and leaving it to distintegrate instead of trying to capture or destroy it—a ploy that saved countless American and Australian lives.

When I finished my filing that morning, Ed Hughes, one of the press officers, handed me a script I had left for broadcast during my absence. On the margin was a pencilled note: "Bill, you ain't a virgin any more. Got thru—rated fair but useable. Ed." "Fair" seemed to be the best I could hope for after ten days of trying, so I reluctantly decided to return south and wait for some technical improvements at the Country Club.

From the time that we established a major base at Cape Gloucester on New Britain in January, 1944, the Japanese were beaten, at least to the extent that they had no longer even a faint chance of ultimate victory. A considerable faction in Tokyo knew it well.

The year 1943 had been a year of unbroken reverses for the emperor's forces. Allied might had driven them out of Guadalcanal, Buna, and the Huon Gulf, had eliminated or neutralized all their bases in eastern New Guinea, and had immobilized them in the remainder of the Solomons. A complete enemy convoy, including its guardian warships, had been destroyed in the Battle of the Bismarck Sea, and Tokyo could not point to even a minor seaborne victory to compensate.

Hirohito's vital air force had been outfought, outmanned, and technically surpassed. The once-lethal Zero could not compare with the modern fighters and bombers America had developed and introduced since the Zero's initial successes.

Finally, Japan had squandered its original corps of trained, seasoned combat pilots, and the replacements, inexperienced and poorly trained, were inadequate. I say squandered because the Japanese with his characteristic attitude toward death developed in the Zero a plane almost completely without protection for the pilot. All armor was discarded for maneuverability and speed. Japanese combat pilots had been fighting for two years in a plane that offered all the protection of a hang-glider. That being so, the loss of a plane usually meant the loss of a pilot, and while Hideki Tojo didn't seem to be wanting for manpower, he never seemed to understand the difference in time necessary to train a combat pilot adequately and that required to teach a foot soldier the basics of his profession.

It may have been an honor to die for the emperor, but the death of an experienced combat pilot meant the loss to the emperor of a fighting specialist in whom long hours of meticulous, specialized training had been invested. In critical contrast, MacArthur's air forces in January, 1944, included many pilots who had had their planes destroyed in enemy action but had survived to become better fighters for their experience. Beyond question, the Japanese combat pilot of 1944 was vastly inferior to the well-trained men who had manned the original Zeros, and he was absolutely no match for the Americans and Australians who were improving with experience and who held complete control of the air.

Without air control the hopes of Japan were utterly doomed, and a great many people in Tokyo knew it. There were those who would have argued for a negotiated peace at that moment had it not been for the all-important matter of saving face, oriental style. Nothing could be worse than to imply publicly that the masters of Japan, with their emperor behind them, had made a fatal mistake.

In truth, the Japanese navy had men in high places who would have supported a peace movement at that time but didn't dare stand against the army who ruled Japan. As James Kawasaki, the Harvard-educated Japanese businessman, had explained to a group of Americans in Tokyo's American Club back in 1941, the Imperial Navy, which had traveled the seas, had a greater understanding of the world at large than the army, led by men whose contacts with the outside world were largely confined to China and Manchuria.

According to Gordon W. Prange, the historian who did probably the most thorough research project on Pearl Harbor and events leading up to that appalling American defeat, Adm. Isoroku Yamamoto, the architect of Pearl Harbor, was not a believer. He drew up the master blueprint for that successful attack only after expressing his conviction that Japan could never win a war with the United States. He too had studied at Harvard, had served as a naval attaché in Washington, and had traveled in the United States. He considered his country too lacking in experienced manpower, technical know-how, and, most of all, in unlimited access to raw materials necessary to challenge a nation that possessed them all. Yamamoto told Prince Konoye while the latter was still prime minister, "If I am told to fight, regardless of the consequences, I shall run wild for the first six months, but I have utterly no confidence in the second or third year."

January, 1944, was the end of the "second" and the start of the "third" year, and Admiral Yamamoto had been proved right on every score. But Yamamoto was gone, shot down on a flight to Rabaul, and the army command, headed by General and Prime Minister Hideki Tojo, was not about to admit any error. It would require another twenty months of senseless bloodshed, climaxed by a merciless pounding of their homeland and a pair of nuclear visitations, to force the ruling warlords to admit what was obvious to any trained military man in January, 1944. Legend tells us Helen of Troy possessed the "face that launch'd a thousand ships." Certainly "face" launched the death warrants of probably a million Japanese in the last two years of the Pacific war.

CHAPTER 24

The Admiralties and the South Pacific

The Admiralty Islands lie at the top of the Bismarck Sea, about 250 miles north of Cape Gloucester, midway between Kavieng and the east coast of Dutch New Guinea. They include scores of tiny islets surrounding Manus Island whose six hundred square miles make up more than half their total territory. They also include Seeadler Harbor, a magnificent roadstead large enough to berth the entire U.S. fleet. Possession of the Admiralties would secure MacArthur's right flank and destroy any enemy hope of reinforcing or relieving the thousands of the emperor's men now isolated and scattered from the Solomons north.

Originally it had been proposed that a full-scale amphibious force comparable to that at Gloucester make the landing, probably in April, 1944, but this was February, and the General didn't want to waste those extra weeks. Instead he directed a reconnaissance-in-force, using less than a regiment with minimal logistic support. A small, mobile force could be carried aboard fast naval combat vessels rather than on the slower troop transports and could effect a withdrawal more quickly if the Japanese proved to be stronger and more resourceful than he believed.

The Fifth Cavalry Regiment, less one squadron, was chosen for the assignment. In this case MacArthur was moving against almost unanimous opposition from a staff who believed he was courting disaster. Even more secrecy than normal was imposed, but I learned enough to understand that something important was brewing, and I wanted to be on top of the story.

I tried pumping one of the General's aides-de-camp, with little success except to learn that I would have to leave my microphone for a week if I accompanied the landing force. (That much was not restricted, since all operations in the Pacific involved amphibious landings.) He suggested I accompany the light bombers that would cover the undefined operation. That would require an absence of only two or three days. With that information and two years' experience, it wasn't hard to make an educated guess, and when I reached the bomb group headquarters in Nadzab across the Owen Stanleys, my hunch was confirmed. Our target was the Admiralties. We would take off before dawn the next morning, fly to the target and rendezvous, bomb and strafe as directed, then return to Nadzab.

Having had no food since leaving Moresby, I was pleased when the colonel invited me to enjoy a sumptuous repast consisting of bully beef and some kind of canned "vegetable" no one could identify. But after a twelve-hour fast even bully beef tasted good!

About four the next morning a sleepy GI aroused me from the luxury of an air mattress and drove me a couple of miles through complete darkness to a tiny, floorless grass shack, dimly lighted by a single electric bulb. A youthful captain stood in front of a large map tacked onto an improvised board, pointer in hand, talking to some two dozen youngsters crouched on the ground before him. As I entered he gave me a brief glance. "Bill Dunn?" "That's right." "Okay, the colonel called me last night. Be with you in a moment." He turned back to his map.

"The weather really isn't good anywhere along the route, as near as we can learn. There's been no word from the naval force, and there won't be until after the landing, so you'll have to keep your eyes open. When you reach the target, keep in tight formation and circle until you hear from the command ship or the ground station, if they've been able to set one up. Be particularly careful approaching any naval vessel if the weather is bad, because it will be hard to identify you and their ack-ack is good. You all have maps of your primary targets. Keep them handy, but stay away from those targets until you hear from the ground. If they give you an objective, go in as low as possible and strafe it good before you drop the bombs. Remember now—tight formation. You don't know how many aircraft will be in the area, so keep in close. Any questions?"

"How long are we to circle before we leave the target?"

"That will depend on your gasoline supply. If you don't hear from the command ship or the beachhead, you'll probably have enough gas for an hour. By that time there'll be someone to relieve you."

"How high do we hit the secondary target?"

"Treetops, too, strafing as you go in. Anything else?"

The men started getting to their feet, so he turned to me, hand extended. "I'm Captain Hiller and this is Lieutenant Boden, who will be your pilot. He'll give you a good ride. Good luck."

Alvin Boden of Adams, Nebraska, was a tall, angular youngster who didn't look old enough to vote. A pair of green coveralls covered his splinter-like frame, and a huge Adam's apple thrust its way through the open collar. The gold bar of a second lieutenant was pinned to his mechanics-type cap, and he really looked as though he might be on his way to do the morning's milking. It was still pitch dark as he led me to a waiting truck loaded with his contemporaries, all dressed the same, all cracking jokes and laughing.

As we drove off through the night someone started singing "I've Been Working on the Railroad" and the others joined in, with harmony that tried to be close harmony. It was quite a distance to the airstrip, and my new friends had placed "someone in the kitchen with Dinah" a half-dozen times before we arrived. If there was any tension in the group, it seemed to be confined in the correspondent who was perched beside a silent pilot Boden and thinking about the doubtful weather, the naval ack-ack, treetop levels, the reported enemy air reinforcements in Hollandia, and a few dozen other subjects that seemed important at that moment.

Finally the shadowy form of a plane loomed out of the graying morning twilight and several flashlights picked it up. "What plane's this?" "Thirty," came the answer. "Best damned plane in the air force," someone shouted, and a half-dozen men piled out to loud cheers. Several numbers and cheers later a voice from the darkness called: "Sixty-three." "That's us," Boden said as he swung over the side. I followed. The B-25 stood waiting, its bomb bay doors open while a half-dozen ground crewmen moved quietly about, making their final checks.

As soon as we reached the plane, Lieutenant Boden's personality changed completely. Gone was the reticent, gangling country boy and here was a combat aircraft commander, a man in full control, whose every manner inspired confidence. He introduced me to his copilot and the other members of the crew, then excused himself to check the bomb bay load and confer with his crew chief. When he returned, he asked me if I had ever made a bombing mission in a B-25. When I replied in the negative, he gave me my instructions.

"You'll ride up front with the copilot, Gwyl Davis, and me, in place of the navigator. The squadron leader navigates today, and we follow. In case of a crash landing, Davis will open the hatch directly overhead, and he'll be the first out to open the rubber boat. You will follow and I'll be last. The gunners and crew chief will use the rear hatch. Of course we don't expect to crash-land, but it's always good to know the procedures. You'll find a parachute inside the plane, but there's no need to wear it unless there's an emergency, in which case I'll warn you. Sergeant Dreibilbies will fit you with a Mae West and give you headphones and throat microphone. I'll tell you more when we get going."

Just then another officer appeared to check the crew list, and everyone climbed aboard. In the distance we could hear the roar of others warming up, and the dawn began to break just as Boden started his own engines. We were second in line as we rolled down the taxi-strip and waited our turn as the lead plane roared down the runway, peppering us with sand and pebbles. A few seconds later we were aloft ourselves, moving into position on the right, just behind and slightly above the leader. Turning out over Huon Gulf we circled once, slowly, while the other planes joined us.

The sergeant clamped headphones on my ears and buttoned a microphone around my throat. A few minutes later Boden was pointing out Finschhafen on our left and Rooke Island just ahead. Almost immediately we ran into the first of the promised bad weather and dropped down to less than a hundred feet above the choppy waters of the Bismarck Sea. All my airline instincts craved more altitude, but the crew chief wasn't perturbed. He produced a comic book from somewhere and settled back to enjoy real adventure as experienced by someone called Captain Marvel.

Boden and Davis began studying maps and pictures of the target area while I watched the other two planes in our immediate formation, to our left. No other planes of the squadron were visible, but these two were so close I could see the facial expression of the top turret gunner in the lead plane. Suddenly my earphones came to life, and Boden warned me, "There'll be plenty of noise when we let loose with all guns, and you'll probably jump a couple of feet. Don't let it bother you—we all do the same. I'll warn you in advance."

This, of course, was to be expected, because these B-25's carried eight 50-caliber guns in the nose instead of the one 30-caliber gun originally mounted by the manufacturer. This heavy firepower was the idea of General Kenney, who called these planes his "commerce destroyers." The guns were installed over the designing engineers' protests that the project was impossible. The innovation proved itself in the Battle of the Bismarck Sea, however, and these modified B-25's immediately became one of the favorite weapons of the Far East Air Forces.

Despite the demanding business of flying a plane in tight formation at an altitude that had dropped below 50 feet, Boden still found time to talk to me about the mission. After Finschhafen there had been no landmarks to point out, but we did sight a B-24 Liberator heading south, uncomfortably close, probably returning from a strike on Hollandia. Aside from that, our three planes seemed to be all alone in a vast world of low-flying clouds and white-capped waves.

On his next communication Boden advised, "When we go in over the target we'll be very close to the treetops, but don't get scared. It's a perfectly normal procedure." I assured him I probably would be the "scaredest" fellow ever to ride a B-25, but not to worry. "Just forget me and fly your airplane." He looked back and grinned. A few minutes later he pointed out, under the clouds, the first of the scores of atolls in the Admiralties group. By this time we were flying so low we had to pull up to clear the trees on a couple of islets, but we still had to continue for several minutes before a welcome break in the clouds revealed Manus and Los Negros islands to our left.

It was a magnificent sight. On the blueberry waters before us stretched the invasion fleet, not as large as the one at Gloucester but still reaching as far as the eye could penetrate the heavy weather. Occasional pinpoints of light sparking about the beaches could have been gunfire, but otherwise the scene was reassuringly peaceful. Somehow it reminded me of my aerial approach to Tarakan Island off northern Borneo three years earlier, but these were warships rather than thirsty tankers. We began making long sweeping circles over an area northeast of the landing area, and for the first time the other planes of our mission came into view, first behind us, then almost dead ahead as we continued the spirals. By swinging my head from the left window to the right, I managed to keep the invasion fleet in sight, but it was a dizzying exercise.

Suddenly we stopped circling and headed south. Boden reported the landing apparently was proceeding well, because a land-based transmitter already had been set up and we had been informed we were no longer needed. Over the roar of the engines I didn't hear him say we would now hit the secondary target, so I *really* executed the predicted leap when the eight fifties blasted simultaneously and the plane zoomed upward, green treetops flashing by the windows! Instead of diving on our target, as expected, we had been forced so low by the weather that we had to climb to clear it. In a split second we had sprayed the target, deposited a ton of bombs, and were on our way back to a breakfast, six hours delayed, of bully beef and the canned "vegetable" no one could identify.

I was on the air with my own report almost immediately after the official communiqué announced our success, carrying with me a new respect for the flying skills of Nebraska farm boys and the navigational genius of an unseen squadron leader.

Those of us who depended on the microphone to reach the American public had hoped that January, 1944, would end or at least ease our transmission problems north of Australia, but the improvement was slight. We could report from Port Moresby with a reasonable chance of success, but Moresby was no longer the answer to combat reporting. The war had moved hundreds of miles to the north and west, and GHQ SWPA remained in Brisbane hundreds of miles to the south.

We were literally in the middle, and under the circumstances we were better served on the mainland, where theater command provided the day-to-day information we had to have and transpacific transmission was always more reliable.

Port Moresby with its Country Club was useful, however, as a midway station from which we could report such major campaigns as Cape Gloucester and the Admiralties without having to travel the equivalent distance of New York City to Denver to reach a microphone. So we alternated.

After the Admiralties had been secured and while we were planning our next forward thrust, I decided to make a reconnaissance tour of Admiral Halsey's South Pacific Area. I was assured there would be good transmission facilities available but little live news to report. The marines had long since purged Guadalcanal, and Halsey's air arm, running out of targets, had joined General Kenney's Far East Air Force in making life miserable for the enemy at Rabaul. Only Bougainville, some five hundred miles northwest of Guadalcanal, was the scene of any ground action.

The route from Australia to Admiral Halsey's command passed through Noumea, capital of New Caledonia, a delightful little French *ville* with a tropical accent. Noumea had missed the ravages of war but not the impact of the personnel who fight a war. Soldiers, sailors, and airmen, many of them on R and R leave, outnumbered the French and almost outnumbered the Melanesians and other south sea island-ers who made the city their home in normal times. The climate was like that of Hawaii, and it would be difficult to imagine a more ideal spot for R and R. Officers' and enlisted men's clubs sold five-cent beer and charged only fifteen cents for the sterner beverages. Charcoal grills produced "genuine home-side" hamburgers, and if a fellow wanted to increase his material worth, great batteries of slot machines stood ready to serve.

But the one feature that set Noumea apart from other R and R areas was the Pink House, a two-story edifice actually painted a garish pink and further recognizable by the block-long queue of servicemen pa-tiently waiting their turn to enjoy the commercial hospitality of a bevy of belles, all reputed to be straight from the Champs Elysèes. Apparently the high command had agreed with the local authorities not to interfere with a cottage industry that had flourished since the French first settled in New Caledonia, but I was assured the high com-mand had reserved the right of clinical examination. *C'est la vie!* I was able to make several broadcasts during my two stopovers in Noumea – the navy did have good transpacific facilities – but I reported on activities elsewhere in the Pacific, certain that CBS News had minimal interest in the Pink House.

Visiting Guadalcanal was exactly that, visiting. There was noth-ing to report except my impressions of a south sea island that would forever be a vital part of American history. It was then being con-verted into a super-base and repository for armament to be used else-where, but its war, happily, was just a poignant memory. Five years earlier, as an American history buff, I had enjoyed leaving my desk in New York and driving to Virginia or Pennsylvania to wander over some of the historic battlefields of the Civil War. Guadalcanal re-minded me of those brief excursions except that the scars of war on these battlefields were still fresh. Nature hadn't had sufficient time to spread her healing hands over the bruised and battered landscape.

True to their promise, navy technicians in Guadalcanal had an operating transmitter capable of putting a broadcast-quality signal into Noumea for relay to the West Coast. Actually I had been assured I could broadcast from Bougainville where there was some fighting to report, but I hadn't counted on "the Canal," where I was merely breaking my journey. I did make two reports from Guadalcanal, the first devoted to the island itself. The second found me anticipating Bougainville, the scene of one of the strangest campaigns in military history.

The Japanese were present in force on the first of November, 1943, when the Fourteenth Corps, consisting of the Thirty-seventh and American divisions, effected landings at Empress Augusta Bay. It was quite a battle for the first weeks, but while the ground fighting was under way, the Allied sea and air forces severed the enemy's line of communications with Rabaul, the line on which the island had to rely for both supplies and reinforcements and its only connection with the outside world. This severance also meant that in the unlikely event of a Japanese breakthrough and ultimate "victory," the enemy would remain an isolated force on a Pacific island with no place to go. It was like playing football on a field with no goal lines—a touchdown was impossible.

You would expect any commanding general, finding himself in such an utterly impossible situation, to strike his colors and try for peace on the best possible terms, above all to conserve the lives of as many of his own men as possible. To the generals who commanded in the field under Hideki Tojo, however, it was infinitely worse to admit defeat than to sacrifice human lives, their own included.

Maj. Gen. Oscar W. Griswold, who commanded the Fourteenth, firmly believed it took more than determination to win a war. He once remarked, apropos of the Jap's steadfast refusal to admit even the possibility of defeat, "I've found that those determined to do or die, too often merely die!" As a soldier who thoroughly understood the enemy, he made the most of the situation. Once the Japs were completely cut off from all assistance, he secured his perimeter and waited for the enemy to destroy himself in futile assaults, which is precisely what the enemy did, suffering enormous and senseless losses. By contrast, the men of the Thirty-seventh and American confined themselves to defending a well-fortified line and making exploratory patrols, with an economy of human life the Japanese could never understand.

The Solomon Sea, off the New Guinea coast, could be delightful with the enemy safely out of range. Here Sgt. Frank Kunz of General Diller's staff and I enjoy the peaceful sunshine. *Courtesy U.S. Army*

When I arrived, the Americans had been on the island for nearly four months and their beachhead, encompassing some eight miles of waterfront and extending about four miles into the jungle, resembled a resort community rather than a combat zone. But two things belied that illusion. First was the profusion of military vehicles of every description, and second the constant roar of artillery on all sides. I was assured the guns were our own, but in such a limited beachhead there wasn't one square foot of turf that wasn't within range of enemy guns.

Three airstrips were connected by an excellent network of hard-surfaced (coral) roads that centered on corps headquarters. The temporary buildings were well constructed, and the entire area had the well-groomed look standard for any American base, given a little time, no matter how primitive its location. A story circulating in the Pacific at that time concerned a Japanese prisoner being questioned by intelligence officers. "Who do you think are the best jungle fighters?" The answer was prompt. "Australians." "Better than the Americans?" Oh, the Americans don't fight in the jungle. They cut it down and build roads." The American GI never missed a chance to improve his situation, and Bougainville was a prime example.

No reporter ever had a war easier to cover. Because the enemy held no territory we wanted, the Fourteenth Corps was fighting a defensive war only, and the battle lines changed very little. Consequently, the correspondent could roll out of a comfortable bunk in the cool of a tropical morning, stop by the mess hall for breakfast, jump into a jeep, and join the GI's on the perimeter before the sun came up. A few hours later he would be back at headquarters for lunch. He could check out another position in the afternoon or rendezvous with his notes and typewriter. Information was immediately available, and the censors were gentlemen.

Finally he had the miracle of Bougainville to carry his voice, broadcast quality, to Noumea where the trans-Pacific relay was excellent. "Radio Bougainville" was rated a miracle because it was never designed for any task harder than providing recorded entertainment and news to the beachhead GI's within a ten-mile radius. However, when Sgt. John Ettlinger, chief engineer, emcee, anchor man, and janitor, finished his inspired tinkering, the one-lung transmitter was carrying a very acceptable voice signal to the Noumea relay, more than a thousand miles distant. There was only one drawback. Nothing was happening on Bougainville that would affect our overall position in the Pacific. The correspondent is expected to report on a war, not a defensive battle of minor import, so I knew I would have to get back soon to the mainstream of the action.

Despite the fact that this primitive, canvas-topped radio station broadcast regularly to the GI's in Bougainville and anyone else who cared to listen, when the technicians decided to take this picture censors made them remove all references to the island. Note the black-out under "The Voice of" and on the sign to the left of the door. *Courtesy U.S. Army Signal Corps*

I don't want to leave the impression that Bougainville was a champagne waltz. Certainly not for the soldier. There were twelve long miles of perimeter to be defended against a fanatical enemy obviously determined to die for his emperor. The GI's of the Thirty-seventh and Americal divisions did long stints in the front-line foxholes and slit trenches with eager death lurking behind the next bunker. While I was on the island a regiment of Negro troops arrived and moved in to relieve a segment of the Thirty-seventh, the first black Americans to fight as a unit in the South Pacific. There was also a battalion of Fiji islanders attached to the corps, famous for their skills on patrol

Sgt. John Ettlinger actually didn't do much singing over his Bougainville special services station, but he did just about everything else, including construction, mainte-
nance, local news bulletins, and record flips. Most important, he provided the broadcasters with a signal that could reach Noumea with sufficient quality to be relayed
to the States.

duty. But for long months the two divisions bore the brunt of the
fighting and the men were quick to testify that life in a foxhole, in
any forward combat position, is never anything but hell. Of course,
the GI didn't have the option of returning to headquarters for lunch.
The point is that seldom in modern warfare do you find the rigors
and dangers of the forward battle lines in such close proximity to the
contrasting comforts of the rear areas.

It took almost no time to realize that lethal fighting, while mostly
one-sided, was near at hand. Within a couple of hours after my arrival
I stood on the bank of a small stream and counted more than thirty

Japanese dead. With those of their brothers who had succeeded in retreating, they had attempted to pierce our perimeter at that point during the night. Now it was the unhappy task of the victors to bury the enemy dead. This I found was standard operational procedure (s.o.p.) all over the island. The enemy never held any position long enough to dig his own graves.

The navy maintained a twenty-four hour patrol of the waters around Empress Augusta Bay to intercept any attempt to reinforce or supply the enemy by sea. I spent a night aboard a PT boat on patrol duty, and although we sighted no intrusive barges, we did spot a Japanese bivouac area above the northern end of the bay. After peppering the location with our own light guns, our skipper called up a nearby destroyer to give the area a real shelling. That was about as close to an offensive action on our part as occurred during my stay. Normally, General Griswold's ground troops manned their posts and waited for the enemy to come to them. And the enemy usually did just that, thus helping hold our casualties to a minimum.

Several unarmed Japanese soldiers were captured inside our lines, obviously searching for something to eat, clear proof that the Japanese were really hurting for supplies. Considering the inbred Japanese fear of capture, a Japanese soldier had to be more than a little hungry to risk the tortures he was taught would result, just in the hope of finding food. It was another strange facet in a strange campaign.

There is one side of military life that doesn't occur to a lot of people, but I learned early in the war that the average soldier usually found some time during the day to consider his spiritual needs. Just before I left the island, I came upon a crew of Seabees constructing a building out of palm logs, canvas, and sheet metal. Even in its unfinished state, it had begun to resemble a church. I stopped to investigate and found they were indeed constructing a chapel. The officer in charge told me that ever since the first landings, the matter of divine worship had been relegated to temporary accommodations—mess halls, tents, any place a group could congregate. The next Sunday, he pointed out, would be Palm Sunday, and his men decided a real house of worship was needed. It was a memory that has never left me: these tough-as-leather construction engineers using their skills to prepare a fitting edifice for Palm Sunday in a palm jungle.

CHAPTER 25

Flight to Nowhere

Back in New Guinea at the Port Moresby Country Club after only three weeks, I could see that the war was moving away *fast*. In mid-April only Hollandia remained as an enemy base of any importance in all of New Guinea, and General Kenney's men were pounding that installation so mercilessly that the Japs hadn't attempted interception in more than a week. There was no doubt in the minds of media observers that Hollandia would be the target of our next forward thrust, and GHQ intelligence indicated we could expect major resistance whenever we made that move. Actually, it didn't work out that way.

There was never the same cloak of absolute secrecy enfolding our Hollandia plans as there had been with the Admiralties. Certainly care was taken with information that might be useful to the enemy, but everyone concerned knew this would be a full-scale amphibious operation, and no one conceded the enemy a chance, even if forewarned. The only real need for secrecy was to minimize casualties, always one of MacArthur's chief goals.

We had gone into the Admiralties on a much different basis. The enemy, we knew, outnumbered the force we would assign to that task, and, as is always true of a reconnaissance-in-force, we had to be ready to withdraw that force and get away if things went wrong. Any chance of success depended on surprise and finesse. This time, however, we would depend on massive force, and all preparations were being made on the premise that the Japanese would be prepared to meet us with comparable force.

Hollandia was even more remote from my microphone than the Admiralties, so I decided to ride the bombers again to get at least a glimpse of the action. In order to join a bomber group, you had to fly to Nadzab, as I had done before the Admiralties mission, or to one of our other bases across the Owen Stanleys, in the absence of Jap interceptors ordinarily a thoroughly routine matter.

I joined several other correspondents at the designated transport strip just outside Port Moresby, and we boarded our C-47 right on schedule. There were only five or six of us, most of the others relatively new to the theater. We perched on our bucket seats and enjoyed a routine takeoff. Then the routine ended. Unknown to us, the weather over the mountains was worse than bad. Not being a pilot myself, I can't give an expert opinion on what happened, but before too long I began to wonder if our pilot had any idea of where we were or where we were heading. We were flying in clouds as thick as vichyssoise and could barely see our wing tips, but it was obvious we were making some unusual maneuvers, and once or twice I had the feeling we were barely missing a few trees.

To make matters worse, my fellow passengers began to get restless, a couple actually bordering on panic. I was certain our pilot was not over-experienced and if there was anything he didn't need, it was a group of panicky passengers. I was just as scared as the others, if not more so, because I probably had spent more time around flying machines, but I didn't want to add to the problem. Finally I took the floor and called for attention. "All right, you guys. You wanted to be war correspondents and you made it. This is what you asked for! Our pilot doesn't want trouble any more than we do, so give him a break and relax. In the meantime, *shut up!* I want to get some sleep." With that, I stretched out on the floor of the plane, shoved something under my head, and closed my eyes. I did not go to sleep, because I feared the Owen Stanleys as much as anyone, but I must have put on a good show because they did calm down, and finally our pilot found the right answer and we came in for a perfect landing—back at Port Moresby!

The pilot gave no explanation except to mutter something about "lousy weather" before he disappeared into the operations shack. The major in charge told us it was too late to reach Nadzab that day even if the weather lifted, and frankly I was just as well pleased. I went back to the Country Club, dug some emergency rations out of my gear, and poured a drink for myself and Will Oursler, one of our better correspondents and a companion in fear. Years later Will told me he had never understood how I managed to go to sleep at such a time, and I told him the truth. It was too late. He told me he had already written the episode into one of his books. I am still trying to locate a copy of that book.

That "flight to nowhere" occurred on April 21, 1944. The following morning our troops moved ashore at Humboldt and Tanahmerah bays, bracketing the village of Hollandia, and at Aitape, about a hundred miles east. The expected opposition never materialized in any strength. Within four cautious days, we had secured the village and both the Cyclops and Sentani aerodromes, our prime objectives, with minimum resistance on the ground and none in the air. The mystery of the missing ground troops persisted for several days until it was finally determined that the enemy, misjudging MacArthur's strategy as usual, had moved the bulk of his troops east from Hollandia to Wewak and Madang in the belief his major blow would center on those bases.

As a result of our success at Hollandia, none of those troops were of any further use to their emperor. They became merely another group among thousands of military orphans—fragments of the shattered Imperial Eighteenth Army—scattered for hundreds of miles along the northern Guinea coast, completely cut off from all outside communication.

"Their situation reverses Bataan," MacArthur said in the communiqué confirming the capture of Hollandia, but of course there was a difference. Our Bataan forces were completely cut off, but they were also subjected to constant attack and forced to fight for survival. The abandoned Japs in New Guinea were given an occasional stick of bombs to divide among themselves, but otherwise were left to cope with an even more ruthless foe, the jungle.

The campaign was almost anticlimactic in the ease with which it was consummated. While there was never a doubt of the ultimate outcome, some fierce fighting had been expected, particularly in the air because the enemy bases were known to have been heavily reinforced before our Admiralties coup. But those planes weren't there to oppose us when the Sixth Army struck.

There was much speculation at that time as to what had happened to Japan's air force, because all over the Pacific in April, 1944, the enemy refused to rise to aerial challenge on any front, no matter the provocation. In retrospect, Tokyo had finally and reluctantly decided its air force was finished below the equator and was withdrawing the planes northward to defend what everyone was certain would be MacArthur's next major target, the Philippine Islands.

There was another factor that could have influenced this decision, and probably did. This, of course, was Japan's utter lack of fossil fuel, one of the main reasons why Tokyo three years before had decided to challenge the world. Their capture of the NEI oil fields in early 1942 had been a long step toward their coveted goal, but only a step. After the Dutch destroyed those fields when their loss became inevitable, the Japanese had to start reconstruction almost from scratch, and the job was far from finished in April, 1944. Furthermore, they had to ship the crude oil back to their own refineries and processing plants, then move the refined fuel to the distant bases where it had to be always available if the Zeros and the Zekes were to continue flying. This becomes increasingly difficult without control of the seas and the airspace above them. The Japanese didn't have an ounce of fuel to spare.

This period certainly didn't mark the end of all enemy air activity south of the equator, however. In fact, our attacks on those same oil fields weeks later brought strong but ineffective air resistance from the enemy. But that was almost the only exception. The time definitely was past when the Japs would, or even could, order strikes of fifty to a hundred planes on distant missions. Instead, there was increasing evidence that the Japanese air command was not the same efficient and effective command responsible for their early successes. There is no room for indecision in aerial warfare, but the men responsible for Japan's air strategy at this time seemed unable to make important decisions promptly.

At Biak, for example, our prime objective was the Mokmer aerodrome, an enemy base that commanded the whole of western New Guinea, a base they were not prepared to surrender without a stern fight. Still, just as at Lae, Cape Gloucester, and the Admiralties, the enemy's planes failed to arrive until we had the situation well in hand, our landings effected and a beachhead established. There was fierce fighting on this island as the Japs used light and medium tanks in their effort to salvage a hopeless situation, but they got little help from their airmen. There's never been any question that defensive air power is most effective when striking at a landing force before it hits the beach. George Kenney's skip-bombers proved that point in the Bismarck Sea battle, if any proof was needed. Still, the enemy had made no attempt to use his planes against an approaching convoy. These were classic examples of too little, too late, every time! It had to reflect command weakness.

While the war moved steadily northward, driving the embattled Japanese before it, plans were being formulated in Brisbane to follow that movement. Since the end of 1943 it had been obvious that the capital of Queensland was too far removed from the action to serve any longer as headquarters for the Southwest Pacific Command. Everyone connected with GHQ, including the press corps, knew a move had to be made. But where? The untamed jungle territory through which we had been fighting for two years offered planners no suitable solutions, so when Hollandia, a bit less wild, was taken, the best-educated guessers signalled thumbs up, and they were right. GHQ admitted nothing at first, but by August there was only the question of when.

I had a long talk with General Diller and Col. A. A. ("Abe") Schechter, his new radio officer, who assured me that if we did move to Hollandia, broadcast facilities would provide a good and dependable circuit to San Francisco with only atmospherics ("circumstances beyond our control") to worry us. The arrival of Abe Schechter at GHQ was probably the best thing that could have happened to us captives of the microphone. He was a seasoned radio newsman who knew and understood our problem intimately. I had known him long before the war when he was Paul White's counterpart at NBC News, and although we had been professional rivals for several years, we were always friends. Furthermore, Abe was a civilian officer whose great ambition was to get this war over fast and exchange his rank of lieutenant colonel for that of mister. While many civilian officers in all branches of the service were unwilling to make waves for fear of official displeasure that might delay promotion, he had no such qualms. Whenever one of the radio correspondents needed material assistance from the army, Abe would go in and fight for us. Consequently, when Colonel Schechter assured us we would have what we needed to report from Hollandia, I was satisfied. It was time to say farewell to Australia, the end of a memorable two and a half years.

CHAPTER 26

Hollandia

The transfer of GHQ SWPA from Brisbane to Hollandia came during the second week in August, 1944, and it was a mass hegira designed to keep the command functioning without interruption.

Ever since the establishment of our first beachhead at Humboldt Bay, the Army Corps of Engineers and the navy's Seabees had been doing an astounding job of carving a military center out of what had been primeval wilderness only days before. Their basic job was nearly finished when the transfer was ordered. Everyone concerned knew they were building the primary staging area for the Philippines invasion, but the possible date and the primary target were as highly classified as the military could contrive.

A new army, the Eighth, had been created under the command of Lt. Gen. Robert Eichelberger, who had led the First Corps at Buna. His job would be to back up Walter Krueger's Sixth Army, fighting the rearguard actions when necessary and conducting the mopping-up operations, but his "Octagon" Army was to go far beyond that. The Fifth and Thirteenth air forces at last were officially combined into the Far East Air Forces under George Kenney, with Maj. Gen. Ennis ("the Menace") Whitehead moving up to command the Fifth. All these officers had been with MacArthur since the Melbourne days, understood his methods, and would know how to implement his game plan in the stern days ahead.

It's doubtful if Hollandia village, as a colonial Dutch outpost, could have mustered more than two hundred in population, and the area probably could have been traversed on foot in five or ten minutes. By the time GHQ SWPA arrived, Hollandia was counting its population by the tens of thousands and its "city limits" extended miles down a great valley from Humboldt Bay along the shores of magnificent Lake Sentani and up the slopes of surrounding hills and mountains that provided a frame for a military base far beyond anything the Japanese could envision.

Lake Sentani is undoubtedly one of the most beautiful freshwater lakes in the southern hemisphere. Along its miles of shoreline Allied industry and yankee ingenuity created a vast community of small cities — military cities — each with its own transportation, housing, sanitation, provisioning, and recreation facilities, all bound together by a chain of dusty highways. Throughout the valley were great airstrips from which every type of plane operated, from the tiny L-5 Cubs to the great four-engine bombers and transports. Nearby, fronting the Pacific at the western end of the Bismarck Sea, were docking, anchorage, and cargo-handling facilities for the huge, ever-changing fleet of vessels necessary to supply a base of that magnitude. It was almost impossible to believe this had all been accomplished in little more than four months.

One major road rose from the valley to scale a small mountain high above Sentani, winding its way to the very top and a nondescript building, nothing more than a couple of prefabricated sheet-metal huts put together to provide living quarters and working space for General MacArthur and members of his immediate staff. This was the mythi-

Lt. Gen. Robert L. Eichelberger (retired with the rank of general), commander, First Corps in New Guinea, Eighth Army in New Guinea, the Philippines, and Japan; first commander, Allied Ground Forces during the occupation of Japan. *Portrait by John Cullen Murphy, 1944*

cal "mansion on the hill." A mile or so down the hill on a plateau overlooking the lake were the accommodations for the rest of the GHQ staff, together with a press shack and billets for the correspondents.

Most important for the radio reporters, of course, was the studio Colonel Abe had assured us would be ready. It was quartered in a GI tent and insulated, more or less, with draperies fashioned from GI blankets. It didn't look too promising, but it did fulfill his promise of a serviceable voice link to the network pick-up stations on the West Coast. It was not a perfect solution—in fact my first broadcast attempt was a failure—but the facilities equalled those at Port Moresby, and Schechter and his staff never eased their efforts to improve them.

Most of us knew nothing of the new facilities when we said farewell to Australia. Although we did have promises, our few glimpses of primitive Hollandia, mostly from air force photographs, gave us little encouragement. Too, the manner of our transfer did nothing to bolster our spirits.

All correspondents were instructed to be in Brisbane on Saturday, August 12, bringing as little gear as was consistent with the knowledge we would not be returning to our base of two and a half years. I am not sure just how many reporters actually made the flight, but I do know that enough of the American, Australian, and British media—press, radio, and photographers—were aboard to ensure global headlines had our pilot misjudged one of those great tropical clouds and found a granite core.

We were all loaded into a C-54, the military verson of the DC-4, and a short briefing told us we would make the flight nonstop, a distance of some two thousand miles. We would fly straight north from Brisbane, across the Coral Sea to the eastern tip of New Guinea, then turn northwest and skirt the north Guinea coast to Hollandia, avoiding the Owen Stanleys entirely. We took off about ten o'clock that night, faced with the prospect of ten or more hours sitting up in bucket seats and looking at each other since there was no external visibility. During my career as a reporter I have spent many nights sleeping on the ground, on steel or wooden decks, even on a bench outside a courtroom waiting for a jury to return. None of these qualify for a hardship rating when compared with trying to sleep sitting up in a bucket seat at five thousand feet in a nonpressurized cabin. Conversation is difficult with four 1,000-horsepower engines roaring outside a nonsoundproof bulkhead, and I wished I'd had the foresight of Alvin Boden's crew chief and invited Captain Marvel to come along.

Gen. George C. Kenney, commander, Fifth Air Force and the Far East Air Forces. *Courtesy U.S. Air Force*

Daylight did nothing to improve visibility. We were still in a persistent cloudbank and could see nothing outside but the misty wing tips. After several hours of this, signs of nervousness began to creep through the cabin. It was impossible to put thoughts of the Owen

Lt. Gen. Ennis ("the Menace") P. Whitehead, deputy commander, Fifth Air Force; commander, Fifth Air Force; commander, Far East Air Forces; General Kenney's right-hand man from Australia to Japan.

Stanleys completely out of mind. Finally, Bill Dickinson of the United Press turned to me and remarked, "You know, Bill, there's one good thing about flying in the tropics. You can often go like this for hours, then suddenly burst out into perfect weather." I nodded my agreement

From this tent came the final broadcast reports from New Guinea—from Hollandia,
the last stop before Leyte. Thanks to Colonel Schechter and his aides, broadcast results
were exceptionally good despite the camp-fire ambience. Standing at the left, above,
are Lt. Col. A. A. Schechter, Arthur Feldman of MBS, Clete Roberts of NBC Blue network, myself, George Folster and Pat Flaherty of NBC, and Gordon Walker of the *Christian Science Monitor*. Kneeling in front are the NCO's who did yeoman duty for too
little credit. *Courtesy U.S. Army*

and probably sighed as I responded, "So do I!" Bill's wishful observation proved prophetic, and the tension soon lifted. The New Guinea
coast was bathed in sunshine, and Hollandia was not far ahead. Most
of us recalled that flight some years later when a plane carrying a
group of correspondents from the NEI to Europe crashed in India killing them all, including George Moorad, who had pinch-hit for me
during my first home leave in 1943. There's a lot to be said for the
modern jetliner that flies high above the rock-centered weather and re-

duces those twelve-hour bucket-seat ordeals to a fraction of the time.

We all knew our sojourn in Hollandia would not be long. Even as our C-54 settled down on one of the multiple airstrips, an amphibious force under the command of Adm. Dan Barbey and carrying Douglas MacArthur as an eyewitness observer was heading northwest from Hollandia to surprise completely a small Japanese force on the island of Morotai, northernmost of the Mollucas (the Spice Islands). It was our first landing north of the equator and gave us a key base within three hundred miles of Mindanao.

A look at a map of the Pacific will show that any seaborne force directed at the Philippine Islands from Hollandia (now Djajapura) must pass between two island groups the Japanese then held in strength, the Moluccas of present-day Indonesia to the west, and the Carolines to the east. Halmahera, the largest of the Moluccas, was Japan's most important base in that area. The Japs obviously expected MacArthur to strike Halmahera and were prepared to contest a landing there at any cost. Instead, MacArthur again chose to "hit 'em where they ain't." Morotai lies about twenty-five miles above Halmahera's northern tip and, as predicted, was taken with hardly a token show of resistance and in such strength that Halmahera was completely neutralized. Another important enemy force was left to wither, cut off from all reinforcement and supply. The left flank of the invasion route was now secured. Since Palau had fallen to Central Pacific forces, after bitter fighting and several thousand casualties, only days before Morotai, the right flank too was secured. The road to the Philippines was wide open.

This meant, of course, our sojourn in Hollandia would be limited to the time necessary to complete the final plans for that move. We correspondents, of course, had no way of knowing how long this would be, so we determined to make ourselves as comfortable as possible, something we had learned during our first days in Port Moresby. The billeting officer had assigned a tent large enough for a dozen persons to the six radio correspondents: George Thomas (or "Jimmy") Folster and Pat Flaherty of NBC, Clete Roberts of the NBC Blue network (predecessor of ABC), Arthur Feldman of Mutual, Gordon Walker of the *Christian Science Monitor,* who was back-stopping Feldman, and me, on my own for CBS News.

We didn't ask to be so segregated, but no one objected. As I remarked before, most of my closest associates during the Pacific war were men in my own line of electronic reporting. We understood each other's problems, and we could provide a united front when we needed something. Curiously, there were no problems of competition. We all had access to the same official information and differed only in how we used that information and what unofficial information we dug out for ourselves.

Our tent was located on the side of a hill with a matchless view of Lake Sentani in the valley below us, a perfect spot for a vacation chalet. All it lacked was a verandah facing the lake on which tired radio reporters could relax each evening and watch the sun drop down behind the Cyclops range, so we built one. Someone produced a couple of bottles of Australian "hospital brandy"—perfectly named—and we visited one of the many portable sawmills that were everywhere turning the jungle into lumber. The brandy, which none of us would touch, produced the lumber we needed for a porch, and we went to work. The wood they gave us was beautiful, but it wasn't South Carolina pine. There are few metals harder than tropical ironwood. I have always hoped our GI sawyers didn't work as hard finishing that brandy as we did finishing our verandah, but I doubt they enjoyed it as much. It's the simple things that make a jungle comfortable.

The secret of living well in a military community, jungle or not, lies in mastering the gentle art of scrounging, the ability to get rid of something you don't want in exchange for something you need. The Radio Shack, as we dubbed our aerie, was inhabited by a half-dozen of the best scroungers in the business, and Jimmy Folster was particularly talented. One of his most memorable coups came when he located a GI on duty at MacArthur's "mansion on the hill" whom he had written a story about for a Chicago newspaper. It was a brief item but had earned the lad's undying gratitude, and that was fortunate because he had access to the ice-making machine. The value of a daily block of ice to a verandah two and a half degrees below the equator cannot be overestimated.

Of all the ridiculous myths that grew up around Douglas MacArthur during that war, none were more outlandish than the fantasies that sprang up about that "mansion on the hill." How they started and circulated so swiftly I never knew, but every one of the tens of thousands of GI's in the Hollandia complex was ready and anxious to tell how Gen. Douglas MacArthur was living in luxury in this hilltop mansion, surrounded by all the amenities of Versailles in the heyday of Louis XIV.

There were two obvious contradictions to the basic story which anybody could have checked out if he had tried, but of course no one tried. First, Douglas MacArthur never lived in Hollandia! During my two months' sojourn the General spent exactly four nights on top of that hill, and those were as a *transient*, two when he returned from his Morotai expedition and another two while waiting to board the U.S.S. *Nashville* for the Philippines. The rest of the time he spent in Brisbane. His basic plan for the Leyte campaign had been completed before Morotai, and there was little for him to do while his staff worked out the details. He could, and did, relax, but not in Hollandia.

Second, on that same road about halfway down was another head-quarters building put together by combining Quonset huts to provide quarters and working space for Adm. Tom Kincaid and his Seventh Fleet staff when they were "afloat ashore." I personally checked out both establishments, as did any other correspondent who was interested, and I came away with no doubt the navy had the best of it by far. The navy carries its amenities along wherever its ships go, and it was no great feat to shift a few up the hillside to ease the discomforts of dry land. But Douglas MacArthur was never reported living with the navy, so the critics never gave the Quonset villa a second glance.

This baseless scuttlebutt was by no means confined to the enlisted man trying to find something to take his mind off the heat, the dust, and the insects. Many of the officers enjoyed this back-fence gossip, too. Another correspondent and I walked into the local office of the air transport command one day and found the officer in charge, a gold-leaf major, almost frothing at the mouth. "You guys want a story? Well, listen to this. Some of our men had to offload a C-54 loaded with combat supplies the other day to haul a load of white gravel up here for the paths around that damned mansion up on the hill."

Neither of us believed him, but we had to check it out. If ever there was an "informed source," you'd think it would be the executive officer of the command that had been ordered to make the shift. If true, it was a story that had to be told, but it would have to be perfectly documented. We began to ask questions, notebooks at the ready, about the exact date and schedule, the name and rank of the pilot and his crew chief, and the identity of the engineer unit that handled the gravel after it arrived. The major admitted it had happened on his day off, but assured us his relief would have all those details and more if we came back the next day. We made three trips back before a sheepish major acknowledged he hadn't been able to locate a single person who had actually seen the gravel or taken part in the operation. A short drive up the hill had already provided the rest of the refutation. If anyone did fly a planeload of white gravel to Hollandia, it certainly didn't wind up around the "mansion."

In all my years covering the armed forces in the Pacific and later in Korea, I was never associated with an officer in high command who showed as little interest as Douglas MacArthur in the ordinary creature comforts some men prize so highly. My opinion is seconded by all the many men who were close to him. He is often accused of being egotistical. I considered it self-confidence, a reasonable characteristic in a man whose belief in himself was based on a sound education, long years of experience, a thorough knowledge of the military science that had dominated his life, and, extremely important at that time, an almost uncanny understanding of the enemy he was fighting. Any man so equipped is not likely to develop an inferiority complex. Finally, Douglas MacArthur was a man of great pride, and his greatest pride was in being a soldier. He never referred to himself as a general or even as an officer. He was a *soldier* and took pride in leading a soldier's life. I believe that if that "mansion on the hill" had been anything close to what the scuttlebutt depicted it, he would have refused to give it even those four transient nights.

October 1, 1944, was something of an anniversary for me. Exactly three years before, on October 1, 1941, I had left Manila on a trip scheduled to take me through China, to Burma and Thailand, and back to Manila in time to fly home for Christmas. I didn't come close. The Japanese, of course, struck while I was still in Burma, and my extended reconnaissance tour became a race with the grim reality of war. October 1, 1942, found us fighting to halt the enemy on New Guinea's Kokoda Trail and drive him out of Guadalcanal and the Solomons. There were still plenty of clouds overhead. October 1, 1943, found us in possession of the Solomons and eastern New Guinea again, the Japs contesting every step but our mastery of the air becoming more and more apparent. On October 1, 1944, after three years, the road back to Manila was visible at last. There was no longer any doubt. Bitter fighting lay ahead, but the only thing then in question was the target. The date had to be almost immediately.

Hollandia by this time was seething with Philippines fever. It was the dominant topic of conversation and conjecture. Maps were studied and guesses made as to the first strike. Mindanao got the most votes,

Here the "top brass" of the Third and Seventh fleets are shown en route to a meeting at Seventh Fleet headquarters, Hollandia, to map the naval strategy that would put the Sixth Army on Philippine soil on October 20, 1944. From the left are Commdr. Homer W. Graf, chief of staff, Seventh Fleet; Rear Adm. Daniel E. Barbey, commander amphibious forces, Seventh Fleet; Vice Adm. Thomas C. Kincaid, commander Seventh Fleet; Vice Adm. Theodore E. Wilson, commander amphibious forces, Third Fleet; Rear Adm. Forrest P. Sherman, deputy chief of staff, Pacific Ocean area; and Brig. Gen. William E. Riley, USMC, War Plans officer, Third Fleet. *Courtesy U.S. Naval Institute*

probably because it was the closest. Not too many fixed on Leyte, which is not prominent on any map because it is surrounded on three sides by Samar, Dinagat, and Mindanao. Not until we had our final briefing by one of the top staff officers did we learn Leyte was, indeed, our target. Once the final briefing was completed, all correspondents were forbidden for obvious reasons to leave Hollandia for any destination where they might possibly fall into enemy hands. I had learned from General Kenney of plans for the Thirteenth Air Force to launch a series of major air attacks on Balikpapan, but no correspondent could accompany a bombing mission once he knew the details of the Leyte campaign.

Actually, those raids on the enemy-held Borneo air fields were the most important development of that last week before we moved north. Not only did they wreak havoc in the installations and on enemy hopes, but they also brought the Japanese air arm out from under the blanket for the first time in weeks. During the first raid, in early October, sixty B-24 Liberators dropped seventy-four tons of bombs despite heavy opposition by Zeros and by some of the most intense anti-aircraft fire our men had yet encountered. Still, we balanced the score by downing seven Zeros with a loss of three Liberators. Obviously, the Japanese had placed defense of their oil supply at the top of the agenda.

The second raid, two days later, cost us seven of the big bombers, but it was the last without fighter support. The final sortie before we took off for Leyte was the fiercest of all. About a hundred Liberators, covered by fighters of the Fifth Air Force, deposited 135 tons of death and destruction, starting fires that were still raging days later. Near-perfect weather aided the bombardiers, fighter support was effective, and the raid brought Balikpapan very near the end of its usefulness to the Japanese. In the combat overhead our score was thirty-six Zeros definitely shot down and ten probable against a loss of three bombers and a single fighter. In that fight Richard Bong, who would become the number one ace in the history of the American armed forces with forty confirmed victories, bagged his twenty-ninth and thirtieth bogies within minutes of each other. Soon after his squadron returned to its base, Dick was informed he had been awarded the Congressional Medal of Honor in recognition of his mounting record. His reaction was typical of the midwestern farm boy whose stated ambition was to get back to the plow. He looked puzzled. "What for?"

With all this activity by the Far East Air Forces, there was no lack of news to report from our GI tent on the mountainside, and our technical facilities were performing well. My personal score was about an 80 percent success in reaching the network at San Francisco, and the quality of the signal was quite good. Still, GHQ was not satisfied. Someone came up with the idea of having all radio correspondents record a stock of broadcasts that could be transmitted across

I interview Maj. Richard Bong at Port Moresby just after he has passed Eddie Ricken-backer's World War I record of twenty-six enemy planes destroyed. *Courtesy U.S. Army*

the Pacific so the Japanese wouldn't realize we were off the normal schedules and suspect something was cooking.

I've always believed General Willoughby was behind that idea, which obviously had come from someone with no understanding of broadcast journalism. "Sir Charles" was an erudite gentleman, born for the military. He was MacArthur's G-2, heading the intelligence division, and I am not criticizing him in that role. In fact he gave me valuable tips several times during the long trek from Melbourne. But Douglas MacArthur would never have believed the Japanese would fall for that ploy.

We protested and pleaded our networks' ban on recordings, but to no avail, so we took our turns and produced a half-dozen recordings each, not one of which could possibly have contained a syllable of spot news. New York, although taken by surprise, obviously divined the situation so no objections were raised. But no one was fooled. After the war a Connecticut housewife remarked to me, "Bill, I used to get a big kick out of your broadcasts when you switched from news to features because I was sure something important was going to happen, and it always did." So much for pulling the kilowatts over anyone's eyes. But, still trying, we had to repeat this artful deception when the time came to move from Leyte to Luzon.

By now it was time to say farewell to lovely Lake Sentani and the verandah, but there was one ritual to be observed before we embarked. Colonel Abe gathered together the four senior network representatives, Folster, Feldman, Roberts, and me, in the press tent to tell us what we already knew, that one of us would represent the combined networks in covering the long-awaited return of General MacArthur to the Philippines aboard his flagship, the U.S.S. *Nashville*. He then pulled an Australian ten-pound note out of his pocket and marked a digit of the serial number. Art Feldman was the first man on his left, so Abe turned to him. "Give us a number." "Five." Folster was next. "Six." Then to me. "Seven." "That's it!" He showed us the indicated number and tucked the ten-pound note back in his pocket. That's what it takes to earn the right to wade ashore at Leyte Gulf with General Douglas MacArthur.

S-P-E-C-I-A-L R-E-P-O-R-T

Apache

The *Apache* didn't look like a former presidential yacht nor did she have the distinctive lines of a coast guard cutter. In fact, with her camouflage coating of jungle greens and browns and her improbable superstructure surmounted by an inexplicable array of masts and antennae, the *Apache* looked like nothing else afloat. Nevertheless, she was the answer to the radio reporter's prayer, and she brought the battle for the Philippines into the American living room as no other segment of the Pacific war had been reported.

The radio correspondent "fought" the Pacific war, at least before Leyte, under transmission handicaps that are almost unbelievable in today's era of satellites and completely mobile communications. First, all types of recordings, the backbone of modern electronic journalism, were strictly forbidden by all major networks on the premise that recordings of sound only could easily be faked and nothing should be allowed on the air that could possibly challenge the integrity of the microphone. That left the Pacific reporter chained to the infrequent live microphones capable of spanning that broad ocean. In my case there was no such mike in all of

She may not have been a "thing of beauty" but the U.S.S. *Apache* was certainly a joy to all captives of the microphone whose chore it was to report the Pacific war for the American public. There also was no doubt she was distinctive both to the eye and the ear. This is the only known picture of the *Apache* and is the cherished property of Maj. Al Pierce, who presided over her transmitters.

Burma, and while the Dutch in what used to be the Netherlands East Indies had excellent facilities within reasonable proximity to the news sources, the battle for the Indies didn't last long. In Australia and New Guinea it was largely a choice between good facilities far from the nearest combat area or combat areas with the nearest microphone hundreds of miles distant. It wasn't until the war was entering its third year that we were able to broadcast from the big island with any consistent degree of success, and by that time the war was continuing northward faster than we could keep pace.

We all knew that the climax would come in the Philippines, and we also knew it would be a campaign impossible to cover by remote control. Fortunately, MacArthur's press chief was

View from the deck of the broadcast ship, the *Apache*, looking straight up. This conglomeration of wires, masts, and antennae is only a part of the aerial decoration the *Apache* carried, incomprehensible to the broadcaster but vital to his mission. *Courtesy U.S. Army Signal Corps*

well aware of the problem and the idea of a floating transmitter was born during a series of consultations between Colonel Diller and Maj. Gen. Spencer B. Akin, the chief signal officer, and approved on one of Diller's trips to the Pentagon.

Akin turned the procurement assignment over to his seaborne communications office, headed by Lt. Col. Orville Davidsmeyer, which located the *Apache* and two 10,000-watt transmitters. The job of design, development of plans, and specifications was assigned to a junior officer, Lt. Sanford T. Terry. Although he lacked seniority, Terry's civilian record included marine radio experience on a U.S. Coast and Geodetic Survey vessel, followed by eight years with the 50,000-watt CBS station in Richmond, Virginia, WRVA, where his duties included transmitter operation as well as a number of design and con-

This quartet of technicians operated the twin transmitters on the *Apache* and kept them fine-tuned all the way from Leyte to Japan. *Standing, left,* Lieutenant Jeungel, Lt. Tony Borgia, and Sergeant Mandelstamm. *Front,* Lt. Al Pierce, crew chief. *Courtesy U.S. Army Signal Corps*

Pat Flaherty of NBC and I arrive aboard the *Apache* to inform the folks back home what's happening in Leyte. *Courtesy U.S. Army*

struction jobs. For two months Sandy Terry sat in a Brisbane office, creating a radio ship on paper while the *Apache* itself was crossing the Pacific.

I never learned exactly what factors governed the choice of the *Apache*, ready availability, probably, but it was a happy choice. When the "tired and retired" old ship was first brought to the attention of Davidsmeyer's scouts, she was little more than a hull with an aging engine. The hull was sound, however, and the engine would propel her halfway around the world from Chesapeake Bay to a Sydney shipyard for an almost complete reconstruction job. The *Apache* had enjoyed a colorful career from the time she was commissioned by the Coast Guard in the 1890s. She had

served President William McKinley as his executive yacht and then became a member of the Newfoundland ice patrol. After nearly a half-century, when she was called up for wartime duty, she was still earning her fuel ration as the reception ship for the Maryland Yacht Club.

Once the *Apache* reached Sydney we radio reporters, whenever south from New Guinea, kept hopeful eyes on her as she was stripped to the skin, rebuilt, and crammed with the most sophisticated broadcast equipment of every type ever crowded into a 185-foot hull, at least to that time. Until now the business of design and reconstruction had been Sandy Terry's concern. Lt. Luther A. ("Al") Pierce was named technical director and given the responsibility of installing the electronic equipment and perfecting the broadcast transmitters. Only a few months earlier, Al Pierce had been in charge of the transmitters at station WABC (now WCBS), the CBS flagship station in New York, and he understood what "broadcast quality" meant in network operation.

Pierce and his men delivered on time, but the margin was narrow. From the first it was understood that the *Apache* was being groomed for the Philippines campaign, but the target date of course was a top-drawer secret, and the engineers and craftsmen were working on a hypothetical schedule probably aimed at late November.

Fortunately when the word came, only minimal days in advance, that the target date would be moved up by more than a month, the reconstruction of the *Apache* was virtually complete, thanks to Sandy's crew, and all that remained was for Pierce's men to complete and perfect the installation of the electronic complex. Thus, when the *Apache* moved out of Sydney harbor and headed north, the technicians and engineers continued their work enroute. They finally completed the job while cruising toward Leyte Gulf with the invasion fleet. By then, as I noted earlier, the *Apache* had moved into the invasion zone of silence.

When Colonel Schechter handed a copy of the first official Leyte communiqué to Lt. Stanley Quinn, who sat down before an untested microphone and read it to a waiting world, no one knew whether the *Apache* could deliver.

In the celebration that followed word from the West Coast that the signal was excellent—everyone on the staff wanted a reliable link to the American public—no one noticed that the communiqué had never been cleared by MacArthur!

We radio reporters were definitely in business! With our transmission problems solved (always barring the better than outside chance some kamikaze would zero in on our new prize), we turned to the business of putting the *Apache* to the best possible use.

The first thing we correspondents learned, after a brief power struggle, was that Colonel Abe and his staff completely outranked us when it came to sleeping accommodations. What few berths were still available after the ship's crew and Al Pierce's technicians were quartered were promptly commandeered by the radio press staff. The broadcast facilities were ours day and night, and we were welcome to enjoy the output of the galley, the comforts of the none-too-spacious wardroom, or the blessings (genuine!) of the community showers, but no beds. For that we could either commute to shore or sleep on the deck.

The trouble with commuting was that the blackout in Leyte Gulf was as complete as military ingenuity could make it, and navigating a small boat through the vast fleet that filled the anchorage was a formidable challenge even in semi-darkness. Consequently, most of us elected to stay aboard overnight (most of our regular schedules came in the early morning or late evening) even though we all had accommodations of a sort in Tacloban.

At first I thought I had found the answer on the thick carpeting on the floor of the broadcast studio where there was the added attraction of air conditioning. But there was just too much traffic, too many of us using the studio too often for special reports. Finally I settled for a corner of the main deck under the bridge, where the steel below me was no harder than any other steel and the steel above me offered some protection from ack-ack, always a greater menace than the bombs.

In an air raid, and we averaged between fifteen and twenty raids or alerts every twenty-four hours, the bombs either hit or they missed, and there was usually only one or two of them in your vicinity at any one time. But the ack-ack from your own guns began when the first bogie was reported and continued until well after the last one had left for whatever destination. It was everywhere and completely invisible until it struck. That steel deck above me was a genuine comfort.

On my first night in that corner I had a rubber mattress I had scrounged somewhere, a prime asset until I found myself rolling off all night. My mattress was appropriated in turn the following day by someone whose need obviously was greater than mine, so I settled for the bare deck with a GI blanket (which I could hide during the day) for a pallet. It would be my main billet for the next sixty-plus nights.

To this day I do not understand why the *Apache* with its amazing complex of electronic equipment fed by two great 10,000-watt generators that radiated excess energy day and night, was never targeted by the Japs. The inability of the engineers to test the installations in advance didn't prevent them from creating a top-rated broadcast signal, but it did result in the appearance of a lot of bugs that might have been avoided. The necessary proximity of all the various and

varied electronic components to each other made for heavy arcing and sparking incidents at strange times and without warning. Lights had a habit of turning themselves on without explanation, and when this happened on the outside deck at night, the popularity of the *Apache* with her neighbors waned swiftly. *Cut those lights you #/& ±: + fools!* One night a very visible glow developed above the main antenna during the peak broadcast time. It agitated the entire anchorage, ourselves included, until it was rectified, but it drew no attention from the enemy.

One memorable evening several of us crouched on the deck outside the studio and watched with something very near terror as a determined kamikaze headed directly at us at an altitude of about two hundred feet. At the very last instant, when the Good Lord must have joined our team, he turned and dived into the after hold of a cargo ship hardly four hundred yards distant, igniting fires that raged all night. Had he continued on to the *Apache*, it undoubtedly would have spelled *finis* to all transmissions even if the *Apache* herself had survived.

The hundreds of broadcast reports that reached the United States via the *Apache* (she also transmitted press copy, but only by voice) attracted a lot of attention from the media back home, most of it highly laudatory. One dissenting vote was cast by *Variety*, then as now the voice of showbiz. When Stan Quinn was given the first official communiqué to read over the untested circuits, he was instructed to read it at dictation speed so it could be copied by hand on the West Coast. He did exactly that, to everyone's complete satisfaction.

Some weeks later a copy of *Variety* showed up in the Southwest Pacific Command which carried a "review" of that first broadcast from the *Apache*. No stars were awarded. *Variety* couldn't understand why Douglas MacArthur would entrust anything as important as his first Leyte communiqué to a Filipino who obviously could read English only syllable by syllable!

When the main combat action moved from Leyte to Luzon, the *Apache* again accompanied the invasion force, this time to Lingayen Gulf where it continued to render yeoman service during the entire Luzon campaign although we no longer went aboard to make our broadcasts. Instead, the Signal Corps provided us with a series of temporary studios, primitive but effective, as we moved southward toward Manila. Our mikes were always connected to the *Apache* by army landlines, thus, she was always with us, at least by remote control, whenever we needed her.

In final fact, the *Apache* appeared in Yokohama harbor very soon after our initial landings at the Atsugi airfield. By that time, however, her vital usefulness was behind her. We then held the keys to Radio Tokyo, and I was soon broadcasting my reports from the same studios I had used more than four years earlier.

I never learned what finally happened to the *Apache* after we reached Tokyo, but, whatever her fate, those of us who lived with her, profited by her peculiar abilities, and formed a bit of affection for the softness of her steel decks will always treasure her memory.

CHAPTER 27

Back on Philippine Soil

On October 15 the four correspondents chosen to accompany the C-in-C back to the Philippines were told to be ready to board his flagship at any moment, but it was after noon the following day before we were directed to the U.S.S. *Nashville* in Hollandia harbor. We barely had time to stow our gear in a large four-bunk cabin before word was passed that MacArthur would be coming aboard almost immediately. We rushed topside in time to see him arriving in a captain's barge.

As the General stepped from the barge to the landing platform at the bottom of the *Nashville*'s ladder a sudden surge lifted the small craft several feet above the platform, throwing him face down on the boards. Everyone of the scores watching from above gasped at the potential embarrassment, but not Douglas MacArthur. With complete aplomb the C-in-C rose to his feet, nonchalantly mounted the ladder, saluted the quarterdeck, and accepted the welcome only the navy can accord.

General MacArthur meets the four correspondents who are to accompany him on the historic landing on a Leyte Island beach, marking his promised return to the Philippines. *Left,* William Dickinson of the United Press, Frank Prist of Acme Newsphotos, Earle Crotchett of Paramount News, and myself, keeping an eye on the General's corncob pipe. Prist was killed by a Japanese sniper two weeks later. *Courtesy U.S. Army*

Frank Prist, the Acme photographer who was standing beside me, gave a low whistle and remarked, sotto voce: "Damitall, Bill, if I didn't know better I'd swear that was the correct way to come aboard."

Soon afterward we weighed anchor and headed north, surrounded by the largest armada the Pacific had seen to that time, more than 700 martial craft ranging from the plodding transports and cargo ships to the great battleships and warships of every ilk, chafing at the necessity for reduced speed so as not to outdistance the carriers of men and munitions they were there to protect.

Three uneventful days later, just before midnight on October 19, we dropped anchor outside the mouth of Leyte Gulf to spend a mostly sleepless night waiting for the dawn attack.

We have already covered the events of that historic October 20— it can never be forgotten—but the bitterest battles for Leyte Island came in the days to follow.

On the second day of the invasion I again accompanied MacArthur on his inspection tour of the forward positions, then returned to the *Nashville* to make my own report to CBS News. The following morning I transferred my gear to the *Apache* after wishing the General good luck and receiving his caution, "Bill, take care of yourself," an admonition he repeated every time we met, through two wars.

Anyone who saw the televised scenes of Manila celebrating the deposition of former president Ferdinand Marcos in 1986 has an idea of what the little city of Tacloban was like when I reached it later that morning, Sunday, October 22, 1944. The First Cavalry had ousted the Japs with minimal damage to the city, and the streets were thronged with happy people. The women were in their native dress, a blend of the East and the West, the men in their Sunday best, most on their way from a celebration mass in one of the city's several churches. Old men and young tossed salutes at every uniform, and children, many too young to remember pre-Japanese days, danced in the streets, waving their fingers in the "V" sign and shouting "Victor-ee! Vic-tor-ee!" They may not have understood the meaning of the word, but they knew this was a moment of great importance in their young lives. Few of the GI's left to guard the city had ever heard the Philippines greeting, *mabuhay*, but they caught on fast. Soon everyone was greeting everyone else with great gusto, and *mabuhay* became an instant and integral part of the GI vocabulary.

Probably the most surprising feature of the day was the appearance of American flags, not just two or three but scores of them all over the city. Flags hidden from the Japanese now appeared in windows, on porches, flying from hastily rigged flagpoles, and waving in the city square alongside the Philippines ensign. It was the greatest exhibition of sincere regard of one people for another people I have ever witnessed.

Tacloban was literally an open city. Homes were thrown open to the Americans, and the citizenry combed through its meager stores —the Japs hadn't overlooked much!—in search of anything to offer the liberators. At the same time the GI's were digging into their packs

This group of seven larger-than-life bronze figures based in a reflecting pool on the beach at Leyte where Douglas MacArthur first waded ashore was designed and sculpted by eminent Filipino artist José Caedo and dedicated in 1977 on the thirty-third anniversary of the General's promised return. *From left:* Pres. Sergio Osmeña, Col. Courtney Whitney, General MacArthur, Brig. Gen. Carlos P. Romulo, myself, Lt. Gen. Richard Sutherland, and Sgt. Francis Saveron. Although I was the only member of the bronzed group present at the dedication, I had not been advised in advance that I was one of the seven. It was the greatest shock of my life. *Courtesy Philippine government*

to find something to offer their new-found friends, which gave birth to the conviction all "GI Joes" carried an inexhaustible supply of chewing gum and cigarettes. ("Vic-tor-ee, Joe. You got cigarette?")

The climax to the day came shortly after noon, when a formal parade was organized, featuring flags, drums, musical instruments of every type, and native noisemakers that defied description. Truly, there was more noise than music, but it was a joyful noise, and I could detect fragments of "God Bless America" and "Land of the Morning," the Philippines anthem, nearly all the way back to Red Beach as I headed for the *Apache* to report on a delirious day that is still vivid in my memory after more than four decades.

George Folster, Arthur Feldman, and I were offered accommodations in the home of the superintendent of Tacloban schools, a large frame house that once had been a comfortable family abode but, like everything else in the city, had been stripped of anything the enemy could use. The First Cavalry, which had liberated Tacloban and held down our right flank, provided us with blankets and mosquito nets that we fitted onto a trio of woven-cane cots. These, together with a couple of chairs and tables, equipped two adequate rooms on the ground floor, rooms we would seldom occupy except for occasional breaks during the day, since we slept aboard the *Apache*, despite her lack of accommodations.

On Tuesday night, however, I did stay in Tacloban and the next morning, October 25, I thumbed my way to Red Beach just before dawn. Even before I reached the waterfront, I was sure something important was happening. There was an undefinable feeling in the night air that reminded me of that night in Java when the Japs began their invasion. When I reached the beach, I found large groups of Americans and Filipinos intently watching the southern horizon. I saw nothing, but a GI told me there had been vivid flashes of light reflected against the sky during most of the night. The consensus was that a major battle was taking place in or near the Surigao Straits just south of Leyte, but no one had any concrete information.

Once aboard the *Apache* I learned that Admiral Kincaid's Seventh Fleet had engaged an enemy force trying to enter the gulf through the straits. There was still no indication of how the fight was going and no official confirmation it was happening. Until that confirmation arrived, I was told, I could not speculate. Accordingly, I based my broadcast on the ground fighting, then went out on deck to see if daylight revealed anything.

San Pedro Bay is situated at the northern tip of Leyte Gulf at the entrance to the San Juanico Straits that separate Leyte from neighboring Samar. The *Apache* was anchored in the bay just a few hundred yards off the Tacloban airfield. I could see an army of workmen in the distance, striving to put the inadequate strip into condition for the Fifth Air Force planes that were to relieve the carrier planes as quickly as possible. There was much to be done.

I decided to inspect the field personally while waiting for some official news from Surigao, so I hailed a small LCM (landing craft, mechanized) heading for Red Beach and climbed aboard. We were only a few yards from the *Apache* when one of the frequent alerts

Vice Adm. Thomas C. Kincaid (left) and Lt. Gen. Walter Krueger, aboard a patrol tor-
pedo boat in Leyte Gulf. Together with Lt. Gen. George Kenney, commander Far East
Air Forces, they were irreverently known throughout the SWPA as "MacArthur's Ku
Klux Klan." The trio made a formidable team, as the Japanese discovered. *Courtesy
U.S. Naval Institute*

touched off a harbor-wide barrage of anti-aircraft fire that peppered
our craft with spent flak and rocked the harbor with concussion. I
never liked flak, spent or not, but before I could find something to
crawl under, a cease-fire was signalled and the barrage ended as quickly
as it had begun. At the same time a flight of small planes appeared
on the northern horizon, heading for the Tacloban strip.

Most of the men aboard our craft began cheering, believing them
to be P-47's—Thunderbolts—of the Fifth Air Force, but square wing
tips disproved that to me. Certainly they weren't bogies, so they had

to be from one or more of the carriers, and the fact that they were heading for an unfinished airport could mean only one thing: they were in trouble. Our LCM would not be allowed near the airstrip under those circumstances, so I asked to be offloaded at the nearest beach. It took me a half-hour to reach the field, and by that time the last of seventy-seven navy Hellcats, Hepcats, and dive bombers were on the ground, not all without mishap, but miraculously all without loss of life.

I reported it as a sight I would never forget, and I never have. Construction material was everywhere, and the work of rebuilding the airfield was even then going right ahead. Bulldozers, graders, and rollers were hard at it. Trucks were arriving with great loads of coral while workmen, members of the engineer units, were swarming like ants. But even more astounding was the business of preparing those planes still operational for immediate return to action. (All damaged planes were immediately bulldozed into San Pedro Bay.) There were no trained ground crews, of course, so the pilots directed infantrymen and engineers as they rolled gas drums to the planes, refueled, fitted bombs into the racks, and re-armed the guns.

The pilots were a story in themselves. All were fighting mad, some in tears of frustration. They had lost their carrier, one of the CVE's, small escort carriers that carried no armor, and they were sure we were losing the battle. They had to get back and fight! I then learned that these men were not engaged in any combat to the south. They were the northernmost echelon of Kincaid's Seventh Fleet, operating to the *north* against an enemy fleet apparently advancing through the San Bernardino Straits above Samar. This was my first realization that we actually were fighting on two fronts.

There was no doubt I had tickets on the fifty-yard line with plenty to hold my attention, but the real scoring was going on beyond the north and south goal lines, and it was difficult to learn anything except what you could see with your own eyes. Everyone was concentrating on the job before him, and few had any time for the questions of an inquisitive reporter.

But one thing was obvious to any observer. Every pilot who roared down that makeshift runway to get back into the fight should have been awarded the Navy Cross. Even the miniature deck of a CVE would seem like Dulles International compared with the fraction of an undersized airstrip they had to work from. They were using a short, rough-surfaced runway barely twenty feet wide, swept for its entire length by light to medium crosswinds off San Pedro Bay. Not all of them made it, but no serious injuries resulted even when one plane, caught in a cross draft, went out of control and crashed into a gas truck without catching fire. The boys merely hung their tail wheels over the last available inch of usable runway and gunned their engines. These take-offs were practically carrier launchings with none of the aids a carrier provides and without the wide smooth surface of a carrier deck. The pilots began their climb the instant they cleared the ground and immediately were on their way back to combat to continue the fight. All hell and a lousy airstrip wasn't going to stop them!

It was a perfect demonstration of all-services cooperation and co-ordination. The army provided the manpower for the hastily organized ground crews, established radio contact with the naval command, and provided food and coffee for the navy fliers. Tom Mitchell, a major general in the Marine Air Corps, present on an inspection tour, grabbed a flag, ran out on the runway, and directed traffic, sending the planes on their way with carrier precision. About this time General Kenney arrived, also on an inspection mission, and helped locate additional fuel and munitions, then quietly exhorted the engineers to even greater efforts. He never raised his voice but he got his message across: nothing was more vital to the *personal* future of each of them than the airfields they were building, and there wasn't a moment to spare. The immediate situation was ample proof, if proof was needed!

As the last of the planes took to the air (I estimated we left at least five at the bottom of San Pedro Bay), Kenney climbed in behind the wheel of his jeep and motioned me to join him. "Come on, Bill, let's see what's happening at the coral pits." After checking the condition and work progress of the entire Tacloban field, we headed inland to inspect the quarries. Leyte is a coral island, and coral takes the place of gravel as nature's one plentiful material with which to surface runways and pave highways. Coral, obviously, was very high on George Kenney's agenda.

As we drove to the various installations, the general filled me in on what he knew of the naval battle, apparently still raging, but there wasn't a great deal I didn't know. We had smashed the enemy in the south, but he had no more information from the north than the naval fliers had given him. He would get a complete briefing when he returned to GHQ, but at the moment his most pressing concern was the coral that would enable him to bring the two Far East Air Forces to Leyte where they were needed. There was reason for concern, as it turned out. The men in the quarries were doing their job, but they weren't giving it the extra effort he wanted, and he let them know it. Again, quietly but forcefully, he spelled it out: "Give me the coral I need and you won't have to dig foxholes!"

CHAPTER 28

Won by the Second Team

The Battle of Leyte Gulf was the greatest naval engagement ever fought, and it was won by the second team! Never in their wildest imaginings did Admirals Ernest King, in Washington, and Chester Nimitz, in Hawaii, foresee that the pivotal battle that would eliminate Japan as a naval power would be fought by Thomas Kincaid, who headed the Seventh Fleet and technically served under the Southwest Pacific Command of Douglas MacArthur!

The navy had placed all its blue chips on Bull Halsey's Third Fleet, larger, more modern, armed primarily for combat and, of course, entirely under naval command. This decision can't be faulted, for Halsey was indeed a great combat admiral of proved ability, but unfortunately he had not kept his superiors fully aware of his plans and movements, and his fleet was almost four hundred miles north of the gulf when the enemy struck.

I shall not explore again the details of this epic battle. That's been done many times and by experts in naval strategy. But those of us on the fifty-yard line believe to this day that we owe an eternal debt to the quiet, soft-spoken sailor who destroyed one major enemy fleet completely, then turned immediately to do battle with a second fleet coming at us from the north. This in spite of the fact that he had exhausted most of his armor-piercing shells (he was armed primarily for shore bombardment in support of amphibious operations) and was served by a crew that had no time to recuperate from a long night of combat at Surigao.

General Kenney dropped me in Tacloban about ten o'clock. I found the press office almost deserted except for a couple of officers. The only concrete information I could glean was that Halsey and his Third Fleet were indeed missing, just as General Kenney suspected, apparently on a sortie to the north of Luzon, certainly too distant to support Kincaid's Seventh. It didn't take much imagination to visualize

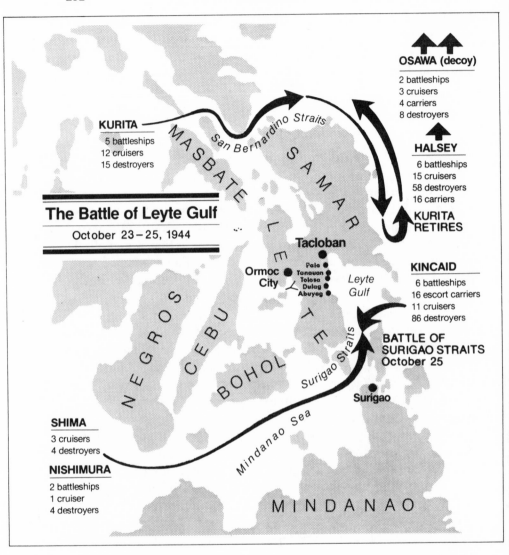

KURITA
5 battleships
12 cruisers
15 destroyers

The Battle of Leyte Gulf

October 23–25, 1944

OSAWA (decoy)
2 battleships
3 cruisers
4 carriers
8 destroyers

HALSEY
6 battleships
15 cruisers
58 destroyers
16 carriers

KURITA RETIRES

Tacloban

Palo
Tanauan
Tolosa
Dulag
Abuyog

Ormoc City

Leyte Gulf

KINCAID
6 battleships
16 escort carriers
11 cruisers
86 destroyers

BATTLE OF SURIGAO STRAITS
October 25

San Bernardino Straits

MASBATE

SAMAR

LEYTE

NEGROS

CEBU

BOHOL

Surigao Straits

Surigao

Mindanao Sea

MINDANAO

SHIMA
3 cruisers
4 destroyers

NISHIMURA
2 battleships
1 cruiser
4 destroyers

what would happen if only a segment of the enemy's fleet should penetrate the gulf where scores of defenseless supply ships, Libertys, LST's, and tankers were waiting like the proverbial sitting ducks. The carnage would have been beyond comprehension and the entire campaign seriously threatened. There was nothing a reporter could do, however, except to continue his quest for information. Anything favorable would be pure gold!

Adm. Thomas C. Kincaid, commander of the victorious Seventh Fleet (a vice admiral at the time) in the battle of Leyte Gulf, the largest sea battle in history. *Courtesy U.S. Naval Institute*

This was the situation when I cleared a message to New York asking for more time on my next schedule. It was then about ten o'clock on Wednesday night, October 24, in New York and our next network news would take the air at eight on Thursday morning, about ten hours later. By that time I should have a more complete picture of the battle, or be in full flight myself.

The break came suddenly and without any preliminary hint. I had just decided to return to the Tacloban airstrip as a possible source of information and was at the steps of the press office when a press officer called me. A message just received, ostensibly from the naval command, announced that Takeo Kurita, the Japanese admiral, had broken contact at 9:11 A.M., and was retiring north and west into the San Bernardino Straits. That was all. No explanation, no details, no conjecture, but that was enough! I knew the details would come later, as they did, but no one was sure, then or later, what made Kurita turn and run just when everything seemed to be going his way.

I have always believed those winged orphans of that hectic morning at the Tacloban strip (the same exercise was duplicated at the unfinished Dulag strip, a few miles south) could have forced Kurita's decision. Despite the damage to their carriers and the necessary use of two caricatures of landing fields, these lads, I learned later, shot down more than a hundred land-based enemy planes and distributed nearly two hundred tons of bombs and more than eighty torpedoes for Kurita's ships to divide among themselves. Further, they were showing no doubt of their ability to continue indefinitely.

Poor communication was always a major weakness in the emperor's seaborne forces, but Kurita must have known about the total destruction of his sister fleet to the south and could only guess at Kincaid's ability to launch his fleet immediately into another major engagement. When one combines that shattering realization with the constant harassment of our carrier pilots, the ceaseless sting of a swarm of PT boats that could and did run rings around the larger craft, and the valor of Kincaid's leading destroyers (all three of them!) which performed like battleships, Kurita's sudden nostalgia for the Inland Sea is easier to understand.

As was true throughout the war, air power was the decisive factor. Neither of the enemy's fleets included any carriers and both depended on planes from land bases on nearby occupied islands. But the land-based planes had long since been proved obsolete. The Japanese were still sending their pilots aloft in aircraft that were not technically advanced over those that caught us observing the Sabbath at Pearl Harbor.

Whatever his rationale, Kurita's decision made a marked difference in the morale of the press corps. The press conference that afternoon was probably the most high-spirited session we'd had since our arrival five days before. Apprehensions had vanished and everyone was relaxed.

I had written my script and was waiting for its return from the censors. Asahel ("Ace") Bush of the AP was sitting beside me, pencilling a few changes in his story before filing it. He suddenly stopped and held out his hands. "Look at those hands, Bill. What the hell am I going to do with them?" Both were covered with the fungus growth we called "jungle crud," an occupational hazard common to hundreds of men assigned to jungle duty, not serious but damned unpleasant. I advised him to see "Doc" Egeberg, the colonel who was MacArthur's personal physician. I had escaped the jungle crud, but Doc (Roger) showed me how to cure the worst case of prickly heat I every heard of (Prickly heat—miliaria—can be frightening when it covers the body with suppurating pustules!), and my faith in him is still unshaken after forty-plus years.

Ace agreed that was a good idea, thanked me, and left to file his copy. When I reclaimed my script from the censor my deadline was near so Phil North, a major on General Diller's staff who had been with us all the way from Melbourne, offered to jeep me to the beach and help locate a boat to the Apache. Before we reached the town limits, however, the air alert sounded and two or three enemy bombers started making deposits in our immediate vicinity, accompanied by the cacaphony of a thousand (or so it seemed) anti-aircraft guns. Phil and I jumped out of the jeep and crawled under it for protection from the ack-ack. Some of the bombs dropped uncomfortably close, but we stayed put until, after what seemed like an hour but was probably no more than five minutes, the all-clear sounded and we continued to the beach.

Ordinarily the incident would have been promptly forgotten, but on the following morning, aboard the Apache, I learned that at least one of the bombs that missed us did strike a house near the press office where several correspondents were billeted. Ace Bush and Stanley Gunn were killed, and Clete Roberts of the NBC Blue network was wounded, fortunately not seriously. Everyone knew Ace, but

Gunn was a newcomer, sent out to represent the *Fort Worth Star-Telegram*, who had arrived in Tacloban only the day before. His first taste of combat had been his last. Coincidentally, Phil North was the son of Jimmy North, editor of the *Star-Telegram* and one of the few who knew Stan personally. Their Texas reunion on a tropical Philippine island had been brief.

Ace and Stan were buried in graves lined with palm fronds, not far from where they died, the first of three correspondents who would die in Leyte. Frank Prist, of Acme Newsphotos, would join them in a few days, shot through the heart by a sniper.

My first thought on hearing of Ace's death was irreverent, perhaps, but founded in sincere sympathy. Now Ace wouldn't have to worry about that damned jungle crud. Almost every correspondent who came directly from New Guinea had some similar problem of greater or less severity, but we were all hoping for a less permanent solution. The fact that Gunn was not yet known in the theater, combined with the marked similarity of our family names, resulted in a report that "poor old Bill Dunn is dead." (All correspondents who die in action automatically become "poor old" to their surviving compadres.) The report was, as Mark Twain observed, exaggerated, but it took a long time to refute. Months later, when we reached Manila's Santo Tomás internment camp, a lot of my newly liberated friends greeted me with various versions of "My God, Bill. I thought you were dead!"

October 25, 1944, had been an emotional as well as an historical twenty-four hours, a day that would go down in history as the date of an overwhelming American victory in the greatest naval battle ever fought. In my report on the battle I included, as seemed quite logical, the statement that Adm. Thomas Kincaid, as the mastermind who engineered that victory, would now take his place in American history with George Dewey, David Farragut, Oliver Hazard Perry, John Paul Jones, and other great soldiers of the sea who contributed to the glory of American naval history. That proved to be one of my greatest misstatements of the war. Today Thomas Kincaid is almost a forgotten figure in American history, and I shall always believe it was his fellows of the naval high command who brought it about, even though I admit I don't know how they did it.

Only a few days after the battle I was talking to a general commanding in the Southwest Pacific, an officer who reported only to MacArthur and whose three stars led me to believe he could speak with authority. I was lauding Kincaid and the magnitude of his victory. His place among America's greatest military heros, I reiterated, was assured for all time. To my surprise the general shook his head in disagreement. He was obviously speaking off the record, and I never had a chance to ask his permission to quote him later, but he was certain what would happen.

"Bill, I agree with you completely. Tom deserves all the credit, but it will never happen." I was astounded. "What do you mean?"

"You must remember, first of all, that Tom Kincaid and the Seventh Fleet are a part of the Southwest Pacific Command and, as such, report to General MacArthur. That means that, technically at least, Leyte Gulf was a victory for the army, and you can be sure the navy will never take that passively." I couldn't believe him. "But, General," I protested, "Kincaid was in sole command. The Third Fleet was four hundred miles away and Nimitz was in Hawaii. How can they take that away from him?"

"All I can say is they'll try. Ernie King has a well-known phobia for MacArthur, and the fact that he himself, as chief of naval operations, probably steered Tom to that command makes no difference. Kincaid is now a MacArthur man in Ernie King's eyes and rates no cheers whatever he does. Remember, only last July when the General was summoned to Pearl Harbor for a meeting with President Roosevelt, King left Honolulu a day earlier and returned to Washington to avoid meeting him. He is not about to let a MacArthur man walk off with the kudoes if he can help it, and he has his staff well indoctrinated in the same ideology."

Today historians agree that Leyte Gulf was the greatest naval battle ever fought from the standpoint of ships and personnel involved, surpassing the Battle of Jutland, in which the British and Germans fought without decision until the Germans withdrew under cover of weather. The British Grand Fleet was commanded by John Rushworth Jellicoe and the German *Kriegsflotte* by Reinhard Scheer, both of whom are included in every standard encyclopedia or reference work, their place in history secure despite having fought without winning. You will not find Thomas Kincaid, who *did* win, in your Britannica, Americana, Columbia, World Book, or any other encyclopedia I have been able to check (and I don't believe today's American schoolchildren are being taught to rank him with John Paul Jones), but you will find Ernest J. King, William F. Halsey, and Chester Nimitz, all of whom moved ahead to five-star splendor and historical acclaim, although not one of them ever fought, much less won, a battle as critically decisive as Leyte Gulf. But Thomas Kincaid will always rank with the very greatest of American military heroes in my personal hall of fame.

Soon after the naval battle was ended and Kurita sent scurrying back to the Inland Sea, someone in GHQ evolved the happy idea of moving the *Apache* from her anchorage out in the gulf into the San Juanico Straits, the narrow strip of water that runs northwest from upper San Pedro Bay and separates Leyte from neighboring Samar.

It was a great break for the microphone reporters, because Tacloban's commercial waterfront faces the straits, only a short distance from the building that housed the press office. Instead of having to drive several miles to Red Beach and take a boat for the last mile, we could jeep to the Tacloban docks to find the *Apache* only minutes distant if we could locate a boat operating at our odd business hours, day and night. The less one had to drive, walk, or wade in the face of Leyte's typhoons and monsoon deluges, the better!

The campaign for the island of Leyte brought the American forces into direct confrontation with two ruthless enemies, a desperate Japanese army and the worst monsoon season to strike the central Philippines in many years. I have always believed that the first could have been reduced without too much difficulty had it not been for the unexpected force of the second. Man can seldom match the ferocity of nature.

Several historians (few of whom, if any, were present) have charged that Douglas MacArthur underestimated the strength of the Japanese on Leyte when he scheduled our return to the Philippines. As a professional observer who was present every day of the campaign, I must disagree. With the aid of an effective guerrilla organization in direct communication with MacArthur's headquarters, plus a number of intelligence observers throughout the islands, we had adequate information on enemy strength and disposition. What neither the guerrillas nor our meteorologists could tell us was that the monsoon season, which we anticipated and believed we were prepared for, would be a record-smasher, bringing with it two typhoons (a third was a near miss) and torrential rains that would pour some fifty inches — more than four feet! — of water on this combat zone in ten weeks.

Leyte was, and still is, strictly an agrarian island, totally unprepared by nature to handle the heavy machinery of war. The highways were intended to carry only such light traffic as carabao carts, the pony-drawn *calesas*, and the limited number of motor cars and light trucks that would be normal to a rural community in a tropical clime. The byroads and side streets collapsed almost immediately, while the main highways required the constant attention of the engineers and Seabees whose skills we had hoped could be concentrated on construction of the airfields we needed so acutely. The same weather, of course, struck the Japanese during those weeks but the enemy was fighting a defensive war, which meant the burden of forward movement was greater for our forces—our whole game plan depended on it. We were the ones driving ahead and this, plus the fact of heavier equipment, made us more vulnerable to weather.

If you could watch, as I did, an empty truck gradually sink below the soft shoulders of a partially paved Tacloban street to be completely swallowed by a thirsty earth in a matter of days, you might get some idea of what fifty inches of rain in ten weeks, with the resulting island-wide quagmire, could mean to foot soldiers trying to advance against an enemy who was dug in and fighting a defensive campaign. This particular truck, a quarter-ton utility vehicle, got itself mired not far from press headquarters and defied all efforts at extrication. It was finally relieved of whatever cargo it carried and abandoned. Each day we would pass and mark its descent to a tropical grave dug by the rains of Leyte. In a week it was buried, and it probably remains in its muddy sepulchre to this day.

The foot slogger has a tough enough job when the ground under his boots is firm, but when he has to maneuver in mud, instant swamp that often swallows him up to his kneecaps, the situation becomes next to impossible. Such conditions explain why it took us a little more than two weeks to capture 85 percent of the island but almost two months to secure the remaining 15 percent.

After all these years it is still impossible to fathom the overall game plan of the Japanese in Leyte. From the first, General MacArthur predicted that the loss of Leyte would cost Japan the whole of the Philippines, and for once the enemy seemed to agree. Radio Tokyo, in a series of surprisingly frank broadcasts, stated flatly that Leyte was the key to the entire archipelago and must be held at all costs. That dictum, undoubtedly coming from one of the military hierarchs in Tokyo, clearly called for an all-out offensive. There was no alternative if the Philippines were to be saved. Yet, from the day the Americans first appeared outside Leyte Gulf, the enemy ground forces fought a purely defensive campaign. With surprisingly little resistance, he retreated

steadily until he reached his prepared defensive enclave based on Ormoc Bay on the westernmost coast of the island, behind a rugged range
of extinct volcanic formations.

With the monsoon deluges making all overland approaches virtually impassable, Ormoc was the perfect site for defense, within overnight barging distance of Cebu and Masbate and still within reasonable supply and reinforcement range of all the rest of the central
islands, the Visayas. But not even an amateur strategist would have
chosen Ormoc as the base from which to launch an attack powerful
enough to menace the American positions, much less to recapture
territory already in our hands. More amazing was the apparent and
mistaken conviction that victory was possible if only sufficient reinforcements could be brought in. No one will ever know, within a
margin of thousands, how many of Hirohito's subjects were sacrificed
by the overall command in this battle zone without even firing a
shot for their emperor.

When we first set foot on Leyte's beaches, the Japanese had one
division commander on the island leading a contingent of men who
had faced nothing more arduous than garrison duty, living off the land
at the expense of the Filipinos and enjoying the stories of their amazing "victories" elsewhere as reported faithfully by Radio Tokyo—not
the best conditioning for unexpected combat. Soon they brought in
Tomoyuki Yamashita, an experienced army commander who had led
the successful conquest of Malaya and Singapore, and they were determined to equip him with an army.

The first major Japanese effort, three weeks after our own initial
landings, was the most nearly successful. An enemy convoy, aided by
heavy weather, succeeded in landing an estimated thirty-five thousand troops at Ormoc on November 10, but at a cost of seven destroyers and four transports. Several thousand troops went down with the
transports. Those who did reach Ormoc would constitute the bulk
of Yamashita's troops, because after that time everything was down-
hill for the Nips. But they never stopped trying. Three days later six
enemy destroyers, escorting three transports, ran head-on into elements of Halsey's Third Fleet and were eradicated. Of an estimated
eight thousand troops, only those who could swim the remaining miles
to shore survived.

Ormoc Bay is a large inlet of the Camotes Sea, shaped like an in-
verted U and measuring some eighteen miles across its southern entrance. The city of Ormoc lies on the extreme northern shore, about

fifteen miles above the mouth. The enemy bases were massed around the northern and eastern shores of the bay, behind the volcanic hills. To the west of the city some fifteen miles, or about twice that distance by road, lies Polompon, a small port that faces directly on the sea. The Japanese preferred to route their convoys into the bay itself to eliminate the overland trek, but they made determined, if unsuccessful, efforts to use both ports.

It's doubtful that more than a scant 10 percent of Japanese efforts were successful after that first big landing on November 10, but they persisted, still convinced the answer lay in sheer numbers. Any informed observer could see that Japan's fatal flaw in Leyte, as it had been all over the Pacific after their first few successful months against inadequate opposition, was an almost total lack of the basic military skills. Had the enemy actually been able to mass several divisions or their equivalent in that cul-de-sac, there would have been no room to maneuver and, most vital, no adequate air cover. His naval support already had been routed, and those volcanic hills which were delaying our progress would have become a barrier to enemy operations instead of a shield.

In short, Ormoc was a potential trap, and any sizable reinforcements would have been doomed. No responsible field commander would ever have continued to pour troops into such an impossible situation unless he was ordered to by a higher command, in this case Kuniaki Koiso, who had replaced Tojo as prime minister, and his military clique, still intent on saving face. Although Koiso was given erroneous information by his top-ranking officers, on which he probably relied to order the Ormoc operation, there is still sufficient evidence that the military fate of the Japanese empire lay in the hands of men with fatally inadequate military knowledge.

The presence of the *Apache* in the San Juanico Straits, if an improvement, didn't solve all the broadcasters' problems. Although the Signal Corps would later provide us with primitive but effective remote studios as we moved southward toward Manila, they never managed to establish a really acceptable remote studio ashore during our stay in Leyte. As long as we were in Leyte, our transpacific signal was almost always better from the ship than from the shore. For that reason we had to stay within a safe distance of the Tacloban docks when bad weather threatened to turn worse, or risk getting weathered in ashore and missing a scheduled broadcast. That limitation still gave us a range of about thirty miles and an area that included Sixth Army headquarters and Kenney's air forces, as well as two corps of infantry. News was not scarce, but it was useless unless you could reach the mike.

On the other hand, there was also the ever-present possibility of being trapped on board the ship for more than twenty-four hours when the windswept waters of the straits halted small boat traffic. I spent more nights aboard the *Apache* than I did ashore, but we all preferred to be ashore during the daylight hours to seek out the information necessary to supplement the bare facts of the communiqué. We had no options, however; we merely met each situation as it arose and hoped for better weather tomorrow.

After their catastrophic encounter with the Third Fleet on November 13, the Japs suspended for about ten days their efforts to force large convoys through our defenses, confining themselves to night runs from Cebu and Masbate with barges and small boats. But it wasn't profitable. When the weather eliminated effective night flying, our PT boats were active, and not enough supplies and troops got through to make any difference. As a result, the Japanese resumed their formal convoy attempts on November 25, and our air forces had a Roman holiday. Our fighter pilots had been running short of Zekes and Bettys to score on, so the fighter command rigged their planes for use as dive bombers and turned them loose on enemy shipping. It cost the Nips dearly.

The daily destruction of an enemy convoy—usually three or four destroyers and the same number of transport-cargo ships with a minimum of air cover—was fast becoming so routine that, as any first-year journalism student will tell you, it was no longer news. Nevertheless, during the last week of November I reported the destruction of seven convoys totalling 47 ships, naval and cargo, as well as an estimated 25,000 Japanese. Also destroyed were countless tons of desperately needed supplies.

The wretched troops didn't even have the honor of dying in combat for their emperor but went to their graves in the Camotes Sea like caged rats, crammed into the holds of overloaded ships. Not one of those convoys had even the most remote chance of success, and at least 95 percent of the men were doomed to certain death as soon as they set foot on their assigned transport. I don't believe there has ever been a more persistently useless sacrifice of life, on such a large scale, in the history of warfare.

And the end was not yet.

S-P-E-C-I-A-L   R-E-P-O-R-T

Liberty Ship

There was one honor too often accorded correspondents in World War II that none of us ever wanted, at least not at the stipulated price. With our nation's shipyards turning out Liberty ships at a phenomenal rate to move the vast resources of men and materiel necessary to support that war, a demand was created for suitable names for these craft. Someone suggested that the names of veteran correspondents might be appropriate, and the idea was adopted. You had to die in the line of duty to qualify.

A short time after our landing in Leyte I was driving in the Tacloban dock area, watching the process of unloading the seemingly endless stream of ships, most of them Liberty ships, that were supplying our military effort. Suddenly I heard my name being shouted, and with a Dutch accent. I jammed on the brakes and jumped out to investigate. The voice was coming from the bridge of a ship moored alongside the dock, and I immediately recognized Captain Jan Praas, the skipper who had carried me to safety from Java. The ship, of course, was the M.S. *Janssens*, reconditioned in a Sydney shipyard and back serving the Allied cause.

I parked my jeep and ran up the gangplank to a welcome that was hard to associate with the grim, unsmiling, unsleeping martinet who had taken that ship through a Japanese blockade to the safety of Fremantle harbor. The captain had no Heineken in his reefer (refrigerator), but he had it well stocked with Australia's finest brews and insisted we salute our re-union although it was only about nine in the morning. Actually, he had business with the port captain that required his early attention, so we split a bottle of Swan lager and I went ashore, promising to return for the midday meal and conversation.

I doubt that many persons have ever enjoyed a bona fide *nasi-goreng* while moored to a cargo wharf on the island of Leyte. Captain Praas's Malayan crew, recruited in Australia, not only served a meal that was incredible in the heart of an active war zone, they also produced several of the native musical instruments used in the *gamelin*, the traditional combo of the Indies, so we had real Indonesian music to accompany our Javanese luncheon, our Australian beer, and the exotic ambience of a freight dock in the central Philippines. The work of stripping the *Janssens* of her war cargo never paused, however. Wars pay little attention to reunions.

We reminisced at great length about the escape from Java. Praas admitted he was as scared as I several times during that voyage. He wanted to know what had happened to the other correspondents, and I told him that Win Turner had returned to his Sydney newspaper, that George Weller and I were still trying to make some sense out of covering a war, but that Frank Cuhel had been killed in the crash of the *Yankee Clipper* in Lisbon harbor in April, 1943, while transferring to North Africa to cover that phase of the war for *MBS*. I told him how Frank and I had occupied adjoining quarters in Melbourne and Sydney, becoming close friends despite professional rivalry. An all-time football great at the University of Iowa, and a medal-winning hurdler in the 1928 Amsterdam Olympics, Frank had a brilliant mind and a genius for friendship. Although reporters have to learn to accept the loss of friends in the ruthlessness of modern warfare, Frank's death was a particularly harsh blow.

The luncheon was all too brief, but both the captain and I had duties so I thanked him for a splendid meal that compensated generously for the long, but necessary, subjugation to sausages, cabbage, and potatoes (mixed!) while we were eluding the Japanese on the Indian Ocean. I went ashore, promising to return the following morning to see if the *Janssens* were still in port. The next day I arrived at the dock just in time to see the *Janssens* moving away from its mooring. Praas and I exchanged shouted farewells—I never saw him again—and the ship moved into the stream. As I stood there waving, another ship— this one a Liberty ship—moved in behind the *Janssens*, preparing to occupy the same berth. I glanced casually at her nameplate and my knees nearly buckled.

The ship was the *Frank J. Cuhel.*

CHAPTER 29

Anniversaries and Ormoc

December 7 (December 8 in the Pacific), as the anniversary of Pearl Harbor, was something of a let-down to most of us on the scene, in both 1942 and 1943. For some reason, or perhaps for no reason at all, an air of expectation attached to the date, an idea that the Japanese would attempt a major strike somewhere in the theater by way of commemorating their one unchallenged, unforgettable victory.

I was in New Guinea on both dates, and it soon became apparent the once-proud enemy was in no mood to celebrate anything. In 1942 he was on the verge of losing Buna, his toehold on New Guinea and the Solomons was slipping, and his overall forward drive had definitely ended. All the celebrating was on our side, and we marked the day with a very successful attack on enemy positions beyond the Owen Stanleys, bagging a half-dozen Zeros in the process, with no loss to ourselves. I mention this because I watched the planes returning, counted the victory rolls, and witnessed the quiet satisfaction evident in any squadron after a successful mission with everyone home safely. But the thing that impressed the event indelibly on my mind was that the next communiqué detailing the raid listed our losses as *light*—superb understatement.

The following year the enemy had even less reason to celebrate.

We marked the anniversary by pouring tons of bombs on Japanese air bases in New Britain in preparation for our landings at Cape Gloucester two weeks later. By this time there undoubtedly were many under the Rising Sun who would prefer to forget entirely a day that launched events now completely out of control.

But the third anniversary was different. Both the Japanese and the Allies scheduled major moves on that day, although it's doubtful the enemy included any "celebration" in his plans.

General MacArthur, according to those close to him, was unhappy with the Ormoc stalemate. Walter Krueger was a sound soldier, but he was above all a conservative soldier. "God's mill grinds slow, but sure" seemed to be his ruling dictum, but MacArthur felt Krueger placed too much emphasis on "slow." That trait would eventually deprive the Sixth Army of the right to lead the planned assault on the Japanese mainland. MacArthur had his own very definite idea of how to break the Ormoc logjam, but Krueger was slow to buy it. The Seventy-seventh Division was on hand, completely equipped and ready for action, serving as Krueger's reserve. Twice MacArthur *suggested* that the Seventy-seventh be moved, by water, around the island and landed on the east coast of Ormoc Bay, directly behind the enemy positions. The proposal was made in the form of a suggestion because MacArthur believed that a four-star army commander should make his own decisions. When two suggestions failed to produce any action, however, MacArthur reluctantly gave the formal order, and the early end of the Leyte campaign was assured.

At the same time, the Japanese launched one more reinforcement attempt with one of the largest convoys of the campaign. Seven destroyers and destroyer-escorts and six transports were on the way down from the China Sea.

The forty-eight hours from December 6 to December 8 produced confusion among the reporters. The high command tried to keep plans under cover for security reasons, but several of us guessed something was under way involving the Seventy-seventh Division, and Ormoc was the obvious answer. But our big surprise came when orders were handed down to issue side arms to all correspondents!

I immediately asked New York for more air time, not sure what I would report but having no doubt there would be plenty of news. Then I went in to Diller's makeshift office to protest the order. We were noncombatants, I explained as if he didn't know, and were forbidden by military law to carry arms. He agreed fully but patiently explained that the matter was completely out of his hands. The orders had come from way up the line, probably Sixth Army headquarters, and there was no appeal. So I walked out carrying a shiny new .38-caliber pistol, which I promptly tucked away at the bottom of my gear, and went back to work trying to find out what was happening. (The pistol stayed buried in my gear until I reached Manila months later, when I presented it to a noncom who had been helpful. I never saw a correspondent wear a gun, and the subject was never again brought up.)

The reason for the original order became evident shortly after noon that same day, when we learned that the Japs had dropped an unknown number of paratroopers in central Leyte not far from Fifth Air Force headquarters. There proved to be about two hundred in the mission, not nearly enough to threaten nearby installations but, as we realized later, its primary mission was to divert attention from the convoy.

Like everything the enemy tried in the latter months of 1944, both the convoy and the diversion were total failures. Patrols set out at once in search of the paratroopers and had little trouble locating and destroying them. The Seventy-seventh was on the water by this time, heading for the Surigao Straits and the west coast of the island. It had been the original plan to leave the protection of the division to the Fifth Air Force, but long before the Seventy-seventh reached its destination, scout planes reported a large enemy convoy coming in from the north, the Jap's desperation fleet of thirteen vessels aimed at the same target, Ormoc Bay.

Immediately Navy Hellcats and Marine Corsairs were called in to support the Fifth, and the enemy moved forward to another total rout on land and on sea, total destruction of the convoy and before many days the loss of his final corner of the island.

Once the Japs realized we were also launching a seaborne offensive, they had to divide their already inadequate air strength for offensive and defensive assignments, both completely outmanned and outgunned. It was again a matter of too little, too late. Caught completely by surprise, as usual, the enemy had no time to maneuver troops into position to meet our landing, and the Seventy-seventh went ashore virtually unopposed at the beach, some three miles south of Ormoc City. Three days later, after some heavy fighting to dispose of the belated opposition, the Seventy-seventh was in Ormoc City with the enemy caught in a completely hopeless situation with the Seventy-seventh at his rear, the Tenth Corps to his north, and the Twenty-fourth Corps to the south. If we had been fighting any enemy except the Japanese that would have been the end to the battle of Leyte.

Actually it *was* the end of the battle, except that the Japanese, as always, refused to surrender, singly or by units, and we had no alternative except to kill them all, one by one. It would take some time to complete that grisly assignment forced on us by the Japanese.

The Japanese attitude toward death is something no Occidental can easily understand. In 1943, when I was on my first home leave, I had a long discussion with Eric Severeid, one of the great CBS News correspondents but a reporter who had never at that time been in Asia. Eric was emphatic in his disbelief that the Japanese were any more willing to die than any other race. That was before the advent of the kamikaze, and Eric obviously believed that accounts of other suicidal exploits had been grossly exaggerated. I certainly couldn't agree with him, and when I returned to the Pacific that conversation stayed with me. Could I be wrong?

Everything that happened from that time forward served to bear me out completely, and the battle for Leyte Island provided the cap, more than any individual kamikaze could ever do. Whether the Japanese actually *wanted* to die is something only the individual could know, but I have always been convinced they were perfectly *willing* to die, and did so without hesitation and for reasons almost impossible for westerners to comprehend.

A lifetime of indoctrination in a religion that stressed the divinity of the emperor and taught that highest honors attended him who died for his emperor, was, of course, the foundation of the Japanese attitude toward the hereafter. But when that lifelong indoctrination was combined with a military creed that rated death as infinitely preferable to the perfidy of surrender, the result was a conception of death that Occidentals, and most Orientals, probably never can comprehend. Furthermore, the Japanese soldier was taught from the first day of training for his intended Pacific conquest that the barbaric enemy, American or Australian, would subject any prisoner captured to untold tortures, agonies from which instant death would be a welcome relief. Finally, he was led to believe that any soldier who did surrender to the enemy and who did survive would be forever a pariah, an outcast who could never return to his family or resume a normal life. And he believed it.

It has been estimated that upward of seventy thousand Japanese perished under the Hiroshima bomb, but that frightful toll did, at least, have the positive effect of convincing most, if not all, of the Tokyo military that the end was at hand. More than a hundred thousand Japanese died in the battle for Leyte, thousands without ever reaching Leyte soil, but that futile and horrible waste of human life, Japanese life, had no visible effect on the Messrs Koiso and Tojo and the militarist clique that continued to rule Japan. With them it was still a matter of face, and the slaughter had to continue.

Thousands of Japanese lives could have been saved had the Japanese simply surrendered when, after the fall of Ormoc City, the situation became demonstrably hopeless. Yamashita retired with his staff to Luzon even before MacArthur declared the battle ended, but he left behind him thousands of troops scattered through the hills of western Leyte, obviously with orders to observe "the creed."

One of the most inexplicable anticlimaxes of this, or any other battle of the Pacific war, came two days after we had completed full possession of Ormoc Bay and were concentrating on hunting down the enemy in those nearby hills. Early on Wednesday morning, under cover of predawn darkness but completely without air cover or naval escort, three small Japanese transports sailed into Ormoc Bay as nonchalantly as if entering Yokohama harbor and headed straight for our batteries on the opposite shore. The batteries picked them up before they were near any land and destroyed them with all hands. If anyone reached shore, he had to be a strong swimmer and would have found a reception party waiting. After more than four decades I am still trying to decide whether we were witnessing a complete breakdown of enemy communications or a waterborne kamikaze-type exercise born of sheer frustration.

General MacArthur observed Christmas Day by declaring the battle won and relieving the Sixth Army from all further Leyte duty. General Eichelberger's Eighth Army took over and spent the next month killing hundreds of recalcitrant Japs who chose death rather than the simple gesture of raising their hands. Finally, the battle for Leyte had passed into history.

The one redeeming feature of Leyte's weather, as far as the radio correspondents were concerned, was its failure to have any pronounced effect on atmospherics across the Pacific. The *Apache* was never in better form, and while we did have some "conditions beyond our control," overall transmission was good and New York made full use of it.

White had promised me an assistant before we left New Guinea,

Merry Christmas, Leyte style! Beer is hardly a holiday substitute for the Yule wassail bowl but, believe your correspondent, it is better than nothing. The tree was a tropical bush plucked from a nearby roadside and the decorations included all the paper clips one could filch from GHQ plus copious quantities of bathroom tissue provided by the navy. *Courtesy U.S. Army*

and he actually sent a man who got as far as Honolulu, where an "informed source" told him the Philippines campaign had been postponed indefinitely. Without telling White, he returned to New York just about the time we were wading ashore at Leyte. As a result, I had the battle of Leyte almost altogether on my own, averaging two broadcast reports a day at roughly twelve-hour intervals, usually from the *Apache*, which I preferred, but sometimes from the makeshift studio the Signal Corps had put together in a Tacloban schoolhouse.

It was strenuous but rewarding. There is nothing a radio reporter hates more than inaction. He is always tethered to his mike and can't wander as far afield as the press reporters could and did. When widely spaced schedules indicate a lack of interest on the part of New York in any particular phase of "his" war, he becomes restless and starts to ask himself questions. ("What the hell am I doing here?")

When my assistant did arrive in mid-December, he was too late to be of much help in Leyte, but he proved to be exactly what I wanted. Jack Adams was a seasoned reporter with diverse experience, including the Washington beat. White had briefed him thoroughly on radio techniques and CBS News procedures. Finally, he had a personality I knew would mesh perfectly with the men on Diller's staff who could make his job much easier.

How Adams escaped the selective service ferrets, I never knew and never asked. Jack was in his early thirties and apparently in robust health, just what the draft boards were looking for. But he was also a damned good reporter, had obviously been cleared by Washington, and was on the spot, and that was my only concern. Now I could break my electronic bonds for a day or two if a good story happened to be breaking in another area. Jack Adams would prove invaluable once we hit the beaches of Luzon.

The final days of the waning Leyte campaign were overshadowed when General MacArthur sired another coup reminiscent of the Admiralties and Hollandia. Despite the misgivings of many senior members of his staff, the General, on December 12, dispatched an amphibious task force under the command of Brig. Gen. Bill Dunkel down through Surigao to move north through the Sulu Sea and effect a landing on the south coast of Mindoro Island.

Mindoro lies directly south of Manila, some two hundred miles at its southern point where the landing was made, and about twice that distance by air, west-northwest of Leyte. It was within easy fighter and bomber range of Manila and southern Luzon, but it was deep in Japanese-held territory. Many on MacArthur's staff expected heavy opposition because of the strategic value of the island. The General didn't agree, and again he was proved right. A few Zekes made passes at the convoy as it steamed north, and General Dunkel was slightly wounded while on the bridge of his command ship, but no important material damage resulted, and there was virtually no opposition at the beach. We were well established before it finally became evident there would be no important opposition on the island at any time.

The coup, of course, cut the Philippines archipelago in two at its waist, the Visayas, and isolated thousands more Japanese to the south. Mindoro's dry season was a welcome relief for our engineers, and we had our first airstrip in operation within four days with others to follow quickly. But the prime reason for the Mindoro move lay in MacArthur's master plan for the invasion of Luzon and the drive to Manila, a plan that was top secret at that time.

His strategy, in part, called for major landings on the beaches of Lingayen Gulf, a large inlet on the western coast of Luzon, almost exactly at its center. Our attacking convoy would follow Dunkel's route around the southern end of Leyte through the Sulu Sea to the South China Sea, then skirt the west coasts of Mindoro and Luzon to its destination. Possession of Mindoro with a full complement of fighter and bomber bases in operation would cover our right flank as the convoy moved into the China Sea.

It was later confirmed that the Japanese once again misjudged MacArthur's intention, believing our objectives would be the islands of Negros and Palawan to the south and west. By the time they realized their error, their available troops were wrongly committed. Further, they undoubtedly were running short of manpower after their massive waste of life in Leyte and the waters surrounding the island. Also, they dared not reduce their Luzon garrison too greatly when Luzon clearly would be our next objective. I doubt even MacArthur expected Mindoro to be secured so rapidly and at such minimal cost.

Although there was no connection between the two events, the announcement of the Mindoro conquest coincided almost exactly with word from Washington that General MacArthur was one of a small, elite group of U.S. Army, Navy, and Air Force commanders to receive the newly created rank that would be marked by five stars, on the land, sea, or in the air. That news created quite a stir at GHQ because the new five-star insignia didn't exist and there were no silversmiths operating in the Leyte quagmire. There seemed to be no alternative except to send back home for the work of a qualified craftsman. That meant, of course, that Douglas MacArthur would have to be content with his four-star device for a few more days.

I never had the feeling that MacArthur considered the delay worthy of a second thought. After all, four stars had marked the highest possible rank since George Washington resigned his command after the Revolution, a rank not again attained until Ulysses S. Grant was so recognized after his triumphs in the Civil War. In Manila, four years earlier, MacArthur had told me he didn't believe the rank (we were talking about the equivalent rank of field marshal) would ever be awarded by our government to an active commander, although possibly to a victorious commander upon retirement, more as a reward for distinguished achievement than as an advance in rank. Now he was being cited for a promotion he avowedly never expected.

But the delay did bother the people close to him, men who regarded the five stars as an accolade for the entire theater as well as a promotion for their commander. Someone in Gen. Hugh ("Pat") Casey's Corps of Engineers decided to find a solution. I never learned exactly who was responsible for the original idea, but a company of engineers made a collection of Australian, Dutch (Indies), and Philippine coins—pounds, guilders, and pesos—melted them down and refined the molten silver, and created two sets of the insignia from patterns made by themselves. The use of Pacific coins was symbolic, of course, but they were also the only silver objects immediately available. The gleaming circlets of stars, twin sets, were presented to the General as Christmas presents one day late. Even the matchless skills of the army engineers can't always produce miracles faster than overnight. I doubt that any other member of that elite group donned his circlet of stars earlier than Douglas MacArthur, who was farthest removed—thanks to the Corps of Engineers in which he began his military career.

One night during that steaming Christmas season, a group of air force officers and I were sitting around Fifth Fighter Command living quarters, masterminding the war and lamenting the fact that the Mindoro foray hadn't flushed out more targets. The conversation turned to kamikazes. Everyone seemed to agree that the doubtful results produced by this type of derring-do were not worth the deliberate sacrifice of a trained pilot and the destruction of his plane, particularly when the enemy was so acutely short of both. One well-placed five-hundred-pounder could be just as effective, if not more so, and the bomber pilot had at least an outside chance of a repeat attack.

"Personally, I've never considered the so-called heroism of the kamikaze any great deal." That was Maj. Gen. Paul B. ("Squeeze") Wurtsmith, who headed the Fifth Fighter Command, a pilot who had been in combat continuously since the first American fighter plane had reached Australia. He was perched on the edge of his cot, beer in hand, clad like the rest of us in the formal evening wear for pilots in the tropics, underwear shorts. He continued, "The Jap pilot may not be too well trained, but he isn't stupid. He knows the odds are stacked against him. He knows from personal experience that he's flying an inferior crate against a better-trained enemy and his chances of finally surviving are minimal. I doubt that Japan has the equivalent of one squadron of pilots who were flying combat back in the days of Port Darwin." No one questioned that premise, so he went on, "If I were in his place, I'd fly with the idea that every mission was probably my last and that I'm certain to buy the farm before too long. So, why not volunteer for K-duty, and get it over with fast?"

Then followed a spirited discussion as to whether the kamis were actually bona fide volunteers or merely victims of the well-known "military volunteer" system, as in "Captain Jones, ten members of your company will volunteer for fatigue duty."

Not being a combat pilot I merely listened, but I had witnessed considerable combat, and I had some very definite ideas of my own, most of which paralleled those of Squeeze Wurtsmith.

I had seen kamikazes crash into three ships during our first week in Leyte Gulf, and while they did cause some damage and a few casualties, not one of the ships was put out of commission. Even more significant, I had seen two kamis, forced off their course by the effectiveness of our anti-aircraft fire, plunge into the bay with no harm to anyone or anything but themselves. The kamikazes were, like most of the other ideas produced by the Japanese in the last year of the war, a desperation ploy. But no such ploy could alter the one fact made plain by the battle for Leyte Island: the Emperor's armed forces were under the control of men who just didn't know how to conduct modern warfare.

CHAPTER 30

Return to Luzon

Shortly after daybreak on the morning of January 10, 1945, I sat down before a microphone aboard the *Apache* and began a pool broadcast to the combined American networks:

> I am speaking to you this morning form the island of Luzon—
> from what's reputed to be the foremost Japanese stronghold in the
> Philippines but which was, less than twenty-four hours ago, the scene

of an almost bloodless landing by the forces of General Douglas MacArthur.

I've taken part in four major amphibious landings out here in the Pacific during the past year, but yesterday's assault was, at once, the dullest and the most thrilling of my experience.

It was dull just as perfection is often prone to be dull. It's the unexpected that makes for drama, and the preparations that preceded this landing left no room for the unexpected.

It was thrilling to be a witness to this great display of amphibious power—greater even than that at Leyte Gulf—but it was most thrilling to splash ashore through the foaming surf and to stand again on the soil of Luzon, to realize that we were only little more than a hundred miles from Manila, where I have many friends who have waited for more than three years in the confines of their internment camp for our return.

I was up on the bridge of our landing craft long before dawn yesterday. The Southern Cross, symbolic of the Southwest Pacific, had followed us far north of the equator and hung directly over the beach. On the dark purple water, as far as the eye could carry through the intermittent moonlight, hundreds of ships of every type surrounded us—transports and cruisers, cargo vessels and battleships, landing craft and destroyers.

Shortly before sunrise the big warships began their methodical pounding of the landing beaches and by the time the sun had climbed above the mountains of northern Luzon, thousands of American boys had begun swarming over the sides of their transports, down the rope nets into the waiting barges.

This was the hour when the Jap air force was expected to strike in force in one last desperate endeavor. Just at sunrise one lone plane showed up and was promptly chased away. A half-hour later another plane appeared and was promptly shot down.

The small barges formed their flotillas and moved off toward the shore, and in their wake came the long lines of LST's, LSM's, and LCI's, the bigger troop and cargo landing craft. Great LSD's—floating dockships—opened their stern gates and disgorged their smaller craft.

Suddenly the deafening cacophony of the warships ended—a signal that the first troops were moving ashore. It was as simple as that —and we are still waiting for enemy opposition. The fate of Luzon and of the Philippines has been settled without any possibility of doubt.

If that final statement seemed a bit overoptimistic at the time, it proved to be accurate. Four years of watching Japanese operations in many parts of the Pacific had convinced me that once again I was witnessing the one exercise at which they excelled—delayed futility.

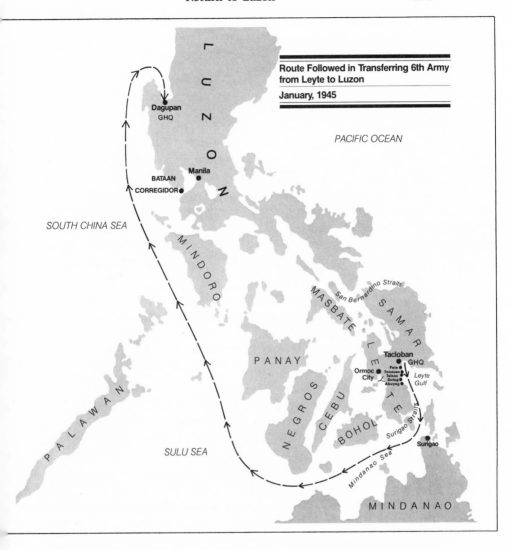

Route Followed in Transferring 6th Army
from Leyte to Luzon

January, 1945

The progress of a convoy is always governed by the speed of its slowest component, and among the nine hundred ships (plus or minus a few dozen) that left Leyte Gulf and other ports for Lingayen Gulf on January 4 and 5 were cargo vessels, vital to the campaign but hardly qualified for a regatta. Consequently, our swift escorts had to throttle back. Our LCI (landing craft, infantry), which carried about a dozen correspondents in addition to staff officers and personnel, spent a restful five days in the waters of the southern Philippines and the China Sea. We saw no more than five enemy planes, none of which paid us the slightest heed.

Other sections of the convoy were not so fortunate, however. The U.S.S. *Boise*, which carried the General and his staff, was attacked so often it seemed certain the Nips had discovered just who she was carrying.

It may seem strange that we, in our own little ship, weren't more aware of attacks on other parts of the armada, but it was perfectly normal given the length of the convoy. I never learned just how much ocean would be needed to float some nine hundred ships in convoy formation, but it had to approach fifty miles in length. From the bridge of our LCI we could seldom see more than a couple of dozen other ships between us and the four horizons. When you divide nine hundred by two dozen, you'll come up with a lot of miles between the "tender and the caboose."

At no time was our convoy more than a half-hour flight from a known Japanese air base, and the fact that it was not subjected to more serious harassment was eloquent testimony to the effectiveness of George Kenney's airmen, who kept those bases under almost constant attack.

As luck would have it, our LCI, on the morning of January 9, moved into the beach right next to the barge bringing General MacArthur ashore from the *Boise*. Engineers by this time had built a pier from the beach into the water, using great steel cubes that were floated empty into their designated positions, then flooded with sea water. As I watched, one of the engineering officers on the pier motioned for the General's barge to move alongside so MacArthur could walk ashore dry-shod. The General vetoed that idea immediately, so the barge moved directly into the beach beside our craft and dropped its ramp. Once again Douglas MacArthur emulated the combat troops, as he had in Leyte, and waded ashore.

Historians of every calibre tend to attribute anything MacArthur did that was at all out of the ordinary to an overdeveloped ego. After serving with him through one entire war and part of a second, I have my own idea. Douglas MacArthur believed strongly that anyone in command of troops should be prepared and able to do anything he ordered his men to do. Thus, wading the surf instead of walking dry-shod was his personal salute to the combat soldier. It was only one of many such gestures he made.

Once ashore, it was the Leyte beachhead repeated but without a formal pronouncement. Ignoring the fine white sand that made walking difficult, the general strode from one command post to another, observing, asking questions, and making an occasional suggestion. Unlike the Leyte landing, however, there were no signs of the enemy, no bodies to inspect, no Jap unit insignia to be identified. There just wasn't any enemy to be found. While I'm sure the General expected the bulk of Yamashita's troops to be elsewhere, he didn't expect them to be entirely missing. I had the feeling he was a bit disappointed.

I've been told that several correspondents were critical of MacArthur for remaining aboard the *Boise* for two or three nights instead of moving ashore permanently. Looking back, I find this hard to believe, or to understand, if true, for almost all the press corps was itself billeted on naval ships, mostly landing craft, for the first week or two after the landing. My bunk aboard the LCI was certainly more comfortable than any cane-bottomed cot I might have found ashore or the steel deck of the *Apache*. I stayed with the navy as long as practical, and I can't fault any commanding officer, army or navy, who elected to do the same.

Shortly after leaving MacArthur on the beach, I was informed by one of Diller's staff that I had been chosen by lot to make the first official broadcast from Luzon. How I could have won a drawing in which I had not participated is still a mystery, but I was the only radio correspondent who had been in Luzon before and had friends waiting for our return, and I had been accredited to GHQ SWPA longer than any of my fellows. I suspect someone stacked the cards in my favor. Regardless of how it happened, it was a great thrill to sit before that microphone and realize I was once again on the island I had left nearly three and a half years before for what was to have been a brief trip to the Chinese mainland and Burma before returning to Luzon—Manila—on my way back to 485 Madison Avenue. I had been mentally reviewing those three and a half years as I waited for San Francisco to give me the go ahead. There had been little room for optimism in those first bitter months, and the flood of memories convinced me I was justified in the optimistic note on which I concluded my report.

CHAPTER 31

Pushing Southward

After four years of covering the world's biggest military theater on
my own an assistant was indeed welcome, and I could not have picked
a better aide than Jack Adams myself. At our first meeting we agreed
we could support each other more efficiently if we operated individually, each choosing his own assignments after the schedules had been
divided. We met at least once every day, usually at the GHQ press
room, to discuss our plans for the day and divide the schedules. In
this way we worked individually but as a team for the remainder of
the war with never a major difference.

Jack was an expert rifleman who had participated in international
competitions throughout Europe before the war, and that interesting
fact was the basis of the only near-disagreement we ever had. Soon
after we began our trek down the Luzon central plains, I began to get
reports of how my righthand man had borrowed weapons from GI's
to indulge in a bit of target practice, usually choosing the enemy,
when available, as his clay pigeon. I believe a noncombatant in a war
zone should remain exactly that, and that no correspondent should
carry arms for any reason. The thirty-eight issued to me in Tacloban
was still at the bottom of my duffle bag and would stay there. Jack
always denied these reports, and I must admit I've never known a man
who could look as innocent, even shocked, at my suspicions. But he
was never able to explain how the stories started or how the GI's
learned of his skills with a rifle. In all my years as a correspondent
covering the Pacific and Korean wars, no soldier ever offered me his
rifle for any reason, and I'm sure Jack had to do some expert selling
to get the chance to shoot. But that was a small price to pay for the
top-notch aide, the good right arm I greatly needed, and Jack Adams
ranked first among my favorite riflemen for the rest of his life.

In his memoirs Douglas MacArthur remarked with apparent satisfaction that our forces reached Tarlac, just under halfway to Manila,
in only twelve days. He is in fact quite laudatory as to the progress
of the Sixth Army and its commander at this point. Those of us who
were working closely with GHQ, however, had quite the opposite impression at the time.

I was in and out of GHQ every day, talking to anyone who might
have information I could use. Krueger's advance of fifty-five miles in

those twelve days was slightly less than five miles a day in the face of no opposition. The impression I had, reinforced several times, could be summed up as, "Why the hell doesn't Krueger get moving? What's holding him up?" That would never have been MacArthur speaking under any circumstances, even if he agreed, but the rest of the staff seemed to be unanimous, and Dick Sutherland, as chief of staff with three shiny stars, didn't hesitate to tell several of us, "If I were commanding the Sixth Army, we'd be in Manila right now."

There was no way to make Krueger accelerate except possibly by direct order, and MacArthur was not about to issue orders to an army commander. After all, we were not bogged down as we had been when he ordered the Seventy-seventh Division into Ormoc. Furthermore, his primary interest in Manila was centered on the Santo Tomás internment camp and thirty-seven hundred American and Allied civilians being held there completely at the mercy of an enemy who had shown no inclination to be merciful.

It was well known around GHQ that the General had been formulating plans to deal with this precarious situation long before we reached the Lingayen beaches, but only those closest to him had any idea what was in his mind. Any successful solution had to depend on complete surprise, however, and the C-in-C had long since proved his ability to surprise the Japanese. Meanwhile, all thoughts of Santo Tomás and Lost Baños, the secondary camp some forty kilometers south of Manila, were top secret.

The fact that MacArthur indicates no dissatisfaction with Krueger in his autobiography is completely in character. In none of his writings does he criticise any subordinate who failed to measure up, and there were many such. He handled such matters in his own way and closed the book. Significantly, however, long before Luzon was secured MacArthur chose Bob Eichelberger and his Eighth Army to lead the invasion of Japan, which happily never became necessary.

One thing MacArthur did that many of his staff didn't approve was to return a general officer he felt had failed to meet his standards back to Washington for reassignment without reducing him to permanent rank. Almost every general officer in World War II, in all wars, actually, served at several grades above his permanent rank. Most were colonels or lieutenant colonels, but in the air corps, particularly, there were permanent captains wearing stars, and at least one (probably more) of George Kenney's brigadiers was a permanent first lieutenant! Most theater and army commanders reduced an erring general to permanent rank immediately as a matter of self-defense. If a major general reported to the Pentagon for reassignment, the chances were great he would be assigned an office commensurate with that rank and be in strategic position to make waves against his former commander. If he reported wearing an eagle or a leaf, however, he probably would never be heard from again. During the war MacArthur felt it necessary to replace several general officers, but they wore their stars back to the Pentagon. One or two did later splash water, as he knew they would, but that was the way he felt about discipline. He truly hated to see anyone fail, particularly a professional soldier.

Regardless of his reaction to Sixth Army progress, MacArthur had more important things on his mind at that moment. Manila was a symbol whose recapture would have significance to outside observers but it had no strategic value. MacArthur had made no attempt to hold it four years earlier for just that reason. He had then declared it an open city in order to prevent the useless destruction of a beautiful capital city and to avoid senseless civilian bloodshed, and he expected Yamashita to do the same now. But Yamashita had no interest in conserving life or property, regardless of any absence of tactical values. This proved to be one of MacArthur's few complete misjudgments of Japanese intentions.

During the battle for Leyte, press headquarters and GHQ had remained in Tacloban for the entire eleven weeks, with the *Apache* just off shore. At Lingayen the *Apache* still was just off shore, and as long as GHQ remained in Dagupan, where MacArthur had established his first Luzon base, we radio reporters had no technical problems. That situation naturally didn't last. Even with Krueger's cautious pace, each day's progress took us farther from the gulf and from our transmitter.

At this time Diller and Schechter, with the authority of GHQ behind them, put a little pressure on Maj. Gen. Spencer Akin, SWPA communications chief, and for the first time we found ourselves equipped with an efficient land-based but portable transmitter, which linked us to the *Apache* by dependable land lines. That transmitter followed us all the way down the central plains, and we no longer had to be amphibious to use the *Apache's* electronic talents.

The studio was first set up in a nondescript frame house in Lingayen town, about ten kilometers from Dagupan on the main north-south highway to Manila. When GHQ moved to a sugar central (refinery for sugar cane) in San Miguel, near Tarlac, our studio went along and set up in a nipa-thatched Filipino house. The third stop was Grace

Park on the northern edge of Manila, and the last a bank building in Plaza Cervantes in the heart of downtown Manila, directly across the plaza from the ruins of the RCAC studio from which I had aired my reports in 1941. All that took weeks, of course, but in the meantime we were always within reasonable reach of a microphone that would connect us with San Francisco and the network. Four decades ago, half a world away, and in a country ravaged by warfare, it really was something of an electronic miracle.

Those three weeks following the January 9 landings produced no really startling news, and we reporters roamed the central plains, checking hospitals, unit command posts, and newly liberated towns and talking with Filipino civilians who had witnessed events from the enemy's side of the lines. In one Dagupan hospital I encountered, quite by accident, Dr. Enrique Romulo, brother of Gen. Carlos Romulo, who didn't know his brother was within a couple of city blocks. "Rommie," the general, was equally uninformed, so I promoted a reunion in exchange for a good human interest story. In another hospital I was approached by a Filipina nurse wanting to know if I, as an American, had any information about the American nurses captured on Corregidor. She was Federica Garcia of Manila with another good story. She had been serving with an American hospital unit when the Japanese came, was transferred to Bataan to serve until that peninsula was lost, then on "the Rock" until that stronghold also fell. Nurse Garcia was held as a prisoner until the American nurses were sent to Santo Tomás, at which time she was freed. Normally you expect to uncover stories of American casualties in those hospitals, stories of GI's and how their part in the war brought them there, but such cases, providentially, were rare in Luzon at that time. Our casualties had been minimal.

To the Filipino, the most important development was the departure, at last, of the despised Japanese. It never occurred to anyone that the Americans might actually lose out in the long run, permitting the enemy to come back. When I posed this "possibility" to several, just to get their reaction, it was always met with derision. The Filipino was deeply impressed by what he had seen of America's military muscle, particularly when contrasted with the rubber-band sinew the Jap had exhibited for three years. One Lingayen businessman told me he had seen more American trucks in the first four days after the landing than he had seen the Japanese operate during the entire war. Our movement of ordnance was an awesome sight to these people and left

Engineers and Seabees bring ashore the war materiel that will carry the Sixth Army from Lingayen Gulf down the central Luzon plain to Manila and eventual liberation of all the Philippine Islands. This is a side of modern warfare that doesn't get too much credit, but without it there would be no victory. I didn't find all my stories under combat conditions. *Courtesy U.S. Army*

them with no doubt that the "blessings" of the Greater East Asia Co-Prosperity Sphere could safely be forgotten.

Late in the month I learned that the Eleventh Corps of Eichel-berger's Eighth Army, under the command of Maj. Gen. William Hall, would make an amphibious landing on the coast of Zambales province, just north of Subic Bay and the Bataan peninsula. I immediately applied for transportation and joined the amphibious fleet, commanded by Rear Adm. Arthur Strubel, which would provide naval support.

If anything can be humorous in connection with modern warfare, the Zambales landings came close. All intelligence reports had predicted minimal opposition, but none had even hinted there would be no opposition whatever. Just before time for the shore bombardment, at dawn, word came from a guerrilla unit that no bombardment would be necessary. Representatives of the guerrillas met with Hall and Struble and the big guns were called off. As the barge flotilla carrying units of the Twenty-fourth (34th Regimental Combat Team) and the Thirty-eighth divisions headed for the beaches, a welcoming party of guerrillas, members of the local military units, and scores of curious citizens was there to meet them.

The military units lost no time in forming ranks and moving inland as directed by their commanders. On the beach there was much handshaking, laughter, and shouts of *mabuhay* and *vic-to-ree!* All we needed was a keg of beer and a throaty political orator to make it a real Fourth of July celebration! Not having to report to Krueger, General Hall gave his men free rein, and they moved swiftly toward the interior. He told me later that the advance covered twelve miles before pausing to tighten its supply lines. Everyone on the beach agreed that was the way a war should be fought!

There was also a humorous aftermath. During my residence in Manila after the war, I attended a reception at which President Ramón Magsaysay was a guest. During the evening a group of us were talking with the president about nothing in particular. Suddenly he turned to me and asked, "Bill, do you remember the first time we met?" As general manager of the Manila Broadcasting Company, I had had considerable contact with Ramón Magsaysay since before he became secretary of national defense, his stepping stone to Malacañan, but I couldn't recall any special "first time." He laughed, "It was on the beach at Zambales when you landed with the Eleventh Corps. I was a captain serving with the guerrillas who greeted you." Then he administered the coup de grace, "You were not so stout in those days!"

S-P-E-C-I-A-L   R-E-P-O-R-T

Gold Braid

"Gold braid on an ordinary campaign cap! No one but Doug MacArthur would ever think of that one." That opinion, variously worded, was expressed thousands of times by thousands of people during the four years of the Pacific war, and long after. "MacArthur's cap" was probably the best-known personal identification symbol to emerge from the whole global conflict, surpassing Montgomery's beret or Georgie Patton's twin silver pistols. Every GI, sailor, airman, or merchant seaman, in the Pacific recognized that cap instantly.

Inasmuch as all general officers who wore as many stars as MacArthur were authorized to design their own uniforms (e.g., the Eisenhower jacket), everyone believed the famous gold braid was MacArthur's inspiration, and a lot of us had a lurking admiration for his taste in headgear. The truth, however, as the truth is often proved to be, was several meters to the left. Not only did the General not specify the braid but he was more than a little disconcerted at what he considered an unnecessary expenditure. The story came out during the New Guinea campaign, when the General had temporary headquarters in Port Moresby, at former Government House. One evening while relaxing and chatting with a few members of his staff, someone mentioned the cap, and MacArthur rather ruefully told the group how it happened to come by its most distinguishing feature. One of those present was Maj. Phil R. North, and this account is his.

During his service with the Philippines Commonwealth Army, MacArthur never wore a uniform although his Philippines rank entitled him to the fanciest livery any designer could conceive. He obviously wasn't interested. His duties were administrative and he never wore anything except ordinary civvies, usually white linens in that tropical clime. When he was called to command the United States Armed Forces in the Far East in July, 1941, he had immediate need of a uniform, a need not easily filled in a foreign station and after several years in civvies. One thing he couldn't find in his gear was a campaign cap. Consequently he sent a rush order to his U.S. supplier for a khaki campaign cap, "the same as my last order." By that, he explained, he meant the same

size and material. He didn't remember that his last order, several years earlier, had been for a dress uniform. Gold braid was, and still is, standard adornment for dress uniform caps.

When the cap arrived it was, indeed, an exact copy of the previous cap, except that its color was khaki instead of blue. It was also accompanied by a bill that included a healthy charge for the gold braid. No Scot ever enjoyed spending money for something he didn't need, and Douglas MacArthur felt no need for gold braid on an ordinary campaign cap. It was, of course, too late to order a replacement, so the General paid the extra charge and put the cap into historic use, still without enthusiasm.

The gold-braided cap was probably one of the General's best investments, however, when measured in terms of the universal recognition it produced. And despite his first reaction, MacArthur eventually developed a genuine affection for the celebrated cap. All through the Pacific and Korean wars and his administration of Japan, he never wore another except when cold weather dictated something warmer than the tropical khaki.

Truly, the cap had a career of its own.

Although General MacArthur returned to uniform in July, 1941, his newly acquired headgear was not immediately prominent. The job of organizing USAFFE kept him close to his desk and his public appearances in Manila were limited.

Once the enemy struck, however, and the military action moved to Bataan and Corregidor, the General became a familiar figure as he strode tirelessly about the "Rock," inspecting installations, conversing with the men, making suggestions (he seldom issued a direct order), with the cap ever present to offer protection from a relentless sun. By the time President Roosevelt ordered him to Australia, General MacArthur's cap was famous far beyond the islands of the Philippines.

The seven-day journey from Corregidor to Melbourne by PT boat and converted bomber, almost spelled *finis* for the cap, just as that arduous trip threatened the lives of the General, his wife, Jean, and their son, Arthur, as well as the few members of his staff who accompanied him. The elements were never kind and the week-long battle with those elements while eluding the Japanese navy and air force, took a heavy toll on everyone and everything, including the cap.

Alternately saturated by salt-water spray, baked by the equatorial sun, and soaked again and again by rains of hurricane proportions, the General's cap almost gave up the fight. First of all, it shrank a couple of sizes and the braid was tarnished beyond recognition. Even the khaki-cloth top looked like any remnant from a rag-bag.

Knowing the affection the General had acquired for the cap in the preceding months, Jean MacArthur turned to Col. Sid Huff, an aide who had accompanied them from the "Rock," for help. Sid searched Melbourne to locate a hat-stretcher—an instrument Jean didn't know existed —and together they set to work.

First the cap was restored to its proper size, then metal polish and elbow grease released the braid from its camouflage. Even the khaki top responded to detergent, and the cap returned to active duty.

It had survived the first of many campaigns in which it would serve with the General during those ten historic years.

An occasional touching-up kept the cap serviceable during the long drive from Melbourne to Tokyo, but at the start of the Japanese occupation Jean MacArthur again decided a major overhaul was necessary and once more she called on Sid Huff.

There was no question the cloth top had to be replaced. It was stained so deeply its very color was doubtful, but both agreed that a brand new top on an obviously aging cap would look out of place. Accordingly, Sid searched through a stack of worn uniform shirts until he found a khaki material they agreed was close to the original, but without the brand-new sheen.

Finding a hat maker in Tokyo wasn't difficult but finding one who would accept the job was another matter. The hatter they chose refused at first even to touch the cap. He was afraid it would fall to pieces. Jean MacArthur is not easily dissuaded, however, and he finally agreed. Working under the personal supervision of both the General's wife and his A.D.C., the hatter actually restored the cap to something near its original condition. It would now serve the General faithfully through his administration of Japan and the Korean war.

During that epochal decade, 1941–51, General Douglas MacArthur probably had as many uniforms (mostly field-duty suntans) as any soldier on active duty, but he would never admit to more than one campaign cap, and that cap truly earned its place of honor in the MacArthur Memorial at Norfolk.

CHAPTER 32
Prisoners of War

A day or two before the Zambales landings, Larry Lehrbas, the colonel who was one of MacArthur's senior aides, called me aside as I walked through the Dagupan GHQ, and told me: "Bill, if you hear of a 'name' division being motorized, join it immediately. I can't tell you any more and you definitely must not mention this to anyone else." With that, he walked into his office and closed the door. I didn't really need anything else. Larry had been a top-flight newspaperman for many years and knew a good story. His accent on secrecy pointed unmistakably to the one subject of top concern to all of us: Manila and the Santo Tomás internees. A few discreet inquiries brought no more information, so I filed Larry's tip in the back of my mind and headed for Zambales.

When I returned to Dagupan after seeing the Eleventh Corps ashore, another correspondent stopped me on the street and asked, casually, "Why would they put the First Cav on wheels?" "Wheels? The First Cavalry? Are you sure?" "No doubt about it. They landed up the coast yesterday and are now rolling toward Cabanatuan." I told him, truthfully, I didn't even know the First Cav had left Leyte, and then I was on my way. It so happened I was carrying my trusty Hermes, so I just kept going. I started hitch-hiking southward in search of the cavalry, taking with me only the typewriter and the not-too-clean suntans I was wearing. I never got back to the LCI on the Dagupan beach to salvage the rest of my gear.

As often happens when a reporter keeps moving, I stumbled, almost by accident, upon the *barrio* (village) where the Sixth Rangers had just brought the American prisoners of war who had been snatched only hours earlier from the prison camp near Cabanatuan. This was a story to rival Santo Tomás and I was faced with an immediate dilemma: how to cover two major stories breaking at the same time.

There was supposed to be a new studio set up by the Signal Corps at San Miguel, Tarlac, scheduled to be the next seat of GHQ and the press headquarters. I had no firm confirmation of this, however, and if I suspended my quest for the cavalry (actually, I knew where they were by now), I might miss the Manila story altogether.

Determined to be ready for any eventuality, I parked my mill on the hood of a jeep and pounded out my report, still wondering. The

answer came when I learned that a courier would leave shortly for
Sixth Army headquarters. The commanding officer agreed to send my
copy, together with an explanatory note to Jack Adams. Then he sent
a radio signal to Dagupan advising Adams to meet the courier. The
solution wasn't perfect, but it did work for most of a week. Jack stood
by at GHQ waiting for my reports and airing them for me. The results
were good enough to prompt a congratulatory message from Paul
White, something as easy to come by as the Congressional Medal!

Fortunately the barrio where the Alamo Scouts (Sixth Rangers) had
taken the liberated prisoners was not far from First Cavalry headquarters and I was able to greet my deliriously happy fellow countrymen,
share their jubilation, prepare my report for Adams to relay, and still
reach my original destination with time to spare. Again my luck was
at a peak, and I was able to file an exclusive report as the only reporter on the scene. It read:

> They were standing in the chow line when I first saw them—511
> Americans who had been prisoners of the Jap for three long, bitter
> years, 511 American men who had been awaiting sudden and vio-
> lent death and who miraculously had been spirited from their barbed-
> wire stockade to the comparative luxury of an American field hos-
> pital hastily set up in a Filipino schoolhouse. They were clad in gray
> hospital pajamas. Some wore shoes or sandals. Most were barefooted.
> In their hands, as they shuffled past the mess attendants, were tin
> plates, granite pie pans, aluminum mess kits, anything that would
> hold the great helpings of canned meat, vegetables, and fruit that
> were being dished out. Their expressions were as varied as the moods
> of man. Some seemed dazed, some alert. Some were somberly silent
> and others jubilantly talkative. I tried to speak to one of them, but
> the words wouldn't come and I turned away and blew my nose vio-
> lently.
> I looked for a familiar face, for anyone I had known in Manila be-
> fore the war. It wasn't easy, because most of these men had changed,
> obviously, in three years of privation and worse. Some wore beards,
> others were merely unshaven. Most were emaciated, and all were
> clearly fatigued after a perilous, strenuous night. Finally I found one.
> Just one out of 511, one of a dozen who might have been there. My
> discovery was Earle Baumgartner, head of RCA Communications in
> Manila, not only the man who had handled all my Manila broad-
> casts four years ago but also a close personal friend. We sighted each
> other almost simultaneously, and it was the warmest greeting I've
> ever received. "B.G." as everyone called him, was one of the healthi-
> est, a bit thinner, of course, but otherwise much the same.
> "Bill," he said, "if you don't think you are standing in the middle

of the five hundred happiest men in the world, you're crazy!"

Our conversation was probably amazing. What do you talk about to an old friend who has just stepped out of three years of hell? The war, of course, communications, golf, rice, mutual friends, the future, a wife who has had no news of him for three years, and more.

Gradually I got his story of the lightning-like rescue by a hand-picked company from the Sixth Ranger Battalion—the Alamo Scouts —which marched deep into enemy territory without being detected and snatched the entire roster right out from under the noses of a considerably larger garrison. All at a cost of one Ranger killed and three Rangers and one prisoner wounded.

"We had just turned in for the night," he told me, "when the whole world seemed to explode outside. Pistols, machine guns, mortars, carbines, all let loose at once. I fell to the floor and tried to dig a hole with my fingers. We had all decided the Japs would kill us when the Americans came too close, so I thought that this was it! Then I decided I really *did* want a hole, so I ducked out the door. As I reached the open air, a big six-foot American grabbed me by the shoulder and shouted, 'You're all right now, friend. We're here! Head for the main gate.' I headed!"

The departure was as precipitate as the arrival. The Rangers held off the garrison until the column moved away in the darkness to begin a march of nearly eight miles to the nearest point where transportation could be provided. Those who were too weak to walk were carried on the backs of individual Rangers the whole distance. It was beyond question one of the greatest feats of stamina and bravery in the long story of the Pacific war.

All the prisoners were bitter in their stories of treatment at the hands of the Japs, and all had verified tales of unprovoked killings and tortures at the whim of their jailers, whom they referred to as "Taiwan guards." But the abuse ended abruptly two days before our landings at Lingayen. The camp commandant announced they were no longer prisoners of war, but were to be regarded as civilians as long as they remained within the stockade. Then the guards disappeared and for forty-eight hours not a Jap was seen. Finally they began drifting back, but with a vastly different attitude. Now they proved to be courteous, even bowed when they entered the stockade. At the time of their temporary disappearance, the prisoners took over the Japs' store of food, and for the final three weeks they ate fairly well with no interference. But the guards remained until the end.

And so, 511 Americans were reclaimed from a living death. We knew there would be no rest until every other American and American ally in Japanese hands had been liberated.

CHAPTER 33

"Lightning Column"

Maj. Gen. Vernon Mudge, commander of the First Cavalry, had his command post in a tent on the outskirts of Cabanatuan. When I reached there that evening of February 1, I found three other friends of many years. Carl Mydans of *Life* magazine had spent a year in Santo Tomás, with Dean Schedler of the Associated Press and Frank Hewlett of United Press, who were newsmen in Manila and escaped from Corregidor to Australia. My own CBS News Far East headquarters still remained theoretically in Manila. Each of us had been tipped off by a friend at GHQ who understood our special interests in this mission.

General Mudge welcomed us but advised us to be sure we realized what we might be getting into. He indicated our projected route, almost directly south from Cabanatuan and east of the main north-south highway, the route of the Thirty-seventh Infantry Division, also heading for Manila. Mudge didn't say so, but the impression was strong we were in a race with the Thirty-seventh, with Manila as the prize. But we also realized we would be on wheels while our competition, commanded by Maj. Gen. Bob Beightler, would have to depend on shoe leather for transport. I never believed MacArthur set it up as a race, because everyone knew that only a major catastrophe could prevent the motorized unit from winning. The important thing was that Beightler's Thirty-seventh would be in perfect position to provide the immediate reinforcement the C-in-C knew would be needed.

Vernon Mudge understood the situation perfectly. He knew the cards were stacked in his favor, and he knew why. Santo Tomás, in MacArthur's mind, had to be taken swiftly, with as little fighting as possible, because he and his staff were certain that if we did have to fight our way into the camp, the Japanese would immediately start the wholesale slaughter everyone feared.

Nowhere else in the history of warfare will you find an instance of a military commander sending a force of barely eight hundred men into a city of more than a million population known to be held by the equivalent of at least two divisions of infantry. It was impossible, and the Japanese knew it was impossible. That was the premise on which MacArthur founded his entire strategy for the thrust. Based on his long association with the Oriental and his study of this particular Oriental, he was sure the Japanese would mark the progress of this fragile column and, from the very first, not believe what they saw. Furthermore, he didn't want the Thirty-seventh to arrive at the same time as the "flying column" because the arrival of a full division while the Japs were trying to solve the enigma of this small force might prompt large-scale fighting before the internees were in protective hands. There was no logistical reason why the Thirty-seventh shouldn't have been put on wheels as well. There was no shortage of transport.

MacArthur's plan worked perfectly, and the arrival of the Thirty-seventh came just at the moment the enemy was ready to believe. Bob Beightler was a great soldier, and he bitterly resented finishing second. But the assignment of his Thirty-seventh was just as important as that of the First Cav, if less spectacular. If the Thirty-seventh hadn't timed its movements perfectly, these words might never have been written and thirty-seven hundred helpless civilians might have found themselves squarely in the middle of disaster.

Back at Cabanatuan, General Mudge told us where the column (mostly the Eighth Cavalry Squadron) would be forming, about six kilometers south of his command post. He told us to report to Lt. Col. Haskett ("Hack") Conner in time for a midnight departure. It was then about seven o'clock. At this point one of his aides entered the tent carrying, to our amazement, a huge tray of turkey sandwiches. I had watched some five hundred newly freed prisoners of war consume prodigious quantities of canned rations down to the last morsel, but had had no food myself all day. You can't ask an emaciated, half-starved POW to share his first square meal in three years. There were no starved competitors for the sandwiches, however, and we all fell to with a will. The general watched us with perfect understanding and advised us to eat all we could. "I don't know when you'll eat again." Encouraging.

It was dark when we reached the rice paddy where the Manila column was being organized, but the moon was coming up and we could tell we were not joining an overpowering legion. It was impossible to size up the entire squadron, but what we could see was not too reassuring. This was the team that was going to strike Manila? Was it smart to place our faith in such a limited force? We stood on the edge of the bone-dry rice paddy and talked in low tones. There was some sentiment for returning to Cabanatuan, but after due deliberation we decided, unanimously, to proceed to Manila with that undermanned column rather than risk snipers lurking along the six kilometers back to Cabanatuan.

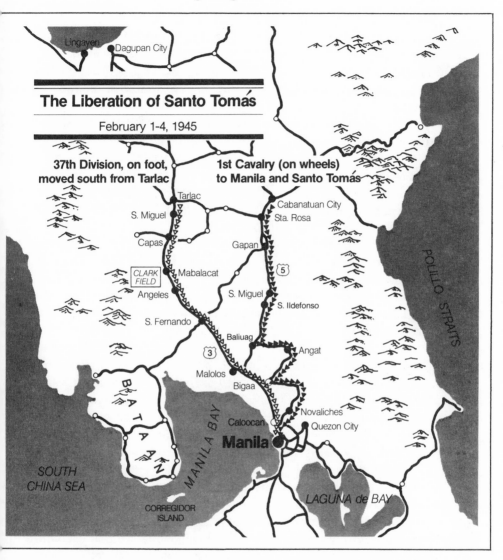

The Liberation of Santo Tomás

February 1-4, 1945

37th Division, on foot, moved south from Tarlac

1st Cavalry (on wheels) to Manila and Santo Tomás

Of such weighty decisions are heroes made!

There was no problem in locating Colonel Conner. His command post was a patch of ground in a corner of the paddy, marked by a map spread on the bristly rice stubble and partially illuminated by a field lantern. He wore the standard jungle greens. He showed no insignia, no silver leaf, but you knew immediately he was in command and after you had talked to him for only a few moments you were glad. We introduced ourselves, but he already had a signal from division command and was expecting us. Just as Mudge had, Conner asked if we were fully aware of what we might be getting into. Again we insisted we were, actually stretching the truth a bit. We really had no solid idea of what lay ahead, but we were not about to admit it.

With two ranking officers questioning our judgment, I suddenly thought for some inane reason of MacMahon at Sevastopol: "*J'y suis, j'y reste.*" We were there, without doubt, and we had little choice except to remain unless we wanted to start out on our own. Sometimes a person comes up with a silly thought like that one as an antidote to the apprehension he isn't willing to admit. At any rate, I decided to keep the good *maréchal* to myself.

Conner assigned our jeep a position in the column and advised us to get some sleep. We would leave in about three hours. We spread our shelter-halfs on the ground with the dirt parapet that enclosed the paddy as a pillow. It had been a strenuous and an emotional day and I was both tired and tense, but fatigue won and I fell asleep almost instantly.

Shortly after midnight an officer wakened us to a brilliant moon and starlit night that almost rivaled daylight. The roar of tanks and the rumble of ten-wheel trucks shook the ground, leaving no doubt that a major operation was building. Colonel Conner was still at his command post checking the formation of the column on the adjacent highway, but his maps had been gathered up and his jeep stood by ready for the signal.

The organizational activity had never eased since we joined the column some four hours earlier. Neighboring rice paddies had been filled with tanks, trucks, and field artillery, plus engineering, medical, and service units, and it was Conner's job to see that each unit found its proper place in the column. Late intelligence indicated the bulk of the enemy force would probably be stationed east of our route, to our left as we moved south, and the marine air arm had assigned units to cover that left flank. Finally, Conner told us a forward patrol had already reached the Angat River some forty miles to the south, and it was our assignment to establish contact with that patrol before dawn to secure that vital crossing.

Our first mortal casualty came before our task force had started to move. We learned that a reconnaissance patrol had been attacked about fifteen miles to the south, and Lt. Col. Tom Ross, whom some of us had known in Leyte, had been killed.

Promptly at one o'clock the signal was given, the lead tanks roared into action, and the "flying" column began to move. The task force was labeled a "lightning" column, but the lumbering tanks fixed the speed of the entire task force. Still, we were on wheels and we knew the enemy had no comparable rolling stock at hand. Although the column had been thrown together in a few brief hours, the organizational procedures and the operation en route were perfect. Tanks units moved ahead to seize threatened bridges, and it was reassuring as we reached those bridges to see the tanks standing sentinel at both ends to guard our crossing. The blackout was supposed to be total, but the moon cheated enough to outline those great machines of war. When we reached rivers where there were no bridges, usually the result of our own demolitions four years earlier, a huge bulldozer would bump off a trailer and begin grading ford approaches without a moment's delay. At one crossing the engineers built a ford approach and a makeshift bridge simultaneously and transferred the entire column in record time.

For the first few miles most of the *barrios* seemed deserted, the villagers apparently having fled to the fields or hills as the first threat of combat approached. But when we reached San Miguel, Bulacan (almost every province in Luzon has its San Miguel), a rich sugar center and capital of the province, we found the darkened streets crowded with Filipinos, mostly civilian but with a generous sprinkle of guerrillas, all cheering and singing with a fervor that bordered on hysteria. From then on we were greeted by delirious Filipinos in almost every community. When the civilians were absent, we knew the Japs were near.

We reached our primary objective, the advance patrol at the Angat River, shortly before dawn, only to find the enemy had retreated. We continued on into the little city of Baliuag, where we were greeted by thousands who thronged the streets, screaming, singing, and dancing around our column, oblivious to danger, until it became almost impossible to move. In the heart of the city our jeep finally was completely surrounded and we were forced to stop. As soon as we did, women and children threw flowers at us and fought to touch our hands, and the same was true of every vehicle in the column. It was the only time our task force was seriously threatened, and by love rather than enmity! The column was completely stalled for several minutes while civilian authorities joined in trying to force a path through this mass of rejoicing humanity.

As we inched our way through, the town people began passing us foodstuffs of every sort. I got two eggs, fortunately hard-boiled, and Schedler some hot sweet corn. Fruits of almost every kind were almost forced on us, and I found particular pleasure in a handful of fresh roasted *camotes*, a type of native yam.

Any member of the column, cavalryman or correspondent, who didn't get a kiss from one of the happy señoritas who stormed the loaded vehicles had only himself to blame. All the way out of the city the street was lined with men and women too old or infirm to join the stampede, who stood waving the V for victory sign, some of them weeping unabashedly. And above all this bedlam two youngsters in the belfry of the town's tallest church were pounding the bell with stones. I shall never forget Baliuag.

During the night the Japanese had been more of a nuisance than a menace. At no time did they attempt a stand, content with random mortar salvos and persistent sniper fire. They succeeded in inflicting some major casualties but never posed any real threat.

During the night this correspondent was just another joe, indistinguishable at rifle range from any of the eight hundred cavalrymen stretched along the highway. But with the arrival of the morning sun, I suddenly became the most conspicuous man in the entire column. When I left Dagupan to catch up with the First Cavalry, I hadn't paused, even to jettison my suntans, perfect attire for rear echelon activity but not recommended for combat areas. I was the only man in the entire task force not clad in jungle greens, and while I would gladly have surrendered a goodly sum for the proper uniform, it was too late. Someone produced a rubber-lined poncho in the accepted colors, and Hewlett and Mydans in the seat behind me tried to get me to wear it over the rest of my attire. I struggled and insisted strongly I would rather be shot than suffer the miseries of that rubber blanket beneath the merciless tropical sun, but my buddies were just as adamant. They didn't give a damn if I did get shot, they didn't want snipers aiming at me and hitting them instead! I couldn't argue with that premise, so we spent most of the day wrestling with the issue and the poncho.

When Colonel Conner told us we had to establish contact with the forward patrol by dawn, I assumed it was to prevent the Japs from blowing the bridge across the Angat, one of the larger rivers of Luzon.

Once we left Baliuag, however, I learned that we ourselves had destroyed the bridge during our retreat to the Bataan peninsula in 1942. Contact was important because the Angat was one barrier at which the enemy might make a defensive stand, in which case the patrol might need important reinforcement when daylight arrived. As General MacArthur expected, however, the Japanese, not anticipating our drive, had no counterplan and elected to withdraw. We knew that General Yamashita was in the mountains to the north, and these isolated enemy units had no organized overall direction.

The river itself was a challenge, however, wider and deeper than the streams we had forded during the night. Engineer patrols were dispatched in each direction and finally located a point suitable for fording. The water was still too high for the jeeps and other light vehicles, a problem solved by forming "trains." A tank was used as the "locomotive" and several heavy trucks were lashed on behind. Then came the jeeps, pulled by the trucks, the water sometimes submerging them above their hoods. It was an unusual operation, but it worked. Once across, the small vehicles usually had to halt for a time to dry out before they could be started again, but that didn't take long in the Luzon sunshine. Most of us in the small vehicles chose to wade rather than sit in water that came above our navels, and we too dried quickly under the Luzon sun. Within an hour or less, our clothing was perfectly dry, shoes included. The only drawback was that my clothing, after a few consecutive baptisms, began to rot, and I had no idea where or when I could find replacements.

Although our mobile column had been tagged with the adjective "lightning" at the very inception and was thus described in my broadcasts and in my colleagues' dispatches, the word is misleading, as was the "flying" appellation. The distance between our organizational rice paddy below Cabanatuan and Santo Tomás University in Manila was about 110 kilometers, something less than 70 miles, plus a few miles for strategic detours. Our column spent just 43 hours covering that distance, which averages out to something over 1.5 miles an hour, hardly Ben Franklin's idea of "lightning" speed. Still, when compared with Walter Krueger's rate of less than five miles per day during our first two weeks on Luzon, our speed wasn't to be despised. The important thing is that we kept moving in spite of enemy gestures. Our pauses were momentary and necessary but in no way an acknowledgment of enemy strength. Bridgeless rivers gave us more pause than Yamashita's entire disorganized army.

We spent most of Friday, February 2, fording rivers and blasting out isolated nests of Japanese who continued to be a headache but nothing more. There was no close combat but both sides suffered casualties, including fatalities, the Jap by far the most.

Once again we found ourselves closer to the front but knowing less about the war, as the old adage has it. The four of us in our jeep, positioned near the center of the column, had firsthand information on whatever was happening a hundred yards ahead or behind us, as well as any enemy action leveled in our direction. The rest of the time we guessed at developments or listened for scuttlebutt. We knew nothing of the decisions that guided our movements.

Brig. Gen. William C. ("Bill") Chase was in overall command of our column, reporting to General Mudge, but he was very little in evidence from our position in the column. We did know we were under the protection of Hack Conner, and that was most reassuring. Chase, of course, was in contact with Conner by radio and with the marine pilots who provided Chase with priceless aerial observation and reconnaissance.

During the day several L-5 Cub artillery observation planes landed beside our column, apparently carrying couriers or special messages. I managed to talk with one of the sergeant-pilots and found he was scheduled to return to Sixth Army headquarters. He agreed to give me a hand, and I was able to send back my first broadcast copy since joining the task force. Jack Adams would be notified to pick it up. Everyone is cooperative when engaged in an operation like this one.

The four of us sharing the jeep were the only reporters with the task force as it started for Santo Tomás. We all had ties to Manila and the Philippines and close friends in the camp. But Frank Hewlett had by far the greatest stake in the venture. His wife, Virginia, was an internee, or at least Frank prayed she was. When he had left Manila on January, 1942, to accompany the U.S. troops to Bataan, he had been forced to leave Virginia behind, praying she would be given the humanitarian treatment supposedly guaranteed by the Geneva convention. Since then Frank had had no definite word of Virginia from any source. None of her letters were delivered, and he had no way of knowing whether she was receiving his.

I had known Frank and Virginia well before the war and had been in their Manila home several times. I knew Virginia as a lovely, gracious lady. Perhaps for that reason he talked to me about her now and then, for he seldom discussed the situation with casual friends. Once in Australia he told me he had learned that Virginia was aboard the *Gripsholm* and he was going to Goa, in what was then Portuguese India, to meet her. He was jubilant!

It must have been the bitterest disappointment of a lifetime. Not only was she not aboard the ship, but he was unable to locate anyone with any information concerning her. Santo Tomás was his last hope, and I could tell that those last few miles were to him maddeningly slow.

On Friday night, February 2, near the town of Bigaa, only twenty miles from Manila, our column came to an unexpected and extended halt. There was no sign of enemy action, so it had to be one of the "hurry up and wait!" situations for which the army has always been famous. Mydans and Schedler had walked back along the column to talk with some of the GI's, while Frank and I were sitting on the hood of the jeep and talking about nothing in particular. Suddenly Frank grabbed my knee in a vise-like grip that almost made me wince. "Bill, this has *got* to be it. Virginia *has* to be there!" I put my arm around his shoulder and assured him everything was going to be right, and quickly. Of course I had no information to back my words but I, too, was praying that the Almighty was about to give a grand person his first real break in three years. Frank had to know my lack of knowledge, but he probably was just looking for moral support and he seemed to relax a bit.

Those last twenty miles into Manila on Saturday produced a lot of enemy action, but nowhere did the Japs mass enough strength to pose a real threat. Still, the closer we came to the city, the more they heckled us. Several times we were out of our jeep and into a ditch a half-dozen times in a single hour. When a bullet smacked into a tree just above Hewlett's head as he jumped for the earth, everyone swore it had been intended for my suntans, and the sweltering poncho appeared again.

A critical point on the route was the village of Novaliches, about six miles north of the Manila city line, where the marine fliers had reported an important bridge over a narrow, deep gorge, still intact but believed to be mined for destruction. As we entered the town the road made an L-turn to the left with the bridge directly ahead. Part of the column made the turn, then the Japs showed up and we stayed pinned to that corner for what seemed like an hour. Conner later told us the bridge actually was visibly mined and the fuses already lighted when we arrived. Naval Lt. James Sutton, a demolitions expert assigned to our column, went out on the bridge in the face of sniper fire and cut the fuses. Again tanks guarded the approaches until the entire column crossed without serious opposition. It was the last natural barrier before Manila.

At this point we made one of the few serious mistakes of the entire operation. Lieutenant Sutton had no orders to destroy the explosives, or at least remove them, after he defused the charges. As a result, the explosives remained on the bridge, and after we crossed the Japs came back and completed the demolition, making it extremely difficult for our needed reinforcements to follow.

The main road from Novaliches angles southwest from the bridge until it intersects Avenida Rizal, the main north-south artery north of the Pasig River. We followed that road past the Grace Park airfield, where scores of demolished Jap planes testified to the effectiveness of Halsey's Third Fleet and explained in part why the enemy had given our task force no trouble from the air. On the other side of the road was a Chinese cemetery that extended for several blocks along our left flank and, we soon learned, covered a nest of Japs. It took us some time to quiet the snipers who were using gravestones for bunkers, but fortunately they proved to be poor riflemen and we did manage to move the entire force into the city with minimum casualties.

Bill Chase told me some time later that we crossed the city limits at exactly 6:35 P.M., Manila time, far ahead of the Thirty-seventh Division, but where he got those figures I never knew. The sun was setting over Manila Bay when we reached the Avenue, but I never did know where the city line was situated.

Once past the cemetery, we realized that Avenida Rizal was deserted, no cheering crowds, no exuberant civilians, no traffic of any sort, a sure sign the Japs were in the area. The university compound is approximately two and a half miles from the Chinese cemetery, but it took us almost an hour and a half to cover that distance, thanks mainly to a series of street fights that stalled us in the heart of north Manila.

Another thing that slowed our progress was our ignorance as to exactly where Santo Tomás was located. The university was, and is, a sizable piece of real estate (approximately 150 acres, walled). But nightfall follows sunset very quickly in early February in the tropics, and before we had quelled our first street fight, the great city was in complete darkness. At this time two Filipino civilians appeared out of the shadows, identified themselves as guerrillas, and offered to act as guides. We had to have direction, so we accepted their offer even though their identification was doubtful. We were still on Rizal and continued south to Quericada, then east about four blocks to Quezon Boulevard, which touches the western corner of Santo Tomás.

Far Eastern University was also located on Quezon, and it was here we encountered our bitterest opposition. As we rode down Quezon I noticed a modern four-story building on our right, the most urban edifice I had seen since Australia. My admiration was halted instantly when we found ourselves the target of machine-gun fire from a half-dozen of those handsome windows. We turned our light artillery on the building, and in moments it was a blazing pyre for whatever enemy force remained inside. But enemy fire seemed to be coming from all sides, and it was some time before we got the situation under control. During this fight Hewlett decided to go find Santo Tomás on his own, but we convinced him his only chance of finding Virginia was to stay with the armament. It was here also that, in defiance of military dictates, we divided our forces in the face of the enemy and sent a good segment of the column with one of the guides to capture and hold Malacañan Palace.

Although we were coming from the north, our guides took us clear around the university to Calle España, on which the main entrance fronts. We were heading north when we finally stopped before a forbidding wall constructed of concrete and cast-iron grills and at least a quarter-mile long and ten feet high. Our jeep, by sheer chance, came to a halt before a huge iron gate, grilled and securely chained, in the middle of the wall. One of the officers shouted a challenge, but there was no response. There wasn't the slightest hint of light or sound of habitation. After another challenge went unanswered, it was decided to force an entrance, but not at the main gate, which might have been booby-trapped. Instead, Battling Basic, a tank that had been our neighbor in the column for most of the way, crashed an opening in the wall itself, then backed out. Its powerful headlights shone inside through the opening, but nothing was visible except trees.

At this point Carl Mydans, a former internee, volunteered for something that was far beyond the call of duty for a noncombatant correspondent. With one of the officers he walked into the opening several feet, a perfect target for enemy fire with those powerful headlights behind him, then cupped his hands and shouted, "Hello, anyone! This is Carl Mydans. Are there any Americans in there?" There was no response. He called again, and when there still was no reaction from inside, he came back out to where I was seated on the ground with my back to the wall. He obviously was emotionally shaken. "Bill, I'm afraid to go in there, afraid of what we're going to find. I don't think there's anyone still alive."

Just at that moment a grenade came over the wall, and a piece of shrapnel struck Colonel Conner. He was not seriously wounded, as it developed, but the very idea of losing our visible commanding officer was chilling. Someone called for water, and I checked my own canteen—empty. I started back along the column to find someone who still had even a little drinking water. I found nothing, at least no one who would admit having any because clean water, like everything else at that particular moment, was in extremely short supply. (Conner later estimated that at that time not only were we out of drinking water, but we probably had just about enough fuel to carry us back to the city limits if we had to retreat. MacArthur's plans board had left no room for miscalculation.)

I was almost at the rear of the column when lights suddenly blazed inside the camp, and the wildest, most *beautiful* screams of joy I had ever heard erupted! Carl's very legitimate fears were instantly put to rest. I dashed back to the main gate and found that Battling Basic had moved ahead into the campus accompanied by a contingent of cavalrymen on foot and by my three colleagues. The tank, once it came within identifiable range, was visual proof we were Americans instead of some enemy ruse.

I stepped inside the opening and stood for a moment with my back to the inside of the wall, my eyes trying to pierce that darkness to the lights and jubilation beyond, some 150 yards away. No other unit showed any sign of entering and, frankly, I was afraid. It didn't take long for a reporter's curiosity to win out, however, and I took off alone. To this day I wonder whether I ran or walked the distance. All I clearly remember is that I was following a long, dark road.

As I cleared the dark, I spotted Battling Basic in front of the main building, a dead Japanese officer sprawled beside it. The tank was surrounded by celebrating internees, none of whom paid any attention to the fallen enemy. Almost unbelievably, the first person out of some thirty-seven hundred who saw me as I emerged from the shadows screamed, "You're Bill Dunn!" Miraculously, I not only recognized her but remembered her name. "You're Marty Roberts—and just as beautiful as ever!" My last luncheon in Manila over three years earlier had been in the home of Bob and Marty Roberts!

In simple truth, everything looked beautiful to me at that moment. Other friends appeared from all directions, including two who had been reported dead. All carried the bitter stamp of malnutrition, and some were hard to recognize for that reason. I was talking with some newly liberated friends when someone clapped me on the back with the force of a sledgehammer. "I found her! *I found her!*" Frank grabbed me in a rugged bear-hug, then literally danced away to break the news to the others. We were in the midst of thousands of deliriously happy people, but not one could top the happiness of Frank Hewlett. The jubilant excitement carried on past dawn—a night that still remains vivid in my memory after four decades.

Most important, however, we had reached another major milestone in our long campaign to force the Japanese back to Japan. I had left Manila on October 3, 1941, for a brief trip through China and Burma before returning to Manila and then home. Now on February 3, 1945, exactly three years and four months later, I was finally back in Manila, after quite a few detours and considerable opposition. Next stop: *Tokyo!*

CHAPTER 34

A City Burns

Almost immediately we reporters learned what the internees had known for long years, that it is always much easier to get into jail than to get out. The greatest story in the world is of no value to the reporter if it doesn't reach the public. None of us had the facilities to move broadcasts, pictures, or the written word. The nearest facilities for any of us would now be at MacArthur's new GHQ, moved from Dagupan to a large sugar refinery at San Miguel, Tarlac, while we were driving on Santo Tomás.

Although the new GHQ was much closer to Manila, it was still inaccessible to us because there was no transport available and there were still too many Japanese operating outside the walls. In other words, we were just as certainly prisoners, for the moment at least, as those thousands we had come to liberate, and would continue as such until the reinforcements—Bob Beightler's Thirty-seventh—arrived, within hours, we hoped. General Chase, who had rejoined our column during the fight on Quezon Boulevard, predicted the Thirty-seventh would be outside our walls on Sunday—the next day—but that it probably would be a couple of days before a regular courier service could be established and perhaps longer before any of us could make the trip to GHQ in person. Accordingly, we all prepared our materials, and on Sunday evening a courier did leave to meet the Thirty-seventh and then proceed to San Miguel. He carried our stories, including my broadcast script which Jack Adams aired, the first vocal report to come out of the first and largest internment camp to be liberated.

On Tuesday, February 6, I was told it would be possible for me to get an escort to the Thirty-seventh command post (CP), which had been set up in a Japanese brewery on the northern city limits. From there I should find transportation to GHQ. I accepted immediately, for two important reasons. First, of course, I wanted to reach a microphone as quickly as possible. Second, I had to get away from the emotionally charged aura that had enveloped me for some sixty hours.

Never have I undergone such emotional extremes in such a short time, and I wanted a break, quickly. Seeing so many old friends in various stages of malnutrition from bad to critical, listening to their stories of those thirty-seven months of trying to keep their spirits alive and their faith in their distant nation unwavering, was something I wasn't designed by nature to handle.

For me, the climax had come on Monday morning when Sam Wilson, a former Manila businessman who had served two years as a colonel of guerrillas in Mindanao (he actually held the rank of captain in the U.S. Naval Reserve, but there was no navy in Mindanao), arrived in camp to join his wife and two sons. One of my greatest privileges on entering Santo Tomás had been to find Susie and the boys and tell them I had seen Sam in Tacloban, that he was in good health and would be with them soom. They had had no word from him for security reasons. The Japs would have been rough on the family of a known, active guerrilla.

With characteristic thoughtfulness Sam had brought with him a large American flag, knowing the Japs would have destroyed any flags found in the camp. Bill Chase was ecstatic at the prospect of a formal review of his troops and a ceremonial flag-raising, but Sam overruled him. This flag, he insisted, was for the *internees*. They must be allowed to raise it themselves. And at nine-thirty on Monday morning the Stars and Stripes waved once more over the heads of Americans who had not been forgotten.

I stood in front of the main building to watch the ceremony. It was simple but unforgettable. A few of the men emerged from a second-story window onto the roof of the front entrance portico, unfurled the flag to the eyes of the throng of half-starved, emaciated internees in the courtyard below, then slowly hauled it to its proud position atop the staff. As it caught the breeze, a breeze still tainted with the smoke of a hundred fires outside the walls, the hungry thousands, without signal, began to sing "God Bless America" in voices choked with emotion. Fred Hamilton, a hard-bitten regular army colonel who was standing beside me, wept unashamedly, and there were few dry eyes among the soldiers standing by. My own reaction is immaterial. That was all. No fanfare, no shouting, just a song that was more than a prayer.

By the time I was able to leave on Tuesday afternoon, the feverish excitement had abated somewhat. Food supplies were expected momentarily, and scores of internees were holding informal meetings, planning for a future that would have to find its phoenix rebirth in the ashes of sadistic savagery. An amazing number of long-time residents indicated they had no interest in returning to the States until they had had a chance to survey shattered businesses, contact former associates, and lay a firm foundation for reconstruction of the American business community that had been the backbone of the Philippine economy before Japanese intervention. Almost every major American and British firm, as well as those of other nationalities, that had operated in the islands before 1942 had representatives in this great prison camp, and they all were anxious to start sifting the ashes and commence rebuilding. The foreign community would lead in the reconstruction of a shattered nation.

Not surprisingly, the jaunt to the city limits and the Thirty-seventh CP was less eventful than our arrival had been. During my two and a half days as a virtual "internee," I climbed several times to the top of the tower that crowns the main building of the university and offers a fairly good view of the city. When I made my last climb shortly before leaving for GHQ, the heaviest fighting was south of the river, although there seemed to be more unbridled enemy devastation than actual combat.

The Pasig River, which bisects the city almost at its center, is not really a river, but a strait that connects Laguna de Bay (neither a lagoon nor a bay, but the nation's largest lake) with Manila Bay, a distance of some eleven kilometers. The Pasig is a broad, forbidding bar-

In 1948 I accompanied Gen. Bob Eichelberger as he revisited Cavite province, where the Eighth Army commander barely escaped an enemy ambush during his 1945 drive into Manila from the South. *Courtesy U.S. Army*

rier as it passes through the heart of the downtown business section, and it formerly had been traversed by four major bridges. As the First Cav and the Thirty-seventh moved in from the north, the Japs, having devastated the commercial area just north of the Pasig, blew up these bridges and moved their major efforts south of that barrier.

Elements of Bob Eichelberger's Eighth Army were moving north from southernmost Luzon, but in the meantime south of the Pasig the enemy had little opposition to his rapine and incendiarism. A sizable enemy contingent had taken positions inside Intramuros, the walled city that lies directly on the south bank of the Pasig. It was obvious that southern Manila was going to suffer most. To the north,

When General Eichelberger retired after a career that led him from West Point to an Army command, he stopped in Manila for a review of some of his most successful campaigns, and I, having accompanied him on many of those campaigns, was there to meet him. *Courtesy U.S. Army*

however, the cavalry and the Thirty-seventh were gaining control, and reinforcements were on their way. When I left Santo Tomás, the most forceful impression I carried with me was of dozens of fires and explosions continuing without apparent opposition and both visible and audible for long miles.

Almost the first person I met at the Thirty-seventh CP was General Beightler himself, whom I had known in Bougainville. He greeted me, "Hey, Bill Dunn! Going into Manila with us?" When I replied, "I just left Manila, General, heading for General MacArthur's headquarters," the atmosphere changed instantly. "You went with the First Cavalry!" It was more an accusation than a statement. With that he turned back to his maps, the interview obviously ended. He was a hard loser and obviously didn't understand, or believe, the cards had been stacked against him. Bob Beightler was a top-notch division commander and the Thirty-seventh second to none in its overall record through several years of tough campaigning, but he didn't want to accept second place, even in a good cause. From then on I never met Bob without being labeled "Dunn of the First Cavalry." Bill Chase, years later, told me the same story. Bob Beightler never forgave the cavalry for being the first in Manila.

I arrived at San Miguel just after dark and found a special press conference being organized. I stowed my meager gear and went in to see what was brewing. To my utter astonishment, I learned that General MacArthur was about to announce, through his press staff, plans for a victory parade through Manila within the next few hours. All at once the emotions and tensions of the past few days broke the dam, and I became almost hysterical. I interrupted the spokesman without ceremony, insisting that such a parade was impossible. The bridges were blown up and the city was in flames.

I realized immediately what had happened. General MacArthur had declared Manila an open city in 1942 and believed the Japanese would do the same, particularly since the city had no strategic value, and none of his immediate staff wanted to tell him he was wrong. It was possible, of course, that most of the staff, stationed some sixty-five miles north of the scene, were not yet fully aware of what was happening. But I had seen his chief of staff doing a reconnaissance close enough to Manila to know the score.

I had usurped the floor and I held it. "If this announcement is released the General is going to look ridiculous! There is *no* possibility, physically, of a parade. Get down on your knees if necessary, let *me* talk to him, do *anything*, but don't release this announcement!"

General Diller was inclined to be adamant. "Calm down, Bill," he said, apparently not certain whether a guy who seemed to have cracked

In 1941 Douglas MacArthur, understanding the absence of any strategic value to the then lovely city of Manila, declared it an open city and moved his forces to Bataan. In 1945, when the situation was reversed, he expected the Japanese to do the same. Instead, the enemy chose futile destruction, barricading themselves in buildings like the City Hall *(top)* and the Legislative Building and refusing to negotiate.

I am surveying the wreckage of Calle Juan Luna, the heart of Manila's prewar financial district. Directly in front of me is the Trade and Commerce Building, completely gutted by incendiaries but structurally sound. U.S. engineers did a miraculous job of rehabilitating it and had GHQ settled within its charred walls in less than three weeks. Smaller buildings like that directly behind me had to be completely rebuilt. *Courtesy U.S. Army Signal Corps*

up deserved anger or sympathy. "You've been through a lot in the past few days, but you mustn't get hysterical. The General knows what he's doing."

"Pick," I replied, "emotion has nothing to do with this. This is plainly a case where the General has been given erroneous intelligence. This statement will only tell the world he doesn't have the facts." To this day I am not sure whether the announcement was ever released, but I do know there was no parade!

Early the next morning I was busy preparing a script, still more than a little numb from the preceding days. As I was studying my notes Colonel Schechter came over and put a hand on my shoulder. "Bill, I've got some bad news for you." I looked up, inquiringly, and he handed me a slip of paper, a message relayed by the Signal Corps. My father had died the preceding day. If there had to be bad news, this was the time for it. I stared at the message, blankly. There was no room for further emotion. I thanked Abe and turned back to my typewriter, then sat there motionless for some moments, trying to sort out some poignant memories. Several days passed before I could fully realize the depth of my loss.

There's something unreal about watching a great city go up in flames. You know it's happening because it's right there before your eyes, but still there's a feeling that your senses must be playing you false. The burning of Manila was an endless series of scattered blazes spotted throughout the southern half of the city. From a vantage point atop an eight-story bank building on the north bank of the Pasig, you could look southward across the river to see the innumerable fires and watch the destruction of the Ermita section, which included the major hotels and apartment houses, the American high commissioner's office (now the American Embassy), and the venerable Army and Navy Club where you first learned to shoot "liar's dice." Worst of all, of course, was the knowledge that in those buildings were men, women, and children unable to escape or shot by enemy riflemen if they did reach the street. The Japs' shortage of explosives forced them to rely mostly on simple arson for their depredations, which left mostly intact the concrete or steel skeletons of those burned-out buildings.

On the night of February 9, one week after our arrival in Manila, I reported to the network: "The fight for the city is progressing, but that progress is slow, because it is necessary to pry these suicidal maniacs out of their every hiding place, one by one and group by group. They are not trying to retreat, withdraw, or reinforce. They are just staying put until such time as we kill them off. And their ultimate death will have served but one purpose—the reduction of the population of an over-crowded Japan. Militarily it will have contributed absolutely nothing to the fast crumbling New Order in East Asia."

Fortunately for the radio reporters, GHQ lost no time moving the microphone south from San Miguel, Tarlac. The Signal Corps took over an abandoned house in Grace Park on the northern city limits,

This section of Manila's financial district doesn't look too bad but appearances can be deceiving. The bank building behind me was completely gutted by fire and the pavement so pitted that just plain walking could be hazardous. *Courtesy U.S. Army Signal Corps*

right across from the airfield that had been the graveyard of more than a hundred Japanese planes. It was a flimsy house of bamboo and galvanized iron, but once a bit of ineffective soundproofing and the electronic equipment had been installed, we had a servicable studio some sixty miles closer to the action.

One feature of this primitive installation was its martial sound effects. An artillery unit positioned its guns on the airfield directly across the street and joined in the business of trying to blast the Japs out of south Manila. The artillerymen had no idea of our schedules, nor would it have made any difference if they had. Consequently, a report to the American public was often punctuated by a salvo from the 155's that made the microphone jump.

Surprisingly, perhaps, the listeners who told us of hearing those blasts all assumed they were caused by enemy shells bursting in our immediate vicinity, and we built up a brief but amazing reputation for bravery for our obvious determination to report the news in spite of "bombs bursting in air."

During our few days in San Miguel, Tarlac, right after I returned from Santo Tomás, George Folster and I had camped out in a brand-new nipa hut (the owners never appeared) and found the floor, made of one-inch bamboo strips, infinitely softer than the steel decks of the *Apache*. When we followed our mikes to Manila, however, the question of quarters became immediate. Manila had no surviving hotels worthy of the name, and thousands of homeless people swarmed the streets. My solution came from Sam Wilson, the guerrilla colonel who had brought the flag to Santo Tomás. Sam had a home in the Santa Mesa area north of the river, in an enclave that had not been torched. Directly across from Sam's house was that of a friend who was then in the United States with his family. It was a nice, sturdy frame house completely without furnishings, thanks to looters, who were the secondary curse of the battle for Manila. Sam got permission for me to occupy the house as a guard against further looting. I invited Folster to join me, and together we revived the art of scrounging that had served us so well in New Guinea and Leyte. The army came through with a few basics, my pals at Far East Air Force provided a small but adequate generator, and our running water still ran! When Federico, the original prewar houseboy, showed up in search of rice for his family, we were really in business. Who needed the Waldorf?

In the meantime, war continued on all sides, particularly to the

Capt. Sam Wilson, U.S.N., the guerrilla leader who brought the first American flag into Santo Tomás, returned to his own S. J. Wilson Building, which he built before the war, to find the banking floor knee deep in Japanese currency, most of it the bogus "Mickey Mouse." Sam served three years as a colonel of guerrillas in Mindanao before he learned he had been promoted to captain in the navy! *Courtesy Acme Newsphoto*

east and north, where the rumble of artillery never ceased day or night. A large contingent of Japanese still operated in the very heart of the city, in Intramuros, the old walled city. In the late sixteenth century, when the Spaniards decided to keep control of these islands Magellan had discovered, they chose a village on the east shore of Manila Bay as their capital and straightway began to build a wall as protection against unfriendly neighbors from nearby islands or the Asiatic mainland. It was then the era of guardian walls: China was still building her serpentine colossus, and Europe was a continent of walled cities. Completed after long years, the wall was an architectural masterpiece, nearly two-and-a-half miles in its roughly oval circumference, twenty-five feet tall, and almost as thick. It was adequate to discourage most potential foes of the era of its construction, but it proved to be little more than a major nuisance four centuries later in its first *real* test, before the guns of the Fourteenth Corps.

It was not known how many enemy troops were crammed into that stone enclave, because there was no communication through those forbidding walls. The wise decision was to take no chances, so a full corps, the Fourteenth, was assigned to duty under the command of Lt. Gen. Oscar W. Griswold, whom I had come to know in Bougainville.

H-hour was set for the morning of February 23, and the general invited me to join him at his command post atop a burned-out hotel just across the river, barely three hundred yards from the northeast corner of the wall. All the action took place on the Pasig River below us and on the narrow strip of land in front of the wall, most of it formerly an elongated nine-hole public golf course.

I had been impressed with the naval shore bombardments at Gloucester, Leyte, and Lingayen, but none of them could compare with the artillery barrage that struck those ancient walls. In a shore bombardment, the shells that streak overhead burst long distances inland and the cacaphony, while deafening, is somewhat muted by distance. In this bombardment the shells were bursting directly in front of us, barely three hundred yards distant. The shelling started exactly at 7:00 A.M. and continued without pause for ninety minutes, slowly grinding holes in the ancient, resisting walls but falling far short of destroying them. In those ninety minutes our artillery, mortars, and light guns poured more than three hundred tons of steel into their target as we watched. In the four-plus decades since that morning I have become increasingly hard of hearing, and several of my fellow correspondents report similar developments. There is no way to prove the concussion of those bombardments, particularly the shelling of Intramuros, was responsible, but it certainly did nothing to improve the hearing of any of the military or civilian personnel that remained within their range.

Suddenly, at 8:30 A.M., the shelling ended as abruptly as it had begun. The sudden silence was almost as disconcerting as the noise itself. For the first time it was possible to talk without screaming. General Griswold, never taking his eyes off the scene, observed with something near a sigh, "Now there's nothing more I can do but sweat.

I've given them all I've got and they're under a higher command." As he spoke, a cloud of magenta smoke rose over the south wall, a signal, and immediately a flotilla of hand-propelled small boats came down the Pasig, moving slowly toward the battered north wall. At the same time, other troops moved across the narrow fairways of the golf course toward the east wall, where they dispersed along the base, moving slowly toward the holes our guns had drilled through the stone.

It was a breathless moment. As the first boats reached the south bank and the men clambered onto the levee, a lone sniper underneath what was left of nearby Jones Bridge opened fire with a machine gun, but he was silenced before doing any damage. It was the only opposition. At this moment a stream of dazed, half-crazed civilians moved out of the north wall toward the boats and freedom. Our troops moved in from all sides, and the battle within the walls began. Beside me, General Griswold wiped the perspiration from his hands and face as he murmured, just audibly, "God bless them! God bless them!" You could sense the unspoken prayer behind those blessings.

The purging of Intramuros was a nasty dig-'em-out operation that occupied the Fourteenth Corps for several days but, fortunately, without too many casualties. As always, the Japanese made no attempt to counterattack but huddled in warrens burrowed among the ruins of the walled city, awaiting extermination. They gave us no choice.

Success of the operation meant that Manila could at last be regarded as secured, but there was no reason for rejoicing and certainly no further mention of a victory parade. The city, especially the business and financial section immediately north of the Pasig, was a heart-rending shambles, particularly to those who remembered the prewar "Pearl of the Orient," a lovely, gracious, peaceful city. North of the shattered business section, great expanses of residential and small business communities had escaped the barbarian torches, thanks to the First Cavalry and the Thirty-seventh Division. To the south, below the Pasig, you could explore scores of square miles and find nothing that hadn't been seriously damaged, if not utterly destroyed.

Such scenes would license the observer to walk the streets of burned-out Tokyo months later with no overwhelming feeling of sympathy for the victims of Allied air raids. Furthermore, while Allied bombers were dropping their incendiaries on Japan's capital, there were no Allied gunmen in the streets forcing innocent civilians to remain in burning buildings or shooting them if they tried to escape. Tokyo, a much larger city, suffered more property damage than Manila in this exchange of lethal devastation, but the civilian casualties were comparatively much worse in Manila, because of Japanese atrocities.

Bitterest of all is the realization that the havoc wreaked in both cities contributed nothing to the matter of victory or defeat. Manila had no strategic value in any campaign to maintain possession of the islands, while Japan was definitely a defeated nation before the first of the heavy bombing raids began. The final result of the conflict would have been the same had both Manila and Tokyo been declared open cities. History must search long and hard to uncover a more pointless waste of human life.

Suddenly I realized I was *tired!*

As the Luzon campaign moved steadily into the month of March, those members of the press corps still with us who had accompanied the first troops onto the beaches of Leyte were approaching their fifth month under combat conditions, five months with no relief from the sounds and rigors of warfare and, for most of them, without spending a single night in a normal bed. As a group, the correspondents were older than the GI's and the junior officers, their average age somewhere in the middle or upper thirties, and they had received none of the boot camp training that conditioned the soldiers. The strain was beginning to show.

Not all members of the original media corps were still with us, however. Four had died in the line of duty (Bill Chickering of Time-Life was the fourth, killed by a kamikaze en route to Lingayen), two had returned home with shrapnel wounds, and several had transferred to the navy and the Okinawa–Iwo Jima campaigns, believing that the worst of the Philippines fighting was ending.

It was not ended, certainly, but with the enemy holed up defensively in the Luzon Mountains and the Eighth Army confined largely to mopping-up activities in the southern islands, our chances of rating prime radio time or page-one headlines were dwindling. From that time forward there would be more and more of the dig-'em-out fighting, fierce and bitter but hardly spectacular enough to compare successfully with Europe, where the Allies were making mincemeat of the Nazis in a fashion that rightly commanded the headlines and dominated the radio news roundups.

With this and visions of rare roast beef and fresh vegetables in mind, I decided to take R and R leave south of the equator. Jack Adams, who had proved himself a more than capable right arm, was ready and eager to handle our schedules for the next two or three weeks. He was particularly anxious to accompany the rescue contingent we knew was being formed to liberate the second and final major civilian internment camp, at Los Baños on the shores of Laguna de Bay about forty miles southeast of Manila. After the intense emotional experience of Santo Tomás, I was perfectly willing to let someone else cover this liberation.

One campaign I certainly didn't want to miss, however, was the return to the Indies, probably to be signalled by an amphibious strike against Tarakan, which had been Japan's first NEI target three and a half years earlier. The Nips had run me out of the Indies, out of Java, with my tail between my legs, and I wanted to be present for the first counterblow. But my sources at GHQ assured me nothing would happen in that direction for at least a month, so I advised New York of my decision and picked up my travel orders from General Diller's office.

Squeeze Wurtsmith had been given his second star and command of the Thirteenth Air Force on General Kenney's recommendation, both within a matter of weeks, so before I headed south I stopped by his headquarters to congratulate him. From the time we had both arrived in Australia in early 1942, he a lieutenant colonel in command of the newly organized Forty-ninth Fighter Group, we had been close friends, and I really think I got as much kick out of his steady advancement as he did.

He had a marked fondness for good music and spaghetti, both almost unknown in the combat areas. From their earliest days in Port Darwin and New Guinea, Squeeze and members of his staff would visit my "mess" in Sydney every time they came south on R and R, and I would swap them generous portions of Schubert and spaghetti for information on what was happening in the northern areas beyond the reach of my microphone. (The same ploy worked with many other staff officers on Sydney leave.)

After I extended my congratulations, he abruptly changed the subject. "What'll you do with your records?" I shrugged. There wasn't much I could do with approximately a ton of the old-fashioned twelve inch shellac records I had collected over the preceding couple of years. (A single album of Beethoven's Ninth in shellac would weigh as much as all nine of his symphonies on vinyl LP's.) "I'll just have to get rid of them. They sure as hell won't fit in my flight bag."

Maj. Gen. Paul B. ("Squeeze") Wurtsmith, commander, 49th Fighter Group; commander, Fifth Air Force Fighter Command; commander, 13th Air Force. As a lieutenant colonel, Wurtsmith brought the first American group of fighter planes (the 49th) to the Southwest Pacific. His men, all rookies, quickly developed into the foremost fighter group in the Pacific, amassing all the combat records. *Courtesy U.S. Air Force*

"I've got to send my plane to Sydney in two or three weeks and my aide will be flying it. He'll have orders to bring you and your gear back with him."

"You mean the records? They're too damned heavy."

"Listen, my friend, this is the Air Force and the plane's a B-17. It can carry more records than you'll ever own. Just get them up here!"

The leave was all I hoped. Australian beef (mostly lamb, in fact) never tasted better; rationing was very flexible now that the war had moved north. I had forgotten how soft spring mattresses could be, and in fact they needed some getting used to. I did a couple of broadcast reports just to remind New York I was still alive and checked in with my friends at the Australia Broadcasting Commission and the Sydney press. Then, suddenly, just as quickly as my original decision was born, I was ready to return. I had to know what was happening up there, firsthand. And at that time my phone rang.

"Mr. Dunn, this is Captain Clark, General Wurtsmith's pilot. I am leaving for Manila day after tomorrow, and I have orders to bring you back together with your gear." "Captain, did the general give you any idea of what my gear includes?" "That makes no difference. Whatever it is we'll take it. General's orders!" I tried to tell him I'd be putting close to a ton of shellac on his flying machine, but he wasn't interested. I was obviously a VIP, at least for this particular flight. The records were packed in fourteen inch wooden cubes, compact and deceptively heavy. The next morning a truck arrived with Clark's crew chief, and my entire musical library, Bach to Wagner, began its journey to war-torn Manila.

When I arrived at Sydney's Mascor airport to board the plane, I found the crew chief had scattered the cubes around the interior of the plane so there was nothing apparent to indicate the overall weight. Clark was already on the flight deck with his copilot. I tried again to make sure he understood the amount of the extra weight he was carrying, but he had already checked the plane and his main interest rested with two of Sydney's loveliest who were standing on the apron, waving their farewells. Once we took off, he advised me, we were coming back to buzz the apron in a salute to the ladies. I crossed my fingers. Clark used every inch of Mascor's longest runway and continued straight ahead for a dozen miles before attempting a gentle turn. By the time we reached our altitude the attractions of Sydney were just a memory and we were on our way back to army chow, army cots, and an unfriendly enemy.

CHAPTER 35

Farewell to a President

"Is it true? Is the President really dead?"

"It's true, all right. GHQ hasn't had any official notification from Washington yet but there's plenty of unofficial confirmation."

"In that case — and you'll probably think I'm nuts — *who* is the President of the United States?"

"No, Bill, I don't think you're nuts. I had to ask, same as you. The President is Harry S Truman."

"Okay, then. Who is Harry S Truman?"

That may seem an unlikely conversation, particularly when you realize that the questions were being asked by an American correspondent representing one of the nation's foremost news media. But it happened, very much as I have reported, and for a few moments I held the dubious distinction of being an American reporter who didn't know who was at the helm of his great nation! On April 12, very shortly after my return from Australia, I was awakened by this message from a Signal Corps friend, telling me that Franklin D. Roosevelt had died a short time earlier in Warm Springs, Georgia. My friend had no details.

I immediately dressed, jumped into a jeep, and headed for Plaza Cervantes in the heart of Manila's burned-out business section, where another temporary press headquarters had been set up in my absence. It was early in the morning, just before daybreak, but the officer on duty had what few facts were available, including the information that Harry S Truman was a senator from Missouri whom Roosevelt had chosen as his running mate for the 1944 campaign.

Actually, my ignorance of the new chief executive wasn't too strange in the circumstances. The months of October and November, during which a presidential campaign traditionally reaches its peak, were also peak months in the Southwest Pacific in 1944, peak months in our drive to return to the Philippines, in our conquest of the Japanese navy at Leyte Gulf, and in our bitter campaign against a stubborn enemy on that typhoon-battered island. Politics had to take second place, if that, in our attention.

Roosevelt's victory over Tom Dewey was a foregone conclusion even among diehard Republicans (he won over 80 percent of the electoral vote), so political talk was minimal, and whatever interest those of us in the SWPA had in the contest, it didn't reach to presidential running mates. I must have heard of Harry Truman before that April morning, but the name had made no impression.

Even before the official word reached GHQ from Washington, New York ordered a special report, but there was really little to report. Press headquarters doubted that General MacArthur had been awakened in the absence of official word, and there was no sign of unusual activity at Casa Blanca, the stately old Spanish mansion in the Santa Mesa section of Manila where General MacArthur had his quarters and which I passed on my way to the studio. United States flags were dropped to half-staff at GHQ, and at Malacañan Palace the flag of the Philippines was similarly lowered. President Osmeña was in the United States at the time, but Maximo Kalaw, minister of instruction and information, spoke for him, issuing a brief but poignant statement even before most Americans heard the news: "The world, and the Philippines especially, now mourns the loss of the greatest man of the present generation. He [President Roosevelt] has crystalized in him[self] the loftiest of American war aims, supported by the mightiest military force of all times. We in the Philippines have lost our best friend—our father."

I concluded my report that morning by saying, "The President's death will be deeply and sincerely mourned throughout the Pacific wherever American men and women are serving. He will be greatly mourned by the Filipinos to whom he brought the realization of their greatest goal—independence."

Almost simultaneous with the news of the president's death, the Eighth Army launched what would prove to be the final drive to clear the Japanese out of the southern islands. On April 14, elements of the Americal Division made an almost unopposed landing on the island of Bohol in the Mindanao Sea, just south of Leyte above Mindanao Island. All other islands were virtually secure except for small pockets of bitter-end resistance.

I had spent considerable time with the Eighth Army during the preceding week and found General Bob Eichelberger greatly pleased at his troops' continued advance on all fronts, far ahead of schedule. Unless Bohol produced some unexpected enemy strength, and it didn't, all semblance of organized resistance would be ended and the Eighth Army left without a worthy opponent. General Bob knew I had spent some time with the Americal in Bougainville, and he emphasized the difference between a defensive stand along a static perimeter, as at

Bougainville, and an offensive drive into enemy territory. The Thirty-seventh Division, which had also served on the Bougainville perimeter, had proved itself beyond question on the drive into Manila and Santo Tomás, and now the Americal was having its own opportunity. The results were exhilarating to the entire command.

It had long been obvious that General MacArthur had been unhappy with the snail-like caution of the Sixth Army on Luzon as well as at Ormoc, and now the Eighth Army was demonstrating how a campaign could be completed far ahead of schedule, with complete success and considerable conservation of life. MacArthur, of course, never aired his displeasure with subordinates, either at the time or later, but the depth of his feeling was revealed some weeks later, after the southern islands had been declared secure and bitter fighting was still going on in the mountains of northern Luzon.

GHQ had finally found a "permanent" home in the Trade and Commerce Building on Calle Juan Luna, just around the corner from press headquarters in Plaza Cervantes. It was another edifice that had been badly burned but was basically sound. I was just entering one day when I met Brig. Gen. Bonner Fellers, MacArthur's military secretary. "Hey, Bill," he greeted me, "Your friend is upstairs." "My friend?" "Yes. General Eichelberger is in with the General right now."

I thanked him and went up to MacArthur's outer office, where a half-dozen staff members were working. Almost immediately the inner door opened and Eichelberger came out, a big smile on his face.

I greeted him. "Nice going, General, but it looks as though you've fought yourself out of a job." His smile broadened as he replied, *sotto voce*, "No, Bill, it looks like I've fought myself *into* a job!" He glanced around the room, then put an arm across my shoulder and led me to the outer hallway. It was obvious he was highly pleased about something, and he didn't keep me in suspense. "General MacArthur has just told me that I will lead the attack on the Japanese mainland. It will be an Eighth Army operation with myself in command." Almost before I could congratulate him, he emphasized what I already suspected. "I'm trusting you, Bill. This is strictly off the record until the General makes the official announcement and that probably won't be until we set the date for the invasion." This, indeed, would be a blow to Walter Krueger and the Sixth Army command, but it didn't really surprise me. It was obvious that Bob Eichelberger was fighting MacArthur's type of war.

Walter Krueger and Robert Eichelberger were the only two army commanders I had come to know personally. My acquaintanceship with Krueger was limited to a few formal interviews and an occasional nod when I happened to encounter him at his headquarters. My friendship with Eichelberger, born in Buna, lasted throughout his life.

It would be difficult to find two men in similar positions who were more dissimilar in personal characteristics. Krueger, born in Poland, had entered the United States Army during the Spanish-American War as a buck private and had earned his successive promotions from the bottom of the ladder to the eminence of four stars and an army command. He was a soldier first and always, and a good one. He was also, despite having spent no time on the Plains above the Hudson, an outstanding example of the "West Point martinet"—everything strictly by the book. He had the reputation of being particularly rough on officers, possibly a result of his years as an enlisted man. Finally, Krueger was a confirmed introvert who was clearly his own best friend. Sixth Army headquarters, wherever positioned, always had a commanding general's mess limited to one table and two chairs, one chair, of course, reserved for the commanding general and the second, more often than not, unoccupied.

Eichelberger was born in Ohio and educated at Ohio State University and West Point, where he earned his gold bar, the first step toward his own army command. There was nothing of the martinet in his approach to necessary discipline; he was available to anyone with a problem or an idea, from the enlisted man to the corps commander. By further contrast, Bob Eichelberger was a complete extrovert who dreaded being alone, particularly at meals and when relaxing. The Eighth Army featured a commanding general's mess as well, but it usually resembled the dining hall in a midwestern college, dominated by a large table that seated the commanding general, members of his staff (not all of whom wore stars), and guests who might include anyone the general or any member of his staff had invited.

Krueger never evinced any great preferences in food, but Eichelberger had an educated palate. He was fond of good food but even fonder of human relationship, and his table was always a place for animated conversation and free exchange of opinions. Formality was left for the parade ground, and the mess sergeant was always beyond reproach! Admirals, aboard their flagships, traditionally eat alone in the privacy of their quarters unless they specifically and personally extend an invitation. Bob Eichelberger would have been a most unhappy commander on the high seas.

CHAPTER 36

Oil of the Indies

The oil of the Indies! Romancers call it black gold, but to the apprehensive war chiefs in Tokyo it was far more precious than any metal, for without it their disintegrating war machine would grind to a dead halt, on the land, the sea, and in the air. The priceless oil of the Indies already was in seriously short supply north of the equator and west of the Philippines and dwindling further as Allied forces tightened their control of the sea lanes over which that oil was transported to Japan. Now the time had come to close the tap completely.

Three years earlier, when the Rising Sun was truly rising and Tokyo was preparing to appropriate the oil of the Indies for its exclusive use, Tarakan Island had been its first target, for two reasons. First, it was ideally situated on the west coast of the Celebes Sea, about three and a half degrees above the equator, easy to reach by sea. Even more important, however, was the quality of Tarakan crude oil, possibly the highest grade to be found anywhere and easily adapted to military use.

Our decision to make Tarakan our primary target in a campaign to deny the oil of the Indies to the Japanese was largely a matter of geography. It was the major oil field closest to our newly established Philippines bases, and it was unquestionably within that portion of the Indies assigned as our responsibility. Most of the NEI, of course, was within the British sphere.

Inasmuch as I had visited Tarakan briefly four years earlier and had been in the Indies when Tarakan was taken, I told Jack Adams this was one landing I *had* to cover. We would be making other landings in Borneo if he wanted an amphibious assignment.

The assault was made on May 2, 1945, by Australian troops transported by an amphibious U.S.-Australia naval force under command of Rear Adm. Forrest B. Royal. That force came to Tarakan from Allied bases to the east and south. To join it I had to fly down to the Celebes Sea, southwest of Mindanao, a long and tedious flight in a Black Cat, a PBY patrol bomber largely used for night attacks and reconnaissance. It was my first opportunity to ride one of those amazingly obsolete aircraft with an unbelievable record all through the Pacific war. A PBY in good condition needed a good tail wind to reach a hundred knots, but it was a master of stealth.

Once I had joined the assault team, transferring at sea to a landing craft, I experienced my final shore bombardment, probably the heaviest of them all. The Japanese were rightly suspected of having underground defenses fronting the beach, so the preliminary bombardment had to be exceptionally heavy and accurate, and it was. The Japanese abandoned their underground positions and took to the nearby hills.

There was virtually no opposition at the beach, but that beach at Tarakan without doubt was the toughest, from a physical standpoint, that I have ever seen. We had to come ashore across a shelf of oily mud, washed by a tide that dropped ten feet in three hours and moved the shoreline a hundred yards out to sea before you realized what was happening. The landing had to be made exactly on schedule or there would have been no chance of getting our landing craft within reach of solid ground.

Even before we could attempt the actual landing, the task force had to clean out a well-laid mine field, a job that took four days, and Australian engineers had to force openings through beach obstructions, principally twenty-five-foot sections of steel rails upended in staggered lines at ten-foot intervals. The Japanese had never confronted us with such elaborate defenses before, probably because they never knew where MacArthur would strike. Tarakan was a different challenge in that respect. There were no alternates. All these handicaps had been anticipated, however, and fitted into a schedule that couldn't be botched. But the menace of ten-foot tides could not be eliminated by engineering skills.

Over three years throughout the Pacific any time a Jap found himself in any kind of hole, he would fight to the death. But subterranean works at Tarakan were virtually empty when the first Australians began to check them, almost immediately after the first wave moved ashore. The exodus must have coincided with the bombardment. The Japanese had fled inland in something very near panic. I saw enemy mess kits with uneaten rice still wet, discarded gear of every type, and two artillery pieces trained directly on our beach from an underground position, deserted by gunners who didn't even pause to fire the shells already in their chambers. But although the Japs ran, they didn't run far. First contact was established no more than a hundred yards inland, and from then on the fighting was bitter. But by then it was too late. The Nips put up a fine defense but on the Diggers' terms. It was almost the only time on record that the enemy abandoned previously prepared works without a struggle. Once they moved to the jungle and hills they played right into the hands of the Diggers, who had long since proved themselves peerless jungle fighters.

Tarakan Island is roughly the size of Staten Island, some eight by twenty miles. The oil wells were mostly situated directly in the center, connected to the coast by what had been fairly good roads and pipelines, but surrounded for the most part by very respectable jungles. Before the war, the village of Taraken was a small Dutch and Malay community that existed only for the oil industry. When I first visited it in March, 1941, it was a small but convenient airstrip where the Dutch planes stopped en route from Manila to Java to fuel both the plane and the passengers. My "fuel" had included sauerkraut, mashed potatoes, and juicy sausages served by healthy, well-fed Malay servants. I mention this because of the contrast between those people and the natives we found on our return.

Not long after the first troops came ashore, the natives — most of them must have been the same people — started coming into our lines. The change was both staggering and pitiful. From the Solomons to Luzon I had never seen newly liberated people in such unanimously bad physical condition. They were obviously starving and most were suffering from beriberi or pellagra with hideous sores gaping through their rags of clothing. Many had been shot by the fleeing Japs, not with intent to kill but to render them a burden on the landing forces. A bullet through the instep was the enemy's favorite treatment. Our medics were much busier with these poor human wrecks than with our own casualties, at least in the first hours of the landing. It was memorable testimony to the glorious benefits of the promised Greater East Asia Co-Prosperity Sphere!

We had not reached the oil fields late that afternoon when I had to start back to my microphone several hundred miles north, so I could not report their condition, but that was less important than the fact that the Australians were moving ahead, slowly but steadily, and there was no question of the outcome. The restoration of the Tarakan fields was always a secondary consideration in this operation, although we would certainly have welcomed another source of fuel for our own armed forces. The primary objective of the campaign was to cut off the Japanese completely from this rich portion of the oil of the Indies, and by sunset on our landing day, that mission had been accomplished.

S-P-E-C-I-A-L   R-E-P-O-R-T

Coffin Nail

Dick Sutherland was hardly what you'd call a garrulous general. Ordinarily you'd be lucky to rate a noncommittal grunt to acknowledge a greeting. That's why I was surprised when he called to me as I passed his door and asked me into his office. The month was January of 1945 and we were in Dagupan where GHQ SWPA was located in a nondescript frame house, the temporary offices of General MacArthur and his staff. As chief of staff, Richard K. Sutherland was always positioned next to the C-in-C, and I was prowling the area in the endless search for broadcast news. Dick was standing beside his desk.

"Bill, I've got a story here that you can't broadcast, but I think some of you correspondents should know about it." He picked up a thick, heavy file that rested on his desk and hefted it. I thought he was going to hand it to me, but he continued to weigh it, provocatively, as he asked the indicated question, "Do you know what this is?" I assured him I had no idea, and he returned it to his desk. "Bill, this is a projected campaign for the liberation of the Netherlands Indies, complete to the last round of ammunition. We have the men, the materiel, the bottoms, and the necessary air-naval support right now. We could secure the islands in less than sixty days, conservatively."

I was surprised, to state it mildly. This was a possibility no one had ever hinted to me. My first thought was for our immediate campaign. "What about the Philippines? We have a fight on our hands right here."

"We can clean up the Philippines with what we have on hand, together with what's on the way. The NEI campaign would be a total plus." Naturally I wanted to know, in that case, just what was holding us up, and of course that was exactly the question he wanted me to ask. "The British," he answered, and he repeated it for emphasis, "The British refuse to give us their permission to strike anywhere beyond Borneo. They say, and they're technically correct, that the remainder of those islands lie within their assigned sphere, and they intend to resolve that situation themselves. The only trouble with that position is that they have neither the men nor the materiel right now, and no one knows when they will. A lot can happen in those islands in the next few months."

"What's the General think about it?"

"He's very unhappy with the British attitude, of course, but they are our allies, and he feels we can't afford a public disagreement—which is why you can't talk about it. But I did think some of you fellows should understand what's happening in regard to the NEI."

I never had occasion to check Dick's story with General MacArthur personally, but MacArthur did confirm the existence of such a projected campaign in his autobiography, attributing the veto to the anonymity of Washington, whence any such order would have had to emanate regardless of what prompted it. Even at that time, however, there was no reason for me to doubt Sutherland who, as head of the SWPA staff, would have played an important part in the organization of any such campaign. Certainly there was nothing tentative about the way he placed the onus squarely on the shoulders of our British allies.

Frankly, Dick Sutherland was never one of my favorite GHQ personalities, although I never had any disagreement with him. He could be quite affable when he chose, but he seldom chose. Technically he was a good chief of staff. Any shortcomings cited by his critics and there were more than a few, were largely personal. He understood MacArthur's methods and was an efficient administrator. I never knew him to mislead a correspondent deliberately, although he sometimes refused to give us the time of day. I don't believe he would have showed me the NEI file or blamed the veto on the British if he hadn't checked with MacArthur in advance.

The idea of such a stand by the British was entirely plausible because of the intense colonial rivalry between the British and the Dutch. It was a rivalry born of completely different concepts of colonial development, the Dutch by resident paternalism and the British by transient efficiency. A British general, Sir Archibald Wavell, had been in titular command of the Dutch-Allied forces when the Indies fell to the Japanese, so it was only natural that the British wanted the restoration to be made by their own command. Many Dutch, however, to this day doubt the sincerity of any British desire to effect the actual restoration. That was the situation with regard to the Indies at the time of my conversation with Dick Sutherland.

Regardless of Sutherland's observations on the Philippines campaign,

we still had a lot of hard fighting ahead before the islands would be free of the enemy. In the intense activity of the next few weeks both the conversation and the vetoed Indies campaign slipped back into that mental file where I kept good stories that couldn't then be released.

Assuming, as I do, that Sutherland was correct, the ultimate results of that British veto boggle the mind. According to the MacArthur plan, as Sutherland reported it to me, the Dutch could have been returned to the Indies as early as March, 1945, instead of six months later, and of course a lot did happen in those months. There can be no reasonable doubt that those six wantonly wasted months cost the Dutch the Indies.

Soon after the Japanese took control of the Indies in March, 1942, intelligence reports confirmed the activities of a group of Indonesians who were openly collaborating with the invaders. Two of the leaders had long records of anti-Dutch activity extending back twelve to fifteen years. The two, of course, were Sukarno and Muhammad Hatta, and it didn't take much imagination to envision what they would do to Dutch sovereignty, given the opportunity. Those crucial six months gave them all the time they needed. By the time Dick Sutherland showed me the NEI campaign file, the Japanese in the Indies knew their tenure was running out and allowed Sukarno the freedom he needed to organize his project. He made the most of it.

In those decisive months Sukarno and Hatta, with Japanese assistance, completed their plan and organized their military force. By the time the Dutch made their tentative return, the nationalist movement had gone too far to be stopped. The Dutch would be expelled after more than four constructive centuries, and thousands of Indonesians would die or find themselves in political prisons so Sukarno could establish his "guided democracy" (he ultimately broke with Hatta) and realize his dictatorial ambitions. Of even more importance was the wanton destruction of one of the world's most efficient economies and the introduction of widespread poverty in a land where poverty had been almost unknown.

As an observer who was in the Indies before, during, and after the Pacific war, I have never considered Sukarno's nationalist movement to be any more representative of the will and desires of the Indonesian peoples than the ever-present independence movement in Puerto Rico reflects the will of the majority in that Caribbean island. As a matter of record, of course, every vote the Puerto Ricans have taken has shown an overwhelming preference for the status quo. But such plebiscites mean nothing to the would-be Sukarnos whose patriotic fervor too often is merely a mask for an overwhelming urge to get control of the gravy train.

The Indonesians, unfortunately, were never given a chance to make a choice. Any attempt at opposition to Sukarno, either by voice or deed, was ruthlessly quelled almost before it started. The world will never know with any degree of accuracy how many Indonesians died or spent long years in prison because they dared try to exercise the vaunted right of self-determination on their own.

Personally, I shall never forget an experience I had during a visit to Java a year or so after the war while the Dutch were fighting their losing battle against the Japanese-armed Sukarno forces, and against mounting pressures from the newly organized United Nations. About a week after my arrival in Batavia (now Jakarta) the Dutch, by force of arms, had advanced their line of demarcation some fifteen kilometers to the little city of Buitenzorg (now Bogor) about fifty-five kilometers south of Batavia. In other words, they had re-conquered a considerable area that had, until then, been held by the Sukarno forces.

On this particular day a Dutch official invited Ed Baker, an official of Time-Life and me to drive with him to Buitenzorg and inspect the newly recaptured territory. As we neared the old line of demarcation the official told us to see what happened when we moved into the newly occupied territory. "What do we watch for?" "You'll see!"

We did! There were four of us in the car: two Dutch officials, Baker and I, who looked more like a Dutchman than many Hollanders. We could never be mistaken for Asians. As soon as we crossed the designated line pandemonium broke loose in the rice paddies and fields that lined our route. The native farmers, men and women, came rushing up to us, cheering, shouting, waving, and pressing forward to touch the car or us. All I could think of was the drive I had made into occupied Manila with the First Cavalry. These people, like the Filipinos, were almost delirious with joy, and the demonstrations were continuous all the way to our destination. For me, that was an unmistakeable plebiscite. There could be no question that these people vastly preferred the ruling hand of the Dutch, under which they had lived from birth, to that of their own self-styled "nationalists," who had governed them since the end of the Japanese occupation. Unfortunately for them, their preferences would come to naught.

The world can never recover fully from the effects of those tragically wasted months when the Allied forces of Douglas MacArthur were required to stand idle while one of the world's greatest island civilizations was being chopped to bits. "Self determination" was to be the rule, and in the Indies, as in countless compara-

ble parts of the world, that "right" unfortunately meant turning defenseless, simple-thinking people of minimal education over to the whims of despots like Sukarno, Hatta, and others of the same ilk. I believe that future historians will record that when the British refused to allow Douglas MacArthur to liberate the Netherlands Indies in the early spring of 1945, they drove a king-size coffin nail into the future of the tottering British empire.

CHAPTER 37

VE Day

The news that the war in Europe at last had ended with the final capitulation of Nazi Germany hit Manila with all the impact of an October snowflake on a tin roof. It had to be the greatest anticlimax of the war. There was no reaction, official or otherwise—no bells or whistles, no shouts or cheering, no dancing in the streets. Manila was a mass of burned-out rubble, and each breeze from the north or east brought the sound of enemy artillery in the not-too-distant mountains. The hospitals were filled with the wounded, civilian and military. No one was in a mood to celebrate anything less than a major improvement of his own personal situation.

The news reached me in my quarters shortly before midnight, May 20, and I immediately started for the studio to prepare the report I knew New York would order. On the way I was stopped by an M.P. for taxing my battered vehicle to its limit. I protested. "Hey, soldier, give me a break. The war in Europe has just ended, and I have to make a broadcast." The M.P. looked doubtful. "You mean it's finished over there?" I assured him it was. "Well, okay, then. Go ahead, but *watch that speed!*" That was the "so what" attitude I would encounter all day.

The studio and nearby GHQ were lighted and active, but the rest of the city was wrapped in almost total darkness, and it would be six to twelve hours before most people got the word. My first report, an hour after the news first arrived, was simply that there was nothing to report. Manila hadn't yet been informed. Even when I made my second broadcast about twelve hours later, there still was nothing to tell America except that the only apparent reaction to the news we had awaited so long was the fervent hope that the military might that destroyed Adolf Hitler would now be focused on the Japanese empire.

Even though I knew that the Nazi collapse eventually would prove a major boon to us in our own theater, my impressions of the campaign we had launched for the Borneo oil fields left me little room for enthusiasm for a ceasefire on the other side of the globe, and there was still a lot of nasty, unspectacular, but lethal fighting to be done right there on Luzon. Some of the fiercest was up in the province of Nueva Viscaya, some 150 miles north of Manila, where the Thirty-second Division, which had learned its combat techniques in the swampy jungles of Buna, was waging a mountain campaign in the Caraballos as different from Buna as up is from down.

In both campaigns the Thirty-second had to fight a foe that was deeply dug in, but there was one major difference. In Buna both sides fought on much the same level of mud and jungle. In the Caraballos, however, the enemy was almost always above the advancing Americans, looking down their throats as they fought an inch-by-inch battle.

I was determined to visit the Thirty-second, particularly when I learned that the Signal Corps had installed a temporary transmitter at the division command post capable of relaying a broadcast report to the *Apache* and on to the States.

Maj. Gen. William H. ("Bill") Gill, division commander, sent an L-5 Cub plane, normally used for artillery spotting and liaison chores, down to San Miguel to pick me up. The pilot was a rosy-cheeked youngster who looked fit to quarterback a high school team but who had, in my opinion, insufficient respect for the basic elements of aerial safety. Flying up the side of a mountain is never a game of croquet, and when you insist on spicing that flight by flirting with treetops just for the hell of it, you are only asking for trouble. Once we reached the foothills and it became obvious the flirtation would continue, I nudged the lad and asked, "Did you lose something down here?" He pulled up and throttled back the engine. "What's the matter? You scared?" I left no doubt. "You're damned right I'm scared. This is no way to fly in the mountains. Get us some altitude!"

He shrugged and pulled up to a reasonable cruising level, and we reached Gill's CP without further incident. I had lost face with my youthful pilot, of course, but that was all I lost. Two days later he learned why his nervous passenger had reason to be scared, but the lesson came too late. They buried him in a mountain grave alongside the trail.

The mountain campaign of the Thirty-second was not as immediately dramatic as an amphibious assault or the First Cavalry's drive into Manila, but what the Thirty-second Division accomplished in some four months of nonstop fighting was as genuinely spectacular as anything the war produced.

In my report from General Gill's CP that evening I told the folks back home, in part:

> I am reporting tonight from the "top of the Philippines," from a point on the Villa Verde Trail in the Caraballo Mountains of north-central Luzon. This is a stronghold that the veteran troops of the Thirty-second Division in 119 days of continuous fighting have wrested from the Japs, inch by inch, peak by peak, and valley by valley.
>
> As a result, the Thirty-second, trained in the deepest jungles, is just about to wind up a *mountain* campaign fought over terrain as rugged as I ever saw in China, Burma, or New Guinea, and to crown its efforts with complete success!
>
> The battle for the Villa Verde Trail has been too much overlooked in the more dramatic developments of those same months on the plains of central Luzon and around Manila. But the battle for the tortuous footpath that bears the name of an ancient Spanish missionary, Father Villa Verde, has been in its own way as astounding a campaign as any the second battle for the Philippines has produced.
>
> Four months ago the trail was a 22-mile footpath winding its way over mountain peaks and valleys and lined its full length with pillboxes, caves, tunnels, heavy and light artillery emplacements, and machine-gun nests. The Nips had spent the years of their Philippines occupation making sure the bastion was impregnable.
>
> Tonight, as I speak, the Villa Verde Trail is a road, 22 miles in length, every inch of which was built by the division's 114th Combat Engineers, always in the full face of vicious enemy fire. Perhaps I can give you some idea of this amazing feat by terming it the "Baby Burma Road." I have now traveled both, and the comparison is not overdrawn.
>
> This microphone right now is situated in the very heart of what Radio Tokyo not long ago referred to as an "impregnable defense line." And Radio Tokyo had reason to boast. The Japs really were dug in and armed as never before in this war. For example, one enemy unit ordinarily armed with eight machine guns was found to have thirty-four in operation, and everything else was in proportion.
>
> This was no campaign of maneuver. When the Thirty-second reached the southern limits of this ancient trail, there was no room to maneuver, nothing in the way of a thoroughfare except a winding footpath, barely wide enough for a carabao. In order to penetrate the

fastness of the Caraballo range, the Thirty-second had to have a road, a road to carry supplies for the advancing infantry and to provide evacuation facilities for the wounded.

Immediately the engineers began the stupendous job of converting the Villa Verde Trail into a highway. Up the first mountain they moved, fighting every foot of the way but carving their road as they went. And as the engineers and infantry moved slowly ahead, they pushed their highway thousands of feet into the air, over passes, around peaks, and down the seemingly bottomless valleys.

Casualties were heavy, particularly among the bulldozer drivers who spent much of their time ahead of the infantry. But the enemy's casualties outscored those of the Thirty-second by a ratio of more than ten to one, and the campaign was completely successful.

That particular broadcast carried a special reward for this reporter. Many of the men of the Thirty-second, if not most, having been confined to a remote mountain assignment with no particular attention from the outside world, were really wondering if that outside world was aware of what they were accomplishing. When the word spread that CBS News had sent a reporter to broadcast their story, interest was intense. General Gill and his staff thanked me for "probably the best morale boost of the campaign."

The conquest of the Villa Verde Trail was a remarkable demonstration of what the American in uniform can accomplish when properly trained, properly led, and properly motivated. No soldier, sailor, or airman can do his best unless he knows what he's fighting for. To the uninitiated, success in warfare may seem to be merely a matter of who has the most guns, and there's no doubt guns are essential. But, as the Japanese proved many times in the Pacific, weapons are useless unless the soldier knows how to use them and is properly led. That's where Bill Gill's division held all the aces in the Caraballos. His men not only had the proper tools; they also had the know-how and leadership, and they knew what they were fighting for.

S-P-E-C-I-A-L R-E-P-O-R-T

Eroica

There was one particularly moving exception to the near-indifference with which Manila greeted the news of the Allied victory in Europe. Dr. Herbert Zipper was a Viennese musician — a refugee who had spent twelve anguishing months in the notorious Dachau concentration camp. While a prisoner of the Nazis he made a vow that one day, somehow, he would mark the fall of Adolf Hitler and the

Nazi regime by conducting a thanksgiving performance of Beethoven's Third Symphony, the *Eroica*. He never wavered from that vow, and on May 10, 1945, after twelve long years, he conducted that thanksgiving performance.

After escaping from Dachau, Dr. Zipper finally arrived in the Philippines, where he became conductor of the Manila Symphony Orchestra. The maestro was just beginning to realize some success with the orchestra when the Japanese invasion forced him to disband. The instruments and the precious library were secreted in a fireproof vault, everything but the score of the *Eroica*, which remained with the conductor through three years of occupation, an ever-present symbol of his vow.

Finally the Americans returned, but Dr. Zipper and his wife spent ten nightmarish days and nights evading the brutal Japanese guns and the sadistic firebrands that destroyed their home, their possessions, their community, everything but their indomitable spirit and the precious score that the maestro carried with him day and night.

When they finally reached safety and he announced he was going to reform his orchestra, most people thought he was crazy and said so. The musicians were scattered, many dead, and all were out of practice. But Herbert Zipper refused to be discouraged. With the aid of the U.S. Army special services branch, he located some seventy of his former one hundred plus players. He banded them together, provided them with instruments miraculously salvaged from the fires, and started rehearsals. Many of his men had just come down from the hills where they had spent three years as guerrillas. Others were still weak from malnutrition when the rehearsals started. All were rusty, fingers out of condition and unaccustomed to ensemble playing. Frankly, it looked like a hopeless task.

But the work went on for four weeks, Zipper tirelessly driving, begging, coaxing, teaching. Finally, out of it all, something began to emerge. The orchestra took form, and the rich, full themes of the *Eroica* gradually began to take on the life and vitality with which Beethoven had endowed them. After long deliberation, Dr. Zipper decided to use his cherished score to commemorate the liberation of Manila. The ultimate fall of the Nazis would merit a second thanksgiving. Then, as the date for the first concert was set and final rehearsals began, the Nazis fell as if on cue! Dr. Herbert Zipper's presentation of Beethoven's *Eroica* fulfilled his greatest ambition —commemorating the fall of Nazism and the end of more than a decade of forced exile from his homeland— in addition to celebrating the liberation of his adopted home.

The *Eroica* has been performed by many greater orchestras but never with greater feeling, and I have heard far greater orchestras perform the *Eroica* and produce far fewer moist eyes. You couldn't be critical when you knew that the former *concertmeister* had been killed by the Japanese, and that the leader of the woodwinds had suffered the same fate. The fact that the horns in the trio of the third movement were less than strong became unimportant when you learned that both the finest horn players in the Philippines had given their lives for their country. What remained of this orchestra performed the *Eroica* from a makeshift stage in the nave of Santa Cruz, what was left of one of Manila's most ancient churches, the music echoing between the shattered walls and soaring to the tropical sky that provided the only roof. It was at once a paean of joy and a prayer of thanksgiving.

CHAPTER 38

At Last VJ Day

There are three reasons why home leave in the summer of 1945 will always remain indelible in my mind. First was the reunion with my two girls after more than two years (the second in four and a half years) and the shock of being greeted by a daughter who had grown another five inches since our last meeting. That was the personal reason. The other two were historic and will always be remembered by anyone who lived through that era: the super-bomb on Hiroshima that changed the course of the world forever and Japan's reluctant decision to lay down its arms after a second super-bomb and the threat of more.

In June, 1945, no one, including Tojo, Koiso, and their henchmen, any longer doubted that the total defeat of Hirohito's empire was inevitable. By then the only question was how long the Tokyo war chiefs would be willing to continue sacrificing Japanese lives merely to delay the loss of face they dreaded.

At that time we were committed only to the eradication of trapped Japanese troops in Luzon and a few scattered islands in the South and the Southwest Pacific commands. Even the end of Germany failed to deflect much attention to the Pacific, so Paul White suggested I take my overdue home leave and let Jack Adams handle the mike until the time arrived for our assault on the Japanese mainland. I was determined to cover that campaign whenever it developed, and I knew that General Eichelberger was even then preparing his Eighth Army command to lead the attack.

I eagerly accepted the idea of a home leave, but I made sure there would be a signal from MacArthur's GHQ or Eichelberger's staff if the date set for the invasion required an early return. Unfortunately I made no support plans for an early return in case the war came to a sudden end. Most of us believed the Japanese would hold out until American forces were actually on Japanese soil.

This was going to be a complete holiday, devoted to my family and a few of my close friends. Of course there are duties that can't be

I returned in 1945 for my second home leave in four and a half years to be welcomed by my two girls, Catherine, a brave and wonderful wife, and Patricia, a daughter who had grown five inches since my previous leave two years before! There still was one more separation ahead. *Courtesy United Airlines*

avoided, even on a holiday. I made my required calls in New York and Washington but held them to a minimum. A couple of broadcasts had to be made, but I cleaned the slate early, and Catherine and I were in South Bend visiting my mother on August 6 when the word *Hiroshima* became a permanent part of the English language.

I realized immediately that all my plans would have to be radically revised. I talked to White, who advised me to go on to Chicago and check in with WBBM, the key station for CBS in the Midwest. Then all we could do was await developments.

Three days later another bomb struck, this time at Nagasaki, and even I was finally convinced the end could not be far ahead. But the Tokyo war chiefs still held out, and it was almost a week before the final capitulation was confirmed. From then on the end would be only a formality.

Chicago went wild! The celebration reminded me, in reverse, of Manila's observation of VE Day. There was nothing left of the war on either side of the globe, and no reason for restraint. The whole city turned out to celebrate with every noise-maker ever devised by cacaphonic man, and the festivities lasted long into the night. I knew the war really had ended when I saw a six-foot ordinary seaman walking down Michigan Boulevard with a lovely naval lieutenant hanging on his arm, looking up at him with adoring eyes.

CBS—in fact all radio stations—pre-empted regularly scheduled programs and devoted the time to its own celebration. Virtually everyone who had ever been to the Pacific, or to Europe either, for that matter, contributed. I spoke several times but spent most of the evening composing a broadcast that came close to expressing what was in my heart. It was the statement I wanted on the record in honor of some of the greatest men the journalistic profession has ever known, a brief tribute to former colleagues of the Southwest Pacific who could not share the universal joy.

The Southwest Pacific, I affirmed, was a rugged theater, and the men assigned to keep the world informed of activities out that way were never surpassed for courage and devotion to duty. It was a devotion that cost eighteen of them the right to live and join our hour of jubilation.

Mel Jacoby of *Time-Life* was the first to go, killed on a Port Darwin airfield by a fighter plane that got out of control and cut him down as he waited for his own plane. Mel was a veteran of the Far East. I had known him in Hong Kong and Manila before he, with his bride of only a few weeks, escaped from Corregidor to make his way in small boats to the saftey of Australia, and death.

Barney Darnton, of the *New York Times,* was a gentleman who will never be forgotten by his colleagues. He was the victim, tragically, of an American bomb that exploded near his small boat near Buna, when that jungle valley was a Japanese stronghold.

As I prepared the script I thought of the makeshift leg on my typewriter that Carl Thusgaard of Acme Newsphotos had fashioned only a few hours before the bomber he was riding was shot down near Salamaua.

Harry Poague and Bob Lewis were correspondents for the Red Cross who met their deaths together, at Port Moresby, in a C-47 transport that faltered on takeoff.

Frank Cuhel of Mutual was one of my closest friends. We escaped together from Java in March, 1942, on the last boat to evade the enemy blockade, and we shared quarters in Australia until Frank left to cover the North Africa invasion and died in the crash of the *Yankee Clipper* in Lisbon.

Brydon Taves was head of the United Press staff in the Southwest Pacific until his death in the crash of a B-17 bomber in which he had planned to cover the Cape Gloucester landing. Ken Raynor, a correspondent for Australian AP, died in the same crash.

Memories of Ken's death wakened memories of all those Aussie correspondents who were as fearless at the Australian Digger. Their number included Keith Palmer, killed by a bomb on the Bougainville beachhead, Harold Dick who died in a New Guinea plane crash, John Elliott and William Smith, both dead in the Borneo invasion. Finally there was Damien Parer, an Aussie working for an American company, *Paramount News*, an outstanding cameraman who spent most of his combat career in the Southwest Pacific but actually died in Saipan, killed by a Jap machine gunner while stalking along with his camera, directly behind the lead tank in an advancing column.

On the night following the epochal battle of Leyte Gulf, Asahel ("Ace") Bush and I were working side by side in Tacloban, pounding out our reports and comparing notes as we wrote. Finished, I left to board our broadcasting ship, and just a few minutes later Ace was killed, almost instantly, by a bomb that struck the correspondents' quarters only a few meters distant. John Terry of the *Chicago Daily News* and Stan Gunn of the *Fort Worth Star-Telegram* (Stan had arrived in Leyte less than twenty-four hours earlier) died in the same attack.

A few days later Frank Prist of Acme Newsphotos was shot through the heart by a sniper while driving a jeep out in front of our most advanced lines in Leyte.

Finally, Bill Chickering of *Time-Life* was killed by a kamikaze that crashed into the bridge of a battleship on which he was riding to the Luzon invasion at Lingayen Gulf. I concluded the report:

These are the "Eighteen of the Southwest Pacific," eighteen correspondents who gave their lives so you people back home, and free people everywhere, might get the news of your heroic sons, husbands, and brothers-sisters, or see the pictorial records of their matchless exploits.

This is a record I believe to be unmatched in any theater of this global war, because the eighteen men represented nearly 4 percent of all the correspondents who saw action out that way.

Brave men, all of them, with a devotion to their profession that was stronger than life. You can't help but have a humble pride in having been one of their number for so many years, to have had the honor to call them friends.

That was my personal requiem for eighteen coworkers who were not so fortunate as I, wonderful friends whose memory is still strong after nearly a half-century.

Now my schedule called for an immediate return to New York and a departure for the scene of the Japanese surrender without delay.

S-P-E-C-I-A-L   R-E-P-O-R-T

Desperation

I'll admit I was frightened (scared as hell is probably more accurate) several times during the war years, but the only time I ever experienced sheer desperation came not under combat conditions but in the CBS newsroom on the seventeenth floor of 485 Madison Avenue! Super-bombs on Hiroshima and Nagasaki had destroyed the enemy's will to resist and even then terms were being fixed for the surrrender of the Japanese empire.

Back in New York, however, it looked as if my too-brief home leave might well develop into a permanent home assignment. Paul White told me it would be useless to try to return because the War Department had issued orders barring any additional correspondents from the theater until after the surrender, and Washington was adamant. I stared at

him in utter disbelief. This couldn't happen to me! I found myself fighting back the bitter tears that were trying to form. "Paul, get this straight! I'm going to be there for the surrender and all hell's not going to stop me!"

"Bill, it's not my idea. We want you there, but Washington is adamant. You don't have a chance." I couldn't believe what I was hearing. Surely the fact that I had covered the war, on the scene, from the first day must carry some weight—but it didn't. My personal call to the War Department only brought word that my travel orders, then dated for the middle of September, would not be revised and, furthermore, I was to make no attempt to return. An order! As I hung up, White, who had been listening on an extension, came over to extend his sympathies. I waved him aside. I was scared and I was mad, desperately scared of missing the climax of four long years and bitterly mad, mad at White, who was merely the bearer of bad news, mad at the War Department, and mad, most of all, at a callous fate that could decree such a monstrous injustice. I again affirmed my determination to return, and Paul, shrugging, left me to lick my wounds.

I closed the door of the office I was using and sat down to study my options, if any. One thing I had learned during my years with the armed forces was not to quit at the first turndown. The lack of valid orders could, of course, become a major headache, but it was not necessarily a fatal handicap. I had traveled thousands of miles during the war without orders. No pilot in a combat area would ever think of asking for formal orders. It was the top brass you had to contend with. I had also learned that the armed forces, at that time, were composed of the army and the navy. Neither was necessarily bound by the individual decisions of the other. If the army turned you down, you could often get a hand from the navy, and vice versa. From that thought came a possible solution.

Some years before, while toiling for American Airlines, I had a friend, Whitey Rimes, who, I suddenly remembered, was now a three-striper at the Patuxent naval air base in Maryland. I knew Whitey to be a free soul who shared my dislike for red tape. It was worth a try. I picked up the phone and asked the operator to get me Comdr. W. Thorne Rimes at Patuxent. Within minutes she had traced him to a New York naval office and had him on the line. Those CBS operators were phenomenal detectives. "Bill? This is Whitey. What's the problem?"

"Whitey, I've got to get back for the surrender, and the War Department won't update my orders. The navy's got to help me!"

"No problem. Meet me at Louis and Armand's."

When we met at the traditional CBS spa a few minutes later, Rimes told me to have the CBS operator contact a certain officer at the Oakland naval base and route the call to us. I began to breathe freely for the first time that day. This was the first positive reaction I had had, and I certainly needed a positive reaction from someone. Almost immediately the call came through, and Rimes, blessed with a roundhouse voice that almost made the telephone unnecessary, informed his Oakland contact, and almost all of Louis's luncheon clientele, that Bill Dunn was going back to the Pacific with the United States Navy, and this despite obvious protests from Oakland. Having left no doubt in anyone's mind that he expected the order to be obeyed, Whitey returned to the bar and handed me a card with a name and phone number. "If you have any trouble—but you won't—call me at Patuxent. Now you owe me a drink."

Naturally the word rose rapidly from Louis's to the seventeenth floor, and White, still dubious, offered no objections except to ask how I expected to reach the West Coast without a travel priority. That was only a minor headache, and again American Airlines came to my aid. An old friend booked me on the next morning's "milk run," a local flight that made every stop en route and was highly unpopular with long-distance travelers. Then he sent word to all stations that I was to be the last nonpriority passenger to be offloaded.

It worked even better than we had

hoped, and the next evening found me trying to book a room at the Palace Hotel, where CBS had its San Francisco headquarters. Failing that, I called the Oakland number and found Whitey's man waiting for me. He told me to report to Oakland operation office before nine o'clock, less than three hours later, and that word was more welcome than any hotel room, tired though I was. Shortly before midnight our plane lifted off the Oakland runway, cleared the Golden Gate, and headed for Hawaii, carrying among others an elated but exhausted correspondent equipped with a set of invalid travel orders. Here I was, at last, heading toward the climax of the more than four and a half years since I first cleared that gateway to the Pacific, my troubles behind me!

Not quite!

As I stepped off the plane at Pearl, however, I heard myself being paged. That in itself was a complete surprise, because I was sure no one knew I was on that plane except the naval officers at Oakland. Someone did know, however, for there beside the loading apron was an air corps jeep with a GI driver standing on the seat and calling for William J. Dunn. When I identified myself, the youngster told me to bring my gear. He had orders to take me to the operations office at Hickam Field, the air corps base. I protested that I didn't want to leave my plane, but the GI was adamant, repeating that he had orders to take me back with him although he didn't know who wanted me or why. Reluctantly I shoved my bag and typewriter into the jeep and, completely baffled, accepted the ride to Hickam. At our destination the airman deposited my gear on the sidewalk, returned to his voiture, and drove out of my life forever.

Once inside the office I realized my troubles were far from over. Not one of a half-dozen officers and men on duty there had any idea who had sent the jeep or why. It took only a few questions to convince myself I would get no help from this quarter, and, worst of all, I knew my naval plane would be gone before I could get back to Pearl Harbor. One of the officers suggested I call Major Durno, base press officer, and handed me a phone.

It was not quite seven o'clock, and it was a sleepy George Durno who answered. He was a former Washington correspondent for the Hearst newspapers, and I knew him well. I explained my complete bewilderment at this unexpected turn of events, and he responded with surprise and sympathy. "That's really tough, Bill, but there's nothing I can do except buy you a breakfast. I'll be over as soon as I get dressed." Durno wasted no time. He pulled up in his own jeep in just a few minutes, complete with the faint glimmer of an idea. He had just encountered a colonel who had been a legal counsel for American Airlines and remembered me from those years. Frankly, his name didn't click, but I was anxious to talk to anyone who had the slightest interest in my predicament. So we forgot about breakfast and headed for the colonel's office.

By the time we met I had placed the colonel in my mind. We had never worked in the same areas at American, but I knew enough about the AA operation to sustain a nostalgic few minutes. After the amenities the colonel explained that while he had no authority to assign priorities, he did have something to say about how those priorities were aligned. If I could get myself a class "B" rating (about the highest I could aspire to), he would place me at the top of the "B" list, which, he explained, would be nearly as effective as an "A." There was little chance of movement with any rating below the "B."

The officer who could, if he chose, issue that priority was a pugnacious little light colonel, crabbed and dour, who looked as if he had just breakfasted on K-rations and battery acid. His greeting was almost a snarl (priority officers have to condition themselves to saying no), and my hopes again began to wane. Durno was a persuasive salesman and he took over the presentation of my case, but I still could detect no gleam of understanding in the colonel's eye. Furthermore, I was convinced this man was one who lived by the book and would not forget to inspect my useless travel orders. Then the proverbial fat would really be rendered.

Instead, the officer scowled through all of George's argument, then growled, "Major, do you mean to tell me that we should move this damned correspondent out ahead of the hundreds of legitimate military personnel who actually have a reason to be out there?" "That's right, Colonel." "Okay. I'll give him a "B." No mention of travel orders.

Once again my spirits lifted, and I left Hickam a few hours later for Kwajalein and Guam aboard a big C-54. I was going to make it after all! But to this day that episode remains a total mystery. Who in Hawaii knew I was on that plane? Who sent that jeep to pick me up? Above all, why?

Another hurdle developed in Guam where I was out-ranked by a bona fide "A" priority and then encountered a loading officer, a sergeant,

who was not at all impressed by a civilian with only a "B" priority. Once again American Airlines came to my rescue. A short time before, while heading home for my leave, I had learned that the air corps commander in Guam was Maj. Gen. Tom Hardin, who had been a senior pilot during my years with the airline and another good friend. I asked the sergeant if I could use his phone to call the general, and he clearly didn't like it. He obviously thought I was going to go over his head. I had learned early in the war that no one ever gains anything by trying to outflank a sergeant, and I watched him out of the corner of my eye. He kept well within listening distance, and I kept my conversation as personal as possible, with that in mind.

"No, Tom, I won't be seeing you this time around. I'm anxious to get to Manila and I expect to get away very soon. No, there's nothing you can do. Your boys will take care of me . . . they seem to be a good gang. I just wanted to say hello and tell you to look me up when you get to Tokyo." When I hung up, the sergeant put the phone back in place and pointed to a bench in front of the counter. "If you'll sit there where I can find you, sir, I think we can get you out before long."

The next stop was Manila, my own territory. And once on my own turf I had no need for orders. I knew a score of officers who could write orders for me if I needed them to get to Japan. I didn't.

The day after the formal surrender I was talking to General MacArthur and was quite surprised to learn that he knew I was in the States when Japan folded. He wanted to know how I got back so quickly, and I'm sure he knew of the War Department order banning correspondents. I told him briefly how I had ignored my nonvalid orders and literally talked my way back. When I finished he chuckled. "Why didn't you send me a message, Bill? I would have sent you a top priority." I knew the answer to that one.

"General, I have no doubt you would have given me the priority *if* you had received my request. But I doubt that such a message would ever have cleared your staff to get your attention." He thought for a minute, then smiled. "I guess you're right."

PART 4

CHAPTER 39

Into the Rising Sun

The flight into the Land of the Rising Sun was exactly that. Our C-54 lifted off an Okinawa runway shortly after 2:00 A.M. on Thursday, August 30, 1945. Three hours later we flew directly into the rays of a brilliant sunrise that seemed to originate right over our distant target and remained with us the rest of the way. It was a blinding sun to those of us inside the cabin, but actually there was nothing to see right up to the final minutes of the flight except the whitecaps of the Pacific. Our route kept us well south of Honshu Island until we were over Sagami Bay, directly south of the Atsugi airstrip, and we were over land only for the last few miles. The five-hour flight gave ample time to review myriad memories and to ponder the welcome that might await us once we touched down on Japanese soil.

I had moved from Manila to Okinawa on Tuesday, two days earlier, after breaking Jack Adams's heart. Jack had been certain I could never get back on schedule and was all packed for Tokyo when I suddenly appeared. I apologized for pulling rank on him, but he understood and even forced what is sometimes termed a hollow smile. "I suppose I should hate you for this," he conceded, "but, hell, I'd have done the same myself. Just give my regards to Hirohito."

My day in Okinawa was spent moving from unit to unit of the airborne troops of the Eighth Army, renewing old acquaintances and checking the morale of the men who would be the first to launch this occupation. There was none of the tension I had seen so often on the eve of amphibious landings in the preceding three years. These boys came fully equipped for battle, but they clearly expected no further trouble from the Japanese. Most of them stacked their arms and gear in the vicinity of their assigned planes and spent the few hours before takeoff in complete relaxation, smoking and swapping jokes, singing to the accompaniment of loudspeakers that blared an endless medley of pop tunes, or just sleeping, flat on the unyielding coral surface of the revetment. Red Cross mobile canteens moved slowly about the island and dispensed coffee and doughnuts throughout the night. The naked glare of the floodlights bathed the great airfields with light in blinding contrast with the blackouts that had wrapped all forward posts

Gen. James H. Doolittle led the epochal 1942 raid on Tokyo. He arrived in the Pacific from Europe just as the Japanese called it quits. An old friend, I met him again in Okinawa just before the return to Japan, for a brief reunion. Here he and I exchange some great memories at the New York Wings Club forty years later. *Courtesy Wings Club*

of the Southwest Pacific in darkness for the past one thousand nights. Japan had announced its surrender, and, for the first time since Pearl Harbor, the American soldier was willing to take the Japanese at his word—although he remained ready to react instantly if the climate changed.

These were a few of the thoughts that drifted through my mind as the plane droned on toward an uncertain future. Suddenly the major who occupied the adjoining bucket seat nudged me in the ribs—I may have been drowsing—and pointed excitedly out the window behind us. "Look, Bill, is *that* it?"

That indeed was *it*, a perfect snowcapped cone rising dimly above the mists that covered most of the distant hills to the north. Old Fujisan in person to greet the incoming recent enemy and assure him this was indeed Japan. Most of those in our plane had never before seen Fujiyama, Nippon's exquisite sacred mountain, but it really wasn't necessary for me to identify it for them. There is only one Mount Fuji on this globe and no chance of mistaking it.

Flying low over the flat coastal plain between Atsugi and Yokohama, we watched closely for signs of recent damage from Allied bombers. We were not close enough to Yokohama to mark that city clearly, but the broad, fertile countryside to the west looked as calm and peaceful as it had on my last visit to Japan in 1941. The villages were intact, and from our plane we could see the peasants working in the fields as far as the eye could reach. Most of them didn't even glance up to mark our great silver occupation plane. Not until we crossed the boundaries of the airfield did we see any considerable damage, this in the form of smashed and bomb-scarred hangars and buildings. The countryside, at least, was not in bad condition.

I am not quite sure what we expected to find on the ground of the single-strip airfield, but it certainly wasn't what we actually did find! Around the field was a guard of Japanese naval personnel armed only with clubs. Along the east and north sides of the field were several hundred trucks, buses, and automobiles in various stages of repair, ready to move the Americans to their assigned areas of duty as quickly as they left their planes. Frankly, these vehicles looked more than a little dubious to those of us used to the huge ten-wheelers, the sturdy weapon carriers, and our own jeeps, but this was the best a completely defeated Japan could muster.

The most amazing feature of this strange situation was the attitude of our supposedly reluctant hosts. Everywhere the Japanese, completely unarmed, were bowing and grinning, giving every outward indication that they too were enjoying this moment. Naturally, our troops, all veterans, were inclined to accept these signs of welcome with more than a few grains of salt, but the grins and bows continued.

Japanese airports were never designed for the heavy bombers, transports, and cargo planes, or even the fighters, that had provided the Allies with the wings of victory—further evidence that Japan's military rulers of 1941 had plunged the nation into a major war without any genuine knowledge of what modern warfare required. There were no storage facilities at Atsugi for aircraft, so the single strip would be in constant use once troops began to arrive, with an empty plane leaving for Okinawa every time a loaded plane deposited its human cargo. How long the flimsy runway would accept this unaccustomed beating before it collapsed was an immediate concern.

For this reason MacArthur dispatched a team of 150 specialists headed by Col. Charles Tench of his own staff and including Col. F. C. ("Red") Gideon, Kenney's chief operations officer, to land at Atsugi two days before the first major landings. This was a considered gamble, but one MacArthur thought necessary for the successful launching of the occupation. This team, with absolutely no military support, would find itself in a country that only days before had been its deadly enemy, completely defenseless if Japan experienced a change of heart. Their assignment was to supervise engineering work to beef up the runway, to set up a radio facility to communicate with arriving and departing planes, as well as both MacArthur and Kenney headquarters at Okinawa, and also to check available ground transportation and set up administrative guidelines to handle all phases of the greatest aerial troop movement in history. The success of this mission was attested on the morning of August 30 when the first C-54 dropped down on the Atsugi runway and the exercise began.

My own plane touched down at exactly 7:19 A.M., Japan time, and was back in the air, empty, in a very few minutes. My first concern was to locate some of General Diller's press officers and see what facilities could be rigged in a hurry to relay my first report to CBS News and the network. Everyone cooperated wholeheartedly but to no avail. The Signal Corps had already sent a unit to Yokohama to locate whatever facilities might be linked to Radio Tokyo and placed in operation as quickly as possible.

This unit scored handsomely, and while the endless stream of C-54's was punishing the Atsugi airstrip, the signal corpsmen were busily engaged in setting up a studio for the radio reporters in Yokohama's Customs House a dozen miles to the east. An attempt was made to link this facility to Atsugi by remote control, and I prepared a script, had it censored, and sat down before a field mike to make the first broadcast report from Japan. But we were asking too much, apparently, in the hubbub of the ceaseless landings and the transfer of troops away from the airstrip. I had to delay my first report until I could reach the Customs House that evening.

My own thought was to remain at Atsugi until General MacArthur arrived. The consensus in Okinawa was that if any recalcitrant holdouts did try to make trouble, they would not strike until the C-in-C was in the target area. I had already bought the MacArthur dictum that the Japanese would play ball as promised, but I had to be on hand if they demurred.

The first VIP plane I spotted was the *Miss Em*, the C-54 bringing Eichelberger and his Eighth Army aides, which arrived not too long after I did. Eichelberger immediately went into a huddle with members of his staff who had preceded him. When he concluded, I greeted him. "It's a long way from Buna, eh, Uncle Bob?" He smiled broadly and, as we shook hands, remarked, "Yeah, and I'm no longer off the record." He told me frankly he had been worried for MacArthur's safety and had tried to get him to remain in Okinawa until there was no doubt the situation was stable, but to no avail. The C-in-C was already in the air and would be with us soon. In the meantime Bob Eichelberger had decided MacArthur was right, as usual, but his staff was leaving nothing undone, just in case.

As we talked, the general suddenly broke off in mid-sentence and stared over my shoulder. Then without a word he motioned me aside and strode to greet someone behind me. I turned and saw a battered and bruised GI, wearing a ragged and dirty uniform and walking with a hand-made crutch. This was our first liberated prisoner of war, and he commanded Eichelberger's complete attention for more than a few minutes. The general moved swiftly to greet the lad, put an arm around his shoulder, led him to an upturned crate of some sort, and sat down beside him. The two engaged in a long conversation, the multi-starred army commander and the ragged, unranked soldier, while the rest of us stood at a distance and allowed them their privacy.

Once they concluded, I spoke with the youngster and learned he had been held for some two years in a prison camp fifty or sixty miles from Yokohama. When he learned his captors had surrendered, he picked up his crutch (he was reticent about his injury, saying only that it had happened some months ago in camp), collected his meager gear, and announced he was leaving. No one offered any objection as he walked through the gate, so he kept moving. He boarded a train for Yokohama with no ticket and no money, and still no one objected. Finally, he commandeered a truck and rode the last dozen miles to Atsugi beside a Japanese driver, a free man at last. As I concluded my interview, word came that MacArthur's plane, the *Bataan*, was expected momentarily, so the POW had to surrender attention to his commander in chief, but you can be sure he didn't mind. The man who would command all American troops during the occupation had shown a genuine concern for his well-being, and he was the happiest GI in all of occupied Japan.

Douglas MacArthur's arrival in Japan was almost anticlimactic, in spite of reports to the contrary. Those of us who had reason to be there knew in advance when the *Bataan* would arrive and where she would park. There was no great rush of newsmen, and I definitely saw no Japanese photographer in the vicinity of the plane. Given General Eichelberger's concern about MacArthur's early arrival, any Japanese carrying a camera (a handy mask for a pistol or grenade) would have received the instant attention of his Eighth Army men, who were watching everything and everybody. If Japanese reporters were present they maintained a low profile, something they often did, of course, with great skill.

Protocol decrees that the ranking officer shall be the first to leave a plane, so it was no surprise when MacArthur, clad in his faded suntans and wearing the famous campaign cap with its tarnished braid, was the first to appear, the current corncob in the corner of his mouth as usual. He paused at the top of the steps to survey the situation, just as he always did when arriving at an unfamiliar airfield, even when no cameras were anticipated. (I was with him on a half-dozen flights during two wars and his routine never varied.) One biographer reported that MacArthur took two puffs of his pipe as he "paused in a dramatic pose for the cameras," but I must admit I wasn't that observant. I would have guessed the pipe wasn't lighted; it often wasn't when he flew. He obviously enjoyed the feeling of a pipestem between his teeth, even when he wasn't smoking.

General Eichelberger was the first to greet him as he came down the steps. They exchanged smiling salutes and a warm handshake, then MacArthur remarked it had been a long distance from Melbourne but that this was the payoff, the end of the road. Bob Eichelberger had first joined MacArthur in Melbourne as commander of the newly formed First Corps, creating an alliance that carried them, in close association, from Australia through New Guinea and the Philippines to this narrow strip of runway on the Japanese mainland.

Coincidentally, I was the only American correspondent on that runway who had covered that long trail with them, as Court Whitney, who was acting as MacArthur's military secretary, and several other staff members who had arrived on the *Bataan* reminded me. It was an emotional moment for all who had covered that distance and shared the grim doubts and soaring elations of those seemingly endless three and a half years.

Once the C-in-C was firmly on the ground and the idea of any immediate trouble had been dispersed, my interest turned to Yokohama. Of all the possible pictures that never came out of the war, I think the one I would have enjoyed most would have been a few feet of film depicting the "Toonerville Trolley" convoy that carried MacArthur and his staff to their new temporary headquarters in Yokohama's New Grand Hotel. Not one of the dilapidated, battered, and wheezing charcoal-burners looked capable of completing the twelve- or fifteen-mile trek, and that included the ancient Lincoln sedan in which Japan's newly arrived commander in chief and his Eighth Army commander actually did travel. But no one complained, and the caravan lost little time coughing its way eastward, led by an antediluvian fire engine!

The first thing that struck me about the jalopy in which I cadged a ride was the lack of rubber on the tires. Only the worn cords remained to cushion the wheels from the road, and I was certain they would never hold up for the fifteen or so miles ahead. I was right.

Much has been written about the honor guard (we weren't at all certain of the honor at first) that lined the road all the way to the city. Two divisions of Japanese infantry, some thirty thousand armed men, lined the road on both sides at intervals of about two meters, each man standing at parade rest, his back to the road. This, we later learned, was an honor reserved for the emperor, never before accorded anyone else. It was a thought-provoking sight (were those guns loaded?), but after a few miles I began to notice something else almost as amazing. During the entire drive into Yokohama not a single curiosity-seeker was to be seen. Civilians obviously had their orders and were obeying.

At first our route passed through a countryside that hadn't been too badly ravaged. Here we saw a few farmers at work in the fields, but they paid absolutely no attention to this vanguard of the army moving in to take over their country. The nearer we got to Yokohama, the greater the devastation on every side. Here, too, we were ignored. When our driver finally had to stop and replace one of our threadbare tires with another equally doubtful, I stood up in the back seat and surveyed an unforgettable scene. There were virtually no buildings remaining in this surburban area, only piles of ashes and unidentifiable rubble in every direction.

On top of each pile of debris, however, there was at least one Japanese busily combing the debris for stones, bricks, or any other usable building material. This was the end of August, and bitter winter can come early to central Japan. Preparing some sort of shelter against that winter was infinitely more important than watching the arrival of a foreign legion.

Central Yokohama obviously had been the target of precision bombing. Most of the extensive devastation had resulted from incendiaries, and certain areas, probably cited for future use by our own forces, had been spared. The waterfront, for example, was hardly touched, yet most of the surrounding city was level. Bomber crews had been carefully briefed and were accurately selective. Facing the harbor was the New Grand Hotel looking almost exactly as I had seen it some four years earlier. This was to be our temporary GHQ and probably had been spared for that specific purpose.

I had hoped to make the New Grand my billet, but it was to accommodate the top brass, and I held merely the simulated rank of second lieutenant. Correspondents were assigned to the Park Hotel about two blocks distant, which also had been saved from destruction. It was reasonably comfortable, and, after all, none of us had accepted our assignment with any promise of permanent residence in the Waldorf. The two drawbacks were, first, the beds, which some of the more generously proportioned correspondents found a bit cramped, and, second, the pillows.

These pillows (the linens were threadbare but clean), also small but stuffed with rice husks and blessed with all the downy softness of a paving brick made us realize the comforts of occupation were still in the future. Those were minor discomforts, of course, and the Park did have as one advantage its location, one block from the New Grand and probably three from the Customs House, at the edge of the waterfront enclave that had not been bombed. It was too early for my broadcast but I wanted to check the exact location of the studio and confirm my schedule.

With that accomplished something even more vital struck me. Nearly eighteen hours had passed since my last bite of food, a couple of doughnuts with black coffee just before I left Okinawa. The immediate problem was *where* to find any food. The Park had no dining facilities, there couldn't possibly be a functioning restaurant in burned-out Yokohama, and I hadn't had time to locate a GI mess. That left only the New Grand. Perhaps I could promote a meal there even if I didn't rate a bed.

As I left the Customs House I met Maj. Luther Reed, a recent addition to the GHQ staff who had once headed the CBS publicity department in New York. Luther, too, was looking for food, so together we decided to try the hospitality at the New Grand. The hotel dining room was by no means small but it was nearly filled, with more top rank than I had ever before seen in one group. Here were the men I had worked with for more than three and a half years, the men who had plotted the course and led the drive up that long road from Melbourne, even before Melbourne for some of us, and they made it plain they wanted me to be a part of their celebration. Reed grabbed my arm and advised me, *sotto voce,* "I'm getting out of here. Too much brass!" It was the understandable reaction of a newcomer to the command, so I just laughed and told him to grab one of the few available tables and relax while I made a few calls. These were friends of mine.

Within the next fifteen minutes I shook hands with and had my back slapped by enough stars to supply a couple of American flags! Present and celebrating the end of that long road were the commanders of the Eighth Army, the Far East Air Force, the Fifth, Seventh, and Thirteenth air forces, as well as a number of smaller units, all of which had made their own major contributions. Finally, at the far side of the room, at the furthermost table, were General MacArthur and a half-dozen of his staff. It was the only time I ever remember seeing the General in a public dining room. Food was never one of his top priorities, and he much preferred privacy when he dined. But this obviously was an event that would never be repeated, an occasion to be shared with the men who had played such a vital role in the ultimate victory. When I reached his table, he extended a hand and smiled. "I thought you would be here, Bill." I have only dim memories of having been served a steak dinner, but after more than four decades, I have a vivid memory of the spirit of quiet but jubilant camaraderie that permeated the dining room and gripped the celebrants it hosted, from a five-star general of the army all the way down to a simulated second lieutenant en route to his microphone.

The Japanese who manned the dining room provided eager, smiling service that belied the knowledge that they represented a nation just brought to total defeat. I have never ceased to wonder how they ever prepared the meal.

Perhaps they were simply exhausted by long years of futile warfare with no visible reward and were ready to accept any alternative. If their feelings really were antagonistic, they skillfully hid them.

Finishing that memorable repast, I returned to the Customs House and tailored the script I had hoped to broadcast from Atsugi to cover the later events of the day and to establish that we really were in Japan and that my report was being relayed to my fellow countrymen through the facilities of Radio Tokyo for the first time in four years.

During those four years I had reported to the American public with the facilities of RCAC in Manila, Radio Chungking, the governor general's mike in Java, the facilities of Australia's Cable and Wireless, the makeshift studios at Bougainville and Guadalcanal, a dozen circuits provided by the U.S. Signal Corps, and finally, the priceless talents of the *Apache*, even then moving toward Yokohama harbor, its value a thing of the past but not to be forgotten. My return to the mikes of Radio Tokyo, even in Yokohama, made the circuit complete.

Once a transpacific circuit from Yokohama was established, New York immediately sent through a schedule that would shield me from ennui for the next week at least. That of course was exactly what I wanted. Between the unpredictable Japanese people themselves and their newly acquired nonpaying guests, there was plenty to report in this recently vanquished nation.

Now that the occupation was well under way with no untoward incidents, the next major story would be the formal surrender of Hirohito's empire. There was one other story, however, we were hoping for first—the return of Gen. Jonathan Wainwright to the command from the Manchurian prison camp where he had been held for some three years. We knew that MacArthur had given orders that everything possible be done to bring him, together with Gen. Arthur Percival, who had commanded the British at Singapore, to Japan to take part in the surrender ceremonies. They were known to be en route from Manila, where they had been taken after liberation, but no one seemed to know the probable arrival time.

For that reason I haunted the ground floor of the New Grand where the GHQ staff were camping out until more adequate offices were prepared. I knew that Wainwright would report to MacArthur immediately on arrival, and I wanted to be there when it happened. Most of the correspondents had gone exploring—there was plenty to be seen, particularly for those who had never before been in Japan—but I moved mostly between the hotel and the Customs House, and it paid off.

I was in the hotel talking to one of the aides when an orderly came rushing in to report that Wainwright's car had just pulled up at the main entrance. Everyone started for the door just as the newly liberated POW slowly walked in, really an emaciated caricature of the man I had known in Manila before the war. "Skinny" Wainwright had never carried an excess pound of flesh in his sixty-two years, but this man, relying on a cane for support, carried no flesh whatever, only parchmentlike skin drawn tight over the six feet of bone. His faded suntans hung on him in folds and his hair was turning gray. But he was in obviously good spirits.

The historic reunion took place in a private dining room where they met as MacArthur rushed out to greet him. Two old friends together again. There was no protocol, no thought of pomp and circumstance. Before Wainwright could organize a salute, MacArthur reached for his right hand and placed an arm around his shoulder. "I'm glad to see you, Jim." Wainwright seemed to swallow a couple of times before he replied, almost inaudibly, "I'm glad to see you, too."

That was all. As they stood, both exhibiting obvious emotion, General Percival joined them and acknowledged MacArthur's warm greeting. MacArthur had an obvious feeling for anyone who had spent years in enemy hands, and Percival had been a prisoner longer than Wainwright, but I don't think they had ever met before. His greeting for Percival was warm, but Jim was a member of his family.

From the standpoint of a reporter, the timing of the reunion was perfect. I was only minutes ahead of a scheduled broadcast report, and I was sure no other correspondent had been present at the meeting. George Folster was away with the navy or he certainly would have been there. I was alone. I rushed back to the Customs House, pounded out a script, passed it through the censors, and headed for the studio.

All through the war years CBS News and NBC scheduled their twice-daily World News Roundup in the same time periods, morning and evening. Thus my immediate rival quite often was in the same studio, usually seated on the opposite side of the microphone while I made my report, and vice versa. We both used the same circuit to San Francisco, where the technicians would feed each report to the proper network, sometimes with only thirty seconds intervening. Neither correspondent knew what the other was going to report until he actually heard the spoken words, and by then it was too late to change a censored script. Actually, the system worked very well, with never a technical slip or mix-up. The engineers on the West Coast really knew their business.

On this evening I was scheduled to speak first with my NBC counterpart, a newcomer to the theater, seated opposite. The instant I started to read my script I knew I had an exclusive. I was watching my honorable rival out of the corner of my eye, and he obviously was stunned. Still, I thought, he could ad lib a lead sentence or two to cover himself and argue with the censors later. After all, the war had ended and security could not be involved. As I concluded, he shook his head in obvious frustration and read without change a script that confessed complete ignorance of Jonathan Wainwright's whereabouts, something his bureau chief, Folster, would never have done. After all this time such pride in "scoops," as the movies always termed them, does seem a bit immature, but competition was, and always will be, a dominant facet of the journalistic profession, whether print, audio, or video, and woe to the reporter who fails to understand that canon.

In the plethora of good stories, stories of both human interest and historic merit, one that was almost overlooked, or at least given less attention than it deserved, was the successful transfer of the entire Eleventh Airborne Division from the Philippines to the plains of Honshu Island by air, by far the longest overwater movement of an entire division in modern military history at that time.

Although I started the third day of our occupation in quest of information about the surrender ceremonies, I suddenly changed direction completely and decided to get the full story of that movement from General Kennedy. Immediately after my early broadcast I went to the general's quarters at the New Grand and found his door open. As I looked in, he saw me and waved a hand. "Come in, Bill, I want you to meet an old friend of mine. This is Touhey Spaatz." My luck was still holding! Not only was Kenney obviously willing to cooperate, but Spaatz was the man who personally coordinated the historic transfer, the head of the U.S. Army Strategic Air Command.

I took the hand that Spaatz extended, then made my personal position clear. "It's an honor to meet you, General, but I want you to understand one thing above all else. I am a Far East Air Force man, first and always!" Both men roared and Spaatz gave my hand another shake. "That's fine, Bill, just as long as you don't say anything good about the navy!" It was a typical air force rejoinder. Between these two four-star commanders I was able to clear a really informative report on September 1 on the strategy, long-term and conclusive, that had brought us so far so successfully.

S-P-E-C-I-A-L   R-E-P-O-R-T

Air Power

Yokohama, Sept. 1, 1945—Dunn reporting. Gen. Douglas MacArthur's march to Japan actually *began* a little less than three years ago when a motley assortment of Fifth Air Force transports, augmented by any other planes that could be commandeered, carried the 128th Infantry Regiment from Australia to New Guinea to launch our first offensive against the Japanese. It was, at that time, the largest overwater movement of troops in military history.

General MacArthur's march to Japan *ended* yesterday when a far-from-motley fleet of giant transport planes brought the entire 11th Airborne Division from the Philippines to the plains of Honshu Island.

The first operation was accomplished under the leadership of a man who had just arrived in the Southwest Pacific to take command of an air force that was lacking in everything except the courage of its personnel. That man was Gen. George C. Kenney, now commander of the Far East Air Force, who is here with me this morning.

The final operation—again the largest and longest overwater transfer of troops by air in military history, this time by a large margin—was made possible through the coordination of all American air power in the Pacific, and one of the chief coordinators in making this tremendous undertaking possible was Gen. Touhey

Spaatz, commander of the United States Army Strategic Air Forces, who also is here with me. I want you to meet these men who, between them, control the almost unlimited air power of the united nations in the Pacific—the air power which did so much toward the total defeat of Japan. General Kenney, how is it possible to dare pick up as small a unit as a division, together with practically all the top-ranking officers of the Pacific theater, and move them into the very heart of what was only days ago an enemy nation, without fear of disaster?

GK: Well, Bill, the obvious answer is because Japan had been defeated. The Japanese were worn down to their bare feet. But the real story lies in how that defeat was accomplished. The part air power played in the march to Japan can be divided into three phases. In every operation from New Guinea —or any other place in the Pacific, right up to the shores of Honshu Island—the air force accomplished these three things in order:

First, we gained control of the air—the primary necessity in all modern warfare. Second, we established and maintained a blockade powerful enough to interrupt the enemy's line of communications, making it impossible for him to reinforce or supply his forward bases. Third, we maintained constant attacks on forward enemy positions, making it possible for our ground troops to move ahead with minimal casualties.

Finally, after this program had been repeated—farther and farther ahead and with continued success—it became possible to place sufficient air strength within easy reach of the Japanese home islands to keep those islands under constant attack, as General Spaatz' strategic air forces, together with my own boys, have been able to do for the past several months.

WD: We've certainly seen the results of your strategic bombing in the past two days around the Tokyo Bay area, General Spaatz. Now, approximately what total tonnage of bombs could we pour on Japan in a single day—right now—if the Japanese decided to make more trouble?

TS: Within the next twenty-four hours the army air forces now within striking distance of Japan could pour a minimum of 8,000 tons of bombs, either dispersed around Japan or concentrated on any single point. [General Spaatz later explained this figure did not include any further use of the A-bomb. He was speaking of the equivalent of 8,000 one-ton bombs, or 16,000 at 500 pounds. He believed Japan didn't quit one day too soon.] That tonnage represents eleven months of growth—eleven months in which our potential tonnage has been increased from a maximum of 735 tons last November, to more than 8,000 tons right at this minute. And we could double that tonnage in a very short time, if necessary.

WD: General Kenney has given us a brief outline of the way the air forces operate in supporting the advance of surface forces. What has been the primary objective of the strategic air forces?

TS: Our primary objective has always been to destroy the ability of the enemy to function within the limits of his own homeland—to destroy industry, transportation, communications. To reduce, as we were able to do, for example, the enemy's ability to build planes from 3,000 tons per month to a bare 750.

WD: General Kenney, I understand the Japs have been very short of aviation fuel for the past several months. Do you regard that as a primary reason for the collapse of their air power?

GK: Well, Bill, it undoubtedly was a major factor. But you must remember that the Japanese became short of gasoline because their air power failed them. Japan had to depend on the Netherlands Indies for 95 percent of their gas and oil. When the Nips lost control of the air over the Philippines, last October and November, they lost their ability to protect their supply lines through the China Sea. Our blockade became completely effective, and Japan was doomed to become a nation with no fuel for its internal combustion engines.

WD: That certainly gave us the answer! And now, General Spaatz, I'd like to ask you just how it is possible to coordinate two great air forces with the combined ability to drop some 8,000 tons of bombs in a single day, over such a relatively small target area, without major conflict?

TS: First of all, very close liaison is maintained between the two headquarters. Second, specific areas of operation based on the capabilities of the forces are established. Third, the intent of each of the forces is known by the other force well in advance of each operation. Fourth, both commanders are in complete agreement on their conception of the correct principles of air power. These principles have long been established in the United States Army Air Forces.

WD: Thank you, General Spaatz and General Kenney. There can be no doubt of the magnitude of the debt the people of America owe to the courage, the abilities, and the effectiveness of the United States Army Air Forces. I return you to CBS News in New York.

CHAPTER 40

Surrender

The first ray of sunshine to fall on Tokyo Bay in forty-eight hours came as a salute to the signing of peace, the formal end of World War II, aboard the U.S.S. *Missouri*, flagship of the Pacific fleet, on the morning of Sunday, September 2, 1945. Dramatically and with a timeliness that seemed almost symbolic, the sun moved from behind a canopy of gray clouds just as Douglas MacArthur, as supreme commander for the Allied powers (SCAP), pronounced the restoration of peace and devoutly asked that God preserve it always. The pronouncement came at exactly 9:19 A.M., Japan time—8:19 P.M., Saturday night, in New York. Exactly 21 minutes had been required for all parties concerned to sign the historic paper, the document that all of us who witnessed the ceremony sincerely hoped would not only mark the end of World War II but would also inaugurate an era of peace unparalleled in the history of mankind. This ephemeral goal actually seemed a possibility at that memorable moment.

There had been considerable worry lest the inclement weather of the past two days might mar the occasion, but at dawn the skies, though still a menacing gray above the chill wind that swept over Honshu Island, appeared to hold little threat of immediate rain, and this time the heavens kept that promise. Those of us who were assigned to cover the surrender arrived on board the *Missouri*, via a destroyer, about seven-thirty to find our places about the verandah deck, just aft of the number two turret and forward on the starboard side. We had held a drawing before coming aboard, and I had been chosen by lot to represent the Southwest Pacific at one of the two mikes set up for the pool report to the U.S. networks.

A large table covered with a green rug had been placed on the deck just forward of the turret. This was the table on which the actual signing would take place, and the microphones were positioned directly above. Immediately complications arose. As I was starting to mount the turret to claim my mike, General Diller came rushing up, obviously agitated. "Bill, you've got to help me!" I turned and realized I had never seen him so upset before. "What's happened, Pick?" "Plenty, Bill. When the men from the South Pacific held their drawing Webley Edwards (CBS correspondent from Pearl Harbor) was the winner, and now CBS has *both* microphones. NBC is really raising hell!" *That* I could believe! With four networks participating in two drawings apparently no one had foreseen the possibility that one network would win both. I knew what was coming.

"Bill, you've got to help me. I don't know Edwards, but you and I have worked together ever since Melbourne. Won't you please let Red Muller (NBC in Folster's absence) take your mike? I know it's a lot to ask but . . ." I cut him short. Basically my duty was to protect CBS, and I knew we'd be well represented with Web. I looked up at the radio perch atop the turret, then forward to the somewhat distant areas where most of the media corps, those without cameras or mikes, were being positioned. "Pick, I'm willing to play ball, but I'm damned if I'm going to move my base. I won this vantage point according to the rules, and I don't intend to cover the surrender from Kobe!" Diller laughed with obvious relief. "You won't be going anywhere, Bill. Climb up on that turret and enjoy a box seat!"

Shortly after eight-thirty the scores of generals, admirals, air marshals, and other officers representing all the Allied nations began to arrive to take their assigned positions around the deck, probably the greatest assemblage of military and naval rank in one group in history. A fellow correspondent pointed out there were more four-star American generals lined up on that deck than this country had ever commissioned up to the start of the war just ending. The navy was equally well represented, including Admiral of the Fleet Chester W. Nimitz who, with General of the Army MacArthur, held the top American rank. Nimitz was actually host to the ceremonies, because the *Missouri* was his flagship, at least for the day.

About ten minutes to nine the shrill notes of the bosun's pipe announced the arrival of the supreme commander, advancing through a full complement of side boys. Moving swiftly across the main deck, the General mounted the ladder to the verandah deck, nodded briefly to his associates, and continued on to the captain's cabin. The suntans he wore, though starched and creased, made me wonder if this uniform might have been one he had worn on some previous memorable occasion. The cuffs of the trousers were frayed and the shirt,

open at the throat, was obviously worn. The breast was completely
bare of ribbons and medals and the circlet of five silver stars pinned
to his collar was all there was to distinguish this uniform from that
of any unranked GI. There could be no question, however, as to who
was wearing the battered campaign cap that had become his hallmark.
The marks of over three years of rugged campaigning were obvious
in the tarnished braid that once was gold.

About five minutes later the Japanese arrived, eleven men, three
in frock coats and towering top hats, one in white linens, the others
in army uniforms. First to mount the ladder was Mamoru Shigemitsu,
foreign minister in the imperial cabinet and personal representative
of the emperor, probably the oldest person on board. He experienced
great difficulty in making the climb, his feebleness accentuated by
his reliance on a wooden leg, the result of a bombing in Shanghai some
fifteen years earlier. Once he reached deck, his aide handed him his
cane, and he limped slowly to his position directly in front of the green-
covered table. Beside him on his left stood Gen. Yoshijiro Umezu, chief
of staff of the Imperial Army headquarters. The other nine attendants
took their positions in a double row behind.

At exactly two minutes before nine General MacArthur came
briskly out of the captain's cabin and moved to his place on the opposite side of the table, directly in front of the other Allied signatories
and officers. The microphones were waiting to carry his words to the
world. Characteristically, he left the world with no doubt of the course
he would follow as supreme commander and what precepts would dic-
tate that course. "We are gathered here, representatives of the major
warring powers, to conclude a solemn agreement whereby peace may
be restored. The issues, involving divergent ideals and ideologies, have
been determined on the battlefields of the world, and hence are not
for discussion or debate. Nor is it for us here to meet, representing
as we do a majority of the people of the earth, in a spirit of distrust,
malice, or hatred. But rather it is for us, both victors and vanquished,
to rise to that higher dignity which alone befits the sacred purposes
we are about to serve, committing all our people unreservedly to faithful compliance with the obligation we are here formally to assume."

He spoke with obvious emotion, his hand shaking as it did that
day when he addressed the people of the Philippines from that rain-
swept beach at Leyte. He spoke of the hope that "a better world shall
emerge out of the blood and carnage of the past, a world founded on
faith and understanding, a world dedicated to the dignity of man and

the fulfillment of his most cherished wish, for freedom, tolerance and justice."

He then presented his personal pledge to strive toward those goals, according to his charge: "As supreme commander of the Allied powers, I announce it my firm purpose, in the tradition of the countries I represent, to proceed in the discharge of my responsibilities with justice and tolerance, while taking all necessary dispositions to ensure that the terms of surrender are fully, promptly, and faithfully complied with."

When he concluded, after little more than two minutes, he invited the representatives of the emperor of Japan and the Japanese Imperial Headquarters to sign the instrument of surrender.

There was a slight flurry as a secretary stepped out of the first row behind the minister to inspect the document. When he moved aside, Shigemitsu took his place and, after much fumbling with pens and checking of the time (plus a bit of direction from General Sutherland), he inscribed his name in Japanese characters, first on the Allied copy and then on the Japanese. General Umezu then signed, and both men returned to their places. There was no show of emotion on the part of either man.

On the other side of the table, however, there was obvious emotion as General MacArthur, who would sign next on behalf of the Allied powers, turned to his left and asked Generals Wainwright and Percival to attend him at the signing. The gray, slim commander of Bataan at its fall stepped from his place in the first line behind the table and advanced a few steps. He seemed to have lost some of that stark gauntness so evident on his arrival from prison camp only a few hours before. He saluted smartly and accepted MacArthur's salute in return. Then they shook hands. General Percival did likewise, and MacArthur resumed his place at the table, fishing in his right-hand breast pocket for an assortment of fountain pens. He appeared only to glance at the instruments of surrender, then bent over to sign. He completed only part of his signature, then turned abruptly and handed the pen to Wainwright; the second pen went to Percival. In all, five pens were used, two, we learned later were for West Point and Annapolis while the fifth, the familiar old red pen that had been with him as long as any of us could remember, went back in his pocket, a present for Jean.

The other signatories followed swiftly, nine in all, led by Admiral Nimitz for the United States. The only hitch in the ceremony came

Gen. Douglas MacArthur watches without emotion as Gen. Yoshijiro Umezu signs the instrument of surrender aboard the U.S.S. *Missouri*. Behind him are the representatives of all the Allied nations. I am seated upper right on the gun turret with General Wurtsmith's camera.

when the Canadian signatory inadvertently signed his name in the space assigned to France, but only on the Japanese copy. The mistake was corrected by transposing the designation of the two countries. Midway through the ceremony a flight of B-29's circled the great armada that surrounded the *Missouri*, having come all the way from the Marianas to salute the peace they had done so much to promote. The entire ceremony was completed in exactly 21 minutes, ending when the supreme commander, having voiced his fervent hope for a record era of peace, declared, "These proceedings are closed."

At exactly this moment the truant sun broke through the clouds, as if by some uncanny signal, and a great flight of some fifteen hun-

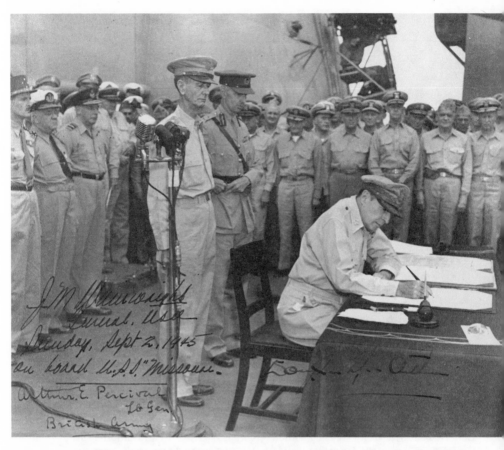

U.S.S. *Missouri*, Sept. 2, 1945. General of the Army Douglas MacArthur signs the instrument of surrender of the Japanese empire. Directly behind him are Lt. Gen. Jonathan M. Wainwright, hero of Bataan, and Lt. Gen. Arthur E. Percival, Commander in Singapore-Malaya. *Courtesy MacArthur Memorial, Norfolk*

dred carrier planes roared in from the east. For the next half hour the air was darkened with one of the greatest displays of air power—*peacetime* air power—ever seen in the Pacific. The planes, from every carrier in Japanese waters, had been on rendezvous east of Tokyo awaiting the signal from Bull Halsey aboard the *Missouri*. Understandably, this exhibition stirred deep memories among those of us who would never forget the days when the thought of putting even a hundred planes in the air at one time was an impossible dream.

Back at the Customs House I found, as expected, a complete madhouse. Every Allied correspondent in Japan, even a couple of cameramen, were jammed into the temporary press room on the fourth floor, and the staccato of typewriters sounded like distant machine guns.

Colonel Abe Schechter was waiting with a schedule from CBS News for the longest report ordered up since the fall of Java. It takes time, of course, to prepare a ten-minute broadcast report, and there wasn't much time remaining before San Francisco would be on the pipe. I sat down and began to type the lead I had been "writing" mentally aboard the destroyer that brought us back from the *Missouri*. I was just getting well into the composition when someone tapped me on the shoulder. I looked up at General Diller. "Excuse me, Bill, but this is important. The General wants you to have lunch with him."

I couldn't believe my ears. Here, on what had to be the climactic day of his entire career, only minutes after accepting the unconditional surrender of the Japanese empire, Douglas MacArthur wanted Bill Dunn to have lunch with him? In three years of major and multiple surprises, this had to rank supreme! "Pick, you can't be serious!" But one look at his face left no doubt. Besides, this was not something any member of his immediate staff would ever joke about. He was deadly serious.

I pointed to my typewriter, to my notes scattered around the desk, and shook my head. "You know, Pick, there's no possibility of accepting with all this demanding immediate action. Give the General my sincere thanks and my congratulations on the surrender. Now, frankly, I haven't a moment to spare." Diller nodded in agreement. "He'll understand, Bill, but I had to relay the invitation. I'll give him your regards." With that he left and I returned to my typing.

Minutes before time to greet San Francisco, Diller returned. "Excuse me again, Bill, but the General wants to make it tomorrow, and we're going to ask Van Atta, Caswell, and Courtenay as well." That, too, was good news. Lee Van Atta of the INS (International News Service, the Hearst Press), Don Caswell of the United Press, and Bill Courtenay of the London *Sketch* had joined the GHQ press corps back in the Melbourne days and like me had remained with the command all the way to Yokohama. Three excellent correspondents, all good friends. It promised to be an interesting luncheon.

My labors for the day didn't end with my delivery of the ten-minute report. New York wanted a follow-up that evening for its Monday morning round-up, and it's always difficult to come up with a new angle on a story you've already covered in unusual depth. You might call it insurance against mental relaxation. When I finally left the studio for the last time for the Park Hotel, I had no trouble falling asleep, despite the questionable comforts of the accommodations.

Shortly after returning from the *Missouri*, General MacArthur transferred his personal quarters from the New Grand to a residence in an outlying surburb that had belonged to one of the American oil companies, a comfortable house that had escaped conflagration. There were quite a few of these small, intact enclaves scattered around the Tokyo-Yokohama area, probably spared because they obviously were not suited for industrial use, even for small home industries. The house would serve MacArthur only a few days until he could move on to Tokyo and the American Embassy, but it would become quite familiar to me in the coming months as the residence of General Eichelberger and Clovis Byers, his chief of staff.

There could be no doubt of the welcome MacArthur accorded our quartet—"comrades in arms" was his term, and it was a warming term even to us who were forbidden to carry arms. He surprised all of us by recalling happenings of the preceding years that had involved us individually and collectively, things of which we thought he had no knowledge.

Almost immediately he turned to me. "Bill, you were in the States when all this started. How did you manage to get back on time?" I am certain he knew of the War Department's ban on correspondents. I told him, briefly, how I had talked my way to Manila, without orders, priorities, or permission. I had the distinct impression he really got a kick out of seeing someone outwit Washington, that invisible presence that is always looking over the shoulder of any field commander.

When he asked why I hadn't wired him for a priority, I expressed doubt that any such message would have passed the scrutiny of his staff, but that was not entirely true. The prime factor was time. I have no doubt that Diller or Willoughby or one of his aides would have acted for me, but there was no time for an exchange of messages. I left New York on the same day that I learned my goal was "impossible" and never really stopped until I reached Manila, just in time to leave for Okinawa and Atsugi. Even one day spent waiting for a message from GHQ could have made my schedule *truly* impossible.

I've been asked what the General served us for lunch, and the answer, of course, was conversation. I actually have no memory of the food, but parts of the conversation will remain with me always. Someone brought up the subject of hari-kari (MacArthur pronounced it "hair-EE-kur*ee*"), which the General assured us was merely a Japanese myth. "There will be suicides in the next few weeks, I'm afraid, but you will never find an authenticated case of hari-kari." Both Prince Konoye and Hideki Tojo proved his view in a matter of days, Konoye swallowing poison while Tojo used a hand gun in his futile attempt. And there were others, none of whom turned to the "purge that only the agonies of *hari-kari* could supply."

I'm not sure just how the navy came into the conversation, but again the General didn't hesitate in expressing his opinions, even to a group of men who were certain to quote him. "Future wars will still be won by foot soldiers, fighting to gain and retain territory, fighting under the protective canopy of air power. The navy will be reduced to a service of supply. The battleship is as obsolete as the bow and arrow."

CHAPTER 41

Stars and Stripes over Tokyo

At eleven o'clock on the morning of September 7, General Eichelberger stepped in front of General MacArthur and saluted. The supreme commander returned the salute and gave the order: "General Eichelberger, have our nation's flag unfurled to fly over Tokyo, and let it wave in its full glory as a symbol of hope for the oppressed and a harbinger of victory for the right."

The First Cavalry band played the "Star-Spangled Banner" and the assemblage stood at attention as the flag was slowly raised to the top of the staff above the chancellory of the American Embassy. It was a simple ceremony but an emotional moment. The chaplain pronounced a benediction and the band turned to Sousa's "Stars and Stripes Forever."

Those present were mostly Americans, with a few of our allies. General Eichelberger represented the army and Admiral Halsey the navy. In a dry swimming pool directly in front of the temporary stand,

members of the media had an unusual point of vantage, while in the
distance crowds of Japanese were watching—the first time I had ever
seen the local people pay attention to American activities.

The ceremony also signalled the total occupation of Japan. Until
this moment, Tokyo had been off-limits to American troops for the
period of a week to avoid the possibility of incidents and therefore
was not formally occupied. Fortunately, this precaution of the supreme
commander proved unnecessary, for none of the Japanese, civilians
or members of the dissolving military, showed any inclination to resist what they clearly realized was inevitable.

Less than an hour after the flag-raising at the embassy, I became
the first free American to send a transpacific broadcast report across
that broad expanse from the studios of Radio Tokyo since December 7,
1941. CBS News had scheduled me for that hour as soon as I advised
New York of the flag-raising time, and it was an eerie feeling to walk
once again into that huge gray edifice and have an American show
me to my studio!

The building apparently had not been hit during the bombardments,
probably due to its proximity to the imperial palace. Still, it showed
marks of physical neglect. The formerly immaculate lobbies and corridors, which had given the edifice a sense of spaciousness, were dingy,
almost grimy, and permeated by an unpleasant odor of cooked fish
that took weeks to eliminate. Obviously the janitors, male and female,
who tended the building, had found more pressing duties once the
hostilities began.

One thing missing was the traditional cup of tea that had formerly
marked every visit to the studios. A reporter was expected to arrive
for his broadcast report in time to share a cup of the Orient's first-
ranking beverage with the Japanese producer before addressing the
mike. The "producers" now were American signal corpsmen who had
never heard of the tradition. You delivered your report with a dry
throat, just as if you still were in studio 9 on the seventeenth floor
of 485 Madison Avenue.

My landmark report, of course, concerned the raising of Old Glory
—you really think of your flag in those terms at times like that—and
the occupation of Japan's capital city by the cavalry. The entrance of
the cavalry effectively disposed of the third in the series of junctures
where trouble, if there was to be any trouble, might be expected. First,
certainly, was the airstrip at Atsugi, and the second the actual signing of the surrender. I doubt that anyone in the high command really

believed our entry into Tokyo would incite any serious trouble, but no conquering troops had ever before set foot in a Japanese capital, and the possibility had to be considered. Tradition is a powerful force in the Orient.

That's why Tokyo had been declared off-limits to Bob Eichelberger's troops for that first week, but the ban had little effect on media members and individual officers. Extended exploration became an immediate diversion.

One of the great paradoxes of the occupation was the sight of modern electric trains, a major segment of the Japanese rail system, operating smoothly throughout the burned-out, bombed-out interurban countryside and in the cities themselves, apparently maintaining regular schedules as though nothing had happened. Our policy of using incendiary instead of explosive bombs in our aerial attacks provided us with a functioning transportation system as well as an almost intact network of utilities, electricity, gas, and water. There could be no doubt our well-laid and well-executed plans for the occupation began to take form almost as soon as Jimmy Doolittle's men dropped the first bomb on the city, and they were formulated from the first with an eye on our future needs when Japan finally saw the light.

It didn't take anyone long to discover that Yokohama's Central Station was only a comparatively short distance from the Shinbashi-Marunouchi section in the heart of Tokyo. Your uniform was your ticket and no one seemed to mind your appropriation of the service. I often wondered, and still do, how we Occidentals would have reacted had the tables been turned.

Clark Lee of the Hearst organization, an old Far East hand whom I had known in both Tokyo and Shanghai before the war, and I were both intent on learning whether the old tap room in the Imperial Hotel had survived. It had, just as if nothing had ever happened, and already had a modest clientele of men who had known it before. On my second expedition I met General Eichelberger coming out of the Imperial and chided him for ignoring the very rule he was supposed to enforce. He grinned and reminded me I had kept him off the record in Buna, but here we were all off the record until Tokyo became legal.

Immediately after the embassy ceremony the city was thrown open to all who had any reason to be in Japan, but again correspondents were relegated to a secondary hotel while the brass vied for space in Frank Lloyd Wright's Imperial. When I term the Dai-Iti a secondary hostelry, I am referring to the size of the rooms and facilities. Actu-

Gen. Bob Eichelberger, commander of the occupation forces, greets Merrill Mueller of NBC and me in front of Tokyo's Imperial Hotel at a time when the city was still off-limits to allied troops. The off-limits ban during the first week of the occupation in fact was directed primarily at organized troop movements.

ally, the Dai-Iti was a modern six-story hotel that included most of the usual amenities, but unfortunately those amenities were designed for people of lesser proportions. I never realized that many Japanese were amusing or educating themselves or satisfying their natural curiosity by tuning in to our transpacific short-wave circuits until I made a kidding report on the troubles Dick Tregaskis, the six-foot-six representative of the *Saturday-Evening Post,* and I with a 42-inch waist, were experiencing trying to bathe in tubs that actually measured 37 inches long and only 17 inches wide. The next day a half-dozen Japanese commiserated with me, having heard my sad story on short wave.

That episode was really an excellent example of our occupation policies. In the Philippines the Japanese had regarded the possession of a radio, regardless of wavelength, as almost a capital offense. The American command had a radically different policy, a complete disinterest in how many radios any Japanese possessed or how they were used. We weren't trying to fool anyone.

It was fortunate for us correspondents that the Dai-Iti Hotel was centrally located, because walking was the only sure method of getting around in one of the world's largest cities during those first few weeks. Taxis didn't exist, and any Japanese who managed to survive the war with an automobile of any vintage was keeping it well hidden until he had some definite idea of what the final decision might be. Streetcars and subways were still running in most areas, but they were not yet equipped with English-language signs, and none of the newcomers had any idea of their destinations. That left us with only the army, and while GHQ tried to be helpful, jeeps and other small vehicles were still in short supply, and the military of course took precedence at the few scattered car pools that were being organized inside the city.

One major story that broke soon after our arrival and one that demanded personal transportation was the attempted suicide of Hideki Tojo on September 11. The word reached me in midafternoon at the Dai-Iti, and I immediately headed for the nearest car pool. By the time I could promote a jeep and driver to take me to the former prime minister's residence, the First Cavalry medics had spirited him away and no one seemed to know where.

I accidently found him just at dusk when I drove into the First Cav headquarters, then in the Meiji Inner Shrine, hoping to get some information from their command post. Strangely, the area inside the main gate was nearly deserted except for a couple of soldiers and a few military vehicles. I asked the nearest GI, "Any idea what they've done with General Tojo?" "Sure," was the reply. "Do you want to see him?"

I stepped out of the jeep and looked around the area. It was almost dark. "Are you kidding?" Without a further word the sergeant (he was, of course, a paramedic) opened the rear door of the vehicle beside him, which proved to be an ambulance. Before I could protest, he pulled a stretcher out nearly three-quarters of its length and tipped it down so I could see for myself the man who had been our arch-enemy for so long, the man who formerly headed the emperor's imperial armed forces. His eyes were closed and there were no visible signs of life. Suddenly I felt like a ghoul. "Put him back." The sergeant grinned at my obvious discomfiture. "It's all right, sir. He's only in a coma. We'll take him on to the hospital as soon as we get the word."

A short time later I was at the First Cav medical center when Tojo was brought in for his second infusion of plasma. He had had his first at his home as soon as the first medics reached him. There was no doubt he was a sick man. His light brown skin, stretched tightly over his prominent cheekbones, gave him the appearance of something very near a death's head. But this time he seemed conscious, and although his eyes remained closed, he did raise his left hand to rub his eyes while the plasma was being injected into his right arm. When the whole story finally developed, it was found that the man had come within half an inch of his heart with the bullet he had hoped would end his earthly cares. But American drugs and American blood saved him for execution as a war criminal. The doctors agreed that while penicillin and other drugs not then available in Japan were important, it probably was the plasma—American blood—that decided his immediate fate.

Observers who were in Japan at the time predicted that the half-inch by which the bullet missed Tojo's heart would cost him a place in Japan's hall of martyred immortals, and nothing has happened since to prove them wrong. It is still difficult for Occidentals to understand, but there was no doubt that the Japanese people wanted him to die. Tojo had undertaken to lead Japan to glorious victory in a war for world supremacy. He failed utterly, and according to the Japanese code, death at his own hand was the only possible atonement.

On the morning following the attempt, Tokyo's *Mainichi Shimbun* spelled out the feeling of the people in a story which read, in part: "The general masses clamored for his death. Letters urging him to kill himself came to his home in abundance. Those close to him also urged his death. But each time the General would say: 'It's easy to die. I can choose any time.' He always turned a deaf ear to such advice."

That was the report of one of Japan's leading dailies, and the other media reflected much the same attitude. As I pointed out in my report to the CBS listeners that morning, "It's a strange psychology—don't try to understand it—that makes a hero out of a man who takes his own life but considers him a bum if he fails." My report continued: "As a matter of fact, Japan's entire military caste is coming in for some strong criticism from among the masses because the expected wave of atoning suicides among high-ranking officers who contributed directly to Japan's first military defeat in history has failed to materialize. As General MacArthur pointed out the other day, there were more suicides among the war criminals of Germany, leaders of a race that does not condone suicide, than among those in Japan, where self-destruction is almost a national virtue."

I don't believe anyone who moved into Japan with the occupation forces, from General MacArthur down through the ranks and including camp followers like myself, really believed we could complete the mechanics of occupation without a single major incident. When you move into a country, uninvited, to appropriate homes, office buildings, real property, almost anything the unwilling hosts possess that meets your needs, you ought to expect some dissent. Further, when you bring thousands of foreign soldiers into a country they have been encouraged to hate and distrust for four years, you can expect some of your own people to get out of line now and then, possibly trying to make up for some of the hardships that marked the long road to Tokyo. But the Japanese obviously had decided that, having lost the war, there was no point in further resistance. They were almost uncanny in their willingness to cooperate. And the American soldier just as obviously had experienced a complete change. To a man, they seemed to consider the past as something to be ignored, if not forgotten, and there was considerable evidence that the combat veteran didn't hold the Japanese civilian responsible for what had happened in those bitter years.

There was, however, one annoying exception. From the very first day, Domei, the Japanese news agency, waged a propaganda war on its own (the daily press, too, was not without lesser fault). To the exasperation of the Allied media, the agency not only ignored censorship regulations but released a flood of stories reporting "incidents" that never happened, characterizing the American soldier as something less than a gentleman, and warning of the dangers he posed to the local citizenry, particularly women and children. A number of correspondents filed complaints about Domei with GHQ, but nothing came of them until five-thirty on the afternoon of Saturday, September 15, when Domei signed off—"30"—for the last time, by direct edict of the supreme commander.

The terminating edict was accompanied by something completely without precedent in my years with MacArthur's headquarters. This was a statement giving the reason for his action and why it had not been taken sooner. The General was not in the habit of explaining his decisions, but in this case reports had begun to circulate, many, of course, from the States, that he was being too lenient with the former enemy. The very fact that he decided to explain indicated to me that he was as impatient with the delay as we or the folks back home were.

Several days earlier he had told some of us correspondents, off the record, why he was not acting with greater speed and more force, and at that time he cited exactly the same points given in the statement that accompanied the Domei edict. The reasons were three, based on the primary objectives of the original occupation agenda. First, and this was always first with MacArthur, was his determination to get every prisoner of war out of the hands of the Japanese as quickly as possible. Second was the urgent need to get as many American troops into Japan as possible without delay. Finally came the necessity of disarming and demobilizing the Japanese armed forces immediately. Once those objectives were met, there could be no chance of even secondary opposition, and the Allied powers could move as desired. That time had come.

The transgressions of the daily press were relatively minor and probably the results of frustration at defeat plus the inability of the average Japanese journalist to accept the fact of atrocities by their troops in the Philippines and the Pacific islands. This was something MacArthur was determined the public should know.

I was surprised, however, when the Domei death sentence didn't convince all of them that the supreme commander was not a man to challenge. I knew many of Tokyo's top journalists, personally if not well. Some I had met during my previous tour of duty, and I considered them as a group to be intelligent, well educated — several in Britain and the States — and fully capable of understanding the facts of life, no matter how bitter. That's why I was surprised when, less than forty-eight hours after Domei's demise, both *Asahi Shimbun* and *Nippon Times* were suspended by SCAP for two days. The *Times'* offense was only in printing a perfectly innocuous editorial without first submitting it for censorship. *Asahi*, however, blatantly cast doubt on a verified atrocity story from the Philippines, hinting it might well be a ploy to detract attention from Americans in Japan. The suspensions wrote an end to that episode, and the Oriental mask moved back into position.

Toward the end of September I received a letter from a French-woman who had lived in Japan since before the war, a French national who, since December, 1941, had lived under the constant threat of arrest and imprisonment. It was dated August 30, the day we arrived at Atsugi-Yokohama, and it vividly expressed how much radio meant to people living in what she called the "mental desert" of wartime Japan.

> Dear Mr. Dunn: We heard you tonight over CBS talking from the Yokohama radio station. It sounded like a dream. For how long did we follow you! From Port Moresby to Buin and all the way up from New Guinea to the Philippines and now to here. We were listening to you, and others, with beating heart, never despairing, always believing that the day of liberation will come. Liberation from the Jap police and the German gestapo.
>
> This sounds surprising to you, but allow me to explain. I am a French national and live together with a German for many years.
>
> The Jap police was persecuting all radio listeners. My set, being a common one [probably no short wave] could not be closed down. So we heard every evening CBS at nine our time and surprisingly clear the station KSL, Salt Lake City, Utah. Sometimes we heard Los Angeles, Dallas, and San Diego but very faintly. KSL came through at nine and ten every evening. We were thankful for the news for we were informed about the progress since Guadalcanal. First this progress sounded slow, but on a sudden it took great strides. And here you are.
>
> We were suffering here from constant watching by the Jap police and the cooperation of the German gestapo with the Japs. Deportation and concentration camp threatening never stopped and only the emperor's speech saved us from the concentration camp where we were ordered to go on the 18th of August. Happy is not enough of an expression for our feeling that America is here now.
>
> Please convey our thanks to CBS, New York, especially to Mr. Allan Jackson for his clear and to the point daily news. It was a welcome message in this mental desert.
>
>   "Thérèse Erinhardt"

That's the sort of gratitude that doesn't come everyday! In the four years I broadcast from various parts of the Pacific I received many letters, but that one I shall never forget.

It's really astounding how quickly and how completely the character of a great army can change when there isn't any war to fight. Three weeks after the *Missouri* signing, I did a broadcast report in which I estimated that nearly 75 percent of the officers I had served with in the Pacific were gone, transferred to other duties or shipped home for the mustering-out process that was the goal of all but the professional soldier. Even on MacArthur's staff the civilian officers were disappearing, and the same was true of every unit assigned to the occupation. These men usually were replaced by "pilgrims" from Washington, anxious to secure their Pacific ribbons to prove they "fought" in a theater in which they had never fought.

Spit and polish didn't exist in the combat areas of the Pacific. You had officers and you had men and it was often difficult to tell them apart, dressed as they were in identical fatigues and covered with Leyte mud. But the Washingtonians brought it back with a bang! After four years with combat troops I still didn't know the difference between a "field grade" and a "company grade" officer, but the new arrivals educated me in a hurry. The dining room of the Imperial Hotel was divided into areas for general officers and field-grade officers—those above the rank of captain. Captains and lieutenants weren't even allowed in the hotel except on duty, on orders, or in certain sections accessible only through the servant's entrance.

The Dai-Iti seated all commissioned ranks, but the "field" and "company" areas were carefully defined and, in addition, four tables were cordoned off behind a sign declaring them off-limits to all except full colonels. Obviously the silver *leaf* didn't rate with the Pentagonians!

I must emphasize that the officers who came to Japan over the combat route didn't think much of this posturing, and they let it be known. Actually, I never saw an "eagle" colonel inside this sacred area who wasn't also wearing the Monument patch on his shoulder. The combat veterans cast their dissenting votes by fending off starvation in the company of their juniors. If you had shared the jungle chow-lines with the nonranking soldier, it didn't seem too demeaning to share a table with a lieutenant colonel.

As nonranked noncombatants, the correspondents were able to steer clear of most of this idiocy. We ate wherever we pleased, and no one ever questioned our decisions. The only objection to our code that came to my attention occurred in the Dai-Ichi building where a couple of correspondents were waiting for the elevator to GHQ. As the elevator door opened a colonel, resplendent in a brand new uniform with shiny silver eagles, put his hand on the arm of one of the two and asked, "Don't you think you should step aside and allow a colonel to enter first?" He picked the wrong man. Spike Hennessey, who represented one of the American press associations, was not known for his finesse. He glared at the colonel's Washington patch briefly, then said, "Well, Colonel, as long as there was any fighting going on out here, that subject was never brought up. Now that you *have* brought it up, the answer is no!" I don't believe the subject was ever brought up again.

While it was possible for a veteran officer who had an interrupted civilian career waiting to get consideration for an early discharge, the only way a GI was going home was by accumulating the required number of "points" in the system the army had established. Time was the greatest contributor to a man's total, and when he reached his magic number he was due, in theory at least, for immediate rotation back to the States. There was nothing the soldier in Japan valued more than his point total, and the number each man had amassed as of any date was of more vital interest and fueled more rap sessions than the results of the World Series.

Several weeks after our arrival in Japan, General Eichelberger invited George Folster and me to accompany him on an inspection tour of the new American bases in Japan, traveling in his personal train, the *Octagon*, formerly the private train of Henry Pu Yi, the puppet emperor of Manchuoko while the Japanese still claimed control of that disputed portion of Manchuria. It was a luxurious train by any standards, and we of course accepted. The steel rails provided an excellent opportunity to see Japan as you can never see it from the air, but to me the ultimate reward came in the opportunity to observe Bob Eichelberger's methods of inspection and review. At every post he devoted most of his attention to the living quarters and recreation facilities provided for the man in the line. Early in the tour he explained, with a characteristic grin, "My officers are the finest in the world. I can always trust them to provide themselves with the best amenities available. I just want to be sure they spread it around."

At each post there was also a formal review when each unit put on its best front for the Old Man. I trailed along behind him as he moved past the formal ranks and was just a bit surprised when he stopped every few feet and asked a soldier, "How many points do *you* have, son?" The answer was always instantaneous. The general would thank him and move on down the line to repeat with another lad. The result was always the same. Finally my curiosity got the best of me. "General, do you really expect to find a soldier who can't remember his point total instantly and accurately?"

"Bill, you don't understand. Every man I questioned is within weeks of his final rotation target. If we had scheduled an armed invasion of Japan, after another three months I would have found myself commanding an army of raw, unseasoned troops. The new men would have had to learn combat by fighting a highly trained army, as we did in Buna. That's been my personal nightmare ever since I was given the command."

About that time General Bob had another problem tossed in his lap, this time by a group of unit commanders who were convinced that boys will be boys. They approached Eichelberger with a request that he issue orders legalizing Yokohama's ancient if not honorable Yoshiwara red-light district. Their argument was familiar: "They'll always find ways to frequent it, or something worse, so why not make it legal so we can police it?" Eichelberger was shocked beyond belief, but not for the anticipated reasons. "Bill," he addressed me in utter disgust, "Are those guys crazy? *What would I tell Miss Em?* She'd kill me if I ever let them make a whorehouse madam out of me!" The lamps of Yoshiwara continued to cast their ruddy invitations, but not with the official approval of Lt. Gen. Robert L. Eichelberger. Miss Em won that one hands down!

My aim, when I first projected this book, was to present my own impressions and observations of the Pacific war and the events leading up to it. The occupation of Japan is another story, which I shall leave to my colleagues who spent more time covering those years. Some things happened during the early days, however, which I believe should be chronicled for the record, developments of which I happened to have unique knowledge.

There was never any doubt that Russia was thoroughly unhappy at the way the occupation was shaping up, unhappy at its smooth progress with no incidents and, hardest to swallow, with no participation by the USSR. Gen. Kuzma Derevyanko, Moscow's representative in Tokyo, was merely an observer, perched on the sidelines muttering threats against SCAP. At the same time there was an insistent faction in Washington convinced that Russia had "reformed" and would henceforth be a trustworthy, valuable ally. This group thought Moscow should be rewarded for its intrepid decision to declare war on Japan a full forty-eight hours before Tokyo signalled it had had enough. During the month of October, reports began to come in from Washington that serious consideration was being given to the establishment of a four-power (United States, Great Britain, USSR, and China) commission to take over administration of the occupation, allowing Douglas MacArthur only to implement its decisions.

My experience with MacArthur and his command convinced me of two things: the General would never accede to such an arrangement, and he would never lift a finger to defend himself. This would be a good story if only I could get solid confirmation of MacArthur's intention, and to me that meant Charles Willoughby. As the staff G-2 he certainly would know the final answer, and he had been a big help to me ever since we arrived in Melbourne almost at the same time.

He welcomed me to his quarters in the Imperial with the usual single drink (he seldom joined in), and I immediately came to the point. "General, do you know what Douglas MacArthur will do if a commission is appointed to take over administration of the occupation?" He didn't hesitate. "I know exactly what he will do. We've discussed it several times. He will resign immediately."

"That's exactly what I thought from the first. Now, can I report this to the American people?" That really was an unnecessary question, because he hadn't given me the information off the record and all Allied censorship had been lifted. Still, I preferred to have his sanction. "Under one condition, Dunn. You must not reveal your source, certainly not quote me." I agreed.

I left the Imperial with what I knew was a good story and almost certainly an exclusive. That knowledge posed another question. Can a story be too exclusive? As every correspondent knows, there's great satisfaction in being first with an important story, but it's also nice to have a respected colleague *follow* with an independent confirmation. I found the answer almost immediately. In the lobby of the Imperial I spotted Frank Kelley of the *New York Herald-Tribune.* My report would go on the network during the daily World Roundup at 6:45 P.M. and the *Trib* wouldn't hit the streets for another hour. Perfect! I clued Frank in on the story, got his promise to protect "Sir Charles," and we had a deal.

At 6:47.30, New York time, on the evening of October 10, I began my report to the network:

> The immediate resignation of General Douglas MacArthur as supreme commander of the Allied forces in the occupation of Japan can be expected if a four-power commission is sent to Tokyo to act in a supervisory capacity. I was given this information only a few hours ago by a ranking general officer on the staff of the supreme commander who, in fact, said there was *no doubt* the General's res-

ignation would be an *immediate* result of any such move by the Allied
powers. General MacArthur feels that his administration has been
eminently successful, that he is achieving his goals without a single
incident worthy of mention, and that any move to place a super-
visory council over him could be nothing less than an indication
of lack of confidence.

Within minutes the *Herald-Trib* was on the street with Kelley's story
iterating the facts I had presented. Then followed some twenty-four
hours of thundering silence on both sides of the Pacific, broken finally by a statement from Washington that completely eliminated the
idea of a commission for all time.

As far as I was concerned the story was ended, and I turned my
attention elsewhere. When I returned to the hotel for lunch a day or
two later, however, I was informed that General Willoughby wanted
me to call him. He answered the phone himself, pretending to be his
aide, but dropped that ruse immediately. "Bill Dunn? Oh, yes, Dunn,
I did want to talk to you. The General has asked me to find out where
you got the information contained in your broadcast concerning the
four-power commission." I felt the hair rising on my nape! Was he going to throw me down? I, too, became formal but emphatic. "General
Willoughby, you know damned well where I got that information!"

"Oh, yes, Dunn, yes. I certainly know one source, but I thought there
might, perhaps, be others." That was different. As long as he wasn't
denying anything I was willing to play ball. "You're right, of course,
General. There was no lack of sources. Everyone at GHQ was talking
about it." That definitely was true. Everyone at GHQ had a personal
interest in the prospect, individual careers were at stake, but "Sir
Charles" was the only one who professed definite knowledge of Mac-
Arthur's final intention. I could almost hear his sigh of relief at the
other end of the line. "That's what I thought, Dunn. I shall talk to
the General myself. We are quite busy right now and I think I can
close the subject."

That was the last I heard of the commission, but it definitely was
not true that MacArthur leaked his intentions to a reporter. Much
has been said by historians and biographers about MacArthur's "pride,"
equating pride with overweening egotism. MacArthur was unquestionably a proud man, in the best sense of the word, and that pride
would never have allowed him to stoop to the ruse of leaking anything
to the media. Information came from him either straightforwardly or

not at all. And any member of his staff who did otherwise was soon set straight, in private but in no uncertain terms.

After almost half a century it is interesting to speculate what would have happened if a commission that included Russia with an equal role and equal authority had taken over. The Russians, since the days of Lenin, have never lost their determination that the game be played by their rules, but there were those in Washington at that time willing to believe the USSR was ready to change its ways. In Japan, however, Kuzma Derevyanko was leaving no doubt as to Russia's ultimate ambitions.

From the day of the surrender Derevyanko not only refused to cooperate with SCAP in any way, but concentrated his energies on trying to make MacArthur's task more difficult. At the time of our discussion of the proposed commission, Willoughby told me that MacArthur had not received one official word on those portions of East Asia occupied by the Russians. This despite the presence of a Russian military mission operating locally, which was being supplied with all official information concerning MacArthur's own activities. Maj. Gen. John R. Hodge, commanding MacArthur's forces in south Korea, was in critical need of coal to provide warmth for his American troops against a fast-approaching winter. But Korea's sources of coal were all located north of the 38th parallel, that section of Korea occupied by the Russians. At the time of my meeting with Willoughby, Hodge not only had been unable to get the needed coal but had never received a single reply to any of his official requests.

This was the type of non-cooperation that could have been expected to wreck even the best efforts of a four-power commission, and MacArthur would have been forced to strike his colors before too long if he had accepted the original concept.

As for what would have happened to Japan and to the Japanese people, a glance at North Korea's dictatorship under Kim Il Sung is sufficient to reveal the Russian blueprint for Japan.

EPILOGUE

The brief but moving ceremony that marked the end of World War II in the Pacific also marked the beginning of a new and exciting era in broadcast journalism. For more than four years there had been few developments in broadcasting techniques and facilities that had not emerged as an adjunct to the war effort. The development of television as a medium for news, information, and entertainment had been on hold ever since Pearl Harbor.

Now the scientists and engineers were free to turn their knowledge and skills to nonmilitary research and development, and the era of modern electronic journalism really took off. Almost everything the listening and viewing public now takes for granted has been developed since that memorable day aboard the U.S.S. *Missouri.* Those who have followed this narrative since its inception can understand the monumental strides made in those few decades, not only in electronics but also in the field of transportation so important to the correspondent.

Both Paul White and I knew he was being wildly optimistic when he estimated my original tour of the Far East at about three months. Today, however, that assignment could be completed in a fraction of that time, and the search for adequate electronic facilities would have been unnecessary. Now the electronic journalist can take his own crew of engineers, if needed, to any part of the globe practically overnight. The development of satellite transmission has eliminated the need for "blind broadcast" techniques and all but wiped out the old "conditions beyond our control" bugaboo that haunted all intercontinental transmission at the end of the Pacific war.

After I left my desk on Madison Avenue in 1941, it took me seventeen days to reach Manila, including five days by ship from San Francisco to Honolulu, three days in Hawaii waiting for the Pan American Clipper, then four daylight flights of from eight to twelve hours from Pearl to Midway, Wake, Guam, and the "Pearl of the Orient." Today a trip from New York's JFK to Manila takes little more time than my original flight from New York to the Golden Gate. All the major destinations on my 1941 itinerary are now connected by jet, and there are no distant places.

Unfortunately, not all post–World War II developments have been equally felicitous. No one who witnessed the Japanese surrender really believed he was present at the end of all wars, but I am certain no one of us, at that time, realized he was witnessing the end of the last war his country would win, at least in his own lifetime!

I shall not comment on the Vietnam debacle, because I was neither an on-the-scene observer nor a participant, but I did spend five months with the microphone trying to make sense out of what Harry S Truman called the Korean "police action," and it was obvious very early that this was one we would never win without the unlikely miracle of a hands-off policy in the White House.

In June, 1950, the formidable Chinese-trained forces of Kim Il Sung, with the full support of the Chinese communists, moved south across the 38th parallel. President Truman acted promptly and, in the majority of opinions, correctly, in ordering U.S. forces to support the minimal United Nations forces (eventually, some 80 percent American and Korean) in the cause of the badly outmanned and outgunned ROK (Republic of Korea) army in its effort to prevent a communist takeover of the entire Korean peninsula. The free world applauded his action, some with reservations, of course, but with the innate feeling that the alternative, a complete communist conquest, could not be considered.

It was a difficult decision, because it meant sending American boys into combat at a time when those lads were not prepared for major war. Politics had ravaged what was once the world's most powerful military force in less than five years, and the occupation troops in both Japan and Korea were sadly lacking in the bare essentials of war. Still, MacArthur, as the supreme commander, made the best of a bad situation. The southward drive was halted, reinforcements were brought in, including the U.S. Marines, two British regiments, and token forces from a number of the UN nations. The situation began to look less hopeless.

Almost at once, however, the White House began to exhibit serious qualms. A series of negative orders began to arrive, orders based on political, not military, reasoning that quickly made a serious situation much more serious. Reports reached the theater that Clement Attlee, snugly ensconced in No. 10 Downing Street, was insisting on

There is no way to cover combat and still maintain any degree of cleanliness, particularly if you make use of the useful foxholes and slit trenches. Here Ed Murrow of CBS News and I demonstrate that axiom down near Masan, having just climbed out of a slit trench wherein we sought refuge from enemy mortar shells. *Courtesy U.S. Army Signal Corps*

appeasing the USSR because a Russian intervention, in his opinion, would certainly trigger a third world war. Truman seemed to be listening, and he was certainly not alone.

Orders were issued putting large areas of Korea off-limits to our bombers, including the bridges over the Yalu River, the gateway to Korea from Manchuria. This, we learned, was because certain factions in Washington were convinced that any move against communist China would bring Russia to the immediate aid of her (at that time) communist ally.

For the second time in two wars I introduce Gen. Douglas MacArthur to a microphone. First time, of course, was on the beachhead at Leyte. In this picture the General is recording the only taped interview he ever granted in the field, this one of the K-2 airstrip in Korea. This was also our first meeting after the start of the Korean War. *Courtesy U.S. Army Signal Corps*

MacArthur made a number of trips to Korea in *SCAP,* his personal Lockheed Constellation, and I was one of the five corespondents who traveled with him. (The others were Carl Mydans of Time-Life, Howard Handelman of INS, Ernest Hobricht of UP, and Russell Brines of AP.) These trips gave us a rare opportunity to learn firsthand how the General was reacting to these seemingly endless interdictions.

Even after the brilliant coup at Inchon, where two divisions of the Tenth Corps were landed successfully in the face of twenty- to thirty-foot tides (a move previously condemned as impossible by the navy and the joint chiefs of staff), doubt and timidity still ruled in Washington. The consensus seemed to be that one false step would bring Russia into the war. MacArthur was worried by this attitude and chafed at each tightening of the rein.

He took particular exception to the premise that Moscow would ever enter a major war merely to help an ally. "Russia," he told me on one flight, "will never voluntarily go to war except to attain a specific personal goal which it is sure can be successful." Furthermore, he believed Russia was still too busy trying to heal the massive wounds of World War II to be looking for immediate military conquests. Finally, he pointed out that Russia already had achieved most of its postwar territorial goals without having to fire a shot.

Before one flight we were summoned to the Dai Ichi building to be briefed by the General himself on an important Allied paratroop drop near Pyongyang, the north Korean capital. He didn't tell us that the mission would not end at Pyongyang. As we left MacArthur's office we were met in the corridor by Lt. Col. Anthony ("Tony") Story, his personal pilot and aide-de-camp, who did some briefing on his own. Tony was emphatic that we keep this flight completely secret; not even our families were to be told. That admonition was both unique and surprising, but the next day we learned the reason.

As we left the Pyongyang area after the drop, Story, instead of heading east toward Tokyo, turned west, aiming at the mouth of the Yalu River, then completely in enemy hands. It was then that MacArthur informed us he was going to make a personal inspection of the Yalu River and the forbidden Yalu frontier. Ernie Hobricht expressed the feeling of all five of us when he shook his head in disbelief and muttered, *sotto voce,* "Is this trip necessary?" The idea of flying deep into enemy airspace in a completely unarmed plane was

This picture was taken at Tokyo's Haneda airport just before the epic flight up the Yalu River in the General's Lockheed Constellation, completely unarmed and with no fighter plane protection, scores of miles behind the Chinese lines. From the left are Russell Brines of Associated Press, Ernest Hobricht of United Press, Howard Handelman of INS, General MacArthur, Carl Mydans of Time-Life, and myself. *Courtesy of U.S. Army Signal Corps*

a typical MacArthur decision. He was certain the risk was minimal, because the enemy would never believe a sane person would authorize it.

Of course he was proved correct again, because we were given the opportunity to inspect the Yalu from its mouth without incident, including the inviolable bridges that would, too quickly, provide an avenue of welcome to the Chinese communist forces which swept down from the north, in spite of Washington's ceaseless attempts to avoid anything that might aggravate Mao Tse-Tung, to help the North Koreans force a stalemate that still remains today after nearly four decades.

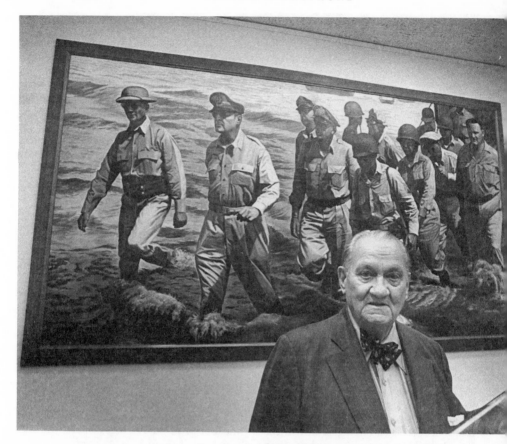

This mural, on the wall of the MacArthur Memorial in Norfolk, was painted by the eminent American artist Alton Tobey and is based on another October 20 photo taken from a different angle. I was visiting the memorial on the occasion of General Mac-Arthur's one-hundredth birthday when this picture was taken. *Courtesy* Norfolk Virginian-Pilot

This, then, was — and still is — the story of the Korean war, plagued and fettered from the first by what irreverent correspondents and other critics referred to as Truman's "Partial Pregnancy Policy," a policy furthered in various ways by later presidents. After all these years, Korea, followed by the tragedy of Vietnam, still stands as absolute proof that there can be no "partial pregnancy" in war.

Historians and biographers have made much of Douglas MacArthur's unique personality and his nonconformist mental processes.

In the quarter-century since the death of Douglas MacArthur, Jean MacArthur has been a constant visitor at the Norfolk memorial, looking after the interests of "my General" in death as carefully as she did during their twenty-seven years together. Here she is at the tomb with Vincent J. Thomas, then mayor of Norfolk on the occasion of her husband's one-hundredth birthday.

Many have found him hard to understand. Many have been distracted by alleged egotism, by the indisputable fact that he did not think or react like the ordinary man. There has always been a tendency to confuse ego with self-confidence. In any estimate of this soldier-statesman, one must never forget that Douglas MacArthur is the only American of international stature whose entire life, excepting only his final years of retirement, was lived as a soldier. His entire education was focused on the military. To him a soldier was always a special type of man, a person to be emulated. I never heard him refer to himself as a general or even as an officer. He was a *soldier* first and always.

George Washington was a great soldier, but it wasn't his whole life. He began as a surveyor and made his overall livelihood as a plantation owner. Andrew Jackson was primarily a frontiersman with an uncanny gift for unconventional warfare. Both Ulysses S. Grant and Robert E. Lee were superb soldiers, but both spent much of their careers in mufti. Soldiering was more of a hobby for Theodore Roosevelt, who is better remembered as a politician. Politics entered Dwight Eisenhower's career relatively late in life, but his pre–West Point days were spent as a normal American schoolboy who probably played at being a soldier.

Douglas MacArthur was born on an army post, the son of a famous soldier and a mother who understood the military establishment better than many soldiers of highest rank. Mary ("Pinky") MacArthur supervised her son's education personally and made certain he was always pointed toward the military eminence she was sure would be his. He had a few brief years in public schools but always under the close supervision of military parents. He already knew more about the art of soldiering when he entered West Point than the average soldier in the ranks.

Fortunately, Douglas MacArthur was also a scholar who studied and read widely, his main interests centering on history, particularly military history, and the classics. He also had to excel in mathematics to earn his high ranking in the Corps of Engineers. His scholastic records are part of the West Point legend and explain the basic intellectual foundation on which he could build his career.

Small wonder, then, that biographers and historians have found MacArthur a breed apart. He never had a chance to be like his civilian brothers, but it may well be conceded that the United States is better off today because of that difference. His place in history is unique and could not have been filled by a man of different background.

The tragedies of Korea and Vietnam lie in the persistent suspicion that we may have become a nation lacking the will to win a war such as Korea, and without the diplomatic finesse to avoid a needless war such as Vietnam. In June, 1951, after Harry Truman abruptly terminated the career of a brilliant soldier without even expressing the thanks of a grateful nation, Douglas MacArthur spoke before a special session of Congress. During that speech he expressed a belief those who knew him best have heard him voice many times, a tenet this nation must understand if future Koreas and Vietnams are to be avoided:

"War's very object is victory—not prolonged indecision. In war, indeed, *there can be no substitute for victory!*"

INDEX

NOTE: *An italicized number indicates photograph on that page.*

Pacific Microphone was composed into type on a Compugraphic digital phototypesetter in ten point Trump Medieval with three points of spacing between the lines. ITC machine was selected for display. The book was designed by Jim Billingsley, typeset by Metricomp, Inc., printed offset by Thomson-Shore, Inc., and bound by John H. Dekker & Sons. The paper on which the book is printed carries acid-free characteristics for an effective life of at least three hundred years.

TEXAS A&M UNIVERSITY PRESS : COLLEGE STATION